The Instant Pot Cookbook:

Healthy Recipes for Instant Pot Pressure Cooker

(4 Instant Pot Cookbooks in 1)

Henry Wilson

Copyright © [Henry Wilson]

All rights reserved. No part of this guide may be reproduced in any form without permission in writing from the publisher except in the case of brief quotations embodied in critical articles or reviews.

Book №1 Contents 17

Introduction 17

Everything you should know about instant pot/pressure cooker 18

Benefits and advantages of an Instant Pot 19

Full Instructions about Using the Various Parts and Settings 20

Instant Pot/pressure cooker use, tips and Safeguards 23

Cleaning Your Instant Pot/Pressure cooker 25

Instant Pot/Pressure cooker times 26

Rice and chicken meals 27

Recipe 1: Teriyaki Chicken with Jasmine Rice 27

Recipe 2: Instant Pot Chicken with Brown Rice 28

Recipe 3: White Rice with Chicken and mushroom cream 29

Recipe 4: Fried white rice with chicken breast 30

Recipe 5: White Rice Chicken Paella 31

Recipe 6: Chicken and Rice Pilaf 32

Recipe 7: Curried Chicken and white rice 33

Recipe 8: Chicken Adobo 34

Recipe 9: Rice with Chicken livers and pine nuts 35

Recipe 10: Chicken Jambalaya 36

Rice and meat meals 38

Recipe 11: Beef and brown rice 38

Recipe 12: Jasmine rice with tomato sauce Beef meatballs 39

Recipe 13: White rice with spicy lamb 40

Recipe 14: Instant cooked white rice with cheese and ground beef 41

Recipe 15: Southern-Style Pork and rice Picadillo 42

Recipe 16: Lamb and white rice curry 44

Recipe 17: Rice with beef and broccoli 44

Recipe 18: Hawaiian Rice with beef 45

Recipe 19: Beef Kajun rice 46

Recipe 20: White rice and Beef meatloaf 47

Vegan rice meals 49

Recipe 21: Jasmine Rice with coconut and veggies 49

Recipe 22: Brown rice with Brussels sprouts 49

Recipe 23: Wild Rice Pilaf with shallots 50

Recipe 24: Rice with mushrooms and cranberries 51

Recipe 25: Green Rice with cilantro and spinach 52

Recipe 26: Rice with olive and cashews 53

Recipe 27: Rice with avocado 54

Recipe 28: Lentil and Rice Curry 54

Recipe 29: Spicy Rice 55

Recipe 30: Lime rice 56

Beans and rice meals 58

Recipe 31: Brown rice with black bean and corn 58

Recipe 32: Jasmine Rice with Red Beans 59

Recipe 33: Rice with white beans and ham 59

Recipe 34: White rice with pigeon peas 61

Recipe 35: White rice and bean chili 61

Coconut rice meals 63

Recipe 36: Coconut rice 63

Recipe 37: Coconut shrimp rice 63

Recipe 38: Sweet Potato and coconut rice 64

Recipe 39: Coconut and orange rice 65

Recipe 40: Coconut and mango rice 66

Risotto meals 68

Recipe 41: Parmesan Risotto 68

Recipe 42: Tuna Risotto 69

Recipe 43: Mushroom Risotto 70

Recipe 44: Salmon Risotto 71

Recipe 45: Sweet Risotto 72

Mexican rice meals 73

Recipe 46: Spicy Mexican Rice 73

Recipe 47: Peri Peri Rice 74

Recipe 48: Mexican Seafood Paella 75

Recipe 49: Enchilada Cheesy Rice 76

Recipe 50: Taco rice with corn kernels and ground beef 77

Asian rice meals 79

Recipe 51: Chinese-Style Rice 79

Recipe 52: Jasmine Rice with fish sauce 80

Recipe 53: Rice dumplings 81

Recipe 54: Brown rice with scrambled eggs 82

Recipe 55: Sushi Bowl 83

Recipe 56: Japanese sticky rice 84

Recipe 57: Rice Balls 85

Recipe 58: Rice with Edamame 86

Recipe 59: Rice with Cabbage and fish 87

Recipe 60: Rice Congee 88

Soups with rice 89

Recipe 61: Rice and chicken soup 89

Recipe 62: Beef Jasmine rice soup 90

Recipe 63: Wild Cauliflower Rice soup 91

Recipe 64: Walnut Rice soup 92

Recipe 65: Mushroom and cashew rice soup 93

Recipe 66: Rice and Carrot Soup 94

Recipe 67: Rice and lentil soup 95

Recipe 68: Rice and Tomato Soup 96

Recipe 69: Rice and miso soup 97

Recipe 70: Beef and spicy rice soup 98

Desserts with rice 99

Recipe 71: Asian Style Rice Cake 99

Recipe 72: Sweet rice with nuts 99

Recipe 73: Sweet rice cubes 101

Recipe 74: Chocolate rice pudding 101

Recipe 75: Sweet Rice with mango 102

Recipe 76: Rice Custard 103

Recipe 77: Sweet rice recipe 104

Recipe 78: Sweet Glutinous Black Rice Biko 105

Recipe 79: Rice with cashews and raisins 105

Recipe 80: Layered Rice Cake 106

Kid-friendly dishes with rice 108

Recipe 81: Fried eggs and rice 108

Recipe 82: Rice cakes for kids 109

Recipe 83: Rice Tikkis 110

Recipe 84: Rice Scotch Eggs 111

Recipe 85: Sweet Rice with pecan nuts 112

Recipe 86: Rice cereal for kids 112

Recipe 87: Kid-friendly Sushi rice balls 113

Recipe 88: Crispy rice for kids 114

Recipe 89: Rice salad with fresh fruits 115

Recipe 90: Rice and Tuna bowl 116

Some other rice recipes 118

Recipe 91: Rice stuffed Pepper 118

Recipe 92: Stuffed grape leaves 119

Recipe 93: Rice Stuffed baby eggplants 120

Recipe 94: Stuffed Cabbage rolls 121

Recipe 95: Wild Rice Stuffed Mushrooms 122

Recipe 96: Rice balls with cheese and pasta sauce 123

Recipe 97: Rice Muffins 124

Recipe 98: Rice stuffed calamari 125

Recipe 99: Rice Stuffed Sausages 126

Recipe 100: Rice guacamole 127

CONCLUSION 129

Book №2 Contents (Asian Instant Pot) 130

Introduction 130

Chapter 1 Asian Cuisine 131

Pakistani Cuisine 131

Indian Cuisine 131

Indonesian Cuisine 131

Malaysian Cuisine 131

Singaporean Cuisine 131

Thai Cuisine 131

Vietnamese Cuisine 132

Filipino Cuisine 132

Chinese Cuisine 132

Japanese Cuisine 132

Korean Cuisine 132

Chapter 2 Asian Spices 133

Chapter 3 Chicken Recipes 134

Chicken Tikka Masala (Indian) 134

Vietnamese Chicken Noodle Soup (Pho Ga) 135

Chicken Biryani (Indian & Pakistani) 136

Ginger Soy Chicken 138

Honey Sesame Chicken 138

Pilipino Chicken Adobo 140

Chicken Afritada 141

Pilipino Chicken Florentine 142

Mongolian Chicken 143

Asian Chicken and Rice 144

Chapter 4 Meat Recipes 146

Chinese BBQ Pork (CHAR SIU) 146

Korean Pork Ribs (Dwaeji Galbi Jjim) 147

Pork Ribs with Black Beans (Chinese) 148

Vietnamese Braised Pork Belly (Thit Kho tau) 149

Malaysian Beef Rendang 150

Beef Caldereta 151

Filipino BBQ Ribs 152

Pilipino Kare Kare 152

Filipino Beef Tapa 153

Korean Short Ribs 154

Chapter 5 Fish and Seafood Recipes 156

- Vietnamese Fish Congee (Chao ca) 156
- Vietnamese Salmon 157
- Indian Coconut Shrimp Curry 158
- Salmon (Singaporean) 159
- Vietnamese Caramel Salmon 160
- Soy-Free Asian Salmon 161
- Ginger Scallion Fish 161
- Fish Biryani 162
- Pressure Cooked Coconut Fish Curry 164
- Chinese Steamed Black Cod 165

Chapter 6 Rice Recipes 167

- Chinese Sticky Rice 167
- Sekihan – Azuki Bean Rice (Japanese) 168
- Indian Lemon Rice 169
- Indonesian Fried Rice (Nasi Goreng) 170
- Hainanese Chicken Rice in Pressure Cooker (Singaporean) 171
- Fried Rice 173
- Black Rice 174
- Chinese Fried Rice 174
- Chinese Chicken Congee 175
- Japanese Pumpkin Rice 176

Chapter 7 Side-Dishes Recipes 178

- Chinese Chicken Soup 178
- Sweet Corn Soup 179
- Filipino Mung Bean Stew 180
- Filipino Arroz Caldo 180
- Sri Lankan Red Lentil Curry 181
- Shanghai Siu Mai (Chinese) 182
- Pork Ribs with Bitter Melon Soup 183
- Cauliflower and Potato Stir Fry 184
- Egg Curry 185

    Lamb Curry (Indian) 187

Chapter 8 Curries 189

    Coconut Chicken Curry (Thai) 189

    Vietnamese Caramelized Pork 190

    Vietnamese Chicken Curry (Ca Ri Ga) 191

    Indian Butter Chicken 192

    Indonesian Curry Chicken (Kari Ayam) 193

    Beef Curry (Hong Kong) 194

    Chicken Curry 195

    Chicken Curry 196

    Beef Potato Curry 197

    Mongolian Beef 198

Chapter 9 Salad Recipes 200

    Vietnamese Chicken Porridge & Salad (Cháo & Gỏi Gà) 200

    Japanese Potato Salad 201

    Chopped Chinese Pork Salad 202

    Paleo Chinese Chicken Salad 203

    Asian Sesame Noodle Salad 204

    Thai Brown Rice Salad 205

    Asian Chicken Salad 207

    Thai Quinoa Mango Salad with Dressing 208

    Asian Spaghetti Salad with Dressing 209

    Asian Slaw Quinoa Salad 210

Chapter 10 Sauces 211

    Homemade Hoisin Sauce (Chinese) 211

    Orange Chicken Sauce (Chinese) 211

    Black Bean Sauce (Chinese) 212

    Filipino White Sauce Recipe 213

    Japanese Sweet and Sour Sauce 214

    Spicy Korean Bibimbap Sauce 214

    Cincalok Dipping Sauce 215

    Thai Chili Sauce (Nam Prik Pao) 216

Thai Sweet Chili Sauce (Nam him kai) 217

Salty Thai Peanut Sauce 217

Chapter 11 Soups and Stews 219

Short Rib Soup (Galbitang in Korean) 219

Indonesian Chicken Noodle Soup (Mie Sop Ayam Medan) 220

Korean Beef Cabbage Radish Soup (Yukgaejang) 221

Pakistani Beef or Mutton Stew (Nihari) 222

Chicken Rendang 224

Chicken Gnocchi Soup 225

Borscht Soup (Hong Kong) 226

Red Bean Soup (Hong Kong) 227

Kimchi Jjigae 227

Indonesian Vegetable Tamarind Soup 228

Chapter 12 Noodles Recipes 230

Spicy Beef Noodle Soup/Bun Bo Hue (Vietnamese) 230

Indonesian Noodles (Mie Goreng) 231

Chicken Curry Soup Noodles 232

Garlic Noodles 234

Chili Garlic Noodles (Chinese) 234

Thai Peanut Noodles 235

Lo Mein (Chinese) 236

Chicken Noodle Soup (Chinese) 237

Chinese Garlic Sesame Noodles 238

Spicy Honey Garlic Noodles (Chinese) 239

Chapter 13 Vegetarian Recipes 240

Broccoli with Garlic 240

Coconut Cabbage 241

Vegan Japanese Curry 242

Butter Chickpeas (Indian) 243

Vegetable Biryani 244

Kidney Bean Curry 245

Vegetable Korma 247

- Spiced Potato and Eggplant 248
- Langar Dal 249
- Egg Biryani 250

Chapter 14 Desserts and Snacks 252

- Filipino Sweet Rice Cake 252
- Filipino Leche Flan 253
- Tofu Pudding (Singaporean) 254
- Watalappan (Sri Lankan) 255
- Chinese Sponge Cake 256
- Rice Pudding (Ba Bao Fan) 257
- Chinese New Year Cake (Kue Bakul) 258
- Chinese Egg Custard 259
- Adzuki Beans Coconut Popsicles 260
- Taiwanese Corn on the Cob 261

Chapter 15 Keto Asian Recipes 262

- Keto Pakistani Karachi Chicken 262
- Pakistani Tandoori Chicken 263
- Chicken Curry (Indian) 264
- Chicken Karachi 265
- Indonesian Oxtail Soup (Sup Buntut) 266
- Filipino Pork Adobo 267
- Pork Chops 268
- Indian Fish Curry 269
- Korean Spicy Pork (Dae Ji Bulgogi) 270
- Taiwanese Beef Stew 271

Conclusion 273

Book №3 Contents (Indian Instant Pot) 274

Introduction 274

Indian Cuisine 275

- North Indian Food 275
- South Indian Food 276

What Food and Spices are Mainly Used in Indian Cuisine? 278
- Using Indian spices 278

Chicken – Indian Style 281
- 1. Butter Chicken 281
- 2. Instant Pot Chicken Masala 282
- 3. Chicken Chettinad 283
- 4. Mughlai Zaafrani Chicken 285
- 5. Chicken Curry with Coconut Milk 286

Meat – Indian Style 288
- 1. Instant Pot Beef Fry Kerala Style 288
- 2. Goan Pork Instant Pot Vindaloo 289
- 3. Instant Pot Gosht 291
- 4. Instant Pot/Pressure Cooker Mutton Korma 292
- 5. Spicy Beef Curry Slow Cooking 294

Indian Fish Curry Recipes 296
- 1. Indian Fish Curry 296
- 2. Instant Pot Fish Tikka 297
- 3. Coconut Milk Fish Curry 298
- 4. Instant Pot Fish Coconut Curry 299
- 5. Fish Molee 300

Rice Indian Recipes 302
- 1. Chicken Biriyani 302
- 2. Jeera Rice 303
- 3. Ghee Rice 304
- 4. Lemon Rice 305
- 5. South Indian Curd Rice 306

Beans Recipes 308
- 1. Beans Thoran 308
- 2. Spicy Green Beans 309
- 3. Beans Patoli Curry 310
- 4. Cluster Beans Fry 311

    5. Green Beans with Potatoes 312

Dal Recipes 314

    1. Guajarati Dal 314

    2. Instant Pot Daal Tadka 315

    3. Daal Makhani 316

    4. Panjabi Dal Tadka 317

    5. Instant Pot Dal Fry 318

Vegetable Recipes 320

    1. South Indian Sambar 320

    2. Avial (Mixed Vegetable) Curry 321

    3. Kadai Mushroom Curry 322

    4. Navaratan Korma 324

    5. Vegetable Korma 326

Indian Desserts 329

    1. Gulab Jamun 329

    2. Instant Pot Gajar Halwa 330

    3. Sweet Pongal 331

    4. Kaju Barfi 332

    5. Paal Payasam (South Indian Dessert in Milk) 333

Soup Recipes 334

    1. Tomato Soup 334

    2. Beetroot Carrot Ginger Soup 335

    3. Mutton Shorba 336

    4. Instant Pot Lentil Soup 338

    5. Curried Chicken Soup 339

Keto Indian Recipes 341

    1. Keto Mutton Masala 341

    2. Keto Instant Pot Paneer Bhurji 342

    3. Spiced Mustard Greens 343

    4. Keto Indian Lamb Curry 345

    5. Keto Indian Butter Chicken 346

Conclusion 349

Book №4 Contents (Vietnamese Instant Pot) 350

Introduction 350

An Insight into Vietnamese Cuisine: 350

Chicken Recipes 356

Caramelized Chicken 356
Marinated Chicken Curry 357
Chicken & Bell Pepper Curry 358
Lemongrass Chicken 359
Glazed Chicken Breasts 360

Meat Recipes 362

Braised Beef Brisket 362
Shredded Chuck Roast 363
Caramelized Pork 364
Braised Pork Belly 365
Shredded Pork 366

Fish Recipes 367

Steamed Sea Bass 367
Caramelized Salmon 368
Catfish in Caramel Sauce 369
Fish Curry 370
Fish & Veggie Curry 371

Rice Recipes 372

Coconut Rice with Peas 372
Veggie Rice 372
Chicken Rice 374
Chicken & Rice Porridge 375
Fish Congee 377

Side Dishes Recipes 378

Glazed Chicken Wings 378
Zesty Meatballs 379
Garlicky Spinach 380

 Soy Sauce Braised Broccoli 381

 Sautéed Mushrooms 382

Salads & Eggs Recipes **383**

 Chicken & Veggie Salad 383

 Chicken & Noodles Salad 384

 Beef Salad 385

 Shrimp Salad 387

 Chicken & Veggie Omelet 388

Soup & Stew Recipes **390**

 Chicken & Noodles Soup 390

 Beef & Noodles Soup 391

 Shrimp & Crab Soup 392

 Beef Stew 394

 Pork Stew 395

Noodles Recipes **397**

 Garlicky Noodles 397

 Noodles with Vegetables 398

 Vermicelli Noodles with Veggies 399

 Honey Noodles with Chicken 400

 Noodles with Shrimp 401

Vegetables & Vegetarian Recipes **403**

 Stewed Squash 403

 Vegetarian Curry 404

 Tofu & Green Beans Curry 405

 Caramelized Tofu 406

 Steamed Spring Rolls 407

Dessert Recipes **409**

 Sweet Soup 409

 Rice Pudding 410

 Rice & Black-Eyed Peas Pudding 411

 Coffee Flan 412

 Coconut Flan 413

Conclusion 415

Book №1

Introduction

Welcome to the Instant Pot/ Pressure cooker Cookbook and congratulations on purchasing your own book and adding it to your bookshelf. You have made the right choice by choosing this book amongst many others. If you are wondering why, let me tell you a small secret; the key to beautiful youthful and rejuvenated skin, a long, safe and sound life resides right here in this book. The recipes in this book are not only easy-to make, but healthy and have excellent results on your well-being. So if you want to figure out the strong bond between the recipes in this book and health, all you have to do is to keep reading this book and you will discover that you have just made the right choice.

This is one of the very few cookbooks you will find that focuses on describing the Instant Pot as a cooking appliance and that explains its different parts one-by-one in detail. Moreover, this cookbook and guide will help you master the use of the Instant Pot hand-in-hand with the art of cooking and mixing different flavours and tastes.

This is the only Instant Pot cookbook that is very-well organized in terms of its function, the benefits of using Instant Pot, the reasons why you should cook rice with an Instant Pot/Pressure cooker and even more. This cookbook has been specially crafted to help you take as much advantage as you can from the use of the Instant Pot/ Pressure cooker.

You won't need to spend your entire day in the kitchen to come up with your favourite recipe, but you will only need the revolutionary cooking appliance known as the Instant Pot/Pressure cooker. Not only are Instant Pots known for being one of the world's easiest to-use cooking appliances, but it can last for your entire life without being damaged if correctly used.

Save your time and your money by downloading your own copy of this cookbook and treat yourself and your family with a wide variety of recipes that you will greatly love. The recipes that you will find in this book come in easy-to-follow directions and instructions and you will be amazed that the ingredients are all affordable.

And don't worry if you are a beginner, because this cookbook will be the best place to start from and will make this cooking journey much easier.

Everything you should know about Instant Pot/Pressure Cooker

Have you ever dreamt of finding a cooking appliance that can save your time, your money and bring you great and healthy results? Have you ever thought of using an Instant Pot/Pressure cooker to cook rice instead of using other sorts of conventional rice cookers? If you have not yet considered using an Instant Pot, it is high time you did. For instance, Instant Pot/ Pressure Cookers are considered as the revolutionary invention of the century with its great innovative cooking proprieties. So what is an Instant Pot?

In fact, Instant Pots are a Canadian invention that were designed to replace conventional cooking appliances and to cook food in a quicker time with the least quantity of water. As its name suggests, an Instant Pot is programmable, dependable, and convenient.

An Instant Pot/ Electric Pressure Cooker is a cooking appliance that combines the properties of a slow cooker, rice cooker, and a yogurt maker with a few settings and functional buttons.

Thanks to the variety of functions it provides, Instant Pot/Electric pressure cookers have become some of the most wanted cooking appliances that you would want to purchase all over the world.

With its unrivalled popularity, Instant Pot sales not only doubled, but tripled in less than four years. By the end of the year 2015, the sales hit the roof of more than three million. And what makes Instant Pots one of the best inventions of the century is that it is designed with unique function settings. So what are the benefits of Instant Pots?

BENEFITS AND ADVANTAGES OF AN INSTANT POT

1. **Instant Pots are safe to use** and to eliminate any possible harm that may spoil your food or burn it. With a safety Lid Lock, the system of your Instant Pot helps prevent any kind of accident while opening your Electric Pressure Cooker.
2. **Instant Pots are programmable and multi-functional**
   Not only are instant pots programmable, but they also combine the benefits of a steamer, yogurt maker, Pressure cooker, Rice Cooker, porridge maker and even Slow Cooker.
3. **Instant pots are energy saving** as it saves up to 80 percent of energy; besides, using Instant Pots helps make healthy recipes simpler by pressing just one button.
4. **Instant Pots can save your time.**
   With the help of your Electric Pressure Cooker, you can cook baby carrots, sweet corn and green peas in no more than three minutes whether frozen or fresh. To make a meal of mashed potatoes, you don't need to boil it into water for more than fifty minutes, but you can steam it in your Instant Pot for about no more than 15 minutes.
5. **Instant Pots can be used for baking desserts.**
   You might be surprised that you can make all varieties of desserts in your Instant Pot. Whether you want a cheesecake, a chocolate fondue and even bread, an Instant Pot can cook it for you in a matter of minutes. You can also make all kinds of puddings in your instant pots and enjoy an incredibly sweet wide range of desserts.

FULL INSTRUCTIONS ABOUT USING THE VARIOUS PARTS AND SETTINGS

The idea of purchasing an Instant Pot/Pressure cooker may be exciting, especially if you are doing it for the first time, but using this cooking appliance may be a bit challenging with the functions it presents. So in order to help you master the use the Instant Pot/ Pressure Cookers properly, we should first study the different functions and settings of this cooking appliance. So what are the main features of Instant Pots and how do they work?

We can generally find eleven buttons on any Instant Pot, but in some brands, we can find more options and functions and these buttons are 'pressure, annual, adjust, sauté, delay time, level indicator, menu, START/CANCEL setting yogurt, rice, porridge, multigrain, keep warm, slow cooker and timer'.

- **The setting "KEEP WARM":**

The setting "Keep warm" helps keep any type of food warm for about 24 hours. And the setting "Keep warm" starts immediately when the cooking process is over and all you have to do to start it is to press the button 'Start/Cancel' to start the warming function. The button 'bb' indicates that the mode, warm is on.

- **The function START/CANCEL:**

This setting "Start/ Cancel" helps cancel any selection that has already been made and it also allows you to cancel any cooking process you want to undo.

- **The setting button "Delay Time":**

The button "Delay Time" is a setting function that allows us to adjust the start of cooking time of. So, in order to use this function feature all you have to do is to press the timer button for about 10 seconds, then use the "+/-"buttons in order to adjust the cooking time and delay it for the number of hours that fit you the most; then just wait a second and press to select the button "delay" to set the minutes count. Besides, you can also cancel this option anytime you want just by pressing the button "Warm/Cancel"

- **The setting button "ADJUST":**

This function allows us to control the consistency of the food we cook. And we can select the buttons "More", "Less" or "Normal" in order to decrease or increase the cooking time.

- **The setting button "MENU":**

The function "Menu" allows the organization of different Instant pot programs. You can press the button "Menu" when you are ready to start the pressure cooking cycle.

- **The button "PRESSURE":**

The button "Pressure" allows you to determine the level of pressure you need throughout the cooking process. To use this function, all you have to do is to press the button "Pressure". There are some other preset functions you can also use to adjust the cooking process to your needs.

➢ **Note:**

Some Instant Pot/ pressure cookers are equipped with default pressure levels that can be adjusted to your liking. For example, if you want to press the normal setting, just press the button "Rice" and the button will indicate will display the time 00:10.

- **The setting button "MANUAL/ PRESSURE COOK":**

This button allows you to set the cooking time to whichever time you want. This function is always utilized with Instant Pots. So in order to use this setting, it is simple; just hit the button "Pressure" and adjust the pressure to Low or high to your liking.

- **The function button "Adjust":**

The button "Adjust" is used to keep the temperature under control and the same applies to the sauté mode, the slow cooking and the yogurt modes.

- **The function button "Sauté":**

This function setting "Sauté" makes a perfect choice if you want to brown meat or to thicken up sauces or even to sauté meat. And to use the sauté function, all you have to do is to press the "Sauté" key. As for the temperature, you can adjust the keys to "Normal", "Less" or "More", after pressing the button "Adjust". When the Instant Pot displays the button "Hot", you can then start sautéing. The sauté process can run for about 30 minutes.

- **The "YOGURT BUTTON":**

The setting "yogurt" can only be used when you want to make yogurt and the cooking process can be processed by pressing the button "Adjust" until the temperature indicates "boil".

- **The timer button:**

The "Timer" button can only be used when you want to delay the cooking process. And to use the function "Timer", just select the button "Manual" or by pressing the "slow cooker" mode. Use the '+/- keys to delay the cooking time to suit your schedule. (The timer option is a subfunction button that relates to the "delay" and as its name indicates adjusts the time of delay, that is why you found it confusing)

So if you want the lunch to be ready in 2 hours, but it only takes 20 minutes to be cooked and no more than 20 minutes to release the pressure, set your timer for about 1 hour.

- **The "Slow cooker Button":**

The setting "Slow cooker" displayed on the Instant Pot, is not equal to the temperatures of a traditional slow cooker. The low temperature is just like the temperature 'Keep warm', the temperature "medium" is like the low and the medium high is like high in conventional slow cookers.

- **The button "Rice":**

The button rice designates the process of cooking rice, so press it whenever you want to cook rice in your Instant Pot. Hit your Slow Cooker Function on your Instant Pot.

INSTANT POT/PRESSURE COOKER USE, TIPS AND SAFEGUARDS

Whenever you want to use your Instant Pot/ pressure cooker, there are some main tips and precautions that you should follow. And below are some tips and safety guards that may help you correctly use of your Instant Pot/ pressure cooker since the beginning and here are some tips that might help you:

- Make sure to prepare all your ingredients before starting to cook, so that the process is swift and efficient.

- Make sure to use a use a kitchen timer or clock. But remember to start the timing right when the cooker reaches full pressure.

- Be careful of certain foods like apple sauce, pearl barley, cranberries, noodles and macaroni; because it should not be cooked in the Pressure. Indeed, the main reason for not cooking these ingredients in pressure cooker is your safety and mainly because these types of foods like noodles can produce froth, sputter or foam which may lead to clogging the pressure release valve and thus you can risk building too much pressure to your Instant Pot.

- The Instant Pot/ Pressure cooker can never be used for any type of medical purpose, especially if you want to sterilize the medical equipment.

- You should remove the pressure cooker from the heat right after you hear the second beep.

- Ensure that the steam-releasing valves are clean and there are no kind of obstructions at all.

- You should also check the rubber gasket as it has to be pliable and clean.

- Never try to repair your Instant pot/ pressure cooker by yourself; and if anything is wrong with it; simply contact the store in order to fix it.

- Most foods benefit from the process of browning before you place your ingredients in a pressure cooker.

- You can apply the depressurizing function; but it is preferred to apply the quick release method. To apply this method; all you have to do is to place your pressure cooker in the sink; and run the cold water on the lid. This procedure will allow the pressure to depressurize in a short time and this method is very effective, especially with grains and veggies.

- Make sure not to touch hot knobs, handles and hot surfaces.

- Keep your children away from the pressure cooker; especially when it is functioning.

- Never put your pressure cooker in a microwave or an oven.

- Use extreme caution when moving your pressure cooker when it contains hot liquids.

- Never use pressure cookers for anything other than cooking.

- Improper use of a pressure cooker can lead to severe burns; so, make sure to follow safety instructions.

- Make sure not to open your pressure cooker until it perfectly cools and all the pressure is released. If the handles are too difficult to push; do not force it to open-up.

- Never use a pressure cooker without pouring enough liquid in or over filling it with liquid, because it can cause a permanent damage to your pressure cooker.

CLEANING YOUR INSTANT POT/PRESSURE COOKER

After using your Instant Pot to cook different types of foods and various dishes, you may find yourself feeling too tired to clean your kitchen or your cooking appliances. On this note, here are some tips that can help you clean your Instant Pot in no time even if it is greasy or grimy.

The good news about Instant Pots are that they are really easy to clean and you know that we can't neglect the step of cleaning because that is an important step if you want to get rid of bacteria and food particles that have gathered all over the sides of your Instant Pot. So here are some steps you can follow in order to keep your Instant pot clean and always looking good as new. Don't worry that you will damage your Instant Pot if you clean it; rest assured because all the parts of the Instant Pot are dish wash safe.

1. The first thing you want to do when you finish using your Instant Pot is to unplug it at the mains; then let the Instant Pot cool to room temperature before cleaning it.
2. So, the first step in cleaning the Instant Pot is to remove its lid and the inner pot; then rinse it with clear water; then wipe it dry with a clean and soft cloth.
3. Wipe the base of the inner cooker rim with a dry cloth in order to prevent any rusting of the exterior part of the rim.
4. Remove the ring from the Instant Pot and remove the anti-block shield from the lid; then wash it with soapy, warm water. Then rinse with clear water and wipe it dry with a soft and gentle cloth.
5. Clean the outer body of the Instant Pot with a soft sponge or soft cloth and make sure never to use harsh chemical detergents or powders.
6. Check that the steam release float and valve are properly positioned and that there are free of any debris.

INSTANT POT/PRESSURE COOKER TIMES

Type of Food or meat	Cooking Time (in minutes)
Beef stew	15 to 20
Beef balls	10 to 15
Dressed Beef	20 to 25
Pot roast beef, beef rump, beef steak, beef chuck, round beef, beef brisket, large beef.	35 to 40
Beef, steak, blade, small beef chunks	25 to 30
Ribs, beef	25 to 30
Shanks, beef	25 to 30
Oxtail beef	40 to 50
Light chicken breasts	8 to 10
Whole Chicken	20 to 25
In bone Chicken	10 to 15
Chicken legs, thighs or drumsticks	10 to 15
Whole Cornish Hen	10 to 15
Duck, chopped with bones	10 to 12
Whole Duck	25 to 30
Sliced Ham	9 to 12
Picnic ham shoulder	25 to 30
Chopped lamb	10 to 15
Lamb stew	10 to 15
Leg of lamb	35 to 45
Pheasants	20 to 25
Pork roast, loin	55 to 60
Butt roast, Pork	45 to 50
Ribs, pork	20 to 25
Boneless turkey breast	15 to 20
Whole turkey breast with bones	25 to 30
Turkey leg drumsticks	15 to 20
Chopped veal	5 to 8
Roasted veal	35 to 45
Whole Quail	8 to 10

Rice and chicken meals

Recipe 1: Teriyaki Chicken with Jasmine Rice

Preparation time: 10 minutes

Cooking time: 20 minutes

Yield: 4 Servings

Ingredients

For the rice:

- 2 cups of jasmine rice
- ½ teaspoon of sea salt
- 2 cups of water
- 1 teaspoon of olive oil

For the chicken:

- 2 lbs of boneless, skinless chicken breast, about 4 pieces
- 1 ¾ cups of water, divided
- 2/3 Cup of soy sauce
- ¾ Cup of honey
- 2 Tablespoons of rice vinegar
- 2 Tablespoons of mirin rice wine
- 1 Tablespoon of minced garlic
- 2 Teaspoons of minced ginger
- 3 Tablespoons of cornstarch
- 2 Tablespoons of thinly sliced green onion
- ½ Teaspoon of sesame seeds

Directions

For the rice:

1. Start by rinsing the jasmine rice in a fine-mesh strainer; then add the rice to the inner pot of your Instant Pot and sprinkle with salt.
2. Pour in the water, and drizzle with the olive oil.
3. Cover your Instant Pot with the lid and make sure the valve is fixed to sealing, and press the button "PRESSURE COOK" for about 4 minutes.
4. Let the rice cool for 10 minutes and naturally release the pressure, then press the button CANCEL, and turn the valve to venting position in order to release the remaining pressure.
5. Set the rice aside.

For the Chicken:

1. Add the chicken breast to your instant pot.
2. Whisk about 1 and ½ cups of water with the soy sauce, the honey, the rice vinegar, the Mirin the rice wine, the garlic, and the ginger in a medium bowl.
3. Add the teriyaki sauce to your instant pot.
4. Check the release valve and make sure it is in a sealing position.
5. Cover the Instant Pot with the lid and press the button "Manual" and set the pressure to HIGH.
6. Set the timer to about 10 minutes by using the '–/+' buttons.
7. When the timer beeps, cover the steam release handle with a clean towel and quick release the pressure by sliding the steam handle to the position "Venting"; make sure all the steam is released; then open the lid and press the button "Keep Warm/ Cancel".
8. Remove the chicken from your instant pot and transfer it to a clean platter; then let rest for about 5 minutes before slicing the meat.
9. In a bowl, mix the cornstarch with 1/4 cup of cool water to make a kind of slurry; then press the button "sauté" on the setting button "more".
10. Gradually add in the cornstarch when teriyaki sauce begins to simmer.
11. Cook for about 80 seconds.
12. Slice the chicken, then drizzle the teriyaki sauce over the top.
13. Garnish with chopped green onions and a dash of sesame seeds.
14. Serve and enjoy your chicken rice dish!

Nutrition Information

Calories: 170 | Fat: 11 g | Carbohydrates 6.51g | Fiber 1.2g |Protein: 17 g

RECIPE 2: INSTANT POT CHICKEN WITH BROWN RICE

Preparation time: 7 minutes

Cooking time: 25 minutes

Yield: 3-4 Servings

Ingredients

- 2 lbs of boneless and skinless chicken breasts or thighs, chopped into pieces
- 1 large and finely chopped white onion
- 2 Minced garlic cloves
- 3 large shredded carrots
- 2 Tablespoons of extra virgin olive oil
- 2 Teaspoons of dried thyme
- 2 Teaspoons of dried oregano
- 2 Teaspoons of cumin
- 1 and ¼ teaspoons of salt

- 1 pinch of ground black pepper
- 2 to 3 bay leaves
- 3 Cups of rinsed and drained long grain brown rice
- 3 and ¾ cups of water

Directions

1. Press the button "Sauté" yon your Instant Pot and let it preheat for a few minutes, you want it hot when you start.
2. Add the olive oil, the onion and the garlic and sauté your ingredients for about 3 to 4 minutes; stir from time to time.
3. Press the button "Cancel"; then add the thyme, the oregano and the cumin; then cook for about 30 additional seconds.
4. Add the chicken, the carrots, the rice, the water, the salt, the pepper and the bay leaves in the same order and make sure not to stir.
5. Lock the lid of your Instant Pot and make sure the valve is in the sealing position; then set the pressure to High and the timer to about 22 minutes.
6. When the Instant Pot displays "OFF", quickly release the pressure through the quick releasing method for about 2 to 3 minutes.
7. Open the lid; then serve and enjoy your delicious brown rice.

Nutrition Information

Calories: 443 | Fat: 10.6 g | Carbohydrates 6.51g | Fiber 2 g |Protein: 28.1 g

RECIPE 3: WHITE RICE WITH CHICKEN AND MUSHROOM CREAM

Preparation time: 10 minutes

Cooking time: 24 minutes

Yield: 4-5 Servings

Ingredients

- 2 Tablespoons of Extra-virgin olive oil
- 2 Cups of white rice
- 1 Large chopped onion
- 2 Cup of low-sodium chicken broth
- 2 Cans of about 10.5 oz of cans cream of mushroom soup
- 1 Pinch of Kosher salt
- 1 Pinch of freshly ground black pepper
- 3 Large skin-on chicken thighs
- 2 Tablespoons of melted butter
- 2 Teaspoons of fresh thyme
- 1 Finely minced garlic clove

- 1 Tablespoon of freshly chopped parsley

Directions:

1. Preheat your Instant Pot by pressing the button "Sauté" for about 3 minutes.
2. When the Instant Pot displays the button hot, add in the rice and the onion.
3. Pour in the broth and the soup and stir the mixture until it is very well combined.
4. Season your ingredients with 1 pinch of salt and 1 pinch of pepper.
5. Place the chicken thighs into the rice mixture and brush it with the melted butter; then sprinkle the garlic on top and season with 1 pinch of salt and 1 pinch of pepper.
6. Lock the lid of your Instant Pot and make sure the seal valve is in position.
7. Set the timer to about 24 minutes and the pressure to HIGH.
8. When the timer beeps, turn off your Instant Pot and quick release the pressure for about 3 minutes.
9. Transfer the rice with the chicken on top to a serving platter and top with chopped parsley.

Nutrition Information

Calories: 303 | Fat: 13.5 g | Carbohydrates 28g | Fiber 1 g |Protein: 18 g

RECIPE 4: FRIED WHITE RICE WITH CHICKEN BREAST

Preparation time: 5 minutes

Cooking time: 25 minutes

Yield: 4 Servings

Ingredients

- 3 Tablespoons of butter
- 4 Minced garlic cloves
- 2 Chopped chicken breasts
- 1 and ¼ cups of chicken broth
- ¼ Cup of low sodium soy sauce
- 1 Cup of dry white rice
- 1 Bag of mixed frozen snap peas and chopped carrots
- 1 Bunch of sliced green onions

Directions:

1. Add the butter, the garlic, the chicken, the chicken broth, the soy sauce and the rice to your Instant Pot.
2. Close the lid of the Instant Pot and cook on High for about 3 minutes.
3. Quick release the pressure for about 3 minutes and open the lid when it is safe.
4. In the meantime; microwave our frozen vegetables for about 4 minutes.

5. Add the veggies and the green onions to the rice in your Instant Pot and stir very well to combine your ingredients.
6. Serve and enjoy our dish!

Nutrition Information

Calories: 325 | Fat: 11 g | Carbohydrates 35g | Fiber 1.2 g |Protein: 22 g

RECIPE 5: WHITE RICE CHICKEN PAELLA

Preparation time: 8 minutes

Cooking time: 18minutes

Yield: 3 Servings

Ingredients

- 1 Tablespoon of olive oil
- 1 Pound of thinly sliced chorizo, or chicken sausage
- 1 Heaped cup of white rice
- 1 Teaspoon of saffron
- ¼ Teaspoon of fine sea salt
- 1 Cup of chunky and thick salsa
- 1 Cup of chicken stock
- ½ Cup of chopped roasted red pepper
- 1 Cup of frozen peas
- lemon cut into wedges
- Chopped parsley

Directions:

1. Heat the olive oil in the inner pot or the Instant Pot by pressing the function 'sauté'.
2. Add the thinly sliced chicken sausage and cook it for about 5 minutes until the chicken sausages look brown.
3. Transfer the chicken sausage to a platter; but do not remove the oil from the Instant Pot.
4. Add the white rice, the saffron, the fine sea salt, the thick and the chunky salsa and pour in the chicken stock into the inner pot.
5. Stir your ingredients very well and lock the lid with the vent in sealed position.
6. Set the Instant Pot Pressure to "High" and the timer to about 8 minutes.
7. When the timer beeps; use the quick release method; then stir in the red pepper, the frozen peas and the chicken sausage; then replace the lid on top and press the button "Keep warm" for about 4 to 5 minutes.
8. Stir your ingredients very well.
9. Serve and enjoy your chicken paella!

Nutrition Information

Calories: 331 | Fat: 20 g | Carbohydrates 17g | Fiber 3 g | Protein: 21 g

RECIPE 6: CHICKEN AND RICE PILAF

Preparation time: 10 minutes

Cooking time: 20 minutes

Yield: 4 Servings

Ingredients

- Pound of chopped chicken breast
- 1 Teaspoon of salt
- ½ Teaspoon of black pepper
- 1 Teaspoon of Cajun
- 1 Tablespoon of vegetable oil
- 1 Large diced onion
- Julienned carrots
- 1 Can of about 15.5 Oz chickpeas
- Cups of rinsed white rice
- 1 Garlic head with the bottom cut off
- 2 and ½ cups of chicken stock
- 1 Cup of chopped parsley

Directions:

1. Dice the chicken breast into 1 cubes of about 1 inch each.
2. Season the chicken breasts with black pepper, salt and Cajun.
3. Set your Instant Pot to the function Sauté on a high heat and to do that, press "sauté" twice and sauté the chicken for about 4 to 5 minutes.
4. Scoop the chicken into a bowl and add the diced onion and the carrots; then sauté for about 4 minutes.
5. Turn off the function "sauté" by pressing the setting button 'cancel'.
6. Add the chickpeas right on top; but do not stir.
7. Add the rinsed rice over the chickpeas and don't stir.
8. Remove the bottom of the garlic head and tightly press it into your mixture.
9. Pour in the chicken stock and season with 1 pinch of salt and 1 pinch of pepper.
10. Cover your Instant Pot with a lid and cook on High for about 12 minutes; but make sure the venting knob is in sealed position.
11. When the timer beeps, naturally release the pressure for about 5 to 7 minutes.
12. Switch the valve knob to venting and quick release the pressure for 3 minutes.
13. Remove the garlic head and stir your ingredients; then top with chopped parsley.
14. Serve and enjoy your Chicken Pilaf!

Nutrition Information

Calories: 312 | Fat: 7 g | Carbohydrates 35g | Fiber 3 g |Protein: 26.8 g

RECIPE 7: CURRIED CHICKEN AND WHITE RICE

Preparation time: 8 minutes

Cooking time: 35 minutes

Yield: 3 Servings

Ingredients

- 2 Tablespoons of olive oil
- 2 Chicken breasts of 6 oz
- ½ Chopped, yellow onion
- ½ Chopped green bell pepper
- Large chopped carrot
- ½ Cup of chopped celery
- Minced garlic cloves
- Cups of white rice
- 1 Teaspoon of turmeric
- 1 Teaspoon of curry powder
- 1 Teaspoon of coriander
- 1 Teaspoon of cumin
- 1 Dash of cayenne
- 2 and ½ cups of water
- ½ Cup of rinsed green peas
- 1 Pinch of sea salt

Directions:

1. Turn your Instant Pot to the function "Sauté" and pour in 1 tablespoon of oil.
2. Place the chicken breasts in your Instant Pot and sauté for about 3 to 4 minutes per side.
3. Remove the chicken breasts from the Instant Pot and set it aside over a platter.
4. Add in one drizzle of oil and add the chopped vegetables of pepper, onion, carrot, celery and garlic.
5. Season with salt and black pepper and sauté for a couple of minutes, but don't over sauté.
6. Chop the chicken into chunks; then add it back to the Instant Pot and add the spices of coriander, cumin, cayenne and curry.
7. Add the rice, and pour in the water.
8. Press the button 'Keep Warm/Cancel' button on your Instant Pot to end the sautéing part; then, press the button 'Manual'.
9. Set the timer to about 22 minutes and the pressure to HIGH and remember to make sure the valve is set to the "Sealing" position.
10. When the timer beeps; naturally release the pressure for about 10 minutes.

11. Release any remaining pressure; then open the lid and add the peas to your Instant Pot.
12. Press the button "Keep warm" and place back the lid for about 2 minutes.
13. Remove the lid; fluff the rice and season with more salt if needed.
14. Serve and enjoy your dish!

Nutrition Information

Calories: 393 | Fat: 7.5 g | Carbohydrates 33.8g | Fiber 3.9 g |Protein: 45 g

RECIPE 8: CHICKEN ADOBO

Preparation time: 10 minutes

Cooking time: 30 minutes

Yield: 6 Servings

Ingredients

- 3 Pounds of bone-in chicken legs and thighs
- Medium sliced yellow onion
- 4 Chopped garlic cloves
- 1/3 Cup of low sodium soy sauce
- Tablespoons of white vinegar
- 1 Tablespoon of brown sugar
- 1 Teaspoon of black peppercorns
- to 3 dried bay leaves
- 1 and ½ cups of long grain white rice
- 1 and ½ cups of water
- Thinly sliced green onions

Directions:

1. Combine the sauce and the chicken ingredients in your Instant Pot; then stir to coat the chicken very well.
2. Nestle a steamer rack in the Instant Pot with the chicken pieces and make sure the chicken legs are not touching the bottom of your Instant Pot.
3. Rinse the rice under water and let it drain for 1 minute; then mix it with 1 and ½ cups of water in a medium bowl.
4. Put the bowl of rice and that of water over the steamer rack and lock the lid of your Instant Pot; make sure the valve is set to "Sealing" position.
5. Press the button "Manual" and adjust the time to about 15 minutes or just to a High pressure for about 15 minutes.
6. When the timer beeps; naturally release the pressure for about 10 minutes or quick release the pressure by releasing the sealed knob to "Venting".
7. Fluff the rice with a fork and check the temperature of the chicken if it is 165°.

8. Prepare the sauce using the bay leaves with the peppercorns, and any chicken; sliced yellow onion; the chopped garlic cloves, the soy sauce, the white vinegar, the brown sugar and cook for about 5 minutes.
9. Serve and enjoy your chicken with rice and sauce!

Nutrition Information

Calories: 263 | Fat: 7.8 g | Carbohydrates 29g | Fiber 0.7 g |Protein: 17.4 g

RECIPE 9: RICE WITH CHICKEN LIVERS AND PINE NUTS

Preparation time: 5 minutes

Cooking time: 40 minutes

Yield: 4-5 Servings

Ingredients

- lb of chicken livers
- Tablespoons of olive oil
- Finely chopped brown onions
- 2 Finely minced garlic cloves
- 12 oz of sliced mushrooms
- ¼ Cup of white wine
- ½ Teaspoon of salt
- to 6 Sprigs of fresh thyme
- 2 Cups of long grain white rice
- 2 Cups of stock
- For the toppings:
- ½ Cup of chopped parsley
- ½ Cup of pine nuts

Directions:

1. Select the function 'sauté' on an Instant Pot of about 6 quarts.
2. Heat the olive oil in your Instant Pot and add in the chicken liver and onion; then sauté for about 7 to 9 minutes.
3. Remove the chicken liver to a platter and set it aside.
4. Add in the garlic and sauté for about 1 to 2 minutes.
5. Add in about ¼ cup of white wine or you can just pour in the stock; then deglaze your Instant Pot for about 1 to 2 minutes.
6. Cancel the function "Sauté" and add in the remaining ingredients.
7. Close the lid of your Instant Pot and cook on High pressure for about 28 minutes.
8. When the timer beeps; naturally release the pressure for 10 to 15 minutes.
9. Add in the parsley and the pine nuts and stir.

10. Top with the chicken livers, parsley and more pine nuts.
11. Serve and enjoy your dish!

Nutrition Information

Calories: 316.8 | Fat: 15.7 g | Carbohydrates 20.6g | Fiber 1.6 g |Protein: 21.5 g

RECIPE 10: CHICKEN JAMBALAYA

Preparation time: 7 minutes

Cooking time: 20 minutes

Yield: 3 Servings

Ingredients:

- 2 Tablespoons of Olive Oil
- 12 ounces of sliced, chopped chicken Sausage
- Medium chopped onion
- 1 Medium seeded and chopped green Bell Pepper
- 1 Medium chopped celery stalk
- Diced garlic cloves
- Teaspoons of Cajun Seasoning
- ¼ Teaspoon of ground Thyme
- 1 Cup of Long-Grain White Rice
- 1 can of 14.5 ounces of undrained diced Tomatoes
- 1 and ½ cups of Low-Sodium Chicken Stock
- ½ Teaspoon of Kosher Salt
- Thinly sliced scallions

Directions:

1. Place the olive oil in your Instant Pot and press the setting function "Sauté" and heat it for about 1 minute.
2. Add in the sliced sausage and sauté for about 2 minutes per side.
3. Transfer the chicken sausage to a platter and set it aside.
4. Add in the onion, the bell pepper, the celery and the garlic.
5. Cook your ingredients for about 3 minutes; then add in the Cajun seasoning, the thyme and finally the rice then stir.
6. Press the button "Cancel" to stop the cooking process.
7. Add in the tomatoes with the juices, the salt and the stock and stir.
8. Close the lid of your Instant Pot and cook on HIGH for about 8 minutes.
9. When the timer beeps, turn off your Instant Pot and naturally release the pressure for about 5 minutes.

10. Stir the rice and add in the scallions and the chicken sausage; then replace the lid over the Instant pot and let your ingredients heat for a couple of minutes.
11. Serve and enjoy your dish!

Nutrition Information

Calories: 263 | Fat: 18.4 g | Carbohydrates 14.9g | Fiber 0.7 g |Protein: 10.3 g

Rice and Meat Meals

Recipe 11: Beef and Brown Rice

Preparation time: 10 minutes

Cooking time: 40 minutes

Yield: 5 Servings

Ingredients:

- 2 and ½ cups of rinsed and drained short grain brown rice
- lb of beef chuck
- 4 Tablespoons of olive oil
- Tablespoons of unsalted butter
- 1 Large, chopped onion
- Large, julienned carrots
- Cups of warm water
- 1 Tablespoon of salt
- ½ Teaspoon of black pepper
- ½ Teaspoon of ground cumin
- ½ Teaspoon of ground paprika
- ½ Teaspoon of ground coriander
- 1 Unpeeled, garlic head; cut into half

Directions:

1. Start by rinsing and draining the rice and set it aside; then set your Instant Pot to the setting 'Sauté' on High; then add in the 3 tablespoons of olive oil.
2. When the oil gets hot; but of course not smoking, add the beef meat into one single layer and sauté it for about 5 minutes.
3. Add in about 4 tablespoons of butter and toss in the chopped onion; then stir for about 3 minutes.
4. Add in the julienned carrots, the salt, the pepper, the cumin, the paprika, the coriander and sauté your ingredients for about 5 minutes.
5. Spread the brown rice in the bottom and pour in warm water; about 1 cup, on top of the garlic cloves in a way that it won't disturb the brown rice.
6. Poke the rice with a wooden spoon 5 times in the bottom and close the lid of your Instant Pot.
7. Make sure the valve is in a sealing position; then press the setting button "Multigrain" and the timer will be set automatically to 40 minutes.
8. 10 minutes before the Instant pot beeps, let your Instant pot rest and naturally release the pressure for 10 minutes.
9. Switch the valve to venting position to release the remaining pressure.

10. Remove the garlic and set it aside; then fluff your ingredients with a fork.
11. Squeeze the garlic on top; then serve and enjoy your dish!

Nutrition Information

Calories: 390 | Fat: 19g | Carbohydrates 22.4g | Fiber 1.4 g |Protein: 30.4 g

RECIPE 12: JASMINE RICE WITH TOMATO SAUCE BEEF MEATBALLS

Preparation time: 8 minutes

Cooking time: 30 minutes

Yield: 4 Servings

Ingredients:

For the meatballs:

- lb of minced beef
- ½ Cup of plain white bread
- 1 Grated onion
- Minced garlic cloves
- ½ Teaspoon of ground black pepper
- 1 Pinch of salt

For the Rice and tomato sauce:

- Cup of Jasmine rice
- Minced garlic cloves
- 1 Chopped onion
- Tablespoons of flour
- 2 Tablespoons of tomato paste
- Tablespoons of vegetable oil
- 2 Cups of water
- ½ Teaspoon of oregano
- 1 to 2 bay leaves
- 1 pinch of salt

Directions:

1. Rinse the rice in a sieve under the water tap until the water runs crystal clear.
2. Start your Instant Pot and preheat it by pressing the button "sauté", then add in the oil and sauté the garlic with the onion for about 4 to 5 minutes.
3. Add in the flour and stir; then add the salt, the oregano, the bay leaf and the tomato paste and pour in the water; close the lid and set the timer to about 10 minutes.
4. Quick release the pressure and open the lid when it is safe to do.

5. Add the rice on top and give a quick stir.
6. Close the lid of your Instant Pot and make sure the valve is in a sealed position; then set the timer to about 25 minutes and the pressure to High.
7. In the meantime; make the meatballs by mixing the minced beef with the onion and the garlic in a large bowl; then add the bread and sprinkle some drops of water with your hand and mix.
8. Season with salt and black pepper; then wet your hands with a bit of oil and start making the meatballs from the meat mixture.
9. Heat a little bit of oil in a large skillet and brown the beef meatballs in it for about 3 to 4 minutes.
10. When the timer of your Instant Pot beeps, quick release the pressure; then open the lid after turning the valve to venting position.
11. Press the button "Keep warm" and fluff the mixture with a fork.
12. Arrange the meatballs on top; then replace the lid and let warm for about 4 minutes.
13. Serve and enjoy your dish!

Nutrition Information

Calories: 321 | Fat: 25g | Carbohydrates 7g | Fiber 2 g |Protein: 15 g

RECIPE 13: WHITE RICE WITH SPICY LAMB

Preparation time: 12 minutes

Cooking time: 35 minutes

Yield: 6-7 Servings

Ingredients:

- Cup of milk
- 1 Cup of plain yogurt
- ½ Teaspoon of turmeric
- 1 and ½ tablespoons of prepared white rice with Masala spice mix
- 1 Teaspoon of Garam Masala
- ½ Teaspoon of chili
- 1 and ½ teaspoons of salt
- Tablespoons of lemon juice
- 9 Dried apricots
- 1 Tablespoon of coarsely chopped ginger
- Tablespoons of chopped garlic
- 1 Teaspoon of white poppy seeds
- ¼ Cup of packed cilantro
- 6 mint leaves
- 2 lbs of chopped lamb

- Tablespoons of olive oil
- 3 Cups of sliced onions
- ¼ Cup of raisins
- ¼ Cup of raw cashews
- ½ Cup of water
- 2 Cups of white rice
- ¼ Cup of chopped cilantro
- 1 Tablespoon of chopped mint

Directions:

1. Start by blending half the quantity of milk, all the quantity of yogurt, the turmeric, the spices, the Garam Masala, the chilli the powder, the salt, the lemon juice, the dried apricots, the ginger, the garlic and the white poppy seeds all together.
2. Add in the cilantro, the mint, the remaining milk and blend your ingredients very well.
3. Preheat your Instant Pot by pressing the "Sauté" mode; then add in the oil and or the ghee when it is hot.
4. Add the sliced onions; then sauté the onions for about 15 minutes.
5. Remove the onions with a spoon; then set it aside; then add in the slotted spoon, and set it aside.
6. Add in the raisins and the cashew and sauté; then remove it with a slotted spoon and set it aside.
7. Press the button "Cancel" to turn off your Instant Pot; then deglaze the inner pot with water and add half of the fried onions to the inner pot.
8. Add the fried onions to the Instant Pot then add in the lamb and pour in the water and lock the lid of the Instant Pot.
9. Set the timer to 15 minutes and the pressure to High.
10. Apply a quick release method; then open the lid and rinse the rice; then add it to the Instant Pot; but this time don't stir; just press the rice down.
11. Close the lid and cook on High pressure for 5 minutes.
12. Apply a 10 minutes natural release the pressure; then wait for about 10 minutes before opening the lid.
13. Open the Instant Pot and stir.
14. Serve the rice in bowls and top with the onions the raisins, the cashews, the cilantro and the mint.

Nutrition Information

Calories: 351 | Fat: 10.2g | Carbohydrates 45g | Fiber 5.6 g | Protein: 20.4g

RECIPE 14: INSTANT COOKED WHITE RICE WITH CHEESE AND GROUND BEEF

Preparation time: 6 minutes

Cooking time: 25 minutes

Yield: 5 Servings

Ingredients:

- Tablespoon of olive oil
- 1 Pound of lean ground beef
- 1 Cup of diced red onion
- 1 Teaspoon of Chili powder
- ½ Teaspoon of salt
- ½ Teaspoon of ground cumin
- Cups of water
- Cups of chunky salsa
- 1 Cup of rinsed and drained long-grain white rice
- 1 Can of about 15 ounces of rinsed and drained black beans
- 1 Cup of cooked corn kernels
- 2 Tablespoons of chopped fresh cilantro
- 1 Cup of shredded Cheddar cheese

Directions

1. Heat the oil in the bottom of your Instant Pot by pressing the function "Sauté".
2. Add the beef, the onion, the chilli powder, the salt and the cumin.
3. Cook your ingredients while stirring from time to time so that you make sure to crumble the meat; the process will take about 5 minutes.
4. Stir in the water, the salsa and the rice.
5. Lock the lid of the Instant pot and select the High pressure; make sure that the valve is in sealed position.
6. Set the timer to about 8 minutes and allow about 10 minutes for the pressure to build up.
7. When the timer beeps, quick release the pressure for about 5 minutes; then unlock the lid and set the function "sauté".
8. Add in the corn, the black beans and the cilantro and cook for about 3 minutes.
9. Serve your rice with ground beef in a serving bowl and top with the cheddar cheese; enjoy!

Nutrition Information

Calories: 358 | Fat: 14g | Carbohydrates 21.3g | Fiber 2 g |Protein: 53g

RECIPE 15: SOUTHERN-STYLE PORK AND RICE PICADILLO

Preparation time: 10 minutes

Cooking time: 30minutes

Yield: 6 Servings

Ingredients:

- 2 Tablespoons of olive oil
- 2 lbs of ground pork
- Cup of minced onion
- 1 Tablespoon of minced garlic
- Tablespoons of minced jalapeno
- 1 Can of 28 Oz of crushed tomatoes
- 1 Cup of bone broth
- 1 Teaspoon of cinnamon
- 1 Teaspoon of pepper
- 1 Teaspoon of garlic powder
- 1 Teaspoon of salt
- 1 Teaspoon of chili powder
- Teaspoon of cumin
- 1 Teaspoon of paprika
- 2/3 Cup of raisins
- ¼ Cup of green olives
- 1 Cup of long-grain white rice
- 1 cup of water

Directions

1. Rinse and drain the rice under cold water until the water runs clear.
2. Heat your Instant Pot by pressing the button sauté and heat the olive oil.
3. Brown the meat in the oil for about 5 to 6 minutes.
4. Add in the rest of the ingredients, cumin, chilli powder, raisins, olive, crushed tomatoes, minced jalapeno, cinnamon and pepper; then pour in the bone broth.
5. Close the lid of your Instant Pot and seal the valve; then set the timer to 10 minutes and the pressure to High.
6. When the timer beeps; quick release the pressure.
7. Open the lid when it is safe doing it and add in the rice; give a quick stir and close the lid again.
8. Set the timer to 8 minutes and the pressure to High.
9. When the timer beeps; naturally release the pressure for 10 minutes.
10. Open the lid of the Instant Pot.
11. Fluff the rice with a fork.
12. Serve and enjoy your rice with ground pork after topping it with chopped cilantro!

Nutrition Information

Calories: 415 | Fat: 16g | Carbohydrates 17g | Fiber 2.1 g | Protein: 18.5g

RECIPE 16: LAMB AND WHITE RICE CURRY

Preparation time: 5 minutes

Cooking time: 20 minutes

Yield: 4 Servings

Ingredients:

- Tablespoons of vegetable oil
- 1 Medium, peeled and thickly sliced onion
- 1 lb of trimmed of fat and chopped lamb neck fillet
- ½ Teaspoon of ground cumin
- 6 Crushed, cardamom pods with the seeds removed
- ¼ Teaspoon of ground cinnamon
- 1 to 2 bay leaves
- 1 and ½ cups of long-grain white rice
- 1/3 Cup of raisins
- ¾ Cup of dried apricots
- Cups of vegetable stock
- Tablespoons of fresh parsley leaves

Directions

1. Heat about 2 tablespoons of vegetable oil in your Instant Pot by pressing the button "Sauté".
2. Toss in the onion and cook for about 8 minutes; then remove it and drain it over a paper towel.
3. Add the remaining quantity of oil; then brown the meat for about 6 minutes.
4. Add the spices and the rice.
5. Add in the raisins and the apricots and the stock; then close the lid of the Instant Pot; make sure to the valve is in sealed position; then set the timer for about 15 minutes and set the pressure to High.
6. When the timer beeps; quick release the pressure for 5 minutes; then when it is safe, open the lid.
7. Serve the rice in bowls and top with chopped parsley; enjoy!

Nutrition Information

Calories: 368| Fat: 11g | Carbohydrates 23.2g | Fiber 2.1 g |Protein: 18g

RECIPE 17: RICE WITH BEEF AND BROCCOLI

Preparation time: 10 minutes

Cooking time: 25 minutes

Yield: 4-5 Servings

Ingredients:

- Tablespoon of olive oil
- 1 lb of stir-fry steak strips
- 4 Minced garlic cloves
- 1 Tablespoon of grated fresh ginger
- ¼ Cup of reduced sodium soy sauce
- ¼ Cup of hoisin sauce
- 1 and ½ cups of water
- 1 Cup of long-grain white rice
- 1 Head of Broccoli
- 1 Diced red pepper

Directions

1. Add the olive oil, the steak strips, the garlic, the ginger, the soy sauce, the hoisin sauce, the water and the rice to your Instant Pot.
2. Close the lid of your Instant Pot and seal the valve; then set the timer for about 15 minutes as the Instant Pot will need about 4 minutes to come to pressure.
3. When the timer beeps; apply a quick release method to release the pressure and open the lid, just when it is safe to do it.
4. Add in the broccoli and the red pepper; then stir very well and place back the lid over your Instant Pot and press the button "Keep warm".
5. Leave the rice for about 5 minutes.
6. Serve and enjoy your dish!

Nutrition Information

Calories: 495| Fat: 19g | Carbohydrates 47g | Fiber 2 g |Protein: 31g

RECIPE 18: HAWAIIAN RICE WITH BEEF

Preparation time: 5 minutes

Cooking time: 30 minutes

Yield: 4 Servings

Ingredients:

- Tablespoon of olive oil
- 1 Finely chopped small onion
- 1 Chopped red pepper

- 6 oz of chopped ham
- Lightly scrambled eggs
- 1 and ½ cups of long-grain white rice, rinsed and drained
- Cups of water
- 2 Tablespoons of soy sauce
- 1 Cup of chopped pineapple
- 1 Tablespoon of chopped scallions

Directions

1. Place the oil, the onion and the red pepper in the bottom of your Instant Pot and press the button "Sauté".
2. Sauté your ingredients for about 3 minutes; then add in the ham and stir your ingredients.
3. Add in the beaten eggs and stir again for about 4 minutes.
4. Add in the white rice; then pour in the water, the soy sauce and the chopped pineapple; then cover your Instant Pot with the lid and seal the valve; then set the manual timer to about 24 minutes.
5. When the timer beeps; quick release the pressure; then let the rice sit in the setting "Keep Warm" for 5 minutes.
6. Serve the rice into bowls; then garnish with chopped scallions.
7. Serve and enjoy your dish!

Nutrition Information

Calories: 273.9| Fat: 12.8g | Carbohydrates: 24.5g | Fiber: 1.7 g |Protein: 14.3g

RECIPE 19: BEEF KAJUN RICE

Preparation time: 6 minutes

Cooking time: 15 minutes

Yield: 3-4 Servings

Ingredients:

- 2 Tablespoons of oil
- and ½ cups of fresh diced onion
- 1 Cup of diced bell peppers
- ½ Cup of diced celery
- 1 Pound of chopped beef
- 1 Tablespoon of salt-free Cajun seasoning
- 1 Cup of water
- 1 Teaspoon of salt
- Bay leaves
- 1 Teaspoon of dried oregano

- Teaspoons of hot sauce
- 1 Cup of rinsed and drained long-grain white rice

Directions:

1. Turn on your Instant Pot by pressing the button "Sauté" and when it displays hot, add in the oil; then add in the chopped beef and stir for 4 minutes.
2. Add in the bay leaf, the Cajun seasoning, the hot sauce, the salt and the rice; then stir for 3 minutes.
3. Pour in the broth and lock the lid.
4. Make sure to seal the valve and cook on High pressure for about 5 minutes.
5. When the timer beeps, let the Instant Pot rest for about 10 minutes.
6. Release the remaining pressure; then fluff the rice with a fork.
7. Serve and enjoy your dish!

Nutrition Information

Calories: 461| Fat: 18g | Carbohydrates: 43g | Fiber: 3 g |Protein: 26g

RECIPE 20: WHITE RICE AND BEEF MEATLOAF

Preparation time: 7 minutes

Cooking time: 20 minutes

Yield: 6-7 Servings

Ingredients:

- Pound of extra-lean ground beef
- ½ Cup of uncooked, instant white rice
- ¼ Cup of finely-chopped onion
- ¼ Cup of minced red bell pepper
- 1 Minced garlic clove
- 1 Teaspoon of salt
- 1 Teaspoon of freshly-ground pepper
- 1 Tablespoon of minced fresh basil and rosemary
- Chopped chives and sage
- Teaspoons of Worcestershire sauce
- 1 Beaten egg
- ¼ Cup of tomato ketchup
- ¼ Cup of non-fat skim milk
- ¼ Cup of dry bread crumbs

Directions:

1. Preheat your Instant Pot by pressing the button "Sauté" and place the trivet or steamer rack in the bottom of your Instant pot.
2. Pour 1 and ¼ cups of water in the Instant pot and place a steamer basket over the rack and place the aluminium oil in the basket in a way that you form an aluminium pack.
3. Lightly grease the aluminium foil.
4. In a large bowl, mix the ground beef with the uncooked rice, the onion, the bell pepper, the garlic, the salt, the pepper, the herbs, the Worcestershire sauce, the egg, the ketchup, the milk, and the bread crumbs.
5. With clean hands, combine all your ingredients and mix very well; then form a shape of a loaf from the mixture.
6. Carefully transfer the loaf to the instant pot and place it over the aluminium foil into the basket and cover the Instant Pot with the lid.
7. Make sure to seal the valve; then select the button "Manual" and cook the meatloaf on High Pressure for about 20 minutes.
8. When the timer beeps, quick release the pressure and once the pressure is completely released, open the lid and check if the temperature of the loaf is 165° F.
9. Let the meatloaf rest for 10 minutes; then slice, serve and enjoy its taste!

Nutrition Information

Calories: 157.2| Fat: 7g | Carbohydrates: 10.9g | Fiber: 1.3 g |Protein: 19.5g

Vegan Rice Meals

Recipe 21: Jasmine Rice with coconut and veggies

Preparation time: 5 minutes

Cooking time: 5 minutes

Yield: 4 Servings

Ingredients:

- 2 Cups of Jasmine rice
- Cup of finely chopped carrots
- 1 Can of about 15 ounces of reduced-fat coconut milk
- ½ Cup of water
- 1 Tablespoon of lime juice
- 1 Cup of frozen peas, defrosted
- 1 and ½ tablespoons of rice vinegar

Directions:

1. Place the Jasmine rice in the Instant Pot; then add in the chopped carrots.
2. Pour in the water and the coconut milk and lock the lid of your Instant Pot.
3. Make sure the valve is in the sealed position; then press the button "Manual/Pressure".
4. Set the timer to about 5 minutes and naturally release the pressure for about 10 minutes.
5. Remove the lid when it is safe to do and add in the peas and the lime juice.
6. Mix your ingredients very well; then add in the rice vinegar and mix.
7. Serve and enjoy your dish!

Nutrition Information

Calories: 298| Fat: 4g | Carbohydrates: 18.7g | Fiber: 2.1 g |Protein: 3g

Recipe 22: Brown rice with Brussels sprouts

Preparation time: 5 minutes

Cooking time: 15 minutes

Yield: 3-4 Servings

Ingredients:

- 2 Teaspoons of minced garlic

- 2 Tablespoons of sesame oil
- 2 Cups of Basmati rice
- 2 Cups of shredded Brussels sprouts
- Small, roughly chopped white onion
- Tablespoons of soy sauce
- to 3 Large beaten eggs

Directions:

1. Add the sesame oil to your Instant Pot and press the button "Sauté".
2. Add the garlic to the Instant Pot and sauté the ingredients and stir for about 1 to 2 minutes; then add in the shredded sprouts and toss very well.
3. Rinse and drain the rice under cold water under it comes out clean.
4. Add in the onion and the rice and close the lid of the Instant Pot and seal the valve.
5. Set the timer to about 15 minutes on High pressure.
6. When the timer beeps; naturally release the pressure.
7. When it is safe, open the lid of your Instant Pot.
8. Fluff the rice with a fork and season with salt and pepper.
9. Add in the soy sauce and give a quick stir.
10. Serve and enjoy your delicious dish!

Nutrition Information

Calories: 112.4| Fat: 10.5g | Carbohydrates: 4.9g | Fiber: 1 g |Protein: 2g

RECIPE 23: WILD RICE PILAF WITH SHALLOTS

Preparation time: 4 minutes

Cooking time: 45 minutes

Yield: 3 Servings

Ingredients:

- ¾ Pound of fennel bulb
- ¼ Cup of minced fresh shallots
- and ½ tablespoons of olive oil
- 1 and ½ tablespoons of minced fresh garlic
- 1 Cup of wild rice
- 1 Cup of dry white wine
- Cups of water
- Teaspoons of balsamic vinegar
- ½ Teaspoon of sea salt
- ¼ Teaspoon of freshly ground pepper

Directions:

1. Trim the end of the fennel bulb and discard the end.
2. Trim the stalks from the fennel bulb and cut the bulbs in portions; then thinly slice it and set it aside.
3. Heat the Instant Pot by pressing the button "Sauté"; then add in 1 tablespoon of oil and sauté the shallots for about 3 minutes.
4. Add in the garlic, the fennel and the rice and stir
5. Pour in the wine in 2 and ½ cups of water; then mix very well.
6. Lock the lid of the Instant pot and set seal the valve.
7. Press the button "multigrain" and the timer to about 35 to 40 minutes.
8. When the timer beeps; quick release the pressure; then when it is safe, open the lid of your Instant Pot and fluff the rice with a fork.
9. Add in the balsamic vinegar, the salt, and the pepper and press the button sauté; then stir for 5 minutes.
10. Serve and enjoy the rice!

Nutrition Information

Calories: 183| Fat: 6g | Carbohydrates: 35g | Fiber: 3 g |Protein: 5g

RECIPE 24: RICE WITH MUSHROOMS AND CRANBERRIES

Preparation time: 5 minutes

Cooking time: 10 minutes

Yield: 4 Servings

Ingredients:

- Cup of long-grain rice
- Cups of water
- 1 Cup of apple juice
- 1 Tablespoon of vegetable oil
- Chopped celery ribs
- 1 Cup of sliced mushrooms
- Chopped scallions
- 1 Cored and chopped apple
- ¼ Cup of dried cranberries
- ¼ Cup of chopped pecan
- ¼ Teaspoon of ground fennel
- ½ Teaspoon of dried sage
- ¼ Teaspoon of ground ginger
- ½ Teaspoon of garlic powder

- 1 Pinch of salt
- 1 Pinch of pepper

Directions:

1. Rinse the rice and drain it very well; then heat the Instant Pot by pressing the button "sauté".
2. Add the rice to your Instant pot; then pour in the water and the apple juice.
3. Close the lid of your Instant pot and make sure the valve is in sealed position.
4. Set the timer to about 10 minutes and set the pressure to High.
5. When the timer beeps, naturally release the pressure and when it is safe, open the Instant Pot and remove the rice from the heat; then drain off any remaining liquid and set aside.
6. Sauté the mushrooms and the celery in 1 tablespoon of oil in a large skillet over a medium high heat for about.
7. Add the rice to the skillet and toss your veggies very well.
8. Season with 1 pinch of pepper and 1 pinch of salt
9. Serve and enjoy your dish!

Nutrition Information

Calories: 190| Fat: 8g | Carbohydrates: 25g | Fiber: 2.7 g |Protein: 7g

RECIPE 25: GREEN RICE WITH CILANTRO AND SPINACH

Preparation time: 7 minutes

Cooking time: 10 minutes

Yield: 3 Servings

Ingredients:

- ½ Cup of tightly packed fresh cilantro
- Cup of tightly packed fresh spinach leaves
- 1 and ¼ cups of chicken stock
- 1 and ¼ cups of milk
- 1 Teaspoon of salt
- 1 Tablespoon of olive oil
- Tablespoons of unsalted butter
- 1 and ½ cups of long-grain white rice
- ¼ Cup of minced onion
- 1 Minced jalapeno with the seeds removed
- Minced garlic cloves
- 1 Quartered lime

Directions:

1. Add the cilantro, the spinach, the chicken stock, the coconut milk and the salt to a blender and puree until you get a smooth mixture and set it aside.
2. Add the olive oil to your Instant Pot and press the button "sauté", and then add in the butter and the onion and sauté for 2 minutes.
3. Add the jalapeno and the garlic and sauté for about 1 to 2 minutes; then add the rice and stir.
4. Pour in the pureed mixture and mix.
5. Lock the lid of your Instant Pot and make sure the valve is in sealed position.
6. Set the timer to about 10 minutes and the pressure to High.
7. When the timer beeps; quick release the pressure; then turn the valve to venting position.
8. Open the lid when it is safe to do.
9. Fluff the rice with a fork.
10. Serve and enjoy your dish with a squeeze of lemon on top!

Nutrition Information

Calories: 126.1| Fat: 6.5g | Carbohydrates: 12.4g | Fiber: 1.3 g |Protein: 5.2g

RECIPE 26: RICE WITH OLIVE AND CASHEWS

Preparation time: 5 minutes

Cooking time: 15 minutes

Yield: 4 Servings

Ingredients:

- 1 Tablespoon of olive oil
- 2 Finely minced garlic cloves
- 1 Cup of rinsed and de-seeded salted olives
- 1 Dash of pepper
- 1 and ½ cups of long-grain white rice, rinsed and drained
- 1 Cup of basmati rice
- 1 Diced red chilli
- 2 Tablespoons of chopped cashews
- 1 Tablespoon of sesame oil

Directions:

1. Heat your Instant Pot by pressing the button "Sauté".
2. Add the oil to the Instant Pot; then add in the garlic and sauté for a couple of minutes.
3. Add in the olives, the pepper and the rinsed rice.
4. Add the sesame oil and toss again; then pour in 1 and ¼ cups of water.
5. Close the Instant Pot and seal the valve.
6. Set the timer to about 12 minutes on a High Pressure.
7. When the timer beeps; naturally release the pressure for about 10 minutes.

8. Turn the valve to the vent position and open the lid.
9. Fluff the rice with a fork; then sprinkle the chilli, the cashews and the sesame oil and mix.
10. Serve and enjoy your dish!

Nutrition Information

Calories: 323| Fat: 14.8g | Carbohydrates: 7.6 g | Fiber: 1.3 g |Protein: 12.4g

RECIPE 27: RICE WITH AVOCADO

Preparation time: 4 minutes

Cooking time: 10 minutes

Yield: 3 Servings

Ingredients:

- 2 and ¼ cups of water
- 1 Tablespoon of butter
- 2 Teaspoons of reduced-sodium chicken stock
- ¾ Teaspoon of ground cumin
- 1 Cup of uncooked long-grain white rice
- 1/3 Cup of picante sauce
- 1 Medium, peeled and cubed ripe avocado
- 2 Sliced green onions

Directions

1. Heat your Instant Pot by pressing the button "sauté"; then pour in the water, the rice and the salt and close the lid of your Instant Pot and seal the valve.
2. Set the timer to about 10 minutes and the pressure to High.
3. When the timer beeps, naturally release the pressure for about 10 minutes.
4. Open the lid of the Instant Pot and add in the picante sauce and stir.
5. Add in the avocado and the green onions and mix.
6. Serve and enjoy your delicious rice!

Nutrition Information

Calories: 188| Fat: 5.9g | Carbohydrates: 12.4g | Fiber: 1.3 g |Protein: 4g

RECIPE 28: LENTIL AND RICE CURRY

Preparation time: 5 minutes

Cooking time: 20 minutes

Yield: 2-3 Servings

Ingredients:

- 1 Cup of long-grain white rice, soaked in water for about 10 minutes
- 2 Tablespoons of coconut oil
- 2 Tablespoons of coconut oil
- 1 Teaspoon of black mustard seeds
- 1 Tablespoon of split chickpeas
- 1 Tablespoon of split and skinless black lentil
- 14 Curry leaves
- 1 and ½ cups of cashews, split into halves
- 1 Green chilli
- 2 Cups of frozen, grated coconut
- 1 and ½ cups of water
- 1 Teaspoon of salt

Directions

1. Soak the white rice in cold water for about 15 minutes.
2. Rinse the rice and drain it; then set it aside.
3. Press the 'sauté' button on your Instant Pot; then add in the coconut oil and once it melts, add in the mustard seeds; then split the chickpeas and the skinless black lentils.
4. Once the mustard seeds start popping up; add in the curry leaves, the cashews and the pepper and stir for about 30 seconds.
5. Add in the grated coconut and stir for about 30 additional seconds.
6. Add in the rice and pour in the water and season with the salt and mix.
7. Secure the lid of your Instant Pot and seal the valve; then set the timer to about 6 minutes at a High pressure.
8. When the timer beeps; then turn naturally release the pressure for about 10 minutes.
9. Open the valve and release the remaining pressure.
10. Fluff the rice with a fork; then serve and enjoy its delicious taste!

Nutrition Information

Calories: 205.3| Fat: 11.9g | Carbohydrates: 21.3g | Fiber: 4.1 g |Protein: 5.6g

RECIPE 29: SPICY RICE

Preparation time: 6 minutes

Cooking time: 15 minutes

Yield: 3 Servings

Ingredients:

- 1 ½ tablespoons of olive oil
- ½ cup of finely chopped sweet onion
- 1 Finely minced garlic clove
- 1 ½ cups of vegetable broth
- ¼ Cup of tomato sauce
- 1 Pinch of Chili powder
- ½ Teaspoon of cumin
- ½ Teaspoon of salt
- 1 Pinch of pepper
- 1 cup of white rice

Directions:

1. Heat your Instant Pot by pressing the "sauté" function on your Instant Pot and heat the oil.
2. Add in the onion and sauté the mixture for about 3 minutes.
3. Add in the garlic and sauté for about 2 additional minutes.
4. Close the lid of your Instant Pot and seal the valve; then press the button "manual" and set the timer for about 8 minutes at a High Pressure.
5. When the timer beeps; quick release the pressure; then naturally release the pressure for 10 minutes.
6. Carefully open the lid of the Instant Pot and fluff the rice with a fork.
7. Serve and enjoy your delicious dish!

Nutrition Information

Calories: 332| Fat: 3.5g | Carbohydrates: 65g | Fiber: 8.7 g |Protein: 13.6g

RECIPE 30: LIME RICE

Preparation time: 5 minutes

Cooking time: 12 minutes

Yield: 4Servings

Ingredients:

- 1 Can of about 14 ounces of vegetable broth
- ¾ Cup of water
- 2 Tablespoons of vegetable oil
- ¾ Cup of water
- 3 Tablespoons of lime juice, divided
- 2 Cups of long grain white rice
- The zest of one lime
- ½ Cup of chopped, fresh cilantro
- ½ Teaspoon of salt

Directions:

1. Place the broth, the water, the oil, about 2 tablespoons of lime juice and the white rice in the bottom of your Instant Pot.
2. Close the lid of the Instant Pot and seal the valve; then press the setting button "Rice" displayed on your Instant Pot, which equals about 12 minutes.
3. When the timer beeps, let the rice rest for about 5 minutes in the Instant Pot and don't attempt to open it; then quick release the pressure by turning the sealed valve to venting position.
4. Let all the steam come out; then transfer the rice to a serving platter.
5. Fluff the rice with the help of a fork; then add in the remaining lime juice, the zest, the chopped cilantro and the salt.
6. Serve and enjoy your lime rice while it is still warm!

Nutrition Information

Calories: 147.6| Fat: 2.9g | Carbohydrates: 28g | Fiber: 4.5 g |Protein: 6g

Beans and Rice Meals

Recipe 31: Brown rice with black bean and corn

Preparation time: 10 minutes

Cooking time: 20 minutes

Yield: 3-4 Servings

Ingredients:

- 2 Cups of canned, drained and rinsed black beans
- 2 Finely minced garlic cloves
- 1 Finely chopped large red bell pepper
- ½ Large finely chopped red onion
- 2 Cups of frozen corn
- 2 Cups of brown rice, rinsed and drained
- 1 Juiced lime
- 1 Tablespoon of Chili powder
- 1 Tablespoon of paprika
- 1 Tablespoon of cumin
- ½ Teaspoon of salt
- ¼ Teaspoon of ground black pepper
- 1 Tablespoon of oil
- ½ Chopped Avocado
- ½ Cup of light sour cream

Directions:

1. In your Instant Pot, add in the oil, the onions and the peppers and press the button "sauté".
2. Sauté your ingredients for about 5 minutes; then add in the garlic and sauté for about 3 minutes.
3. Add in the chilli powder, the paprika, the cumin, the salt, and the black pepper and stir for about 3 minutes.
4. Add in the black beans and the brown rice and pour in 1 cups of vegetable stock.
5. Close the lid of the Instant Pot and make sure the valve is sealed.
6. Set the timer for about 20 to 25 minutes at High pressure.
7. When the timer beeps; quick release the pressure for about 10 minutes.
8. Turn the valve to venting position and release any remaining pressure.
9. Open the lid of the Instant Pot and add in the corn, the lime and the juice.
10. Fluff the rice with a fork; then serve and enjoy your dish with chopped avocado!

Nutrition Information

Calories: 127.9| Fat: 4g | Carbohydrates: 24g | Fiber: 3.7 g |Protein: 8g

RECIPE 32: JASMINE RICE WITH RED BEANS

Preparation time: 5 minutes

Cooking time: 25 minutes

Yield: 4 Servings

Ingredients:

- 1 and ¼ cups of dry Red Kidney Beans
- 1 and ½ cups of dry Jasmine Rice
- 1 Cup of Salsa
- ½ Bunch of Cilantro with the stems and the leaves divided
- 3 Cups of Vegetable Broth
- 2 Cups of water

Directions:

1. Start by chopping the Cilantro, but make sure to keep the leaves and stems separated.
2. Add in the dried beans and the rice to the bottom of your Instant Pot.
3. Pour in the Vegetable Broth and the Water on top of the Rice and the Beans; then combine very well.
4. Add in the cilantro stems and the salsa to the Instant Pot and stir.
5. Close the lid of your Instant Pot; then set the valve to sealing position and press the setting "Manual" at a High pressure for about 25 minutes.
6. When the timer beeps, let the pressure release for about 10 minutes; then press the button "Keep warm".
7. Turn the valve to venting position and open the lid of your Instant Pot.
8. Fluff the rice with a fork.
9. Garnish the rice with chopped cilantro; then serve and enjoy!

Nutrition Information

Calories: 367.8| Fat: 12.2g | Carbohydrates: 45g | Fiber: 4.9 g |Protein: 22.4g

RECIPE 33: RICE WITH WHITE BEANS AND HAM

Preparation time: 7 minutes

Cooking time: 40 minutes

Yield: 3 Servings

Ingredients:

- 2 Tablespoons of vegetable oil
- 1 lb of sliced Andouille
- 1 Cup of chopped onion
- 1 Cup of chopped bell pepper
- 1 Cup of chopped celery
- 1 Tablespoon of minced garlic
- 1 Teaspoon of dried thyme
- ½ Teaspoon of cayenne pepper
- 1 Teaspoon of salt
- 1 Teaspoon of black pepper
- 4 Cups of chicken broth or water
- 2 large bay leaves
- 1 lb of white beans soaked into water overnight
- 1 Smoked ham shank
- 4 Chopped green onions
- ¼ Cup of chopped parsley
- 3 Cups of Wild rice

Directions:

1. Rinse the rice and drain it until the water becomes clear.
2. Select the "Sauté" mode of your Instant Pot and let the Instant Pot heat.
3. Add the oil to the inner pot of your Instant Pot.
4. Add the Andouille sausage and sauté until it is browned for about 6 minutes.
5. Remove the sausage with a spoon to a medium bowl and set it aside.
6. Add in the onion, the bell pepper, the celery and the garlic and stir and sauté for 2 minutes.
7. Add the thyme, the cayenne pepper, the salt, the black pepper and stir for about 30 seconds.
8. Add in the broth, the bay leaves, the beans and the ham shank.
9. Add in the wild rice and close the Instant Pot.
10. Make sure the valve is in sealed position; and pressure cook at High pressure for about 40 minutes or just press the button "Multigrain".
11. When the timer beeps; naturally release the pressure; then open the lid of the Instant Pot.
12. Remove the ham shank and chop it into small pieces and set it aside.
13. Fluff the rice with a fork; then top it with the chopped shank.
14. Serve and enjoy your dish!

Nutrition Information

Calories: 421| Fat: 22g | Carbohydrates: 37g | Fiber: 5 g |Protein: 18g

RECIPE 34: WHITE RICE WITH PIGEON PEAS

Preparation time: 5 minutes

Cooking time: 20 minutes

Yield: 4 Servings

Ingredients:

- 1 Teaspoon of oil
- 1 Small chopped Onion
- 4 Sprigs of thyme
- 2 Teaspoons of crushed garlic
- 2 Cups of long grained white rice
- 1 Teaspoon of black pepper
- 1 Cup of coconut milk
- 2 and ½ cups of water
- 1 Can of 15oz of pigeon peas
- ½ Teaspoon of salt
- 1 Chopped scallion

Directions:

1. Place the oil in your Instant Pot and press the button "Sauté" and when the oil is hot, add the onion and sauté the mixture for a couple of minutes.
2. Add the rice, the black pepper, the coconut milk, the water, the pigeon peas, the salt and the scallion and combine very well.
3. Close the lid of your Instant Pot and make sure the valve is in sealed position.
4. Set the timer to about 20 minutes and the pressure to High.
5. When the timer beeps, quick release the pressure for about 10 minutes.
6. Open the lid of your Instant Pot when it is safe to do.
7. Fluff the rice with a fork; then serve and enjoy your dish!

Nutrition Information

Calories: 160.2| Fat: 6g | Carbohydrates: 34g | Fiber: 1 g |Protein: 4g

RECIPE 35: WHITE RICE AND BEAN CHILI

Preparation time: 5 minutes

Cooking time: 20 minutes

Yield: 4 Servings

Ingredients:

- 3 Tablespoons of canola oil
- 1 Finely minced red onion
- 1 Minced seeded jalapeno
- 1 Finely minced green bell pepper
- 1 Minced red bell pepper
- 2 Tablespoons of minced garlic
- 1 Cup of diced Roma tomatoes
- 2 Cups of long-grain white rice
- 8 Ounces of kidney beans
- 2 Cups of chicken stock
- 1 and ½ cups of water
- 1 Teaspoon of paprika
- 1 Tablespoon of chili powder
- 1 Tablespoon of salt
- 1 Teaspoon of freshly ground black pepper
- 3 Tablespoons of finely sliced green onion

Directions

1. In your Instant Pot, press the setting button "Sauté", then add in the oil, the onion and the peppers and sauté the mixture for 2 minutes.
2. Add in the garlic and the tomatoes and stir for 2 minutes.
3. Add the rice, the beans, the chicken stock and the seasonings and close the lid of your Instant Pot.
4. Seal the valve and set the timer to about 20 minutes and the pressure to High.
5. When the timer beeps; quick release the pressure.
6. When it is safe, open the lid and mix with a spoon or a fork.
7. Serve and enjoy your dish!

Nutrition Information

Calories: 114.2| Fat: 3g | Carbohydrates: 30.6g | Fiber: 3.5 g |Protein: 4.9g

Coconut rice meals

Recipe 36: Coconut rice

Preparation time: 3 minutes

Cooking time: 15 minutes

Yield: 3-4 Servings

Ingredients:

- 2 Cups of Jasmine rice
- 1 Can of coconut milk
- 1 and ½ cups of cold water
- 1 Teaspoon of salt
- 1 Teaspoon of granulated sugar
- 1 Tablespoon of chopped fresh cilantro

Directions

1. Rinse the jasmine rice until the water runs clear; then drain any excess of water.
2. Add the rice, the coconut milk, the water, the salt and the sugar to your Instant Pot.
3. Close the lid of your Instant Pot and ake sure the valve is in sealed position.
4. Set the timer to about 10 to 15 minutes and the pressure to High.
5. When the timer beeps, naturally release the pressure; then press the button "Keep warm" and set it aside for 5 minutes.
6. Open the lid of your Instant Pot.
7. Fluff the rice with a fork; then transfer it to a serving bowl.
8. Garnish the rice with chopped cilantro.
9. Serve and enjoy your dish!

Nutrition Information

Calories: 210| Fat: 8g | Carbohydrates: 20g | Fiber: 1.3 g |Protein: 4g

Recipe 37: Coconut shrimp rice

Preparation time: 5 minutes

Cooking time: 20 minutes

Yield: 5 Servings

Ingredients:

- 1 lb of deveined, tail-on shrimp
- 1 Tablespoon of Oil
- 1 Teaspoon of Mustard Seeds
- 1 Sliced Green chilli pepper
- 1 Cup of chopped onion
- ½ Tablespoon of minced Ginger
- ½ Tablespoon of minced garlic
- 1 Cup of chopped tomato
- ¼ Can of 3.5 oz of Coconut Milk
- 1 Tablespoon of lime juice
- ¼ Cup of chopped Cilantro
- ½ Teaspoon of Ground Turmeric
- ½ Teaspoon of Red Chilli powder
- ½ Teaspoon of Garam Masala
- 1 Teaspoon of Coriander powder
- ½ Teaspoon of salt
- 2 ¼ Cups of long-grain white rice

Directions

1. Rinse the rice and drain it very well.
2. Start your Instant Pot by pressing the setting function "Sauté"; then let it heat for a couple of minutes.
3. Add the oil and the mustard seeds to your Instant Pot and sauté for about 4 minutes.
4. Add the green chilli, the onions, the ginger and the garlic to your Instant Pot and sauté for 3 minutes.
5. Add in the tomato and the spices and sauté for about 2 to 3 minutes.
6. Add the rice, the coconut milk and the shrimp to your Instant Pot.
7. Start the Instant Pot by pressing the button "Manual" at a High pressure and set the timer to about 8 minutes; make sure the valve is sealed.
8. When the timer beeps; naturally release the pressure for about 10 minutes.
9. Open the lid of the Instant Pot when it is safe to do it and pour in the lime juice and garnish it with cilantro and mix.
10. Serve and enjoy your dish!

Nutrition Information

Calories: 226| Fat: 10g | Carbohydrates: 20g | Fiber: 1g |Protein: 24g

RECIPE 38: SWEET POTATO AND COCONUT RICE

Preparation time: 6 minutes

Cooking time: 10 minutes

Yield: 4 Servings

Ingredients:

- 1 Sweet; large, cooked, peeled and cubed potato
- 2 Cups of long-grain white rice
- 3 Cups of vegetable broth
- 3 Cups of water
- ½ Teaspoon of salt
- 1 Teaspoon of garlic powder
- 1 and ½ teaspoons of ginger powder
- ⅛ Teaspoons of cayenne
- ¼ Teaspoon of pepper
- 2 Bay leaves
- 1 Large, finely chopped sweet onion
- ½ Cup of maple syrup
- ½ Cup of full-fat coconut milk
- ½ Cup of golden or black raisins
- 1 Cup of shredded unsweetened coconut
- 1 Cup of cashews

Directions:

1. Heat your Instant Pot by pressing the button "Sauté".
2. Add in the rice, the water, the vegetable broth, the salt, the spices and the bay leaves.
3. Close the lid of your Instant pot and make sure the lid is in sealed position.
4. Set the timer to about 12 minutes at High pressure.
5. When the timer beeps; quick release the pressure for about 10 minutes.
6. Open the lid of the Instant pot when it is safe to do it.
7. Stir in the coconut milk, the raisins, the shredded coconut, and the cashews, if using and mix with a spoon.
8. Add in the cubed sweet potatoes and gently mix again.
9. Serve and enjoy your dish!

Nutrition Information

Calories: 125.3| Fat: 5.6g | Carbohydrates: 16.6g | Fiber: 0.7g |Protein: 3.3g

RECIPE 39: COCONUT AND ORANGE RICE

Preparation time: 5 minutes

Cooking time: 9 minutes

Yield: 2-3 Servings

Ingredients:

- 1 Finely chopped small onion
- 1 Chopped celery stalk
- 1 Grated ginger knob
- 1 Grated Turmeric knob (the size of a thumb)
- 1 Tablespoon of oil
- 1 Cup of white rice, rinsed and drained
- 2 Cups of coconut water
- 2 Juiced oranges
- ⅓ Cup of desiccated coconut

Directions

1. Turn on the Instant Pot by and press the function setting "Sauté".
2. Add a little bit of oil; then add the onion, the ginger and the turmeric and sauté for about 2 minutes.
3. Add in the rice and stir; then pour in the coconut water and the orange juice.
4. Close the lid of your Instant Pot and seal the valve.
5. Set the timer for about 7 minutes at a High pressure.
6. When the timer beeps, naturally release the pressure for 10 minutes; then turn the valve to the venting position.
7. Open the lid of the Instant Pot when it is safe to do, then fluff the rice with a fork.
8. Add the grated coconut, a little bit of orange zest and 1 pinch of salt and mix.
9. Serve and enjoy your delicious coconut rice!

Nutrition Information

Calories: 125.3| Fat: 5.6g | Carbohydrates: 16.6g | Fiber: 0.7g |Protein: 3.3g

RECIPE 40: COCONUT AND MANGO RICE

Preparation time: 3 minutes

Cooking time: 8 minutes

Yield: 3 Servings

Ingredients:

- 1 Tablespoon of olive oil
- 1 and ½ cups of long-grain white rice
- 1 Can of 14 ounces of unsweetened coconut milk
- 2/3 Cup of water
- 1 Teaspoon of salt
- 1 Large, peeled and diced ripe mango

Directions

1. Heat your Instant Pot by pressing the button "sauté"; then add in oil and add the rice and coat very well with oil.
2. Pour in the coconut milk, the mango, the water and the salt and stir; then close the lid of the Instant Pot and pressure cook for about 7 to 8 minutes at a high pressure.
3. When the timer beeps; quick release the pressure; and when it is safe to do, open the lid of the Instant Pot.
4. Transfer the rice to a separate dish and fluff it with a fork.
5. Serve and enjoy your dish!

Nutrition Information

Calories: 230| Fat: 10g | Carbohydrates: 15.3g | Fiber: 2g |Protein: 5g

RISOTTO MEALS

RECIPE 41: PARMESAN RISOTTO

Preparation time: 7 minutes

Cooking time: 10 minutes

Yield: 4 Servings

Ingredients:

- 4 ½ cups of vegetable broth
- 1/8 teaspoon of salt
- 2 tomatoes
- 4 tbsp of butter
- 1/3 cup of finely sliced onion
- 2 cups of uncooked Arborio rice
- 2/3 cup of dry white wine
- 2 and 1/2 cups of fresh asparagus, cut into pieces of 1 inch each.
- 2/3 cup of frozen peas
- 1 cup of Parmesan cheese (grated)
- A pinch of Salt
- A pinch of ground black pepper

Directions

1. In your Instant Pot, place the broth and add a pinch of salt and press the button "sauté".
2. Add around 3 tbsp of butter and let it melt.
3. Add the onion and cook for 2 minutes until you see the onion getting softer and tender.
4. Keep stirring at a low speed.
5. Add the rice and cook for 3 minutes.
6. Add in the wine and cook for 2 minutes.
7. Now add ½ cup of hot broth.
8. Cook all the ingredients until the broth starts to be absorbed in the risotto.
9. Keep stirring at a low speed.
10. Add 1 other cup of broth and stir every time you add until the entire quantity of broth is absorbed.
11. Close the lid of your Instant Pot and set the timer to about 8 minutes and the pressure to High.
12. Make sure the valve is in sealed position
13. When the timer beeps, quick release the pressure and when it is safe, open the lid and add the asparagus and the peas.
14. Add in the tomatoes.

15. Press the sauté for about 5 minutes.
16. Season with salt, cheese and butter.
17. Enjoy your risotto!

Nutrition Information

Calories: 199.6| Fat: 10.2g | Carbohydrates: 18.4g | Fiber: 0.9g |Protein: 7.3g

RECIPE 42: TUNA RISOTTO

Preparation time: 6 minutes

Cooking time: 25 minutes

Yield: 3-4 Servings

Ingredients:

- 1 tbsp of olive oil
- 300 g of risotto rice
- 3 cups of stock
- 1 cup of water
- 1 Pinch of salt
- Black pepper
- ½ cup of vinegar
- 50 g of black olive
- 1 can of Tuna

Directions

1. Pour 1 tbsp of oil in the Instant Pot and press the button "sauté".
2. Heat the oil for about 2 minutes.
3. Add the quantity of rice and cook it for 3 more minutes.
4. At this point, you can add slices of onion and keep heating the ingredients all together.
5. Pour in 1 cup of water and keep stirring.
6. Close the lid of the Instant Pot and seal the valve.
7. Set the timer for about 20 minutes and the pressure to High.
8. When the timer beeps; quick release the pressure for 10 minutes.
9. Open the lid when it is safe to do and add 4 tbsp of grated parmesan cheese.
10. Add one can of peas; you can also add corn kernels, mushrooms and carrots.
11. Check the rice if it is soft and creamy.
12. Add tuna if you want, it a very special taste to the risotto.
13. Season your risotto with a pinch of salt and pepper to taste.
14. Serve your risotto and enjoy its delicious taste!

Nutrition Information

Calories: 161.9| Fat: 6.5g | Carbohydrates: 16.8g | Fiber: 0.8g |Protein: 9.4g

RECIPE 43: MUSHROOM RISOTTO

Preparation time: 5 minutes

Cooking time: 35 minutes

Yield: 3 Servings

Ingredients:

- 8 Cups of vegetable broth
- 2 Tablespoons of olive oil
- 4 Tablespoons of butter
- 2 Minced shallots
- 4 Cups of chopped shiitake, Portobello, and button mushroom
- 1 Pinch of salt
- 1/3 Cup of minced, fresh Italian parsley
- 2 Cups of short-grain Arborio rice
- ½ Cup of dry white wine
- 1 Cup of heavy cream
- ½ cup of grated cheese
- 1 Pinch of salt
- 1 Pinch of ground black pepper
- 1 Cup of peas

Directions

1. Turn on your Instant Pot and press the button "Sauté".
2. Pour in the oil with 2 tablespoons of butter and sauté the rice until the mixture starts bubbling.
3. Add in the shallots and the mushrooms; then add in the peas and stir for 1 minute.
4. Add 1 pinch of salt and mix; then add the parsley and close the lid of your Instant Pot.
5. Make sure the valve is in sealed position.
6. Set the timer for about 15 minutes and the pressure to High.
7. When the timer beeps; naturally release the pressure for 10 minutes.
8. Open the lid of the Instant Pot and add in the parsley, the wine and broth and press the button "sauté".
9. Sauté for about 5 minutes, then serve and enjoy your risotto and enjoy it!

Nutrition Information

Calories: 257.6| Fat: 13g | Carbohydrates: 13g | Fiber: 2g |Protein: 21g

RECIPE 44: SALMON RISOTTO

Preparation time: 8 minutes

Cooking time: 40 minutes

Yield: 4 Servings

Ingredients:

- 1 tbsp of olive oil6 finely green sliced onions
- 3 Minced garlic cloves
- 2 ½ cups of Arborio rice
- 4 and ½ cups of rice
- 1 Finely minced lemon rind with the juice
- ¼ Pound of smoked salmon
- 2 Tablespoons of baby capers
- 2 Tablespoons of finely chopped dill
- 1 Pinch of pepper
- 1 Pinch of salt
- ½ Cup of grated parmesan cheese

Directions:

1. Press the button sauté on your Instant Pot.
2. Add in the oil, half of the onions you have and the garlic; then sauté all together for around 3 minutes.
3. Add in the rice keep stirring.
4. Pour in the stock and the lemon.
5. Keep stirring until everything is combined.
6. Lock the lid and Press the "MENU" button to "RISOTTO" again.
7. Set the timer to about 5 minutes at High pressure.
8. When the timer beeps; quick release the pressure and open the lid; then add in the onion, the lemon juice and the capers.
9. Add the dill and season then add the remaining onion, the capers, the lemon juice and the dill.
10. Season your risotto with the salt and the pepper
11. Lock the lid and set the timer for about 30 minutes.
12. When the timer beeps, release the pressure; then open the lid and serve your risotto with the parmesan cheese.

Nutrition Information

Calories: 368.7| Fat: 21.7g | Carbohydrates: 19.6g | Fiber: 1.7g |Protein: 22.4g

RECIPE 45: SWEET RISOTTO

Preparation time: 4 minutes

Cooking time: 15 minutes

Yield: 3 Servings

Ingredients:

- 1 Cup of butter
- 2 cups of rinsed Arborio Rice
- 7 cups of milk
- vanilla bean
- 1 cup of cream
- $1/3$ cup of sugar
- 1 to 2 star anises

Directions:

1. Press the MENU to the button SAUTÉ.
2. Melt the butter in your Instant Pot.
3. Add the rice and keep stirring until it is well coated.
4. Gradually add the milk and the vanilla bean.
5. Keep stirring until everything to combine it.
6. Lock the lid of the pan.
7. Press the MENU button to the setting "Risotto".
8. Let the mixture boil for around 15 minutes.
9. Stir in the cream and the sugar.
10. Remove the lid and let the risotto be cooked again.
11. When the rice is perfectly cooked after 15 more minutes, sprinkle with one star anise on top.
12. Top your risotto with star anise; then serve and enjoy!

Nutrition Information

Calories: 222.8| Fat: 5g | Carbohydrates: 36g | Fiber: 1.2g |Protein: 8.7g

Mexican Rice Meals

Recipe 46: Spicy Mexican Rice

Preparation time: 5 minutes

Cooking time: 30 minutes

Yield: 2-3 Servings

Ingredients:

- 1 Tablespoon of olive oil
- 1 Small chopped red onion
- 3 Chopped garlic cloves
- 1 De-seed, and chopped jalapeno
- 1 Can of 14.5 oz of fire roasted tomatoes
- ¾ Cup of corn kernels
- 1 Can of 15 Oz of rinsed and drained black beans
- ½ Teaspoon of cumin powder
- ½ Teaspoon of smoked paprika
- ¼ Teaspoon of red chili powder
- 1 Pinch of salt
- 1 Pinch of black pepper
- 1 Cup of brown uncooked rice
- 1 and ½ cups of vegetable broth or water
- 2 to 3 Tablespoons of chopped cilantro
- 1 Juiced lime
- 1 Chopped avocado

Directions:

1. Start your Instant Pot and press the button "sauté" and when it displays 'hot', add in the oil and add in the chopped onion, the garlic and the jalapeño.
2. Sauté your ingredients for about 2 minutes.
3. Add in the black beans and the corn kernels and mix very well; if the kernels are frozen, put it into warm water for about 4 minutes before adding it to the Instant Pot.
4. Add the tomatoes and do not mix; then add the cumin, the spices, the smoked paprika, the chilli powder, the salt, the pepper and the rinsed and drained rice; then mix.
5. Pour in the vegetable broth and mix; then close the lid of your Instant Pot and press the button "Manual" and cook on High pressure for about 20 minutes and make sure the valve is in sealed position.

6. When the timer beeps, naturally release the pressure and when it is safe to open the lid, open it; then fluff the rice with a fork and add the lime juice and the cilantro.
7. Add in the chopped avocado.
8. Serve and enjoy your Mexican dish!

Nutrition Information

Calories: 374| Fat: 11g | Carbohydrates: 43g | Fiber: 5.4g |Protein: 14g

RECIPE 47: PERI PERI RICE

Preparation time: 8 minutes

Cooking time: 25 minutes

Yield: 3 Servings

Ingredients:

- 1 Large finely chopped onion
- 1 Large finely diced bell pepper
- 1 Can of 8 Oz of drained and diced tomatoes
- 2 Tablespoons of spicy peri peri sauce
- ½ Cup of long-grain white rice
- 1 Cup of water

Directions:

1. Press the button 'sauté' of your Instant pot; then heat the oil until it starts shimmering.
2. Add in the onion and the bell pepper, and sauté for about 5 minutes.
3. Add in the canned tomatoes, the canned tomatoes, the peri peri sauce, and the rice, and stir.
4. Sauté the rice with the rest of the ingredients for about 4 minutes.
5. Pour in the water and mix; then close the lid of the Instant Pot and set the timer for about 15 minutes at a High pressure.
6. When the timer beeps, quick release the pressure for about 5 minutes.
7. Open the lid of the Instant Pot and.
8. Stir your ingredients very well and fluff the rice with a fork.
9. Top the rice with chopped cilantro and fresh parsley.
10. Serve and enjoy your delicious Mexican rice!

Nutrition Information

Calories: 124| Fat: 8g | Carbohydrates: 27.3g | Fiber: 2.8g |Protein: 4g

Recipe 48: Mexican Seafood Paella

Preparation time: 10 minutes

Cooking time: 20 minutes

Yield: 3-4 Servings

Ingredients:

- 4 Tablespoons of olive oil
- 1 Pound of sliced cured Spanish chorizo
- 1 Chopped yellow onion
- 3 Finely minced garlic cloves
- 1 Pinch of salt
- 1 Pinch of freshly ground pepper
- 2 Teaspoons of smoked paprika
- 1 Teaspoon of sweet paprika
- ½ Teaspoon of granulated garlic
- ½ Teaspoon of saffron threads
- ½ Cup of dry white wine
- 14 Ounces of crushed tomatoes with the juice
- 2 Cups of long-grain white rice
- 2 Cups of chicken broth
- 1 Pound of clams
- ¾ Pounds of large peeled and deveined shrimp with tails
- 1 and ½ cups of frozen peas
- ½ Cup of chopped fresh flat-leaf parsley
- Sliced lemon wedges

Directions:

1. Select the button "Sauté" of your Instant Pot and warm about 2 tablespoons of oil.
2. Add in the chorizo and sauté your ingredients for about 3 to 4 minutes; then transfer the chorizo to a plate and warm the remaining quantity of oil.
3. Add in the oil and the minced garlic and cook for about 3 minutes.
4. Season your ingredients with 1 pinch of salt and 1 pinch of pepper, then add in the smoked paprika, the sweet paprika, the granulated garlic, and the saffron.
5. Cook for about 3 minutes, then pour in the wine, the tomatoes, the rice, the clams and the broth and close the lid in its place; then make sure the valve is in sealed position.
6. Press the button "Keep Warm/Cancel" to reset the cooking program and press the button "Manual/ Pressure" and set the timer for about 8 minutes at a High pressure.
7. When the timer beeps, turn the valve to the Venting position and manually release the pressure.

8. Carefully remove the lid and press the button "Keep warm/Cancel", then press the button "sauté".
9. Add the remaining quantity of broth, the peas and the shrimp and cook for about 5 minutes.
10. Serve and enjoy your Paella!

Nutrition Information

Calories: 357| Fat: 10.1g | Carbohydrates: 45g | Fiber: 3.6g |Protein: 19.3g

RECIPE 49: ENCHILADA CHEESY RICE

Preparation time: 5 minutes

Cooking time: 22 minutes

Yield: 4 Servings

Ingredients:

- 2 Cups of long grain white rice
- 2 and ½ cups of water
- Can of 15 oz of enchilada sauce
- 1 Can of 14.5 oz of rinsed and drained black beans
- 1 Teaspoon of cumin
- ½ Teaspoon of salt
- ½ Teaspoon of pepper
- 1 Teaspoon of garlic powder
- 1 Tablespoon of lime juice
- 1 to 2 cups of sharp grated cheddar cheese
- 1 Chopped avocado, diced
- Tablespoons of sour cream
- 1 Chopped lime
- Chopped Cilantro

Directions:

1. Add the rice, the water, the enchilada sauce, the black beans, the cumin, the salt, the pepper and the garlic powder to your Instant Pot, but don't over stir.
2. Cover your Instant Pot and make sure the valve is in sealed position.
3. Press the button "Manual" and set the timer to about 12 minutes.
4. When the timer beeps; naturally release the pressure for about 10 minutes; then turn the valve to "venting" position.
5. When the timer beeps let the pressure release naturally for 10 minutes and then move the valve to "venting."
6. Carefully remove the lid, and add in the lime juice and the cheddar cheese.

7. Serve and enjoy your Mexican dish with chopped avocado, sour cream, cilantro and lime wedges!

Nutrition Information

Calories: 312| Fat: 7.2g | Carbohydrates: 40g | Fiber: 2.1g |Protein: 8.7g

RECIPE 50: TACO RICE WITH CORN KERNELS AND GROUND BEEF

Preparation time: 10 minutes

Cooking time: 12 minutes

Yield: 3 Servings

Ingredients:

- 1 Small diced Onion
- 1 lb of ground beef
- ¼ Cup of taco seasoning
- 1 Can of 14 Oz of undrained diced tomatoes
- 1 Cup of fire roasted, drained corn kernels
- ¾ Cups of uncooked long white rice
- 2 Cups of beef broth
- 1 and ½ cups of shredded Colby jack cheese
- For the Taco toppings:
- ½ cup of sour Cream
- 1 Diced Avocado
- 1 Cup of sliced Black Olives
- A little bit of chopped Cilantro
- Salsa

Directions:

1. Start your Instant Pot by pressing the setting button "sauté"; then cook for about 2 minutes.
2. Add in the ground beef and crumble it for about 2 minutes.
3. Drain the beef and discard any fat; then add in the taco seasoning, the chopped tomatoes, the corn kernels, the rice and the beef broth.
4. Close the lid of the Instant Pot and set the timer to about 10 minutes and the pressure to High, make sure the valve is in sealed position.
5. When the timer beeps; quick release the pressure for about 5 minutes and turn the valve to venting position.
6. Add in the shredded cheese and mix very well.
7. Top the rice with cheese, then serve and enjoy its delicious taste!

Nutrition Information

Calories: 131| Fat: 7.2g | Carbohydrates: 15.6g | Fiber: 0.8g |Protein: 3g

ASIAN RICE MEALS

RECIPE 51: CHINESE-STYLE RICE

Preparation time: 5 minutes

Cooking time: 15 minutes

Yield: 2-3 Servings

Ingredients:

- 1 Cup of long grain rice
- 1 Cup of water
- A piece of about 3 inches of pork belly, pork
- 1 Link of sweet Chinese sausage
- 1 Tablespoon of regular soy sauce
- 1 Tablespoon of seasoned soy sauce
- ½ Tablespoon of dark soy sauce
- 1 Tablespoon of fish sauce
- 1 Pinch of sugar
- 1 Pinch of white pepper
- 1 Chopped scallion

Directions:

1. Soak the rice in about 1 cup of water for about 1 hour.
2. Start the Instant Pot by pressing the button "sauté".
3. Add in the cured meat and pour in 1 cup of water.
4. Close the lid of your Instant Pot and seal the valve.
5. Set the timer for about 8 minutes and the pressure to High.
6. When the timer beeps, naturally release the pressure for about 10 minutes.
7. Carefully open the lid of your Instant Pot and take a small bowl, then add the soy sauces, the fish sauce, the sugar and the white pepper and mix very well.
8. Pour the sauce into the Instant Pot evenly on top of the rice and cover the Instant Pot with the lid once more.
9. Set the timer to about 4 minutes and the pressure to High.
10. When the timer beeps; quick release the pressure; then open the lid when it is safe doing it.
11. Transfer the rice to a serving dish; then serve and enjoy your delicious dish with sauce and scallions!

Nutrition Information

Calories: 160.7| Fat: 5.4g | Carbohydrates: 18.7g | Fiber: 0.0g |Protein: 8.6g

RECIPE 52: JASMINE RICE WITH FISH SAUCE

Preparation time: 10 minutes

Cooking time: 30 minutes

Yield: 3 Servings

Ingredients:

- 1 Cup of Uncooked Jasmine Rice
- ½ Piece of chopped Fresh Chicken
- 2 Preserved sausages of medium size
- ¼ Piece of Salted Fish Cutlet
- 2 Cups of water
- 2 Slices of shredded fresh Ginger
- 1 Sliced, small Red Onion
- 1 section of spring onion
- For marinating the Chicken:
- ½ Teaspoon of Soy Sauce
- 1 Heap teaspoon of Corn Flour
- ¼ Teaspoon of Sesame Oil
- ½ Teaspoon of Cooking Wine
- ½ Teaspoon of Dark Soy Sauce
- 1 Dash of Pepper

Directions:

1. Wash the rice and drain it very well for about 1 hour.
2. Start your Instant Pot and press the button "sauté".
3. Add a small quantity of water and blanch the sausages in it for about 1 minute.
4. Remove the skin of the sausages and cut it into slices; then set it aside.
5. Remove the fats and the skin of the chicken and cut it into small pieces; then marinade it with the prepared marinade for about 20 minutes.
6. Drain the Instant Pot, then pour 1 teaspoon of oil in it and press the button "sauté".
7. Sauté the preserved sliced sausages; then remove it and set it aside.
8. Add in the salted fish; then sauté the onion and the ginger; then add in the rice.
9. Arrange the chicken on top of the rice.
10. Pour in 1 cup of water and stir; then close the lid of the Instant Pot and set the timer for about 10 minutes and make sure the valve is in sealed position.
11. When the timer beeps, naturally release the pressure for 10 minutes; then turn the valve to venting position.
12. Garnish the rice with chopped spring onion, chilli and coriander; then drizzle with dark soy sauce.
13. Serve and enjoy your dish!

Nutrition Information

Calories: 357| Fat: 8.6g | Carbohydrates: 44.5g | Fiber: 0.6g |Protein: 24.6g

RECIPE 53: RICE DUMPLINGS

Preparation time: 15 minutes

Cooking time: 60 minutes

Yield: 10 Servings

Ingredients:

- 80 dried bamboo leaves
- 10 cups of sticky glutinous rice
- 2 Tablespoons of salt
- 1 Pound of skinned mung beans
- ½ Cup of dried shrimps
- ½ Cup of dried scallops
- 25 salted egg yolks
- 3 Sliced Chinese sausages
- 1 and ½ cups of peanuts

To marinate the pork belly:

- 2 Pounds of chopped into pieces, pork belly
- 1 Tablespoon of soy sauce
- 1 Teaspoon of salt
- 1 Tablespoon of five spice powder
- 1/2 tsp freshly ground black pepper

Directions:

1. Soak the bamboo leaves for an overnight and make sure to wash and rinse them before using them.
2. You can use about 3 to 4 bamboo leaves per one dumpling wrap.
3. Soak the rice overnight; then drain it in a colander and add about 2 tablespoons of salt; then set it aside.
4. Marinate the pork belly with the soy sauce overnight with the salt, the five-spice powder, and the black pepper powder.
5. Soak the beans and the peanuts overnight; then drain them in a colander and add about 1 tablespoon of salt.
6. Soak the dried shrimps, the shiitake mushrooms and the scallops in separate small bowls for about 1 to 2 hours.
7. To wrap the dumplings:

8. Fold one leaf up so that you create a cone; then fill it with a layer of rice right into the bottom.
9. Add the beans, the egg yolks, the pork belly, the dried scallops, the shrimps, the shiitake mushrooms and the Chinese sausage.
10. Add a second layer of leaf just around the top and top with rice and mung beans.
11. Top with another bamboo leaf; then fold the bottom with the side up; then place the two sides into the middle and pinch the leaves on the other side and fold it down.
12. Tie the dumpling with the twine.
13. Arrange the dumplings into the bottom of your Instant Pot/pressure cooker; then pour in 2 cups of water and lock the lid.
14. Set the timer for about 60 minutes and make sure the valve is in sealed position.
15. When the timer beeps, quick release the pressure for 5 minutes; then carefully open the lid.
16. Serve and enjoy your dumplings!

Nutrition Information

Calories: 246.2| Fat: 3.4g | Carbohydrates: 40g | Fiber: 3.6g |Protein: 12.4g

RECIPE 54: BROWN RICE WITH SCRAMBLED EGGS

Preparation time: 5 minutes

Cooking time: 46 minutes

Yield: 3 Servings

Ingredients:

- 3 Cups of brown rice
- 3 Large eggs
- 4 finely chopped scallions
- 1 Tablespoons of vegetable oil
- 1 Tablespoon of soy sauce
- 1 Pinch of salt
- 1 Pinch of pepper
- ½ Tablespoon of sesame oil
- ½ Teaspoon of sesame seeds

Directions:

1. Rinse the rice and drain it.
2. Finely chop the scallions.
3. Boil the rice into a pan of boiling water for about 30 minutes.
4. Crack the eggs and beat them in a bowl with a fork.
5. Heat your Instant Pot by pressing the button "Sauté" and pour in 2 tablespoons of oil.
6. Add in 2/3 of the scallions and sauté for about 2 minutes.
7. Add in the eggs and sauté while stirring for about 1 minute.

8. Add in 2 tablespoons of oil; then stir in the remaining scallions and sauté for about 1 tablespoon of soy sauce.
9. Add in the rice and give a quick stir; then close the lid of your Instant Pot and set the timer for about 3 minutes and the pressure to High.
10. When the timer beeps, naturally release the pressure; then open the lid and season with salt, sesame oil, and pepper and sprinkle with sesame seeds!

Nutrition Information

Calories: 365| Fat: 19.4g | Carbohydrates: 27.1g | Fiber: 2.4g |Protein: 19.8g

RECIPE 55: SUSHI BOWL

Preparation time: 12 minutes

Cooking time: 20 minutes

Yield: 6 Servings

Ingredients:

- 2 Sheets of nori seaweed of 4 inches each
- 6 Ounces of extra-firm tofu
- The grated zest and the juice of an orange
- The grated zest and the juice of ½ Lemon
- 2 Tablespoons of brown or regular sugar
- 2 Tablespoons of shoyu or soya sauce
- 2 Tablespoons of brown rice vinegar
- 4 Cups of white, rinsed and drained rice
- 4 Chopped green onions
- 1 Peeled, pitted and thinly sliced avocado
- 3 Tablespoons of toasted sesame seeds

Directions:

1. Start by toasting the nori in a preheated oven at a temperature of 300° F for a couple of minutes.
2. Crumble the nori or chop it coarsely; then drain the tofu and pat it dry with paper towels.
3. Cut the tofu through the middle to make about 4 thick sheets.
4. Heat your Instant Pot by pressing the button "sauté" and brown the tofu sheets for a couple of minutes.
5. Remove the sheets of tofu and set it aside.
6. Add in the rice and pour in 1 cup of water and season with salt.
7. Close the lid of your Instant Pot and set the timer to about 7 minutes at a High pressure and when the timer beeps, quick release the pressure and when it is safe, carefully open the lid.

8. Make the dressing by combining the orange juice, the lemon juice, and the sugar in a small pan and bring to a boil for 1 to 2 minutes.
9. Add in the shoyu and the vinegar and boil for 1 additional minute.
10. Add in the zests and stir 1/3 cup of the seasoning into your rice.
11. Serve and enjoy your rice with the toasted nori, the green onions, the tofu, the avocado slices, and 1 sprinkle of sesame seeds!

Nutrition Information

Calories: 379| Fat: 10.8g | Carbohydrates: 44.6g | Fiber: 6.2g |Protein: 27.5g

RECIPE 56: JAPANESE STICKY RICE

Preparation time: 8 minutes

Cooking time: 13 minutes

Yield: 4 Servings

Ingredients:

- 2 ½ Cups of glutinous rice
- ¼ Cup of azuki beans
- 2 and ½ cups of water
- 1 Teaspoon of salt
- 1 Dash of Black sesame

Directions:

1. Start by washing the azuki beans and drain them very well.
2. Pour 2 and ½ cups of water to your Instant Pot; then add in the azuki beans.
3. Close the lid of the Instant Pot and press the button "+" "-"to adjust the timer and make sure the valve is in sealed position.
4. Set the timer to about 10 minutes and when the timer beeps, quick release the pressure and turn the valve to venting position.
5. Open the lid of your Instant Pot and discard the water with a ladle, but don't dry it completely, you can just keep about ½ cup back into your Instant Pot.
6. Add the salt and the rice and close the lid of your Instant Pot and seal the valve.
7. Set the timer for about 3 minutes at High pressure and when the timer beeps; press the button "Cancel" and wait for a few minutes so that the pressure comes out naturally.
8. Once the pressure is released, give the rice a quick stir.
9. Sprinkle the rice with black sesame; then serve and enjoy it!

Nutrition Information

Calories: 240| Fat: 11.2g | Carbohydrates: 43g | Fiber: 2g |Protein: 6g

RECIPE 57: RICE BALLS

Preparation time: 10 minutes

Cooking time: 20 minutes

Yield: 8 Servings

Ingredients:

For the Rice Balls:

- 1 Cup of short-grain Asian rice
- 3 to 4 large cabbage leaves
- 1 Pound of ground pork
- 4 Minced scallions
- 6 Minced water chestnut
- 2 Teaspoons of finely grated peeled fresh ginger
- 2 Finely minced garlic cloves
- 2 Teaspoons of soy sauce
- 2 Teaspoons of sake
- 1 Teaspoon of toasted sesame oil
- 1 Teaspoon of sugar
- 1 Teaspoon of kosher salt

For the sauce

- ½ Cup of soy sauce
- 2 Tablespoons of water
- 2 Tablespoons of minced scallions
- 1 Tablespoon of finely grated fresh peeled ginger
- 2 Teaspoons of hot sesame chile oil
- 2 Teaspoons of unseasoned rice vinegar
- 1 Teaspoon of sugar

Directions:

1. Cover the rice with water in a medium bowl; then set it aside for 30 minutes; then drain the rice with paper towels.
2. Transfer the rice to a shallow dish; then turn on your Instant Pot and pour 1 ¼ cups of water in it.
3. Place a wire rack in the bottom of your Instant Pot and place a steamer basket over the rack.
4. Line the basket with cabbage leaves or with parchment paper.
5. Combine the rest of your ingredients in a bowl and form balls from the mixture; then coat the balls into the rice and press very well to prevent the rice from falling out.
6. Arrange the rice balls in the basket and leave a small space between the balls.

7. Cover your Instant Pot/Pressure cooker with the lid and turn the valve to a sealing position; then set the timer for about 20 minutes and set the pressure to High.
8. When the timer beeps, quick release the pressure; prepare the sauce by mixing the water with the soy sauce, the minced scallions, the ginger, the chile oil, the rice vinegar and the sugar and mix.
9. Serve and enjoy the rice balls with the sauce on top!

Nutrition Information

Calories: 240| Fat: 11.2g | Carbohydrates: 43g | Fiber: 2g |Protein: 6g

RECIPE 58: RICE WITH EDAMAME

Preparation time: 8 minutes

Cooking time: 12 minutes

Yield: 5 Servings

Ingredients:

- 3 Cups of uncooked long-grain white rice
- 2 Scrambled egg whites
- 1 Scrambled whole egg
- 1 Tablespoon of oil
- ½ Chopped onions
- 2 Diced garlic cloves
- 5 Chopped scallions with the greens and whites separated
- ½ Cup of shredded carrots
- 1 Tablespoon of cooking spray
- 1 Cup of shelled edamame
- 2 Tablespoons of low sodium soy sauce
- 1 Pinch of salt and 1 pinch of pepper

Directions:

1. Start your Instant Pot and press the button "sauté", then pour in 1 cup of water and close the lid.
2. Set the timer for about 8 minutes and the pressure to High.
3. When the timer beeps, quick release the pressure and when it is safe to do, open the lid of the Instant Pot.
4. Remove the rice from the Instant Pot and clean the Instant Pot.
5. Whisk the whole eggs and the egg whites; then season it with 1 pinch of salt and 1 pinch of pepper.
6. Spray your Instant Pot with the cooking spray and press the button "sauté"; and when the oil heats up, add in the eggs and cook for about 1 minute.

7. Remove the egg mixture and add the onions, the oil, the scallion whites, the carrots and the garlic and sauté for about 30 to 60 seconds.
8. Add the rice and stir; then add the cooked eggs with the soy sauce, the scallion greens and the Edamame and mix for 1 minute.
9. Serve and enjoy your delicious dish!

Nutrition Information

Calories: 210| Fat: 5.9g | Carbohydrates: 4.5g | Fiber: 1.1g |Protein: 8.7g

RECIPE 59: RICE WITH CABBAGE AND FISH

Preparation time: 5 minutes

Cooking time: 21 minutes

Yield: 3 Servings

Ingredients:

- 1 Tablespoons of olive oil
- 1 Large finely diced onion
- 1 Finely diced red pepper
- ½ Teaspoon of five-spice powder
- 5 Chopped cherry tomatoes
- 1 Cup of shredded cabbage
- 3 Cups of long-grain white rice
- 2 Cups of chicken stock
- 3 to 4 frozen basa fillets, defrosted
- 1 cup of barbecue sauce
- Chopped spring onions
- Toasted sesame seeds and shredded cabbage for the topping

Directions:

1. Start your Instant Pot, then add in the oil and press the button "Sauté" and heat the olive oil in it; then add the onion and the pepper and sauté for about 4 to 5 minutes.
2. Add in the five-spice powder, the cherry tomatoes, the cabbage, the rice and the stock.
3. Cover the instant pot with a lid and set the timer for about 10 minutes; make sure the valve is in sealed position.
4. When the timer beeps; quick release the pressure for about 5 minutes; then turn the valve to venting position.
5. Open the lid of your Instant Pot and transfer the rice to serving bowls.
6. Top the rice with the sesame seeds, the chopped avocado, the shredded red cabbage and the spring onions.
7. Serve and enjoy your dish!

Nutrition Information

Calories: 313| Fat: 7.9g | Carbohydrates: 11g | Fiber: 2g |Protein: 21g

RECIPE 60: RICE CONGEE

Preparation time: 4minutes

Cooking time: 30 minutes

Yield: 2-3 Servings

Ingredients:

- 1 Cup of long-grain white rice
- 1 Cup of water or stock
- 1 Pinch of salt to taste

Directions:

1. Rinse the rice and drain it very well until the water runs clean.
2. Place the 1 cup of rice in the Instant Pot.
3. Pour in about 9 cups of water in the Instant Pot.
4. Close the lid of the Instant Pot and seal the valve.
5. Set the timer to about 30 minutes and when the timer beeps; naturally release the pressure for about 10 minutes; then turn the valve to venting position.
6. Season the Congee with salt.
7. Serve and enjoy your rice congee!

Nutrition Information

Calories: 313| Fat: 7.9g | Carbohydrates: 11g | Fiber: 2g |Protein: 21g

SOUPS WITH RICE

RECIPE 61: RICE AND CHICKEN SOUP

Preparation time: 5 minutes

Cooking time: 25 minutes

Yield: 2 Servings

Ingredients:

- 3 Cups of chicken broth
- 2 Sliced carrots
- 2 Sliced celery ribs of celery
- 1 Diced medium onion
- 1 Teaspoon of dried oregano
- ½ Teaspoon of garlic powder
- 3 Skinless, frozen and boneless chicken thighs
- ¾ Cup of brown rice
- 1 and ½ cups of milk
- ½ Cup of basil pesto

Directions:

1. Turn on the Instant Pot by pressing the button "sauté".
2. Pour in the broth, the carrots, the celery, the onions, the oregano, the garlic powder, the chicken and the brown rice to your Instant Pot.
3. Lock the lid of your Instant Pot and turn the valve to sealing position.
4. Turn off the function "sauté" and set the timer to about 22 minutes by pressing the button "manual".
5. When the timer beeps, naturally release the pressure and turn the valve to the venting position; then remove the lid and chop the chicken into pieces.
6. Add in the milk and add in the pesto; then combine very well.
7. Serve and enjoy your soup!

Nutrition Information

Calories: 326| Fat: 19.8g | Carbohydrates: 29g | Fiber: 3.6g |Protein: 7.2g

RECIPE 62: BEEF JASMINE RICE SOUP

Preparation time: 4 minutes

Cooking time: 18 minutes

Yield: 3 Servings

Ingredients:

- 4 Cups of chicken broth
- 1 Pound of chopped into small pieces, beef shank
- 1 Cup of Jasmine rice
- 1 Chopped onion
- 3 Large, finely chopped carrots
- 3 Chopped celery ribs
- 1 Teaspoon of garlic powder
- 2 Teaspoon of dried parsley
- 1 Teaspoon of dried thyme
- ½ Teaspoon of dried rosemary
- ½ Teaspoon of dried sage
- 1 to 2 bay leaves
- 1 and ½ teaspoons of salt
- 2 Tablespoons of butter

Directions:

1. Turn on your Instant pot and press the button "sauté"; then pour in the chicken broth.
2. When the chicken broth starts heating up, add in the rest of your ingredients and turn off the setting function "sauté".
3. Cover your Instant Pot with its lid and secure it in its place; and make sure the valve is in sealed position.
4. Set the function button "manual/pressure" to about 18 minutes.
5. When the timer beeps; quick release the pressure for about 5 minutes; then turn the valve to venting position.
6. Remove the lid of the Instant Pot when it is safe to do it; then discard the bay leaves and mix very well.
7. Serve and enjoy your delicious soup!

Nutrition Information

Calories: 130| Fat: 4g | Carbohydrates: 18g | Fiber: 2.7g |Protein: 8g

RECIPE 63: WILD CAULIFLOWER RICE SOUP

Preparation time: 10 minutes

Cooking time: 30 minutes

Yield: 4 Servings

Ingredients:

- 2 ½ cups of chicken stock
- 1 Chopped large head of cauliflower
- 1 Finely chopped onion
- 2 Chopped celery stalks
- 2 Chopped carrots
- 3 Finely chopped garlic cloves
- 1 Tablespoon of soy sauce
- 1 Tablespoon of lemon juice
- 1 Pinch of salt
- 1 Pinch of cracked black pepper
- 1 Cup of rinsed wild rice
- 3 Chopped spring onions

Directions:

1. Pour the chicken stock in your Instant Pot; then add in the cauliflower.
2. Add in the cauliflower, the onion, the celery, the wild rice, the carrots and the garlic and close the lid of your Instant Pot.
3. Set the timer for about 25 minutes and make sure the valve is in sealed position.
4. When the timer beeps; quick release the pressure for 5 minutes; then open the lid when it is safe to.
5. Add in the rice, the soy sauce and the lemon juice; then cover the Instant Pot with the lid and turn it on by pressing the button "Manual" and adjust the timer to about 8 minutes.
6. When the timer beeps, naturally release the pressure for 8 minutes; then open the lid of your Instant Pot and puree the mixture with a blender.
7. Ladle the soup in bowls; then garnish with chopped green onions.
8. Serve and enjoy your soup!

Nutrition Information

Calories: 98| Fat: 5.3g | Carbohydrates: 11.2g | Fiber: 4g |Protein: 3.1g

RECIPE 64: WALNUT RICE SOUP

Preparation time: 5 minutes

Cooking time: 14 minutes

Yield: 3 Servings

Ingredients:

- 1 Finely chopped onion
- 1 Cup of long-grain white rice
- 1 Pound of potatoes
- 1 Tablespoon of butter
- 4 Tablespoons of cream
- 2 Cups of vegetable stock
- ¼ Teaspoon of nutmeg
- 1 Pinch of salt
- 1 Pinch of ground black pepper
- 1 Cup of walnuts
- 1 Bunch of chives

Directions:

1. Start your Instant Pot by pressing the button "Sauté".
2. Slice the onion and the potatoes and sauté it into warm butter for about 2 minutes.
3. Add in the rinsed and drained rice and pour in the vegetable stock.
4. Close the lid of your Instant Pot and make sure the valve is in sealed position and set the timer to about 12 minutes.
5. When the timer beeps, quick release the pressure; then open the lid of your Instant Pot.
6. Pour the soup into bowls; then serve the soup in bowls.
7. Add the cream and the nutmeg and season with salt and pepper.
8. Garnish the soup with walnut cream and chives.
9. Serve and enjoy your soup!

Nutrition Information

Calories: 364| Fat: 25g | Carbohydrates: 23g | Fiber: 3.8g |Protein: 23g

RECIPE 65: MUSHROOM AND CASHEW RICE SOUP

Preparation time: 7 minutes

Cooking time: 20 minutes

Yield: 3-4 Servings

Ingredients:

- 1 Cup of long grain white rice
- 1 Cup of raw cashews
- 2 Tablespoons of olive oil
- 1 Finely chopped medium onion
- 2 Chopped large carrots
- 2 Chopped celery ribs
- 2 Cups of finely chopped cremini mushrooms
- 3 to 4 minced garlic cloves
- 2 Cups of low-sodium chicken stock
- ½ Teaspoon of dried marjoram, dill or oregano
- ½ Teaspoon of salt
- ½ Pound of raw boneless skinless chicken breast
- 1/3 Cup of finely chopped fresh parsley

Directions:

1. About 12 hours before cooking, place the rice and the cashews in a medium bowl and cover them with water.
2. Add in the olive oil to your Instant Pot; then press the button "sauté" and when the oil heats up, add in the chopped onion, the carrots, the celery, the mushrooms and the garlic.
3. Season your ingredients with 1 pinch of salt and 1 pinch of pepper and sauté for about 1 minute and stir.
4. Pour in the stock, the dried herbs and about ½ teaspoons of salt and taste with more herbs and salt if needed.
5. Drain the already soaked rice; then rinse it with fresh water and add it to the Instant Pot together with the chicken.
6. Cover your Instant Pot with the lid and make sure the valve is in sealed position.
7. Set the timer to about 20 minutes and when the timer beeps, naturally release the pressure.
8. Prepare the cashew cream and to do that, drain the cashews and place it in a food processor with about 2/3 cup of water and 1 pinch of salt and puree for about 30 seconds.
9. Remove the chicken breasts and dice into pieces; then add it back to the Instant Pot.
10. Stir in the cashew cream.
11. Serve and enjoy your soup!

Nutrition Information

Calories: 244.8| Fat: 4g | Carbohydrates: 40g | Fiber: 2.6g |Protein: 7.3g

Recipe 66: Rice and Carrot Soup

Preparation time: 5 minutes

Cooking time: 7 minutes

Yield: 3 Servings

Ingredients:

- ½ Diced small yellow onion
- 2 Diced celery stalks
- 4 Peeled and finely chopped medium carrots
- 2 Finely minced garlic cloves
- 1 Can of 15 Oz of drained and rinsed beans
- 1 and ½ cups of frozen peas
- 1 Cup of white rice
- 2 Cups of water
- 1 Cup of chicken or vegetable stock
- ½ Teaspoon of dried thyme leaf
- 1 Teaspoon of dried parsley flakes
- ½ Teaspoon of dried basil
- ¼ Teaspoon of garlic powder
- ¼ Teaspoon of salt
- ¼ Teaspoon of black pepper

Directions:

1. Place the diced onion, the celery stalk, then chopped carrots in your Instant Pot.
2. Add in the garlic cloves, the rinsed and drained beans, the peas, the white rice, the water, the dried thyme leaf, the dried basil, the garlic powder, the salt and the pepper.
3. Add in the rice and mix all your ingredients together.
4. Put the lid on your Instant Pot and make sure the valve is in sealed position and set the timer for about 7 minutes.
5. When the timer beeps; quick release the pressure for about 5 minutes.
6. Turn the valve to a venting position; then serve and enjoy your soup!

Nutrition Information

Calories: 211| Fat: 8.7g | Carbohydrates: 23g | Fiber: 3g |Protein: 10g

RECIPE 67: RICE AND LENTIL SOUP

Preparation time: 4 minutes

Cooking time: 14 minutes

Yield: 4 Servings

Ingredients:

- 3 Tablespoons of unrefined, extra-virgin olive oil
- 3 Peeled and diced large carrots
- 3 Diced celery stalks
- 1 Diced large onion
- 3 Minced garlic cloves garlic
- 1 Pound of peeled, seeded and chopped tomatoes
- 3 Cups of vegetable stock or water
- 2 Cups of chopped squash
- 2 Sprigs of fresh thyme
- 1 Pinch of sea salt
- 1 Pinch of freshly ground black pepper
- 2 Handfuls of chopped kale
- ½ Cup of long grain white rice

Directions:

1. Start your Instant Pot and press the button "sauté"; then add in the oil, the carrots, the celery, the onion and the garlic and sauté for about a couple of minutes.
2. Stir in the tomatoes and cook for about 1 minute.
3. Pour in the stock, the chopped squash, the uncooked white rice, the thyme and the 2 teaspoons of salt.
4. Close the lid of your Instant Pot and seal the valve.
5. Set the timer for about 13 minutes and when the timer beeps, quick release the pressure and, open the lid carefully.
6. Discard the thyme sprigs and season with 1 pinch of salt and 1 pinch of ground black pepper.
7. Ladle your soup in bowls; then serve and enjoy it!

Nutrition Information

Calories: 299| Fat: 4.8g | Carbohydrates: 38g | Fiber: 7g |Protein: 10g

RECIPE 68: RICE AND TOMATO SOUP

Preparation time: 5 minutes

Cooking time: 10 minutes

Yield: 4 Servings

Ingredients:

- 1 Tablespoon of ghee
- ½ Teaspoon of cumin seeds
- 1/8 Teaspoon of turmeric
- 1 Chopped green chili
- 4 Finely chopped garlic cloves
- 3 Curry leaves
- 1 Diced plum tomato
- 1 Teaspoon of kosher salt
- 2 Cups of water
- ½ Cup of red lentils
- 4 Ounces of baby spinach
- 1 Cup of white rice
- 1 Teaspoon of kosher salt
- 1 and ½ cups of water

Directions:

1. Add the ghee to your Instant Pot and press the button "sauté".
2. Add the cumin, the turmeric, the green chilli, the garlic, the curry leaves, the tomatoes, the lentils, the salt and the water and stir.
3. Close the Instant Pot with the lid and seal the valve.
4. Set the timer to about 10 minutes.
5. When the timer beeps, allow about 5 minutes of releasing pressure; then open the lid of your Instant Pot and add the chopped the chopped spinach.
6. Puree your ingredients with a blender.
7. Mix your ingredients very well; then Serve and enjoy your delicious soup!

Nutrition Information

Calories: 202| Fat: 7.9g | Carbohydrates: 13.8g | Fiber: 2.6g |Protein: 16.7g

RECIPE 69: RICE AND MISO SOUP

Preparation time: 4 minutes

Cooking time: 7 minutes

Yield: 3 Servings

Ingredients:

- ½ Thinly sliced leek
- 2 Roughly chopped Chinese cabbage leaves
- 4 Roughly chopped shiitake mushrooms
- 1 Vegetable stock cube
- 1 Teaspoon of miso
- 1 Tablespoon of sesame oil
- 1 Teaspoon of sesame seeds
- 1 Tablespoon of soy sauce or tamari
- 1 Pinch of salt
- 1 Pinch of pepper
- 10 oz of firm or silken tofu
- 1 Cup of white rice

Directions:

1. Start by draining the tofu; then cut it into cubes and set it aside.
2. Place the Chinese cabbage, the mushrooms, the leeks, the stock cube, the miso, the sesame oil, the sesame seeds, the rice, the tamari and the salt to your Instant Pot.
3. Season with 1 pinch of pepper and pour in 2 cups of water.
4. Close the lid of your Instant Pot and set the timer to about 7 minutes.
5. When the timer beeps; naturally release the pressure for about 10 minutes.
6. Open the lid of your Instant Pot and add the tofu; then stir.
7. Season with salt and pepper.
8. Serve and enjoy your soup!

Nutrition Information

Calories: 128.5| Fat: 3.1g | Carbohydrates: 8.9g | Fiber: 1.7 g |Protein: 18.9g

RECIPE 70: BEEF AND SPICY RICE SOUP

Preparation time: 6 minutes

Cooking time: 14 minutes

Yield: 5 Servings

Ingredients:

- ½ Pound of beef
- ½ Cup of oil.
- 1 Medium, finely chopped onion
- 1 Large peeled and chopped tomato
- ½ Chopped red bell pepper
- 1 Medium carrot, chopped
- 1 Medium chopped potato
- 1 Cup of long grain white rice
- 2 ½ cups of water
- ¼ Teaspoon of smoked paprika
- ¼ Teaspoon of cumin powder
- 1 Pinch of salt
- 1 Pinch of black pepper
- 1 Teaspoon of dried basil
- ½ Teaspoon of dried mint
- Chopped cilantro and dill for garnishing

Directions:

1. Chop all the vegetables and the beef meat into chunks.
2. Start your Instant Pot by pressing the setting button "sauté".
3. Add in the oil and heat it; then add the meat and sauté for a few minutes.
4. Add in the chopped onions and stir for about 2 minutes; then add in the garlic and sauté for 1 minute.
5. Add in the sliced tomatoes and press it to crush it into the Instant Pot.
6. Add in the diced peppers and the salt; then add in the cumin and the smoked paprika.
7. Add in the rice and the chopped carrots; then stir.
8. Pour in the water and close the lid of your Instant Pot, make sure the valve is in sealed position.
9. Set the timer to about 12 minutes and pressure cook on High.
10. When the timer beeps; quick release the pressure for about 5 minutes.
11. Open the lid of your Instant Pot; then serve and enjoy your rice soup!

Nutrition Information

Calories: 268| Fat: 11g | Carbohydrates: 25g | Fiber: 2 g |Protein: 17g

DESSERTS WITH RICE

RECIPE 71: ASIAN STYLE RICE CAKE

Preparation time: 5 minutes

Cooking time: 30 minutes

Yield: 10 Servings

Ingredients:

- 3 Cups of water
- 1 and ¾ cups sugar
- 1 Pound of sweet rice flour
- ½ Cup of oil flavourless
- ½ Teaspoon of vanilla
- 2 and ½ cups of cooked adzuki beans

Directions:

1. In a large bowl, mix the water with the sugar and gradually add in the rice flour and combine until your ingredients are very well combined.
2. Add the vanilla, the adzuki beans and stir to combine it.
3. Divide the obtained batter between an 8" round pan lined with a plastic wrap.
4. Spray the plastic wrap with oil and place a steam trivet in the bottom of your Instant.
5. Pour in 1 cup of water in your Instant Pot; then place the cake pan on top of the trivet.
6. Cover your Instant Pot with the lid and make sure the valve is in sealed position.
7. Set the timer to about 30 minutes at a High pressure.
8. When the timer beeps; naturally release the pressure for about 10 minutes.
9. Carefully open the lid of your Instant Pot.
10. Serve and enjoy your delicious cake!

Nutrition Information

Calories: 237| Fat: 5.2g | Carbohydrates: 41g | Fiber: 2.1 g |Protein: 3.1g

RECIPE 72: SWEET RICE WITH NUTS

Preparation time: 10 minutes

Cooking time: 35 minutes

Yield: 9 Servings

Ingredients:

- 3 Cups of short grain glutinous, sweet rice
- 2 Cups of water
- 2 Tablespoon of pine nuts
- 4. 2 Ounces of peeled chestnuts, chopped into pieces
- ¼ Cup of raisins
- ¼ Cup of dried cranberries
- 10Rinsed, and pitted dried red dates; halved

For the sauce:

- 1 Tablespoon of soy sauce
- 2 Tablespoon of honey
- 1/3 Cup of dark brown sugar
- 2 Tablespoons of sesame oil
- ½ Teaspoon of cinnamon powder
- 1/8 Teaspoon of fine sea salt

For the toppings:

- 1 Tablespoon of pine nuts
- 2 Pitted dried, rinsed and vertically cut dates

Directions:

1. Start by placing the sweet rice in your Instant Pot after rinsing it with running water.
2. Pour in the water and add the seasoning including the soy sauce, the tablespoon of honey; the dark brown sugar, the sesame oil, the cinnamon powder and the sea salt.
3. Mix your ingredients very well; then add in the nuts and sprinkle the nuts on top.
4. Close the lid of your Instant Pot and set the timer to about 35 minutes and make sure the valve is in sealed in position.
5. When the timer beeps, quick release the pressure for about 6 minutes.
6. Carefully open the lid of your Instant Pot and stir.
7. Place the rice in a square mould; then let the rice cool for about 20 minutes.
8. Top the rice with the dates and with the pine nuts.
9. Slice the cooled rice into squares.

Nutrition Information

Calories: 280| Fat: 6g | Carbohydrates: 32g | Fiber: 1 g |Protein: 5g

RECIPE 73: SWEET RICE CUBES

Preparation time: 15 minutes

Cooking time: 40 minutes

Yield: 12 Servings

Ingredients:

- 1 Pound of Mochiko glutinous rice flour
- 2 and ½ cups of sugar
- 12 Oz of canned coconut milk
- 1 and ¾ cups of water

Directions:

1. Place the steamer trivet in the bottom of your Instant Pot/pressure cooker; then pour in 2 cups of water.
2. Sift the rice flour in a large bowl and add in the sugar; then add in the sugar and the coconut milk.
3. Add the water and whisk until you get no lumps in your batter.
4. Line a 6" baking pan with a foil and spray it with a cooking spray; then place the batter in the pan on top of the foil.
5. Cover the batter with another pieces of foil sprayed with cooking spray.
6. Place the pan over the trivet; then close the lid of your Instant Pot and make sure the valve is in sealed position.
7. Set the timer for about 40 minutes and the pressure to High.
8. When the timer beeps; quick release the pressure; then turn the valve to venting position.
9. Carefully remove the pan from the Instant Pot and remove the top foil.
10. Dust a counter with potato starch; then carefully flip the pan on the counter and remove the bottom foil.
11. Cut into cubes; then toss the cubes into the potato starch.
12. Serve and enjoy your delicious rice cubes!

Nutrition Information

Calories: 293| Fat: 6.4g | Carbohydrates: 19g | Fiber: 2.9 g |Protein: 6g

RECIPE 74: CHOCOLATE RICE PUDDING

Preparation time: 5 minutes

Cooking time: 7 minutes

Yield: 2 Servings

Ingredients:

- 1 Cup of arborio rice
- 1 and ½ cups of water
- 1 Pinch of salt
- 1 to 2 cinnamon sticks
- 2 and ½ cups of Nesquik chocolate milk
- 2 Large eggs
- ½ Teaspoon of vanilla extract

Directions:

1. Add the water, the rice, the salt and the cinnamon sticks to your Instant Pot.
2. Lock the lid of your Instant Pot and turn the valve to sealing position.
3. Set the timer to about 4 to 5 minutes on High pressure.
4. When the timer beeps; naturally release the pressure for about 10 minutes.
5. Open the lid of your Instant Pot and add in two cups of Nesquik chocolate milk with the eggs and the vanilla extract to a medium bowl.
6. Gradually add the rice to the bowl and constantly stir.
7. Press the button "sauté" and let it boil for no more than 1 to 2 minutes.
8. Remove the rice pudding from the Instant Pot and ladle into small bowls.
9. Serve and enjoy your delicious chocolate rice pudding!

Nutrition Information

Calories: 160.2| Fat: 3.9g | Carbohydrates: 26g | Fiber: 0.8 g |Protein: 5g

RECIPE 75: SWEET RICE WITH MANGO

Preparation time: 10 minutes

Cooking time: 22 minutes

Yield: 3 Servings

Ingredients:

- 1 Cup of sweet glutinous rice
- 1 and ¼ cups of water
- ¼ Teaspoon of sea salt
- 2 Tablespoons of canned pandan extract
- 2 Drops of green food coloring
- 1 Cup of coconut milk
- 3 Tablespoons of granulated sugar
- 1 Peeled and thinly sliced mango

Directions:

1. Pour the rice in a deep bowl and set it aside to soak for about 30 minutes.

2. Pour 1 and ½ cups of water in your Instant Pot and season with salt, green food colouring, pandan extract and mix.
3. Close the lid of your Instant Pot and seal the valve; then set the timer to about 22 minutes on High pressure.
4. When the timer beeps; quick release the pressure.
5. Warm the milk in a saucepan with the sugar; then remove from the heat and let cool.
6. After the rice cooker finishes the cooking cycle, allow the rice to stand 5 more minutes.
7. Place a scoop of rice in serving bowls and drizzle with the coconut milk.
8. Arrange the mango slices by the side of the rice drizzled with milk.
9. Serve and enjoy your dessert!

Nutrition Information

Calories: 220.7| Fat: 12.8g | Carbohydrates: 26g | Fiber: 1.1 g |Protein: 2.9g

RECIPE 76: RICE CUSTARD

Preparation time: 8 minutes

Cooking time: 48 minutes

Yield: 3-4 Servings

Ingredients:

- 1/3 Cup of long-grain white rice
- 3 Cups of milk
- 1/3 Cup of caster sugar
- 4 Large eggs
- 1 Teaspoon of vanilla extract
- ¼ Cup of sultanas
- 1 Pinch of ground nutmeg

Directions:

1. Pour 1 cup of water in the bottom of your Instant Pot; then add in the rice.
2. Close the lid of your Instant Pot and set the timer to about 8 minutes on High pressure, the valve is in sealed position.
3. When the timer beeps, quick release the pressure; then turn the valve is in a venting position.
4. Mix the milk with the eggs and vanilla in a bowl; then add the mixture to a sieve and strain into a jug.
5. Add in the rice and the sultanas; then line the base of a 6" baking pan with a tea towel.
6. Clean the Instant Pot and pour in 2 cups of water.
7. Place a trivet in the bottom of your Instant Pot and then place the custard mixture in the pan and cover it with a foil; then place it on top of the trivet in your Instant Pot.
8. Close the Instant Pot and set the timer to about 35 to 40 minutes.

9. When the timer beeps, quick release the pressure for 5 to 10 minutes.
10. Open the lid of your Instant Pot and remove the pan from it; then set aside for 1 hour to cool.
11. Serve and enjoy your delicious custard!

Nutrition Information

Calories: 187| Fat: 6.4g | Carbohydrates: 27.14g | Fiber: 1.8 g |Protein: 4.7g

RECIPE 77: SWEET RICE RECIPE

Preparation time: 10 minutesCooking time: 10 minutes

Yield: 4 Servings

Ingredients:

- 1 Cup of long-grain white rice
- 1 Cup of hot water
- 1 cup of milk
- ¾ cup of sugar
- 1 Pinch of saffron
- 1 Handful of nuts
- 1 Handful of dry fruits
- 2 Tablespoons of Dried Coconut
- 2 Tablespoons of ghee
- ½ Tablespoon of orange zest
- ¼ Teaspoon of Cardamom powder
- 1 Pinch of food colouring, orange
- 2 Tablespoons of chopped orange chunks

Directions:

1. Start by washing the rice and soaking it into a medium bowl filled with water for about 15 to 20 minutes.
2. Drain the rice; then add it to your Instant Pot with the saffron strands and the sugar.
3. Add in the milk and the saffron.
4. In a separate and medium pan, heat the butter or ghee and when it heats up, add the nuts; then fry it for a couple of minutes.
5. Transfer the nuts to the Instant Pot and pour in the hot water and the orange zest.
6. Give the mixture a quick stir; then close the lid of your Instant pot and seal the valve.
7. Set the timer to about 10 minutes on High pressure.
8. When the timer beeps; quick release the pressure for about 5 minutes.
9. Open the lid of your Instant Pot; then fluff the rice with a fork and garnish with dry fruits, dried coconut and chopped orange chunks.
10. Serve and enjoy your dessert!

Nutrition Information

Calories: 149.8| Fat: 4g | Carbohydrates: 37g | Fiber: 0.0 g |Protein: 5g

RECIPE 78: SWEET GLUTINOUS BLACK RICE BIKO

Preparation time: 10 minutes

Cooking time: 25 minutes

Yield: 3 Servings

Ingredients:

- 1 Cup of Black Glutinous Rice, rinsed and soaked in about 1 cup of water for about 1 hour
- 2 and ½ cups of water
- 1 Can of Coconut Milk
- ¾ Cup of packed light brown sugar
- ½ Teaspoon of salt

Directions:

1. Start by draining the water from the soaked glutinous rice.
2. Place the rice in a 6-quart Instant Pot, then pour in the water.
3. Close the lid of your Instant Pot and set the timer for about 15 minutes and make sure the valve is in sealed position.
4. When the timer beeps, quick release the pressure and turn the valve to venting position.
5. Meanwhile, combine the coconut milk with the brown sugar and the salt and bring the mixture to a boil for about 3 minutes.
6. Add the milk mixture to the Instant Pot and stir; then close the lid of your Instant Pot and set the timer to about 5 minutes on High pressure.
7. When the timer beeps; naturally release the pressure for 7 minutes.
8. Open the lid when it is safe to do; then serve and enjoy your dessert!

Nutrition Information

Calories: 159| Fat: 5g | Carbohydrates: 22g | Fiber: 1 g |Protein: 2g

RECIPE 79: RICE WITH CASHEWS AND RAISINS

Preparation time: 12 minutes

Cooking time: 17 minutes

Yield: 2-3 Servings

Ingredients:

- 1 Cup of Raw long grain white Rice
- 2 Cups of Coconut sugar
- 2 Tablespoons of Ghee
- 1 Cup of Cashew nuts
- 1 Cup of Raisins
- ½ Teaspoon of Cardamom powder

Directions:

1. Wash the rice and drain it very well; then add it to your Instant Pot.
2. Pour 3 cups of water in your Instant Pot and close the lid, make sure the valve is in sealed position.
3. Set the timer for about 8 minutes on High pressure.
4. When the timer beeps, naturally release the pressure for 10 minutes and in the meantime, place the coconut sugar in a small saucepan and pour ½ cup of water to it; then bring the mixture to a boil for about 4 to 5 minutes.
5. Remove the pan from the heat and add the syrup to your Instant Pot.
6. Mix your ingredients very well; then press the button "sauté" and cook for about 3 minutes while continuously stirring.
7. In a large non-stick skillet, break the cashew nuts and fry them with the raisins with a teaspoon of ghee.
8. Add the nuts to the rice mixture; then add the remaining quantity of ghee and cardamom powder to the rice.
9. Serve and enjoy your delicious dessert!

Nutrition Information

Calories: 216| Fat: 5.4g | Carbohydrates: 36g | Fiber: 2.4 g |Protein: 5g

RECIPE 80: LAYERED RICE CAKE

Preparation time: 90 minutes

Cooking time: 15 minutes

Yield: 6 Servings

Ingredients:

- 3 Cups of long-grain white rice
- ½ Cup of chopped pecans
- 8 Ounces of softened cream cheese
- 1 Can of about 21 ounces of cherry jam
- 1 Cup of confectioners' sugar
- 1 Carton of 12 ounces of frozen whipped topping

- 1 and ½ cups of cold milk
- ½ Teaspoon of coconut extract
- 1 Cup of shredded and toasted sweetened shredded coconut
- 1 Can of instant pudding mix

Directions:

1. Rinse the rice until the water runs clean; then add the rice to and Instant Pot.
2. Pour in 1 and ½ cups of water; then close the lid of your Instant Pot and set the timer to about 10 minutes on High pressure; make sure the valve is sealed.
3. When the timer beeps, quick release the pressure for 5 minutes; then transfer the rice to a large bowl and combine it with pecans, third the quantity of the cream cheese and spread into a greased pan; then refrigerate for about 25 minutes.
4. Remove from the refrigerator and spread with the jam; then refrigerate for about 15 minutes.
5. In a separate bowl, mix the sugar with the remaining quantity of cream cheese; then add in half of the whipped toppings and spread on top of the refrigerated filling and refrigerate again for 20 minutes.
6. In a medium bowl, mix the milk with the coconut extract and the pudding mix and mix very well; then pour the mixture on top of the layered rice pie, then refrigerate the rice pie for about 30 minutes.
7. Remove your rice pie from the refrigerator and sprinkle coconut on top.
8. Serve and enjoy your delicious dessert!

Nutrition Information

Calories: 250| Fat: 12g | Carbohydrates: 33g | Fiber: 1 g |Protein: 3g

KID-FRIENDLY DISHES WITH RICE

RECIPE 81: FRIED EGGS AND RICE

Preparation time: 8 minutes

Cooking time: 35 minutes

Yield: 4 Servings

Ingredients:

- 2 Large eggs
- 1 cup of brown rice
- 1 teaspoon of ginger paste
- 1 Teaspoon of garlic paste
- 4 Crushed peppercorns
- 1 Medium finely chopped onion
- 1 Pinch of salt

Directions:

1. Wash the rice under running water until it runs clear.
2. Add the rice to your Instant Pot and pour in 1 and ½ cups of water.
3. Season with 1 pinch of salt and close the lid of your Instant Pot.
4. Set the timer to about 30 minutes on High pressure.
5. When the timer beeps; quick release the pressure for 5 minutes; and when it is safe to do it, open the lid and fluff the rice with a fork.
6. Sauté the eggs with 1 pinch of salt and a little bit of butter until the eggs are perfectly scrambled.
7. Sauté the chopped onion in a large skillet with pepper in hot oil.
8. Add in the ginger; then add the garlic paste and give a quick stir.
9. Sprinkle with 1 pinch of salt and transfer the cooked rice to a serving platter.
10. Place the fried eggs right by the side of the rice in the serving dish.
11. Serve and enjoy your kid's delicious dish!

Nutrition Information

Calories: 189.2| Fat: 8.5g | Carbohydrates: 22g | Fiber: 1.4 g |Protein: 6g

RECIPE 82: RICE CAKES FOR KIDS

Preparation time: 15 minutes

Cooking time: 20 minutes

Yield: 8-10 Servings

Ingredients:

- 2 Cups of uncooked short-grain sticky rice
- 1 Seeded and pickled plum
- 1 Pinch of bonito flakes
- ½ Teaspoon of soy sauce
- ½ Teaspoon of Mirin
- 1 Sheet of Nori, seaweed
- 1 Cup of tinned tuna

Directions:

1. Place 2 cups of rice in the bottom of your Instant Pot and pour in 1 ¼ cups of water.
2. Close the lid of your Instant Pot and set the timer to about 20 minutes on High pressure, make sure the valve is in sealed position.
3. When the timer beeps, quick release the pressure; then open the lid when all the pressure is released.
4. Fluff the rice with a fork; then transfer it to a bowl and let cool.
5. Prepare the filling by mixing the bonito flakes with the soy sauce and the mirin.
6. Drain the tuna and mix with 1 tablespoon of mayonnaise.
7. Prepare a seaweed sheet nori and place a cling wrap on top of a rice bowl.
8. Place about ½ cup of the cooked rice on top of the centre of the cling wrap.
9. Place 1 teaspoon of the filling, tuna, bonito flakes, mayonnaise and soy sauce into the centre of the rice and top it with ½ cup of rice.
10. Wrap the prepared cling wrap over the stuffed rice and carefully squeeze; then shape a triangle from the rice with your hands.
11. Remove the wrap and cover the bottom of the cooked and stuffed rice with a nori sheet; then set it aside.
12. Repeat the same process with the remaining quantity of rice.
13. Serve and enjoy your delicious onigiri!

Nutrition Information

Calories: 220| Fat: 3g | Carbohydrates: 18g | Fiber: 2 g |Protein: 7g

RECIPE 83: RICE TIKKIS

Preparation time: 40 minutes

Cooking time: 25 minutes

Yield: 9 Servings

Ingredients:

- ½ Cup of jasmine rice
- ½ Cup of split red lentil
- 2 Teaspoons of oil
- 3 Finely chopped green chillies
- 1 Teaspoon of ginger garlic paste
- 1 Teaspoon of roasted cumin powder
- 2 Tablespoons of fresh chopped coriander leaves
- 2 Teaspoon of lemon juice
- 2 Tablespoons of chopped mint leaves
- ½ Teaspoon of black pepper powder
- 2 Tablespoons of chickpea flour
- 1 Cup of bread crumbs
- 1 Pinch of salt

Directions:

1. Place the rice and the lentils in an Instant Pot and pour in 2 cups of water.
2. Close the lid of your Instant Pot and set the timer to about 12 to 14 minutes on High pressure.
3. When the timer beeps; quick release the pressure for about 5 minutes; then open the lid and fluff the rice with a fork.
4. Clean the Instant Pot and press the button "sauté" and heat the oil; then add the green chillies and the ginger garlic paste and sauté for about 1 to 2 minutes.
5. Add the rice, the lentils, the salt, the cumin and the pepper powder, and mix very well; then sauté for about 3 minutes.
6. Add in the lemon juice, the coriander and the mint leaves; then mix very well.
7. Press the button "Cancel" and mash the obtained mixture with a potato masher.
8. Sprinkle the chickpea flour over the rice mixture and mix gently.
9. Make the shape of round Tikkis from the rice and roll each of the Tikkis into bread crumbs.
10. Refrigerate the Tikkis for about 30 minutes; then fry the Tikis in hot oil for about 5 minutes.
11. Serve and enjoy your rice Tikkis!

Nutrition Information

Calories: 241| Fat: 11g | Carbohydrates: 31g | Fiber: 1 g |Protein: 3g

RECIPE 84: RICE SCOTCH EGGS

Preparation time: 35 minutes

Cooking time: 30 minutes

Yield: 6 Servings

Ingredients:

- 1 Cup of finely chopped spicy smoked sausage
- ¼ Cup of finely chopped sweet onion
- ¼ Cup of finely chopped celery
- ¼ Cup of finely chopped bell pepper
- 2 and ½ cups of long grain white rice
- 1 Tablespoon of Worcestershire sauce
- 1 Teaspoon of Cajun seasoning
- ¼ Teaspoon of dry mustard
- 2 Eggs
- ¼ Cup of fine and dry bread crumbs
- 6 Large eggs
- 1 Cup of vegetable oil
- 1 ¼ cups of chicken stock

Directions:

1. Start your Instant Pot and press the button "sauté"; then place in 1 to 2 tablespoons of vegetable oil.
2. Sauté the sausage for about 3 to 4 minutes.
3. Add the onion and the celery and stir for 2 minutes.
4. Add in the rice and pour in 1 ¼ cups of chicken stock.
5. Close the lid of your Instant Pot and set the timer to about 7 minutes on High pressure.
6. When the timer beeps; quick release the pressure.
7. Open the lid of your Instant Pot and fluff the rice with a fork.
8. Remove from heat, and stir in rice, the Worcestershire sauce, the Cajun seasoning and the dry mustard.
9. Let your mixture cool for about 30 minutes.
10. In the meantime, boil the eggs in 1 ¼ cups of water in your Instant Pot for 4 to 5 minutes.
11. Peel the eggs and remove the rice mixture from the refrigerator.
12. Add in the eggs and the breadcrumbs to the rice
13. Press the mixture of the rice around the hard-boiled and peeled eggs.
14. Pour 1 cup of oil in a large skillet and when it heats up, fry the eggs in batches.
15. Serve and enjoy your delicious dish!

Nutrition Information

Calories: 344| Fat: 22.5g | Carbohydrates: 18.7g | Fiber: 0 g |Protein: 13.6g

RECIPE 85: SWEET RICE WITH PECAN NUTS

Preparation time: 5 minutes

Cooking time: 10 minutes

Yield: 3-4 Servings

Ingredients:

- 2 Cups of long-grain white cooked
- 1 Finely diced pink lady apple
- ¼ Finely diced red onion
- ½ Cup of currants
- ¼ Cup of chopped unsalted pecan nuts
- 1/3 Cup of olive oil
- 1 Teaspoon of curry powder
- 1 Tablespoon of brown sugar
- 1 Teaspoon of white vinegar
- 1 ½ cups of water

Directions:

1. Start your Instant Pot and place the rice in it after rinsing and draining it.
2. Pour in the water and close the lid of the Instant Pot.
3. Set the timer to about 8 minutes on High pressure and make sure the valve is in sealed in position.
4. When the timer beeps, quick release the pressure for 5 to 6 minutes and when the pressure is entirely released, open the lid and fluff the rice with a fork.
5. Transfer the rice to a serving bowl; then toss in the dressing and mix very well.
6. Top the rice with the pecan nuts.
7. Serve and enjoy your delicious sweet rice with nuts!

Nutrition Information

Calories: 170.8| Fat: 3g | Carbohydrates: 34g | Fiber: 5.8 g |Protein: 5.7g

RECIPE 86: RICE CEREAL FOR KIDS

Preparation time: 5 minutes

Cooking time: 7 minutes

Yield: 3 Servings

Ingredients:

- 1 and ½ cups of white Rice
- 1 and 1/2 cups of water
- 1 Tablespoon of butter, divided
- ¼ Cup of sugar
- 1/4 Cup of milk
- 1 Dash of cinnamon sugar

Directions

1. Pour the water into your Instant Pot; then add half a tablespoon of the butter.
2. Add in the rice; then close the lid of your Instant Pot and set the timer to about 7 minutes on High pressure.
3. When the timer beeps; naturally release the pressure for 10 minutes.
4. Transfer the rice to a large bowl; then fluff it with a fork.
5. Add the sugar and the remaining tablespoon of butter and stir.
6. Pour in the milk and sprinkle with cinnamon and sugar.
7. Serve and enjoy!

Nutrition Information

Calories: 123| Fat: 5.9g | Carbohydrates: 18.7g | Fiber: 0.4 g |Protein: 5.7g

RECIPE 87: KID-FRIENDLY SUSHI RICE BALLS

Preparation time: 20 minutes

Cooking time: 12 minutes

Yield: 12 Servings

Ingredients:

- 10.5 oz of sushi rice
- 1/3 Cup of rice vinegar
- 2 Tablespoons of granulated sugar
- ¼ Cup of toasted white sesame seeds
- ¼ Cup of black sesame seeds
- 3.5 oz of sliced and finely chopped smoked salmon
- 1 Finely chopped cucumber
- 2 Tablespoons of mayonnaise
- ½ Teaspoon of wasabi paste
- ½ Cup of soy sauce

Directions

1. Rinse the rice under cold water until the water runs clear; then drain the rice and add it to your Instant Pot.
2. Pour 2 cups of water in your Instant Pot; then close the lid and seal the valve.
3. Set the timer for about 12 minutes on High pressure.
4. When the timer beeps, quick release the pressure for 5 minutes; then reduce the heat to a low setting.
5. Set the rice aside to cool for 10 minutes; then spread it in a baking dish.
6. Combine the sugar with the vinegar and 1 pinch of salt in your Instant Pot; then stir until the sugar dissolves.
7. Drizzle the mixture on top of the rice and toss very well.
8. Divide the rice mixture into about 17 portions and cover with a clean towel.
9. Combine the sesame seeds over a large platter; then combine the salmon, the cucumber, the mayonnaise, and the wasabi paste in a medium bowl.
10. Shape each of the portions of rice into a small ball; then make a small hole into the centre and fill it with ½ teaspoon of the salmon mixture.
11. Shape the rice again in the form of balls.
12. Roll the rice balls in sesame seeds; then arrange the rice balls on top of a tray and cover it with a plastic wrap; then let chill for about 1 hour.
13. Serve and enjoy your sushi balls with soy sauce!

Nutrition Information

Calories: 267.6| Fat: 3.4g | Carbohydrates: 23g | Fiber: 0.7 g |Protein: 17.5g

RECIPE 88: CRISPY RICE FOR KIDS

Preparation time: 7 minutes

Cooking time: 3 minutes

Yield: 10 Servings

Ingredients:

- 6 Cups of brown crispy rice
- 2/3 Cup of almond butter
- 2/3 Cup of brown rice syrup
- 1 Teaspoon of vanilla
- 1 Teaspoon of cinnamon
- Mini chocolate chips
- Dried cranberries
- Flax seeds and blueberries for the toppings

Directions

1. Spray your Instant Pot with cooking spray; then start the Instant Pot and press the button "sauté".
2. Mix the almond butter and the rice syrup in your Instant Pot and sauté for about 2 to 3 minutes.
3. Press the button "Cancel"; then add in the vanilla and the cinnamon, sprinkle with the chocolate chips and the dried cranberries.
4. Pour the mixture over the crispy rice in a 6-inch tray sprayed with cooking spray.
5. Cover the tray with a plastic wrap and refrigerate the rice for about 30 minutes.
6. Remove the tray from the refrigerator and top it with the flax seeds and blueberries slice the rice into squares.
7. Serve and enjoy your delicious dish!

Nutrition Information

Calories: 120| Fat: 3g | Carbohydrates: 16g | Fiber: 0.1 g |Protein: 3g

RECIPE 89: RICE SALAD WITH FRESH FRUITS

Preparation time: 5 minutes

Cooking time: 10 minutes

Yield: 3-4 Servings

Ingredients:

- 1 Can of about 15 ounces of drained, crushed pineapple
- ½ Cup of sliced strawberries
- ¼ Cup of sliced fresh peaches
- 1 Cup of uncooked long-grain white rice
- 1/3 Cup of golden raisins
- 2/3 Cup of flaked coconut
- 5/8 Cup of heavy whipping cream
- 2 Tablespoons of white sugar
- ¼ Teaspoon of vanilla extract
- 1/8 Teaspoon of ground ginger
- 1 Pinch of salt
- ¼ Cup of slivered almonds or pinenuts
- 11 to 12 leaves lettuce
- ¼ Cup of sliced almonds

Directions:

1. Pour 1 and 1/47 cups of water in your Instant Pot and season with 1 pinch of salt.
2. Add the rice and cover the Instant Pot with the lid.
3. Set the timer for about 10 minutes on High pressure.

4. When the timer beeps, quick release the pressure for about 6 minutes.
5. Open the lid of your Instant Pot and fluff the rice with a fork.
6. In a large bowl, add the pineapple, the strawberries, the peaches and add in 1 cup of rice to the mixture.
7. Add the raisins and the coconut.
8. In a second bowl, mix the cream with the sugar, the vanilla, the ginger and the salt and fold the mixture into that of the rice.
9. Stir in the slivered almonds.
10. Spoon the mixture on top of lettuce leaf beds, and sprinkle each with the sliced almonds or with the pine nuts.
11. Serve and enjoy your dish!

Nutrition Information

Calories: 154| Fat: 7.6g | Carbohydrates: 18.6g | Fiber: 1.7 g |Protein: 3.1g

RECIPE 90: RICE AND TUNA BOWL

Preparation time: 4minutes

Cooking time: 8 minutes

Yield: 2 Servings

Ingredients:

- 1 Can of Tuna
- ½ Tablespoon of sesame oil
- 1 Thinly sliced green onion
- ¼ teaspoon of kosher salt
- 1 tablespoon of soy sauce
- ½ teaspoon of roasted sesame seeds
- 1 Diced avocado
- 2 Cups of long grain white rice
- 1 Cup of pitted and sliced olives (optional)

Directions:

1. Start by rinsing and draining the rice; then place it in your Instant Pot.
2. Pour 1 and ½ cups of water over the rice and season with 1 pinch of salt.
3. Close the lid of the Instant Pot and make sure the valve is in sealing position.
4. Set the timer for about 8 minutes on High pressure.
5. When the timer beeps, quick release the pressure for about 5 minutes.
6. Open the lid and fluff the rice with a fork.
7. Drain the tuna in a bowl and mix it with the sesame oil, the green onion, the salt, the soy sauce, and the sesame seeds; top with the olives(optional).

8. Pour the mixture over the rice and mix very well.
9. Serve and enjoy your delicious meal!

Nutrition Information

Calories: 142| Fat: 6g | Carbohydrates: 31g | Fiber: 1 g |Protein: 7g

SOME OTHER RICE RECIPES

RECIPE 91: RICE STUFFED PEPPER

Preparation time: 15 minutes

Cooking time: 27 minutes

Yield: 8 Servings

Ingredients:

- 2 Pounds of ground beef
- 1 Medium, finely chopped onion
- 1 Small, finely chopped green pepper
- 2 Minced garlic cloves
- 1 Teaspoon of salt
- ½ Teaspoon of pepper
- 3 and ¾ cups of water
- 1 Can of about 14 ounces of undrained diced tomatoes
- 1 Can of 10 ounces of undrained green chiles and diced tomatoes
- 1 Can of 15 ounces of tomato sauce
- 1 Tablespoon of ground cumin
- 3 Cups of uncooked long-grain white rice
- 8 Medium green peppers

For the Cheese sauce:

- 1 and ½ pounds of cubed American cheese
- 1 Can of 10 ounces of chopped green chiles and diced tomatoes

Directions

1. Rinse the water and drain it very well, then add the rice to your Instant Pot.
2. Pour 1 and ½ cups of water over the rice and season with 1 pinch of salt.
3. Close the lid of your Instant Pot and set the timer to about 7 minutes; make sure the valve is in sealed position.
4. When the timer beeps, quick release the pressure for about 5 minutes and open the lid.
5. Fluff the rice with a fork and transfer it to a bowl.
6. Clean your Instant Pot and press the Start button "sauté"; then add in the onion, the chopped green pepper, the garlic, the salt and the pepper and sauté the mixture for about 4 to 5 minutes.
7. Add in the water, the tomatoes, the tomato sauce and the cumin and sauté the mixture for about 5 minutes.

8. Add in the rice and close the lid of your Instant pot again.
9. Set the timer to about 5 minutes on High pressure and when the timer beeps, naturally release the pressure for 6 to 7 minutes.
10. Remove the tops and the seeds from the green peppers; then place the peppers in a saucepan filled with hot water and let boil for 3 minutes.
11. Drain the peppers and stuff it with the meat mixture, if you have any quantity of the remaining meat mixture, place it in the bottom of a 6" baking pan.
12. Arrange the peppers on top of the meat mixture and carefully place the cheese on top of each stuffed pepper.
13. Place a trivet in the bottom of your Instant Pot and pour in 1 and ¼ cups of water; then place the baking pan on the top of a trivet and lock the lid.
14. Set the timer for about 6 to 7 minutes and when the timer beeps, quick release the pressure and open the lid of your Instant Pot.
15. Pour the tomato sauce on top of the cooked stuffed peppers.
16. Serve and enjoy your dish!

Nutrition Information

Calories: 242.7| Fat: 9g | Carbohydrates: 22g | Fiber: 3.1 g |Protein: 19g

RECIPE 92: STUFFED GRAPE LEAVES

Preparation time: 10 minutes

Cooking time: 15 minutes

Yield: 12-13 Servings

Ingredients:

- 1 Jar of about 15 oz of grape leaves
- 1 Cup of long-grain white rice
- 2 Pounds of ground beef
- 2 Teaspoons of chopped fresh mint
- 2 Tablespoons of chopped fresh parsley
- 1 Cup of golden raisins
- 2 Teaspoons of finely minced garlic
- 2 Teaspoons of cinnamon
- 2 Teaspoons of oregano
- 1 Teaspoon of garlic
- 1 Teaspoon of onion powder
- 1 Teaspoon of sea salt
- ½ Cup of water
- The juice of 2 lemons
- Thinly sliced lemon slices for garnishing

Directions:

1. Rinse the rice and drain it very well; then mix the white rice with the ground beef, the herbs, and the spices and combine the mixture with both your hands in a large bowl.
2. Rinse the jarred grape leaves and separate each.
3. Cover the bottom of your Instant Pot with some grape leaves.
4. Stuff the grape leaves and to do that, spread out each grape leaf and remove the stem.
5. Fill each of the grape leaves with 1 tablespoon of the meat filling.
6. Roll in the sides at the first place; then tightly roll the grape leaf over the meat mixture.
7. Place the rolled grape leaves in your Instant Pot and make sure to pack it tightly.
8. Repeat the same process until you finish with the rest of the peppers.
9. Pour ½ cup of fresh water over the grape leaves; then add about ½ cup of the lemon juice.
10. Close your Instant Pot and set the timer to about 15 minutes by pressing the button "Manual"; make sure the valve is in sealed position.
11. When the timer beeps; let the pressure release naturally for about 25 minutes.
12. Remove the grape leaves to a serving platter and top it with the fresh lemon slices
13. Serve and enjoy your dish!

Nutrition Information

Calories: 160| Fat: 8g | Carbohydrates: 20g | Fiber: 2 g |Protein: 3g

RECIPE 93: RICE STUFFED BABY EGGPLANTS

Preparation time: 8 minutes

Cooking time: 5 minutes

Yield: 6 Servings

Ingredients:

- 6 to 8 small baby eggplants
- 1 Cup of long grain white rice
- 1 Medium, finely chopped or grated onion
- 1 Teaspoon of grated ginger
- 1 Teaspoon of finely minced garlic
- 1 Teaspoon of red chili powder
- ¼ Teaspoon of turmeric powder
- 1 Teaspoon of garam masala powder
- ½ Teaspoon of ground coriander
- ½ Teaspoon of ground cumin
- 1 Tablespoon of fresh grated coconut
- 1 Teaspoon of brown sugar
- 1 Teaspoon of kosher salt

- 1 Tablespoon of oil
- ½ Teaspoon of mustard seeds
- Chopped cilantro for garnishing

Directions:

1. Rinse the rice and drain it very well; then add it to your Instant Pot and pour in 1 Cup of water
2. Close the lid of the Instant Pot and set the timer for about 6 minutes on High pressure.
3. When the timer beeps, quick release the pressure for 5 minutes.
4. Open the lid of the Instant Pot and fluff the rice with a fork.
5. Wash the baby eggplants and trim the extra stems; but make sure to leave about half an inch of the eggplant stems.
6. With a sharp knife, make 2 vertical cross slits.
7. Now, prepare the stuffing by mixing the rice with the grated onion, the ginger, the garlic, the red chilli powder, the turmeric, the Garam Masala, the ground coriander, the ground cumin, the fresh coconut, the brown sugar and the salt in a large bowl.
8. Mix the ingredients of the stuffing; then stuff the eggplants with the prepared stuffing.
9. Turn on your instant pot to the "Sauté" mode and heat the oil in it.
10. Add the mustard seeds and sauté for 1 minute; then add the stuffed eggplants to your Instant Pot and layer any remaining quantity of the stuffing over the top.
11. Add about ½ cup of water in your Instant Pot; then close the lid of your Instant Pot and turn the valve to sealing position.
12. Set the timer for about 4 to 5 minutes on Low pressure; then garnish with chopped cilantro.
13. When the timer beeps; quick release the pressure for 7 minutes.
14. Open the lid of your Instant Pot; then serve and enjoy your delicious meal!

Nutrition Information

Calories: 230| Fat: 5g | Carbohydrates: 30g | Fiber: 4 g |Protein: 7g

RECIPE 94: STUFFED CABBAGE ROLLS

Preparation time: 20 minutes

Cooking time: 30 minutes

Yield: 10 Servings

Ingredients:

- 1 Medium head of cabbage
- ½ Pound of ground beef
- ½ Pound of hot Italian sausage
- 2 Cups of long-grain white rice
- 1 Can of 14 ounces of diced tomatoes and green chiles

Directions:

1. Wash the rice and drain it very well; then add the rice to your Instant Pot and pour 1 cup of water on top of it.
2. Close the lid of your Instant Pot and set the timer to about 5 minutes on High pressure.
3. When the timer beeps, naturally release the pressure for 7 minutes.
4. In the meantime, remove the core of the cabbage and put the head of cabbage into a pan filled with boiling water and blanch for about 3 to 4 minutes.
5. Open the lid of your Instant Pot and transfer the rice to a bowl; then clean your Instant Pot and press the button "sauté" and add in the sausage and the ground beef and mix very well.
6. Transfer the mixture of sausage and ground beef to the bowl filled with cooked rice and mix together very well.
7. Lay the cabbage leaves over a surface and stuff the leaves with the rice and meat mixture.
8. Fold both ends of the cabbage leaves over and tightly roll up the stuffed cabbage.
9. Arrange the cabbage rolls in a heat-proof dish that fits your Instant Pot.
10. Pour 1 and ½ cups of water in the bottom of your Instant Pot.
11. Arrange the cabbage rolls in the dish and pour the diced tomatoes on top of it.
12. Place the dish in your Instant Pot and close the lid.
13. Turn the valve to seal position and set the timer to about 25 minutes on High pressure.
14. When the timer beeps, allow a natural release.
15. Serve and enjoy your healthy stuffed cabbage rolls!

Nutrition Information

Calories: 233| Fat: 10g | Carbohydrates: 23.1g | Fiber: 2.1 g |Protein: 13.2g

RECIPE 95: WILD RICE STUFFED MUSHROOMS

Preparation time: 20 minutes

Cooking time: 30 minutes

Yield: 10 Servings

Ingredients:

- 6 large white mushrooms
- ½ Cup of wild rice
- Cup of sliced, chopped ham
- 1 Cup of shredded cheddar cheese
- 1 and ½ ounces of softened cream cheese
- 1 Teaspoon of garlic salt
- ½ Tablespoon of butter for greasing
- 1 ¼ cups of water

Directions:

1. Add the wild rice with water and 1 pinch of salt to your Instant Pot.
2. Lock the lid of your Instant Pot and turn the valve to sealing position.
3. Press the button "Manual" and adjust the cooking time to about 35 minutes on High pressure.
4. When the timer of the Instant Pot beeps, let the pressure release naturally.
5. Clean the Instant Pot and grease it with butter; then press the button "sauté" and add in all your ingredients except for the mushrooms and sauté for 2 minutes.
6. Remove the stems of the mushrooms and stuff it with the sautéed rice mixture.
7. Transfer your stuffed mushrooms in the bottom of your Instant Pot and pour in ¼ cup of water and secure the lid with; then set the timer to about 23 minutes on High pressure.
8. When the timer beeps, select the button "Cancel" and quick release the pressure.
9. Remove the lid of the Instant Pot; then serve and enjoy your dish!

Nutrition Information

Calories: 220| Fat: 12g | Carbohydrates: 12g | Fiber: 0.5 g |Protein: 2g

RECIPE 96: RICE BALLS WITH CHEESE AND PASTA SAUCE

Preparation time: 5 minutes

Cooking time: 15 minutes

Yield: 8-9 Servings

Ingredients:

- 1 lb of ground turkey
- ½ Cup of uncooked white rice
- 1 Teaspoon of salt
- ¼ Teaspoon of pepper
- 1 Jar of about 26 oz of pasta sauce
- 1 Cup of water
- 1 Cup of finely chopped parsley
- 5 Oz of shredded mozzarella cheese

Directions:

1. Pour the water into your Instant Pot.
2. In a large mixing bowl, mix the ground turkey with the rice, the salt and pepper.
3. Shape the mixture of the rice and meat into balls and carefully arrange it into the bottom of your Instant Pot.
4. Pour the pasta sauce on top of the rice balls and close the lid.
5. Turn the valve to sealing position; then press the button "Manual" and set the timer to about 15 minutes.
6. When the timer beeps; press the button "cancel"; quick release the pressure.
7. Open the lid of your Instant Pot; then serve and enjoy your delicious rice balls!

Nutrition Information

Calories: 124.3| Fat: 6.8g | Carbohydrates: 9.6g | Fiber: 0.4 g |Protein: 6.7g

RECIPE 97: RICE MUFFINS

Preparation time: 10 minutes

Cooking time: 40 minutes

Yield: 9 Servings

Ingredients:

- 1 Cup of uncooked organic wild rice
- 2 Large organic eggs
- 1 Finely chopped medium organic white onion
- 1 Cup of reduced fat shredded organic mozzarella cheese
- 1 Minced garlic clove
- ½ Cup of finely chopped fresh organic basil
- 1 Small, diced organic tomato
- ½ Teaspoon of sea salt
- ½ Teaspoon of freshly ground pepper
- 1 Teaspoon of chilli powder
- 2 Finely chopped chives
- 1 Cup of organic tomato sauce

Directions:

1. Rinse the wild rice and drain it very well; then add it to your Instant Pot.
2. Pour 1 and ¼ cups of water in your Instant Pot and close the lid.
3. Set the timer for about 30 minutes and make sure the valve is in the sealed position and when the timer beeps, let the pressure release naturally for 10 minutes.
4. Prepare a muffin pan with a non-stick cooking spray; then pre-heat an oven to a temperature of 350° F.
5. In a mixing bowl, combine the cooked rice with the remaining ingredients except for the chives and the tomato sauce and mix very well.
6. Transfer the mixture of the rice to the prepared muffin pan and with a tablespoon; fill each of the muffin cups to its top; then press down and bake the muffins for about 20 minutes.
7. Remove the muffin pan from the oven and set aside for about 10 minutes.
8. Transfer the muffins to a serving platter; then sprinkle with fresh chives and organic tomato sauce.
9. Serve and enjoy your delicious rice muffins!

Nutrition Information

Calories: 213.2| Fat: 7.6g | Carbohydrates: 34g | Fiber: 1.5 g |Protein: 2.4g

RECIPE 98: RICE STUFFED CALAMARI

Preparation time: 15 minutes

Cooking time: 45 minutes

Yield: 5-6 Servings

Ingredients:

- 2 Pounds of cleaned, medium-sized calamari with the tentacles cut off (finely chopped and reserved aside)
- 2 Finely chopped dry onions
- 1 Cup of long grain white rice
- 1 Cup of chopped fresh parsley
- 3 Chopped spring onions
- ½ Cup of white wine
- The juice of 2 lemons
- 10 Tablespoons of extra virgin olive oil
- 1 Pinch of salt
- 1 Pinch of pepper

Directions:

1. Place 5 tablespoons of olive oil in your Instant Pot and press the button "sauté".
2. When the oil heats up, sauté the onions for about 2 minutes.
3. Add in the chopped tentacles and sauté for 2 additional minutes.
4. Add in the rice and sauté while stirring for 1 minute.
5. Add in the wine and keep sautéing until the wine evaporates; then mix in the onions, ¾ cup of the parsley, the salt and the fresh ground black pepper.
6. Press the button "cancel" and let the mixture cool for 5 minutes.
7. Stuff the Calamari to about ¾ full, but don't overfill.
8. Secure the tops of the stuffed calamari with toothpicks.
9. Arrange the stuffed calamari in the bottom of your Instant Pot with 5 tablespoons of olive oil; then add the lemon juice and 3 cups of water and close the lid; make the valve is in the sealing position; then set the timer for about 35 minutes.
10. When the timer beeps; naturally release the pressure for 6 minutes; then open the lid when it is safe doing it and remove the stuffed calamari from the Instant Pot.
11. Remove the toothpicks, then transfer the calamari to a serving dish and garnish it with chopped parsley.
12. Serve and enjoy your delicious meal with a salad of your choice!

Nutrition Information

Calories: 108| Fat: 3g | Carbohydrates: 7g | Fiber: 1.1 g |Protein: 11.3g

RECIPE 99: RICE STUFFED SAUSAGES

Preparation time: 20 minutes

Cooking time: 50 minutes

Yield: 7 Servings

Ingredients:

- 5 to 6 piece Sheep's intestines, about 30cm long
- 1 Pound of minced beef meat and chopped liver
- 2 Cups of long grain white rice
- 1 Teaspoon of salt
- ½ Teaspoon of seven spices
- 1 Cup of small size soaked chick peas
- 1 Medium, chopped onion
- 1 Tablespoon of vegetable oil
- 1 Medium peeled onion
- 1 Cinnamon stick
- 2 Bay leaves
- 1 Teaspoon of salt
- ¼ Cup of chopped parsley for garnishing

Directions:

1. Start your Instant Pot and press the setting button "sauté".
2. Add in the oil and heat it for about 2 minutes.
3. Wash the rice and drain it very well; then add the rice and mix it with the meat, the chopped onion, the chickpeas, the salt and the spices and sauté the mixture for a couple of minutes.
4. Now, hold the already cleaned intestines from its smaller end; then start stuffing it by pushing it through the opening with your thumb.
5. When you finish the quantity of mixture; tie the intestine sides with a clean twine string and place the stuffed intestines in a bowl and wash it again to remove any stuffing on the outside skin.
6. Place the stuffed intestines in your Instant Pot and poke it with a toothpick in a few places.
7. Cover the stuffed intestines with 3 to 4 cups of water.
8. Close the lid of your Instant Pot and turn the valve to sealing position.
9. Set the timer to about 10 minutes on High pressure and when the timer beeps quick release the pressure for 6 minutes; then open the lid when it is safe doing it.
10. Add in the peeled onion, the cinnamon stick, the salt; the bay leaves and add 2 cups of water to your Instant Pot.
11. Place back the lid on the Instant Pot and turn the valve to the sealing position.

12. Set the timer for about 35 minutes and when the timer beeps; let the pressure release naturally for 10 minutes.
13. Garnish the sausages with chopped parsley.
14. Serve and enjoy your stuffed sausages!

Nutrition Information

Calories: 226| Fat: 5.7g | Carbohydrates: 7g | Fiber: 0.8 g |Protein: 35.6g

RECIPE 100: RICE GUACAMOLE

Preparation time: 12 minutes

Cooking time: 30 minutes

Yield: 3 Servings

Ingredients:

- 1 Cup of dried brown rice
- 1 Minced shallot
- 1 Seeded and finely chopped jalapeño
- 1 Peeled and pitted avocado
- 1 Small, finely chopped tomato
- ½ Teaspoon of ground cumin
- ¼ Teaspoon of paprika
- The juice of 1 lime
- 3 Tablespoons of chopped fresh cilantro or parsley
- 1 Pinch of sea salt
- 1 Pinch of fresh ground black pepper

Directions:

1. Wash the rice and drain it very well in a strainer; then transfer the rice to your Instant Pot.
2. Pour in about 2 cups of water in your Instant Pot and cover with a lid.
3. Turn the valve to sealing position; and set the timer to about 30 minutes on High pressure.
4. When the timer beeps, naturally release the pressure; then open the lid and fluff the rice with a fork.
5. Add in the shallot and the jalapeño and cover the Instant Pot without turning it on.
6. Mash the avocado and add in the tomato, the cumin, the paprika, the chilli powder, the lemon or the lime juice and the cilantro or chopped parsley.
7. While the rice is cooking, mash the avocado and stir in the tomato, cumin, paprika and parsley; then add the mixture to the cooked rice and add the salt and the pepper.
8. Garnish with additional parsley; then fluff with a fork.
9. Serve and enjoy your delicious guacamole!

Nutrition Information

Calories: 226| Fat: 5.7g | Carbohydrates: 7g | Fiber: 0.8 g |Protein: 35.6g

CONCLUSION

When we think of food we associate it with security, hospitality, and sustenance. We think of home-cooked food, and what could be better than the warmth of a hot rice bowl with family and friends. Yes indeed, rice brings the family members together. Sometimes happiness resides in the tiniest details and to many people, rice brings happiness.

Rice varies from one continent to another and from one culture to another; for example, rice is extremely important in the Asian culture and it is served almost every day for breakfast, lunch, dinner, snacks and even desserts. This cookbook offers you useful information which you need to know about rice from the way it is cooked to a large array of rice dishes that you will enjoy.

If you are wondering what this book offers in comparison to many similar books, the answer is very simple, this book uses Instant Pot/Pressure cooker to prove to you that using this cooking appliance is much better than using a Rice cooker to cook rice. For instance, using an Instant Pot, you can boil, steam, sauté, fry and even bake rice recipes like you never thought you could do.

Whether you are a beginner in using an Instant Pot or a professional, you will absolutely find something to interest you; especially because this book offers you 100 rice recipes, cooked to perfection. If you are keen on desserts, this book will please you, because thanks to this cookbook, you are going to learn some of the most innovative ways to make desserts with rice.

If your children do not like rice and you find it difficult to convince them to have their Rice Meals, worry no more, because in this cookbook, you will find some recipes that genuinely appeal to your kids. So use your Instant Pot/Pressure cooker and treat your family to a large array of sumptuous recipes that everyone will enjoy.

So, in a few words, rice is the hero ingredient of this cookbook and together with an Instant Pot/pressure cooker, rice makes a perfect marriage of a new cooking technology with one of the most versatile ingredients all over the world. Not only will this cookbook help you to master various techniques of cooking rice, but it will also help you eat healthy food with the amazing and affordable ingredients each recipe uses.

Book № 2

Introduction

For beginner home cooks there is nothing more satisfying than cooking authentic and delicious Asian dishes within minutes. Whether you are craving a Thai, Japanese, Chinese, Vietnamese, or Korean dish or in the mood to try something new, this Asian Instant Pot cookbook teaches you all you need to make authentic Asian cuisine meals right at home! This Instant Pot cookbook will help you make Asian dishes in the comfort of your own kitchen, without hard-to-find ingredients or overly complicated instructions. Best of all – Instant Pot cooking makes sure your meal is ready within minutes. With the help of an Instant Pot, you can make authentic dishes that are healthier and tastier than their restaurant counterparts.

The recipes in this book will allow you to experience a wide variety of flavors: choose from chicken, beef, noodles, rice, curries, soup, stews, vegetarian, keto, and even desserts. This book helps readers find the perfect Asian dish for any occasion. This first-ever Asian Instant Pot Cookbook makes it easy to explore the culinary delights of Asian cuisine with easy recipes for hassle-free Instant Pot cooking. This Asian Instant Pot recipe book is sure to become the go-to book for home cooks interested in creating authentic and delicious Asian dishes at home. You can have fast, delicious Asian meals every day of the week! Join the Asian adventure and learn the unique style of Asian cooking in an Instant Pot. Click the Buy Now Button immediately!

Chapter 1 Asian Cuisine

Pakistani Cuisine

Pakistani cuisine is not well known, but the dishes are diverse and full of flavors. Pakistani cuisine is a blend of cooking tradition that includes Central Asia, the Indian subcontinent, and the Mughal dynasty. Main Pakistani dishes include biryani, nihari, keema, Haleem, naan, chicken jalfrezi, curry, chicken Karachi, seekh kebabs, kofta, and chicken tikka.

Indian Cuisine

Indian cuisine is one of the diverse cuisines of the world. Indian dishes vary according to the use of vegetables, grains, spices, fruits, and geographical location. India's cuisine evolved through cultural interactions with neighboring West Asia, Persia, Mongols, and ancient Greece. Famous Indian dishes include Butter chicken/ Murg Makhani, Tandoori chicken, Chicken tikka masala, red lamb, Malai kofta, chickpea curry, palak paneer, kaali daal, papdi chaat, naan, vindaloo, chicken biriyani, chicken tikka, kebabs, maili kofta, and more.

Indonesian Cuisine

Indonesian food is full of intense flavor and one of the most colorful and vibrant cuisines in the world. Indonesian cuisine offers a blend of Dutch, English, Spanish, Portuguese, Arab, Chinese and Indian dishes. Famous Indonesian dishes include Indonesian Satay, Beef Rendang, Fried rice, Nasi Rawon, Oxtail Soup, Siomay, Indomie, Nasi Uduk, Sweet Martabak, and Pempek.

Malaysian Cuisine

Malaysian cuisine reflects the multiethnic characteristics of its population. Malaysian cuisine is a melting pot of Indonesian, Chinese, European, Indian, and Middle Eastern dishes. Famous Malaysian dishes include banana leaf, nasi Dagang, Bakuteh, Hokkien Mee, Sang, Har noodles, Satay, Nasi Kandar, Charsiew rice, Tanjung Tualang, Nasi Lemak, Hainanese chicken rice, beef rending and more.

Singaporean Cuisine

Singaporean cuisine is derived from several ethnic groups. Influences include the Chinese, Malays, Indonesian, Indian, and others such as Thailand, Eurasian, and the Middle East. Famous Singaporean dishes include Hainanese chicken rice, chili crab, laksa, Char Kuay Teow, Hokkien Prawn Mee, Barbecued Stingray, Fish Head Curry, Satay, Char Siew Rice/Noodles, and Oyster Omelette.

Thai Cuisine

In the 1980s, Thailand became a tourist hub and its cuisine become famous. Thai cuisine is one of the most popular cuisines in the world. Strong aromatic components, an abundance of spices and light preparation are the main features of Thai Cuisine. Popular Thai dishes include: Noodle soup, spicy shrimp soup, chicken in coconut soup, spicy green papaya salad, fried catfish with green mango salad, spicy seafood salad, spicy salad, stir-fried pumpkin, Thai style fried noodles, thick noodle dish, morning glory, fried rice, Thai curry, green curry, and more.

VIETNAMESE CUISINE

Vietnam is divided into 3 distinct sections: Southern, Central, and Northern. Each region differs in its main ingredients, flavors, and taste. However, they have a lot of things in common, such as soy sauce, shrimp paste, and fish sauce. Just like many Asian countries, Vietnamese cuisine emphasizes the balance of yin and yang. Famous Vietnamese dishes include Pho, Cha ca, Banh Mi, Banh Xeo, Goi Cuon, Mi Quang, Bun Thit Nuong, Com Tam, Banh Cuon, Xoi Xeo, Ca Kho To.

FILIPINO CUISINE

Filipino cuisine is composed of cuisines of various ethnolinguistic groups scattered around the Philippines. Filipino dishes employ three main tastes: sugar, salt, and vinegar. Famous Filipino dishes include Kinilaw, sinigang, kare-kare, Sisig, adobo, humba, lechon, pancit guisado, sinangag, balut, and Buko.

CHINESE CUISINE

Chinese cuisine is as diverse as China. With over 5000 named dishes, Chinese cuisine is extremely varied. Traditionally, Chinese cuisine is meant to be enjoyed for its taste and texture, appearance and aroma, its nutritious properties, and balance and harmony of yin and yang elements. Popular dishes include Sweet and sour pork, Kung Pao Chicken, Ma Po Tofu, Wontons, Dumplings, Chow Mein, Peking Roasted Duck, and Spring Rolls.

JAPANESE CUISINE

Japanese cuisine incorporates the traditional and regional foods of Japan, which have developed through centuries of social, economic, and political changes. There are so many unique and fascinating Japanese dishes and they are becoming popular to the West over recent years. Favorite dishes include Sushi & Sashimi, Ramen, Tempura, Kare-Raisu, Okonomiyaki, Shabu Shabu, Miso Soup, Yakitori, Onigiri, Udon, Soba, Gyudon, and Gyoza.

KOREAN CUISINE

Korean cuisine refers to the traditional foods and preparation techniques of Korea. Korean food has an emphasis on fermented vegetable kimchi, cooked meat without much oil, and vegetables, and considered as one of the healthiest food on earth. Popular foods include Kimchi, mixed rice, marinated beef barbecue, stir-fried noodles, sweet syrupy pancakes, spicy rice cake, ox bone soup, soft tofu stew, pork strips, seafood vegetable pancake, pumpkin porridge, cold buckwheat noodles, blood sausage, and ginseng chicken soup.

CHAPTER 2 ASIAN SPICES

Let's learn about widely used Asian spices:

1. Chilies: Chilies are used widely in Asian cooking. There are small chilies, medium chilies, large chilies, and bird's eye chilies.
2. Chinese chives: Chinese chives are more pungent than European chives.
3. Cinnamon: Cinnamon sold in American markets is usually cassia bark. True cinnamon is from Sri Lanka.
4. Fresh coriander/cilantro: Coriander is used widely in Asian cuisine. The leaves, stalks, and roots, all are used in cooking.
5. Curry leaves: They are an essential part of Indian cooking.
6. Fenugreek: Fresh leaves are used extensively.
7. Galangal: They look like ginger but different.
8. Ginger: Ginger is a popular cooking ingredient in Asian cooking.
9. Kaffir lime leaves: These leaves widely used in Thai cooking
10. Lemongrass: Lemongrass is an essential cooking component.
11. Star anise: You can use them whole or ground.
12. Thai basil: They are used widely in Thai cooking.
13. Green cardamom: This spice adds a subtler flavor to a dish.
14. Cloves: They are used in many parts of Asia.
15. Ground coriander: The seed form is popular in Asian cooking.
16. Cumin: There are two types of cumin black and white. White cumin is commonly used in Southeast Asia.
17. Fenugreek seeds: They are a popular spice ingredient.
18. Five spice: Five-spice contains cloves, anise pepper, fennel seeds, star anise, and cassia.
19. Nigella: Nigella is black cumin.
20. Seven-spice: Seven-spice is known as Japanese shichimi.
21. Turmeric: Turmeric adds a distinctive flavor to Asian dishes.

Chapter 3 Chicken Recipes

Here is a classic Asian recipe. Chicken tikka masala. Enjoy a popular Asian meal without leaving your home.

Chicken Tikka Masala (Indian)

| Cook time: 20 minutes | Servings: 2 |

Ingredients for marinating
- Boneless, skinless chicken – ½ lb. chopped into smaller pieces
- Greek yogurt – ½ cup
- Garam masala – 1 ½ tsps.
- Lemon juice – 1 ½ tsps.
- Black pepper – ½ tsp.
- Ground ginger – ¼ tsp.

For the sauce
- Canned tomato puree – 7 ounces
- Garlic – 2 cloves, minced
- Garam masala – 2 tsps.
- Paprika – ¼ tsp.
- Turmeric – ¼ tsp.
- Salt – ¼ tsp.
- Cayenne to taste
- Heavy whipping cream – ½ cup

For serving
- Basmati rice
- Naan
- Freshly chopped cilantro

Method
1. Except for the chicken, combine all the marinade ingredients in a bowl and mix well.
2. Add chicken chunks and coat well. Marinate in the refrigerator for at least 1 hour.
3. Press the sauté mode on your Instant Pot (IP).
4. Add the chicken and marinade. Sauté until 5 minutes or cooked on all side. Stirring occasionally. Turn off the sauté mode.
5. Except for the cream, add all the sauce ingredients to the IP, pour over the chicken.
6. Cover and cook at high pressure for 10 minutes at manual.
7. Release pressure when cooked.
8. Add the cream and mix. Simmer on sauté for a few minutes.

9. Serve with basmati rice or naan.

Nutritional Facts Per Serving
- Calories: 460
- Fat: 27g
- Carb: 19g
- Protein: 32g

With traditional stovetop cooking, these flavorful recipes need hours to cook. With Instant Pot, can enjoy this rich and complex dish within a few minutes.

VIETNAMESE CHICKEN NOODLE SOUP (PHO GA)

| Cook time: 30 minutes | Servings: 2 |

Ingredients
- Canola oil – 1 tbsp.
- Yellow onion – 1 medium, halved
- Ginger – 1-inch, sliced
- Coriander seeds – ½ tbsp.
- Star anise pods – 2
- Cloves – 3
- Cinnamon – ½ stick
- Cardamom pods – 1, smashed
- Bone-in, skin-on chicken thighs – 3
- Fish sauce – 1 ½ tbsps.
- Sugar – ½ tbsp.
- Water – 4 cups
- Kosher salt to taste
- Black pepper to taste
- Rice noodles – 2 servings, cooked

For toppings
- Sliced jalapeno, lime wedges, fresh herbs and sliced scallions (to taste)

Method
1. Press Sauté to preheat the Instant Pot.
2. Add oil to the hot pot. Add ginger, onions and cook for 4 minutes or until charred. Don't stir.
3. Add the cardamom, cinnamon, cloves, star anise, and coriander. Stir and cook for 1 minute.
4. Add the sugar, sauce, and chicken. Add water and cover.
5. Press Manual and cook on high pressure for 15 minutes.
6. Once cooked, do a natural release for 10 minutes.
7. Remove the chicken and strain the broth.

8. Season with salt and pepper.
9. Arrange the chicken with cooked noodles in 4 bowls.
10. Pour over the broth and garnish with toppings.
11. Serve.

Nutritional Facts Per Serving
- Calories: 620
- Fat: 8g
- Carb: 57g
- Protein: 25g

The epitome of a one-pot meal is chicken biryani. This dish is made with tender chicken, aromatic basmati rice, herbs, and spices. Chicken biryani is one of the favorite dishes in India, Pakistan, and Bangladesh.

CHICKEN BIRYANI (INDIAN & PAKISTANI)

| Cook time: 40 minutes | Servings: 2 |

Ingredients
- Garam masala – ½ tsp.
- Ginger – ¼ tbsp. grated
- Garlic – ¼ tbsp. minced
- Red chili powder – ¼ tbsp.
- Turmeric – a pinch
- Mint leaves – a few
- Chopped cilantro - a few
- Lemon juice – ½ tbsp.
- Plain yogurt – 1 tbsp.
- Kosher salt – ½ tsp.
- Chicken – ½ pound, bone-in, skinless (cut into bite-sized pieces)

Remaining ingredients
- Basmati rice – ¾ cup, extra-long variety (washed and soaked in water)
- Ghee – ¾ tbsp. divided
- Yellow onion – ½, sliced
- Bay leaves- 1
- Salt – ½ tsp.
- Saffron – ¼ tsp. mixed in 1 tbsp. warm milk
- Eggs - 1 ½ boiled and shelled
- Jalapeno – ¼, sliced

Raita
- o   Plain yogurt – ½ cup
- o   Yellow onion – ¼, finely diced
- o   Tomato – ½ diced
- o   Kosher salt to taste
- o   Chopped cilantro – ¼ tsp.

Method
1. In a bowl, add the mint leaves, turmeric, chili powder, garlic, ginger, garam masala, half of the lemon juice, chopped cilantro, salt, and yogurt.
2. Add chicken and coat well. Marinate in the refrigerator for at least 30 minutes.
3. Press sauté and add ghee and onions to the hot pot.
4. Cook for 10 minutes or until the onion is caramelized.
5. Remove and set aside about half of the onion for garnishing.
6. Add the rest of the ghee to the Instant Pot and add sliced jalapeno.
7. Add half of the marinated chicken, marinated liquid and bay leaf to the pot. Press Cancel and mix well. Deglaze the pot with a spatula and remove all the brown bits from bottom of the pot by scraping.
8. Add the remaining chicken and close the lid.
9. Press Manual and cook for 4 minutes on High.
10. Do a quick release, and open.
11. Mix the chicken well and remove any stuck food from the bottom.
12. Drain the rice and add to the chicken. Add 1 cup of water and salt. Adjust water if necessary.
13. Close and cook on Manual on High for 6 minutes.
14. Do a quick release when cooked.
15. Open and gently mix the rice and chicken.
16. Garnish with saffron liquid and caramelized onions
17. Serve with lemon wedges, hard-boiled egg, and Raita.
18. To make the Raita: in a bowl, whisk the yogurt. Add salt, tomatoes, and onion and mix well. Garnish with cilantro.

Nutritional Facts Per Serving
- o   Calories: 503
- o   Fat: 18g
- o   Carb: 60g
- o   Protein: 20g

This Malaysian ginger soy chicken is delicious and takes only 8 minutes to cook. Ginger gives an amazing aroma to the dish and soy sauce and sweet soy sauce complements the flavor.

GINGER SOY CHICKEN

Cook time: 8 minutes	Servings: 2

Ingredients
- Chicken – 1 lb. (wings drummettes and wingettes and drumsticks) chopped into pieces
- Oil – ¾ tbsp.
- Ginger – ¾ inch, sliced
- Soy sauce – 1 1/3 tbsps.
- Sweet soy sauce – 2 tbsps.
- Ground white pepper – 2 dashes
- Water – ½ cup
- Sesame oil – ½ tsp.
- Scallion – 2/3 stalk, sliced

Method
1. Press sauté on the Instant Pot.
2. Add oil to the hot pot.
3. Add chicken and sear until slightly brown.
4. Add the ginger and sauté a little bit.
5. Add the sesame oil, ground pepper, sweet soy sauce, soy sauce, and water.
6. Cover and press Manual Cook 8 minutes on High pressure.
7. Do a quick release.
8. Open and stir in scallion.
9. Serve.

Nutritional Facts Per Serving
- Calories: 400
- Fat: 16.7g
- Carb: 19.8g
- Protein: 43g

This Malaysian chicken dish with sticky sweet and savory honey sauce will be your family favorite. If you love moist, juicy, soft, and tender chicken thighs in sauce this meal is for you.

HONEY SESAME CHICKEN

Cook time: 8 minutes	Servings: 2

Ingredients
- Boneless, skinless chicken thighs – 0.75 lbs.
- Salt and ground pepper to taste
- Oil – ¾ tbsp.
- Garlic – 1 clove, minced
- Toasted white sesame – ½ tsp.
- Chopped scallion - ½ tbsp.

Honey sesame sauce
- Chicken broth – ¼ cup
- Honey – 1 ¼ tbsps.
- Soy sauce – 1 tbsp.
- Dark soy sauce – ¼ tsp.
- Apple cider vinegar – ½ tbsp.
- Sriracha – ½ tsp.
- Sesame oil – ½ tsp.
- Corn starch – ½ tsp.

Method
1. Season the chicken with salt and pepper. Set aside.
2. Mix all the sauce ingredients together. Make sure the corn starch and honey are mixed completely. Set aside.
3. Press sauté on your Instant Pot.
4. Add the cooking oil.
5. Sear chicken on all sides.
6. Add the garlic and sauté for a minute.
7. Pour in the sauce and add sesame.
8. Cover and press Manual.
9. Cook on High pressure for 8 minutes.
10. Do a quick release.
11. Add chopped scallion and serve.

Nutritional Facts Per Serving
- Calories: 302
- Fat: 12.8g
- Carb: 13.2g
- Protein: 34.3g

This chicken recipe is a simplified version of traditional Filipino comfort foot. An Instant Pot cooks it in no time at all and one pot means less time to clean.

PILIPINO CHICKEN ADOBO

Cook time: 25 minutes	Servings: 2

Ingredients
- Chicken legs – 2, thighs and drumsticks separated
- Salt and pepper to taste
- Vegetable oil – 1 tbsp.
- Soy sauce – 2 tbsps.
- Sugar - 1 tbsp.
- White distilled vinegar – 1 tbsp.
- Garlic – 2 cloves, smashed
- Bay leaves – 1
- Yellow onion – 1/2, sliced
- Scallions -1, sliced
- Cooked rice for serving

Method
1. Season the chicken with salt and pepper.
2. Press Sauté on your Instant Pot and add the oil.
3. Add half the chicken and brown on both sides, about 7 minutes.
4. Remove to a plate and brown the remaining chicken pieces.
5. Return the chicken to the pot and add the onion, bay leaves, garlic, vinegar, sugar, soy sauce, and pepper.
6. Cover with the lid and cook on High for 8 minutes.
7. Do a quick release and open the lid.
8. Press sauté and reduce the sauce for about 20 minutes, or until the sauce is dark brown and fragrant.
9. Arrange on serving plates.
10. Sprinkle with scallions and serve with rice.

Nutritional Facts Per Serving
- Calories: 424
- Fat: 27.1g
- Carb: 11.7g
- Protein: 32g

This is a Filipino dish made with potatoes, peas, bell peppers, carrots, and chicken.

CHICKEN AFRITADA

| Cook time: 35 minutes | Servings: 2 |

Ingredients
- Chicken drumsticks and thighs – 4 pieces
- Garlic – 1 tbsp. minced
- Onion – ½ sliced
- Tomato paste – 4 ounces
- Chicken broth – ½ cup
- Soy sauce – 1 tbsp.
- Fish sauce – 1 tbsp.
- Dried bay leave – 1
- Carrots – 2, chopped
- Potato – 1, diced
- Bell pepper – ¼, sliced
- Frozen peas – 1 tbsp.
- Cornstarch – ½ tbsp. mixed in cold water (optional)

Method
1. Press sauté and oil and brown the chicken on all sides.
2. Add onion and garlic.
3. Remove the chicken from the pot.
4. Add broth and deglaze the pot. Remove all stuck bits from the bottom of the pot.
5. Add tomato paste, bay leaves, fish sauce, and soy sauce to the pot. Mix well. Return the browned chicken to the pot.
6. Close the lid and press poultry, cook for 10 minutes.
7. Do a quick release and open the lid.
8. Add peas, bell pepper, potato, and carrots.
9. Cook on Manual for 1 minute.
10. Do a quick release and open.
11. Taste and season if necessary.
12. Serve.

Nutritional Facts Per Serving
- Calories: 315
- Fat: 3.6g
- Carb: 40.5g
- Protein: 31.5g

After a hard day's work, you may not find you have much energy, but you will find time to cook this delicious chicken dish. Once you have tasted this dish, you will never buy that frozen pre-made pasta again.

PILIPINO CHICKEN FLORENTINE

Cook time: 20 minutes	Servings: 2

Ingredients
- Boneless chicken – 1 lb.
- Oil – 1 tbsp.
- Onion powder – 1 tbsp.
- Garlic powder – 1 tbsp.
- Tie Noodles – ½ box
- Cream of mushroom soup - 1 can
- Milk – ¾ cup
- Fresh spinach – 1 cup
- Salt and pepper to taste

Method
1. Press sauté on your pressure cooker.
2. Add oil, then brown chicken on all sides.
3. Add the garlic, onion, and season with salt and pepper. Mix well.
4. Add the cream of mushroom soup.
5. Top with noodles, then add the milk and sprinkle with pepper.
6. Close and cook 15 minutes on Manual.
7. Do a quick release and open.
8. Stir everything and shred the chicken.
9. Stir in the fresh spinach and mix.
10. Serve.

Nutritional Facts Per Serving
- Calories: 412
- Fat: 15g
- Carb: 36.3g
- Protein: 32.5g

This Instant Pot Mongolian chicken dish takes only 30 minutes to cook. The dish produces flavorful, juicy and tender chicken.

Mongolian Chicken

| Cook time: 20 minutes | Servings: 2 |

Ingredients
- Boneless skinless chicken breasts - 1 1/3, cut into cubes
- Extra virgin olive oil – 2/3 tbsps.
- Brown sugar – ½ tbsp. or to taste
- Garlic – 1 clove, minced
- Fresh ginger – ½ tsp. minced
- Soy sauce – ½ tbsp.
- Broth – 1/6 cup
- Carrots – 2 tbsps.
- Red pepper flakes – ½ tsp.
- Garlic powder – 1/3 tbsp.

Cornstarch slurry
- Cornstarch – 2/3 tbsp.

Optional
- Green onion – 1 tbsp.
- Sesame seeds – to taste

Rice
- Basmati rice – 2/3 cup
- Water – 2/3 cup
- Butter – 2/3 tbsp.
- Salt – 1 pinch

Method
1. Press sauté on your Instant Pot.
2. Add oil.
3. Add chicken and sauté for 2 to 3 minutes. Stir constantly.
4. Deglaze the pot if necessary.
5. Add red pepper flakes, garlic powder, carrot, water, brown sugar, soy sauce, garlic, and ginger to the pot.
6. Stir to mix.
7. Rice: Add the rice, salt, and water in a pot.
8. Stir to combine.
9. Add a trivet to the instant pot and place the rice pot onto the trivet.
10. Cover with aluminum foil and pinch a few times with a fork.

11. Close and cook at High for 5 minutes.
12. Do a natural release.
13. Open the lid and remove the pot with the rice.
14. Rest and fluff the rice with a fork.
15. Press sauté.
16. In a bowl, combine water and cornstarch, whisk to mix.
17. Add the mixture to the pot and stir to combine.
18. Sauté for a few minutes without the lid.
19. Turn of the heat.
20. Garnish and serve.

Nutritional Facts Per Serving
- Calories: 538
- Fat: 11g
- Carb: 84g
- Protein: 24g

This is a hearty Instant Pot meal with an Asian twist. It is perfect for a lunch or a dinner dish.

ASIAN CHICKEN AND RICE

Cook time: 10 minutes	Servings: 2

Ingredients
- Uncooked jasmine rice – ½ cup (drained and rinsed)
- Skinless chicken thighs – 2, boneless
- Salt – ¼ tsp.
- Ground black pepper – 1 pinch
- Peanut oil – ½ tbsp.
- Yellow onion – ¼, chopped
- Minced garlic – 1 ½ cloves
- Minced ginger – 1 tsp.
- Cumin powder – 1 tsp.
- Chicken broth – ½ cup
- Carrot – 1, chopped
- Bell pepper – ½ chopped
- Soy sauce – ½ tbsp.
- Sesame oil – ½ tsp.
- Chopped green onion – 1 tbsp. for garnish

Method
1. Season the chicken with salt and pepper. Marinate for 10 to 15 minutes.

2. Add peanut oil in the Instant Pot.
3. Press Sauté and place onion in the pot.
4. Stir fry for 3 minutes.
5. Add the cumin, ginger, and garlic. Cook until fragrant.
6. Turn off sauté and add broth.
7. Deglaze the pot if necessary.
8. Add the pepper and carrot.
9. Spread the rice in the pot evenly.
10. Top with chicken. And drizzle with soy sauce. Don't stir.
11. Close and press Manual.
12. Cook on High for 10 minutes.
13. Release pressure naturally.
14. Shred the chicken with forks.
15. Drizzle with sesame oil.
16. Add the sesame seed and green onions.
17. Mix and serve.

Nutritional Facts Per Serving
- Calories: 417
- Fat: 10.9g
- Carb: 46g
- Protein: 32g

CHAPTER 4 MEAT RECIPES

This is a moist and tender pressure cooker Chinese BBQ pork. This sweet and savory dish goes great with noodles or rice.

CHINESE BBQ PORK (CHAR SIU)

| Cook time: 45 minutes | Servings: 2 |

Ingredients
- Pork butt meat – 1 pound, split the longer side in half
- Honey – 3 tbsp.
- Light soy sauce – 2 tbsps.
- Water – 1 cup
- Kosher salt to taste

Marinade
- Chu Hou pastes – 1 tbsp.
- Chinese fermented red bean curd – 2 cubes
- Char siu sauce – 3 tbsps.
- Sesame oil – ½ tsp.
- Shaoxing wine – 2 tbsps.
- Garlic powder – 1 tsp.
- Light soy sauce -1 tbsp.

Method
1. Make lots of deep holes in the meat with a fork.
2. Marinade the pork for up to 2 hours in a Ziploc bag.
3. Remove the pork and marinade from the bag. Add 1 cup water in the Ziploc bag and mix to get the remaining marinade.
4. Add the marinade mixture into the pressure cooker.
5. Place the meat in the pressure cooker on a steamer basket.
6. Season the meat with salt on both sides.
7. Cover with the lid and cook on high pressure for 18 minutes.
8. Then do a natural release for 12 minutes.
9. In a bowl, mix honey and 2 tbsp. soy sauce.
10. Brush the meat with this mixture.
11. Preheat the oven to 450F.
12. Place pork in the oven and cook until both sides are browned, about 4 to 6 minutes.
13. Serve over noodles or rice with leftover sauce.

Nutritional Facts Per Serving
- Calories: 804

- Fat: 58.3g
- Carb: 40.1g
- Protein: 27.3g

This Korean meat dish is accentuated by black pepper, fresh ginger, green chili pepper, and shishito pepper. It is a childhood favorite for most Koreans.

KOREAN PORK RIBS (DWAEJI GALBI JJIM)

| Cook time: 25 minutes | Servings: 2 |

Ingredients
- Pork ribs – ¾ lb. fat trimmed and cut into pieces
- Soy sauce – 65 ml. (jin ganjang)
- Water – ½ cup
- Green chili peppers (Korean) – 2, cut into pieces
- Shishito peppers – 3 to 4, chopped
- Fresh ginger – 1/3 oz. chopped
- Black pepper – 1/6 tsp.

Method
1. Soak ribs in cold water for 10 minutes.
2. In the Instant Pot, add soy sauce, water, ribs, ginger, black pepper, and ½ the green peppers.
3. Close and press Meat/Stew. Cook for reduced time – 20 minutes.
4. Release pressure when cooked.
5. Oven and add rest of the chili peppers and all the shishito peppers.
6. Close the pot again and cook on manual at low pressure for 5 minutes.
7. Serve.

Nutritional Facts Per Serving
- Calories: 301
- Fat: 17g
- Carb: 1g
- Protein: 30g

This Chinese dish is made with fermented soybeans, black beans, and pork ribs. This dish is fuss-free, super easy and fork tender delicious.

PORK RIBS WITH BLACK BEANS (CHINESE)

Cook time: 50 minutes	Servings: 2

Ingredients
- Pork ribs – 2/3 lbs. cut into bite size pieces
- Shao Hsing cooking wine – ½ tbsp.
- Salt to taste
- Ginger – 15 g, minced
- Garlic – 1 clove, minced
- Red chili – ½, seeded and minced
- Fermented black beans – 25 g, minced
- Fermented soybeans – 15 g, minced
- Sugar – ¼ tsp.
- Sesame oil – ½ tsp.
- Water – 1 ½ cups

Method
1. In a bowl, combine the salt, wine and pork ribs.
2. Place minced soybeans, black beans, red chili, garlic, and ginger and stir in sugar. Pour mixture over pork rib pieces. Coat well and marinate for 30 minutes.
3. Add water to the Pressure Cooker and drizzle sesame oil over the ribs.
4. Cover the bowl with a piece of aluminum foil.
5. Place bowl on a steaming rack.
6. Transfer the rack into the pressure cooker pot.
7. Close and lock the lid.
8. Press Steam and set time for 50 minutes.
9. Once finished cooking, allow the cooker to Keep Warm.
10. Press Cancel after 10 minutes and release pressure naturally.
11. Serve.

Nutritional Facts Per Serving
- Calories: 268
- Fat: 13.2g
- Carb: 8.2g
- Protein: 25.1g

When traveling to Vietnam, you won't find this delicious pork belly dish in many Vietnamese restaurants. However, every Vietnamese family makes this dish at home. Cooking this dish is a part of the Lunar New Year celebration.

VIETNAMESE BRAISED PORK BELLY (THIT KHO TAU)

| Cook time: 35 minutes | Servings: 2 |

Ingredients
- Lean pork belly - ¾ lb. cut into 1-inch squares
- Large eggs – 3 (semi-soft boiled and peeled)
- Garlic – 1 clove, minced
- Shallot – ½, diced
- Fish sauce – ½ tbsp.
- Coconut water – 1 cup
- Granulated sugar – 2 tbsps.
- Ground black pepper – ¼ tsp.
- Kosher salt to taste
- Soy sauce – ½ tsp.
- Thai chili pepper for garnish

Method
1. In a bowl, add the pork belly pieces, black pepper, salt, soy sauce, shallot, garlic, and fish sauce. Mix and coat the meat well and set aside.
2. To make the sauce: add the sugar into the Instant Pot and press Sauté.
3. Melt the sugar and let it caramelize, about 5 minutes.
4. Once the sauce takes a coffee color, add the marinated meat and sauté for 5 minutes. Stir and coat well. Add the coconut water and stir. Turn off the sauté mode.
5. Press Manual and cook on high pressure for 35 minutes.
6. Once cooked, do a natural release for 15 minutes.
7. Open the lid and the eggs.
8. Cover and press Keep Warm.
9. Wait about 15 minutes so the eggs can absorb the flavor of the dish.
10. Skim the fat from the sauce.
11. Serve the dish with steamed vegetables and/or rice.
12. Garnish with Thai chilis.

Nutritional Facts Per Serving
- Calories: 428
- Fat: 13.3g
- Carb: 26.9g
- Protein: 51g

This is fall-apart tender, delicious, Malaysian Instant Pot Beef Rendang. With the traditional cooking method, this recipe usually takes several hours. but without Instant Pot, this recipe takes only a few minutes.

MALAYSIAN BEEF RENDANG

| Cook time: 30 minutes | Servings: 2 |

Ingredients
- Onion – ½ cup, chopped
- Minced garlic – ½ tbsp.
- Minced ginger – ½ tbsp.
- Jalapeno – ½
- Vegetable oil – 1 tbsp.
- Rendang curry paste – ½ package
- Skirt steak – ½ pound, cut into 2-inch chunks
- Water – ½ cup, divided
- Full-fat coconut milk – ½ cup, divided
- Shredded coconut – 1 tbsp.

Method
1. Press sauté and add oil to the hot pot.
2. Add the vegetables and stir to coat with oil.
3. Add the rendang paste and stir. Roast the paste for 3 to 4 minutes.
4. Add the steak and stir to coat with spices, about 2 minutes.
5. Pour in ¼ cup water and deglaze the pot well. Remove any burned bits.
6. Add half the coconut milk and remaining water.
7. Cook on High pressure for 25 minutes.
8. Do a natural release for 10 minutes.
9. Open the lid and add the remaining coconut milk and mix well.
10. Garnish with shredded coconut and serve.

Nutritional Facts Per Serving
- Calories: 391
- Fat: 29g
- Carb: 7g
- Protein: 26g

This Instant Pot Beef Caldereta is your go-to dish if you are looking for a faster way to cook and enjoy Filipino food.

BEEF CALDERETA

| Cook time: 45 minutes | Servings: 2 |

Ingredients
- Extra virgin olive oil – ½ tbsp.
- Unsalted butter – ½ tbsp.
- Beef short ribs – 1 pound, cut in pieces
- Worcestershire sauce – 1 tbsp.
- Garlic – 2 cloves, minced
- Onion – ½, sliced
- Bell pepper – 1, seeded and sliced
- Tomato paste – 3 ounces
- Canned liver spread – 2 tbsps.
- Beef broth – 1 cup
- Potato – 1, quartered
- Pitted Spanish green olives with pimiento – 2 tbsps.
- Red pepper flakes – ½ tsp.
- Salt – ½ tsp.
- Ground black pepper – ¼ tsp.

Method
1. Press the sauté on your Instant Pot.
2. Add oil and butter.
3. Braise the beef short ribs and brown on all sides.
4. Drizzle with Worcestershire sauce.
5. Add the bell peppers, onions, and garlic and stir and cook for 2 minutes.
6. Turn off the sauté mode.
7. Add the liver spread and tomato paste. Pour the beef broth.
8. Add the olives and potato. Season with salt, pepper, and red pepper flakes.
9. Cover and cook on High pressure for 45 minutes.
10. Do a quick release when done.
11. Serve.

Nutritional Facts Per Serving
- Calories: 472
- Fat: 18.6g
- Carb: 33.9g
- Protein: 42.5g

This is a Filipino style BBQ rib recipe. It is so easy to make, and you can make them sweet or savory.

FILIPINO BBQ RIBS

Cook time: 45 minutes	Servings: 2

Ingredients
- Spare ribs – ½ rack, cut into portions
- Filipino soy sauce – 2 tbsp.
- Lemon juice – 1 tbsp.
- Ketchup – 2 tbsp.
- Brown sugar – 1 tbsp.
- Garlic cloves – 2, minced
- Onion – 1/2, minced

Method
1. Preheat the oven to broil.
2. Press salute on your pressure cooker.
3. Add oil and sauté the onion and garlic.
4. Then add the lemon juice, sugar, ketchup, and soy sauce. Mix well.
5. Add the ribs into the pot.
6. Press Chicken/Meat and cook for 35 minutes on Manual setting.
7. Do a quick release.
8. Remove the ribs and place on a baking sheet.
9. Broil them for 5 to 10 minutes in the oven.
10. Press sauté on the pot and thicken the sauce.
11. Serve with the sauce.

Nutritional Facts Per Serving
- Calories: 228
- Fat: 6.9g
- Carb: 14.9g
- Protein: 25.7g

Kare Kare is a traditional Pilipino dish. Traditionally it is cooked in a pressure cooker, but it is possible to cook the dish in the Instant Pot.

PILIPINO KARE KARE

Cook time: 50 minutes	Servings: 2

Ingredients
- Oxtail – 150 grams

- Stew meat – 150 grams
- Water – 1 cup
- Onion – ½, sliced in wedges
- Peanut butter – 1 tbsp.
- Green beans – 1 tbsp.
- Eggplant – 100 grams, sliced
- Bok Choy – 1, prepared and cut in half
- Madrecita chicken seasoning – 1 tsp.
- Fish sauce – 1 tsp.

Method
1. Place the oxtail in the pot and add water and stew meat.
2. Close and press Meat. Cook on High pressure for 35 minutes.
3. Release pressure when cooked and open.
4. Remove the meat and oxtail and set aside.
5. If you want, you can refrigerate the broth overnight and skim off the fat.
6. Press sauté and heat the broth.
7. Add the sliced onion when the broth starts to boil.
8. Add the peanut butter after 1 minute. Continue to stir.
9. Add back the meat and oxtail and add the remaining ingredients.
10. Add the beans, bottom stalks of the bok choy, and eggplant after 2 minutes.
11. Add the chicken seasoning, fish sauce and stir to mix.
12. Top the dish with Bok Choy leaves. Gently press and cook for a few minutes.
13. Turn off the heat and serve.

Nutritional Facts Per Serving
- Calories: 211
- Fat: 9.9g
- Carb: 9.7g
- Protein: 21.8g

In the Philippines, people love to eat rice. This is a finger licking good, breakfast dish.

FILIPINO BEEF TAPA

Cook time: 22 minutes	Servings: 2

Ingredients
- Beef sirloin – 1 lb. thin sliced
- Oil – 1 ½ tbsps.
- Minced garlic – 3 cloves
- Water – 1 cup

- o   Soy sauce – 1/3 cup
- o   Salt and pepper to taste
- o   Brown sugar – 1 ½ tbsp.
- o   Oyster sauce – ½ tbsp.
- o   Half lime – juiced
- o   Cornstarch – ½ tsp.
- o   Water – 1 tbsp.

Method
1. Press sauté on your pressure cooker.
2. Add the oil and garlic and cook for 2 minutes.
3. Add sliced sirloin and cook until both sides are brown.
4. Then add the oyster sauce, lime juice, water, soy sauce, salt, pepper, and brown sugar. Mix well.
5. Cover and cook on Manual High for 12 minutes.
6. Do a quick release and open the lid.
7. Mix cornstarch with water and add to the pot.
8. Turn on Sauté and let boil for 5 to 10 minutes. Continue to stir.
9. Remove from heat and serve.

Nutritional Facts Per Serving
- o   Calories: 320
- o   Fat: 17.7g
- o   Carb: 13.4g
- o   Protein: 26.5g

This short rib rice is tender and delicious. The sticky sauce makes it a favorite meal for most Koreans.

KOREAN SHORT RIBS

Korean Short Ribs

Cook time: 55 minutes	Servings: 2

Ingredients
- o   Bone-in beef short ribs – 500 grams
- o   Carrots – 80 grams, chopped
- o   Korean radish – 66 grams, chopped

Sauce

- o   Water – 3 tbsps.
- o   Red apple – 1/3, chopped
- o   Onion – 1/3, chopped

- o   Soy sauce – 2 tbsp.
- o   Brown sugar – ½ tbsp.
- o   Honey – ½ tbsp.
- o   Rice wine – ½ tbsp.
- o   Minced garlic – 1/3 tbsp.
- o   Sesame oil – ½ tsp.
- o   Whole black peppercorns - 1

Method
1. Boil the short ribs in boiling water for 6 to 8 minutes. Then drain and rinse in cold water. Place in the Instant Pot.
2. Blend the sauce ingredients in a mixer until smooth.
3. Pour sauce over the short ribs.
4. Cover with the lid and cook on High for 35 minutes.
5. Do a quick release and remove the lid.
6. Transfer the meat to a bowl, cover and set aside.
7. Add the vegetables into the pot.
8. Press Sauté and cook for 20 minutes.
9. Garnish with toasted sesame seeds.
10. Serve the ribs.

Nutritional Facts Per Serving
- o   Calories: 448
- o   Fat: 15.6g
- o   Carb: 22.7g
- o   Protein: 52.1g

CHAPTER 5 FISH AND SEAFOOD RECIPES

Rice porridge or Vietnamese fish congee is so flavorful and comforting. This delicious fish bowl will be cooked in 25 minutes.

VIETNAMESE FISH CONGEE (CHAO CA)

| Cook time: 25 minutes | Servings: 2 |

Ingredients
- Short grain white rice – 0.38 cup, Washed and drained
- Mung bean – 1 tbsp. Washed and drained
- Fish bones – 0.75 lb. scrub with salt and rinse in cold water
- Ginger – 1, thumb-sized piece, chopped
- Shallot – 0.5, chopped
- Water – 3 cups
- Salt – 0.5 tsp.
- Fish sauce – 0.5 tbsp.
- Fish fillet – 0.5 lb. sliced diagonal into ½ inch thick pieces

For toppings and herbs

- Black pepper
- Vietnamese perilla, sliced
- Chopped cilantro
- Sliced scallion
- Fried shallot

Method
1. Add the rice and bean to the Instant Pot.
2. Add the fish bones, sliced ginger, and chopped shallot.
3. Add fish sauce, salt, and water.
4. Cook on porridge mode for 20 minutes.
5. Season the fish fillets with salt and pepper. Set aside.
6. Release the pressure once cooked. Open, remove and discard fish bones.
7. Add fish fillets and cook on sauté for a couple of minutes or until fish is cooked.
8. Adjust seasoning.
9. Serve topped with herbs of your choice.

Nutritional Facts Per Serving
- Calories: 419
- Fat: 14.5g
- Carb: 52.6g

- o   Protein: 20.3g

This is a Vietnamese Salmon dish cooked in an Instant Pot. The fish is served with a Vietnamese sauce. The salmon is perfect served with rice.

VIETNAMESE SALMON

| Cook time: 15 minutes | Servings: 2 |

Ingredients
- o   Olive oil – ½ tbsp.
- o   Light brown sugar – 2 tbsps.
- o   Asian fish sauce – 1 ½ tbsp.
- o   Soy sauce – ¾ tbsp.
- o   Grated fresh ginger – ¼ tsp.
- o   Finely grated zest of 1 lime
- o   Juice of ½ lime
- o   Freshly ground black pepper – ¼ tsp.
- o   Skinless salmon fillets – 2

For garnish:
- o   Fresh lime wedges
- o   Fresh cilantro leaves
- o   Sliced green onion

Method
1. Press Sauté on your Instant Pot.
2. Add oil, ginger, black pepper, lime juice, lime zest, soy sauce, fish sauce, and brown sugar to the IP. Bring to a simmer, then turn off the cooker.
3. Place the fish (keep the skin side up) into the cooker. Use a spoon to drop some sauce over the fish.
4. Cover and cook on Low for 1 minute. Do a natural release for 5 minutes.
5. Press Sauté and cook the fish for 30 seconds to 1 minute or until the fish is cooked.
6. Remove the fish and reduce the sauce until thickens, about 3 minutes.
7. Arrange the fish and sauce in serving bowls.
8. Garnish with cilantro leaves, sliced green onion, and fresh lime wedges.

Nutritional Facts Per Serving
- o   Calories: 225
- o   Fat: 6.5g
- o   Carb: 15.3g
- o   Protein: 27.7g

This is an Indian cooker shrimp curry dish. It is made in just 20 minutes. This dish is made with tomatoes, onions, garlic, ginger, and flavorful spices.

INDIAN COCONUT SHRIMP CURRY

Cook time: 20 minutes	Servings: 2

Ingredients
- Shrimp, deveined tail-on – ½ lb.
- Oil – ½ tbsp.
- Mustard seeds – ½ tsp.
- Green chili pepper – 1, sliced
- Onion – ½ cup, chopped
- Ginger – 1 tsp. minced
- Garlic – 1 tsp. minced
- Tomato – ½ cup, chopped
- Coconut milk – 4 oz.
- Lime juice – ½ tbsp.
- Cilantro – 1 tsp.

Spices
- Ground turmeric – ¼ tsp.
- Cayenne – ½ tsp.
- Garam masala – ¼ tsp.
- Coriander powder – ½ tsp.
- Salt – ¼ tsp.

Method
1. Press the Sauté on your Instant Pot and add oil and mustard seeds.
2. Sizzle for a few seconds, then add the garlic, ginger, onions, and green chili.
3. Stir-fry until onions are golden brown, about 5 minutes.
4. Add the spices and tomato and mix. Stir-fry for 3 minutes.
5. Add the shrimp and coconut milk to the pot. Stir and press cancel.
6. Close the lid and press Manual.
7. Cook on low pressure for 3 minutes.
8. Do a natural release and open the lid.
9. Stir in lime juice and garnish with cilantro.
10. Enjoy with rice.

Nutritional Facts Per Serving
- Calories: 226
- Fat: 10g
- Carb: 8g
- Protein: 24g

Perfectly cooked moist and juice Instant Pot salmon. This succulent salmon is cooked in sweet-savory, caramelized teriyaki sauce.

SALMON (SINGAPOREAN)

Cook time: 5 minutes	Servings: 2

Ingredients
- Salmon steaks – 2, 1 to 1.5 inch thick
- Garlic – 4 cloves, crushed
- Ginger – 1 to 2 slices

Method
1. Soy sauce – ¼ cup
2. Mirin – ¼ cup
3. Japanese cooking sake – ¼ cup
4. Sesame oil – ¼ tsp.
5. White sugar – 2 tbsps.

Garnish
- Toasted sesame seeds
- Green onion – 1 stalk, sliced

Thickener
- Cornstarch – 2 ½ tbsps.
- Water – 3 tbsps.

Method
1. In the Instant Pot, add ginger and garlic.
2. Layer salmon steaks on the garlic cloves.
3. To make the sauce: mix the sauce ingredients and pour over salmon.
4. Pressure cook at High for 0 (zero) minute and do a natural release for 10 minutes.
5. Check the fish with a food thermometer (around 145F).
6. Place the salmon on serving plates.
7. Thicken the sauce over Sauté button.
8. Serve.

Nutritional Facts Per Serving
- Calories: 657
- Fat: 20g
- Carb: 39g
- Protein: 67g

This salmon dish is cooked with ginger, lime, and Asian fish sauce. The fish cooks very quickly and is wonderfully tender.

VIETNAMESE CARAMEL SALMON

Cook time: 10 minutes	Servings: 2

Ingredients
- Olive oil – ½ tbsp.
- Light brown sugar – 2 tbsps.
- Asian fish sauce – 1 ½ tbsps.
- Soy sauce – ¾ tbsp.
- Grated fresh ginger – ½ tsp.
- Zest of half a lime
- Juice of ½ lime
- Black pepper to taste
- Salmon fillets – 2, skinless (6 to 8 ounces each)
- Fresh cilantro and sliced scallions for garnish

Method
1. Press Sauté on your pressure cooker.
2. Add the oil, sugar, soy sauce, fish sauce, ginger, black pepper, lime zest, and juice in the pressure cooker and whisk to mix.
3. Bring to a simmer and turn off the heat.
4. Place the fish in the pressure cooker.
5. Spoon the sauce over the fish.
6. Cover and cook on Low for 1 minute.
7. Do a natural release for 5 minutes.
8. Remove the fish.
9. Press sauté and thicken the sauce for 3 minutes.
10. Spoon the sauce over the fish.
11. Garnish with cilantro and scallions.
12. Serve.

Nutritional Facts Per Serving
- Calories: 399
- Fat: 23g
- Carb: 19.3g
- Protein: 29.5g

This healthy Asian Salmon dish is delicious and free from gluten and soy.

SOY-FREE ASIAN SALMON

Cook time: 10 minutes	Servings: 2

Ingredients
- Salmon fillets – 2 (6 oz.)
- Coconut oil – 1 tbsp.
- Brown sugar – 1 tbsp.
- Coconut aminos – 3 tbsps.
- Maple syrup – 2 tbsps.
- Paprika - 1 tsp.
- Ginger – ¼ tsp.
- Sesame seeds – 1 tsp.
- Fresh scallions

Method
1. Press sauté on your IP.
2. Add oil and brown sugar. Stir and melt the sugar.
3. Add the aminos, ginger, paprika, and maple. Mix.
4. Add the salmon, skin side up.
5. Season with salt and pepper.
6. Cover and cook on Low for 2 minutes.
7. Do a natural release for 5 minutes.
8. Serve garnished with parsley and sesame seeds.

Nutritional Facts Per Serving
- Calories: 438
- Fat: 25.9g
- Carb: 11g
- Protein: 40.2g

This Chinese Steamed fish recipe is high protein, low-carb, gluten-free and paleo.

GINGER SCALLION FISH

Cook time: 10 minutes	Servings: 2

Ingredients
Mix and marinate

- Soy sauce – 1 ½ tbsps.
- Rice wine – 1 tbsp.

- o Chicken black bean paste – ½ tbsp.
- o Minced ginger – ½ tsp.
- o Garlic – ½ tsp.
- o Firm white fish – ½ pound

Vegetables
- o Peanut oil – ½ tbsp.
- o Julienned ginger – 1 tbsp.
- o Julienned green onion – 2 tbsps.
- o Chopped cilantro – 2 tbsps.
- o Water – 1 cup

Method
1. Place fish pieces on a plate.
2. Mix the ingredients for the sauce in a bowl.
3. Pour over the fish and marinate for 30 minutes.
4. Meanwhile, chop the vegetables and set aside.
5. Add 1 cup water in the IP and add a steamer.
6. Remove the fish from the marinade. Reserve the marinade.
7. Place the fish in the steamer basket.
8. Cook the fish on Low for 2 minutes.
9. Do a quick release.
10. Heat a saucepan.
11. Add oil and add ginger in the hot oil.
12. Sauté for 10 seconds, then add the cilantro and scallions.
13. Stir fry for 2 minutes and add the reserved marinade.
14. Allow to boil until cooked through.
15. Pour over the fish and serve.

Nutritional Facts Per Serving
- o Calories: 171
- o Fat: 5g
- o Carb: 4g
- o Protein: 24g

This delicious Instant Pot Indian fish biryani is made with brown basmati rice.

FISH BIRYANI

| Cook time: 30 minutes | Servings: 2 |

Ingredients
- Butter – ¾ tbsp.
- Onion – ¼, chopped
- Grated ginger – ¼ tsp.
- Brown basmati rice – ¾ cup, rinsed and dried
- Water – ½ cup
- Thin coconut milk – ¼ cup
- Salt – ¼ tsp.
- Roma tomatoes – ¾, chopped

Fish and marinades
- Boneless, skinless firm white fish fillet – ½ lb. cut into large chunk
- Turmeric – a pinch
- Chili powder - 1/2 tsp.
- Salt to taste

Spices
- Bay leaves – 1
- Cinnamon stick – ¼
- Clove – 1
- Turmeric – 1 pinch
- Cardamom pod – 1
- Coriander powder – a pinch
- Garam masala – a pinch

Fresh herbs
- Mint leaves and cilantro leaves

Method
1. Marinade the fish in marinade ingredients for 20 minutes.
2. Press sauté on your Instant Pot and add butter.
3. Add onion and stir fry until soft.
4. Add ginger and all the spice ingredients and sauté until fragrant.
5. Add the fish and gently mix.
6. Cook until cooked through, 2 minutes, remove the fish and turn off the sauté mode.
7. Pour in liquid and salt. Deglaze the pot.
8. Add mint leaves, cilantro, and tomatoes.
9. Sprinkle the rice on top. Make sure the rice is covered by liquid.
10. Cover and cook on High pressure for 20 minutes.
11. Do a natural release.
12. Open the lid and gently fluff the rice.

13. Place the cooked fish pieces into the pot.
14. Garnish with cilantro leaves and serve.

Nutritional Facts Per Serving
- Calories: 477
- Fat: 15.8g
- Carb: 55.4g
- Protein: 24.5g

This Southeast Asian fish dish is spicy, coconutty and filling.

PRESSURE COOKED COCONUT FISH CURRY

| Cook time: 10 minutes | Servings: 2 |

Ingredients
- Fish fillets or steaks – ½ lb. cut into bite size pieces
- Tomato – ½, chopped
- Green chilies – 1, sliced
- Onion – ½, chopped
- Garlic – 1 clove, minced
- Grated ginger – 1 tsp.
- Curry leaves – 2
- Ground coriander – ½ tsp.
- Ground turmeric – 1 pinch
- Chili powder – a pinch
- Ground fenugreek a pinch
- Unsweetened coconut milk – ½ cup
- Salt to taste
- Lemon juice to taste

Method
1. Preheat the pressure cooker.
2. Add oil and drop the curry leaves.
3. Fry for 1 minute.
4. Add the ginger, garlic, and onion and sauté until onion is soft.
5. Add all the ground spiced and sauté for 2 minutes.
6. Deglaze the pot with coconut milk.
7. Add fish pieces, tomato, and green chili. Mix.
8. Cover and cook on 5 minutes on Low.
9. Do a natural release.
10. Add salt, and lemon juice before serving.

11. Serve.

Nutritional Facts Per Serving
- Calories: 160
- Fat: 4.1g
- Carb: 5.3g
- Protein: 23.6g

This steamed black cod only take 2 minutes and cooks perfectly in the Instant Pot.

CHINESE STEAMED BLACK COD

Cook time: 10 minutes	Servings: 2

Ingredients
- Black cod fillet – 2
- Ginger – 2 tsps. minced (divided)
- Goji berries to taste
- Water – 1 cup

Sauce

- Soy cause – 2 tbsps.
- Sugar – 1 tsp.
- Canola oil – ½ tbsp.

Method
1. Add 1 cup water to the IP.
2. In a dish, place the fish.
3. Top with goji berries, and ginger slices.
4. Place a steamer rack in the IP.
5. Place the dish with the fish on top of the steamer rack.
6. Cover and press steam.
7. Cook on Low for 2 minutes.
8. Mix in sugar and soy sauce. Taste and adjust accordingly.
9. Once cooked, do a natural release.
10. Open the lid and remove the fish.
11. Heat oil in a pan over the stove. Turn heat off.
12. Place the remaining ginger slices on the fish.
13. Pour with hot oil.
14. Add sugar and soy mixture to the hot pan on the stove.
15. Let it bubble, but don't burn.
16. Pour sizzling sugar-soy mixture over the fish.
17. Serve.

Nutritional Facts Per Serving
- Calories: 246
- Fat: 4.4g
- Carb: 15.8g
- Protein: 20.3g

CHAPTER 6 RICE RECIPES

This rice dish is made with sweet rice and features mushrooms, chicken, and sausage. For many Chinese, this dish is a favorite lunch meal.

CHINESE STICKY RICE

| Cook time: 12 minutes | Servings: 2 |

Ingredients for chicken
- Skinless, boneless chicken thighs – 3 ounces, cut into pieces
- Soy sauce – ½ tsp.
- Rice wine – ½ tsp.
- Sesame oil – ½ tsp.
- Salt and black pepper to taste

Sticky Rice
- Oil – 1 tsp.
- Chopped scallion – 1
- Ginger – 1 tsp. minced
- Short grain sweet rice – ½ cup, rinsed 4 to 5 times, drained
- Chinese sausage – 1 link, chopped
- Dried shitake mushrooms – 2, chopped (soak them in hot water for 30 minutes then, reserve the liquid)
- Dried shrimp - 1 tbsp. (soak them in hot water and reserve the liquid)
- Chicken broth – ½ cup, mixed with reserved liquids
- Soy sauce – 1 tsp.
- Rice wine – 1 tsp.
- Sesame oil – ½ tsp.
- Pepper to taste

Method
1. Mix chicken pieces with sesame oil, rice wine, soy sauce, salt, and pepper. Set aside.
2. Press sauté on your Instant Pot.
3. Add oil and add ginger and scallion in the hot Instant Pot.
4. Sauté until fragrant.
5. Add marinated chicken and sauté until lightly browned.
6. Add shrimp, mushrooms, sausage, and sweet rice.
7. Sauté a few minutes. Stir a few times.
8. Add the broth and liquid mixture, sesame oil, rice wine, soy sauce, and pepper.
9. Press Cancel and press Rice. Cook for 12 minutes.
10. Release pressure and serve.

Nutritional Facts Per Serving
- Calories: 302
- Fat: 5g
- Carb: 41g
- Protein: 17g

This is a Japanese rice dish made with azuki beans and glutinous rice. Japanese eat this dish as a part of the New Year celebration.

SEKIHAN – AZUKI BEAN RICE (JAPANESE)

| Cook time: 40 minutes | Servings: 2 |

Ingredients
- Glutinous rice - 2/3 cup
- Azuki beans – 2 tbsp.
- Water – ¾ cup
- Salt – 1/3 tsp.
- Black sesame to sprinkle

Method
1. Wash the beans and drain.
2. Add the beans and water in the Instant Pot.
3. Close the lid and cook on low pressure for 10 minutes.
4. Meanwhile, wash the rice and drain.
5. Do a quick release when cooked.
6. Open the lid and add the rice and season with salt.
7. Close the lid and cook on low for 3 minutes more.
8. When finished cooking, do a natural release.
9. Serve sprinkled with black sesame.

Nutritional Facts Per Serving
- Calories: 240
- Fat: 1g
- Carb: 52g
- Protein: 4g

This Indian rice dish is tangy, light and refreshing. You can eat it as a meal or a side dish. Add pickles or yogurt when eating.

INDIAN LEMON RICE

Cook time: 20 minutes	Servings: 2

Ingredients
- Basmati rice – ½ cup, soaked for 30 minutes and rinsed
- Olive oil – 1 ½ tbsp.
- Black mustard seeds – ½ tsp.
- Split chickpeas – ½ tbsp.
- Split and skinless black lentils – 1/2 tbsp.
- Raw peanuts – 2 tbsp.
- Curry leaves – 5
- Green chili – 1, sliced
- Minced ginger – ½ tsp.
- Salt – ½ tsp.
- Coriander powder – ½ tsp.
- Turmeric – 1 pinch
- Lemon juice – 1 tbsp.
- Lemon zest – 1 tsp.
- Water – 1 cup

Method
1. Press the sauté button on the IP and add the oil.
2. Add the black lentils, chickpeas and mustard seeds in the hot oil. Stir-fry for 2 minutes. Add the raw peanuts and stir-fry for 2 minutes.
3. Add the salt, turmeric, coriander, ginger, green chilies, and curry leaves and stir-fry for 30 seconds.
4. Add the rice, water, lemon juice, and zest. Mix well.
5. Cover with the lid and cook on high pressure for 6 minutes.
6. Do a natural release for 10 minutes.
7. Fluff the rice with a fork and serve.

Nutritional Facts Per Serving
- Calories: 332
- Fat: 8g
- Carb: 55g
- Protein: 7g

This is Indonesian fried rice, known as Nasi Goreng. Made with brown rice, this healthy and flavorful dish is made quickly using Instant Pot.

Indonesian Fried Rice (Nasi Goreng)

Cook time: 22 minutes	Servings: 2

Ingredients
- Oil – 1 ½ tbsps.
- Onion – ½, chopped
- Minced garlic – ½ tbsp.
- Fresh chilies – 1, minced
- Boneless, skinless chicken thighs – 1, cut into small pieces
- Carrots – 1, chopped
- Beet – ½, chopped
- Chopped mushrooms – 2 tbsp.
- Brown basmati rice – ½ cup
- Kecap Manis – ½ tbsp. sweet soy sauce
- Tamari or fish sauce – ½ tbsp.
- Tamarind paste – ½ tsp.
- Water – ½ cup

To garnish
- Chopped scallions
- Lime wedges
- Chopped cilantro
- 1 egg per person

Method
1. Press the sauté and add the oil. Heat it for 1 minute.
2. Add in the onions and sauté for 3 minutes.
3. Add in the chili and garlic and sauté for 1 more minute.
4. Add the vegetables and chicken and mix well.
5. Add the rice and mix well.
6. Add the tamari, tamarind, soy sauce, and ½ cup water.
7. Cancel sauté. Cook on high for 7 minutes.
8. Then do a natural release for 10 minutes.
9. Open and mix well.
10. Crack the eggs on top of the rice.
11. Cover so the eggs get cooked via steam.
12. Serve garnished with lime, cilantro, and scallions.

Nutritional Facts Per Serving
- Calories: 328

- Fat: 15.7g
- Carb: 37.7g
- Protein: 10.1g

This easy recipe is comfort food for many Singaporeans. The chicken is tender and moist, and the sauce has spicy, sweet and savory flavors.

HAINANESE CHICKEN RICE IN PRESSURE COOKER (SINGAPOREAN)

| Cook time: 40 minutes | Servings: 2 |

Ingredients

Chicken

- Whole chicken legs – 2
- Green onions – 3 stalks, cut into 2 inches long
- Shallot – 1, roughly minced
- Garlic - 6 cloves, roughly minced
- Ginger – 2 tbsps. sliced
- Unsalted chicken stock - 1 ½ cups
- Sea salt – 1 tbsp.
- Olive oil – 1 tbsp.

Rice
- Jasmine rice – 1 cup
- Chicken stock from the pot – ½ cup
- Water – ½ cup
- Olive oil – 1 tbsp.
- Garlic – 2 cloves, minced

Chicken stock soup
- Remaining chicken stock
- Water
- Lettuce or cabbage
- Chopped green onions for garnish

Sweet soy sauce
- Dark soy sauce – 1 tbsp.
- Shaoxing wine – 1 tbsp.
- Chicken stock – ½ tbsp. from the pot
- Sugar – 1 tsp.
- Sesame oil – 2 drops

Green onion ginger sauce

- Green onions – 1 stalk, finely chopped
- Ginger – 1 tbsp. grated
- Peanut oil – 1 ½ tbsps. heated
- Salt to taste

Chicken chili sauce

- Hot sauce – 2 tbsps.
- Ginger – 2 tbsps. grated
- Garlic – 3 cloves, minced
- Lime – 1 juiced
- Chicken stock – 1 tsp. from the pot

Method

1. Press Sauté and heat up the pressure cooker.
2. Add oil and sauté the garlic, ginger, shallot, and green onions for 2 minutes.
3. Add 1 ½ cups of chicken stock and deglaze the pot. Add salt and mix well.
4. Place the chicken legs into the pot.
5. Close and cook on High pressure for 8 minutes.
6. Do a natural release for 10 minutes.
7. Open the lid and remove the chicken legs from the pot.
8. Cool the chicken in cold water, then place on a cooling rack.
9. Strain the chicken stock.
10. Mix ½-cup water and ½ cup of chicken stock together. Don't make it too salty.
11. To make the rice: Clean the pressure cooker and add 1 tbsp. olive oil.
12. Sauté garlic and add 1 cup of jasmine rice, and 1-cup water-stock mixture.
13. Close lid and cook at High pressure for 3 minutes.
14. Do a natural release.
15. For the ginger sauce: place all the ingredients in a bowl and mix well.
16. To make the soy sauce: mix all the ingredients together.
17. Prepare the chicken chili sauce: mix all the ingredients.
18. Prepare the chicken soup: in a pan, heat the chicken stock and add water if it is too salty.
19. Add cabbage and cook for 1 minute
20. Garnish with chopped onions and serve on the side.

Nutritional Facts Per Serving

- Calories: 859
- Fat: 51.9g
- Carb: 35.5g
- Protein: 60.3g

This is a delicious and easy Instant Pot Chinese fried rice recipe.

FRIED RICE

Cook time: 43 minutes	Servings: 2

Ingredients
- Jasmin rice – 1 cup
- Cold water – 2 cups
- Salt to taste
- Peanut oil – 1 tbsp. plus 1 tsp.
- Eggs – 2 mixed with rice, 2 scrambled
- Frozen vegetables – ½ cup, thawed
- Green onions – 1 stalk, sliced
- A dash of white pepper

Method
1. Add 1 tbsp. peanut oil, and rice in a bowl. Mix well.
2. Add enough water in the bowl and make sure the rice is submerged.
3. Add 1 cup water in the Instant Pot and steamer rack.
4. Layer the rice bowl on the rack.
5. Cook at High for 8 minutes, then do a 10-minute natural release.
6. Meanwhile, prepare the eggs and sliced green onions.
7. Beat the eggs and separate in two bowls.
8. Mix the very hot rice with 2 beaten eggs. Mix well.
9. Discard the hot water and dry.
10. Cook the remaining two eggs in the Instant Pot on Sauté setting with oil. Scramble the eggs and set aside.
11. Add the remaining oil.
12. Add egg mixed rice in the Instant Pot.
13. Wait 1 minute and give it a quick stir.
14. Repeat step 13, for 5 times.
15. Add the vegetables and mix well.
16. Sprinkle with salt and pepper and add the scrambled eggs.
17. Mix well.
18. Add in the sliced green onions and mix well.

Nutritional Facts Per Serving
- Calories: 381
- Fat: 13g
- Carb: 53g
- Protein: 10g

Also known as forbidden rice, this black rice is a superfood. The rice is nutrient-packed and high in antioxidant.

BLACK RICE

Cook time: 34 minutes	Servings: 2

Ingredients
- Black rice – 1 cup, washed and rinsed
- Water – 1 cup

Method
1. Add the rice and water in the inner pot.
2. Cover and pressure cook at High pressure for 18 minutes, then do a natural release for 10 minutes.
3. Open the lid, fluff and serve.

Nutritional Facts Per Serving
- Calories: 397
- Fat: 3g
- Carb: 83g
- Protein: 8g

This recipe is cooked with raw white Jasmine rice. You can cook it in a pressure cooker or Instant Pot in under 15 minutes.

CHINESE FRIED RICE

Cook time: 5 minutes	Servings: 2

Ingredients
- Jasmine rice – 2/3 cup
- Peanut oil – ½ tbsp. divided
- Onion – 2 tbsps. diced
- Fresh garlic – 1/3 tbsp. minced
- Freshwater or broth – 4 oz.
- Soy sauce – ½ tbsp.
- Carrot – 1, finely chopped
- Frozen peas and or corn – ½ cup

After pressure release
- Egg – 1
- Cabbage – 1/3 cup, chopped

- o   Scallions – 1, chopped
- o   Bean sprouts – 1/3 cup
- o   Toasted sesame oil – 1/3 tsp.

Method
1. Press Sauté on your pressure cooker and heat.
2. Add oil and diced onions.
3. Stir fry for 3 minutes.
4. Add rice and toast for 2 minutes.
5. Add garlic and toast for 15 seconds more.
6. Add water and soy sauce and deglaze the cooking pot.
7. Mix in corn, peas, and carrots.
8. Cover and cook on High pressure for 1 minute.
9. Do a natural release.
10. Whisk the egg in a small bowl and set aside.
11. Remove lid and press Sauté.
12. Push rice to one side of the pot.
13. Add the rest of the peanut oil and pour in half of the whisked egg.
14. Scramble until soft and then mix into the rice.
15. Pour the rest of the whisked eggs over the rice and mix well.
16. Add bean sprouts, scallions, and cabbage.
17. Mix until cabbage has wilted.
18. Drizzle sesame oil over rice and serve.

Nutritional Facts Per Serving
- o   Calories: 361
- o   Fat: 7g
- o   Carb: 59g
- o   Protein: 12g

This rich Congee dish is simple with 6 ingredients and 6 steps.

CHINESE CHICKEN CONGEE

Cook time: 30 minutes	Servings: 2

Ingredients
- o   Jasmine rice – 1/3 cup, rinsed and drained
- o   Cold water – 2 1/3 cup
- o   Chicken drumsticks – 2
- o   Ginger – 1 tsp. sliced
- o   Green onion for garnish

- o Salt to taste

Method
1. Add water, rice, ginger, and chicken into the IP.
2. Close the lid and cook on High for 30 minutes.
3. Do a natural release.
4. Open the lid and press sauté.
5. Stir and sauté until thickens.
6. Season with salt
7. Remove the bones from the meat and remove the skin and bone.
8. Garnish and serve.

Nutritional Facts Per Serving
- o Calories: 138
- o Fat: 2.3g
- o Carb: 16g
- o Protein: 12.2g

This dish is known as Kabocha Squash. This Japanese pumpkin rice dish is easy to make and delicious.

JAPANESE PUMPKIN RICE

Cook time: 10 minutes	Servings: 2

Ingredients
- o Japanese pumpkin – 2 cups, cubed
- o Japanese short grain rice – 1 ½ cups, rinsed
- o Cold water – 1 ½ cups
- o Japanese cooking sake – 1 tbsp.
- o Sea salt – 1 tsp.
- o Sesame oil – 4 drops

Method
1. Add the sake, water, rice, sea salt, and sesame oil in the IP.
2. Mix and add squash.
3. Close the lid and cook at High for 7 minutes.
4. Do a natural release.
5. Remove the lid.
6. Mix and serve.

Nutritional Facts Per Serving
- o Calories: 341
- o Fat: 3g

- o Carb: 76g
- o Protein: 6g

Chapter 7 Side-Dishes Recipes

This recipe uses chicken, vegetables, and broth and makes a flavorful, healthy, and delicious Chinese chicken soup within only 30 minutes.

Chinese Chicken Soup

Cook time: 40 minutes	Servings: 2

Ingredients for broth
- Bone-in, skin-on chicken thighs – 2
- Chicken stock – 1 cup
- Ginger – 1 slice
- Green onions- 2, chopped

Soup
- Carrots – 2, sliced
- Zucchinis – 1, sliced
- Mushrooms – ½ pound, sliced
- Salt and black pepper to taste

Method
1. In the Instant Pot, combine green onion, ginger, water, chicken stock, and chicken.
2. Press manual and set the timer for 30 minutes.
3. When cooked, remove ginger and green onion from the soup and discard.
4. Add mushroom, zucchini, and carrot to the soup.
5. Cover and sauté until vegetables are cooked through.
6. Adjust the seasoning and serve.

Nutritional Facts Per Serving
- Calories: 192
- Fat: 3.4g
- Carb: 15.1g
- Protein: 27.1g

This Indo-Chinese soup is perfect for the winter season or during a rainy day. This soup is very similar to the restaurant style sweet corn soup.

Sweet Corn Soup

| Cook time: 20 minutes | Servings: 2 |

Ingredients
- Sweet corn – 1 1/3 cups, divided
- Water – ½ cup
- Oil – ½ tbsp.
- Ginger – 1 tsp. minced
- Garlic – 1 tsp. minced
- Carrots – ½ cup, diced
- Spring onions – 2 ½ stalks, chopped, green and white parts separated
- Vegetable broth – 1 2/3 cups
- Salt to taste
- Black pepper to taste
- Sugar – 1/3 tsp.
- Vinegar – 2/3 tsp.
- Cornstarch – 2 tsps. mixed with ¼ cup water
- Red chili paste to taste

Method
1. Blend ¾ cup sweet corn and ½ cup water in a blender to make a paste.
2. Press sauté on your Instant Pot.
3. Add oil to the hot pot and add garlic and ginger. Stir-fry for 30 seconds.
4. Add spring onion whites, carrots, sweet corn paste, and remaining corn.
5. Add the vinegar, sugar, salt, black pepper, and broth. Stir to mix well.
6. Press cancel and cover with the lid.
7. Press Manual and cook on High for 2 minutes.
8. Do a natural release for 10 minutes.
9. Add the water-cornstarch mixture and mix well.
10. Press sauté and let it come to a quick boil.
11. Use the green part of spring onions to garnish and add chili sauce to taste.
12. Serve.

Nutritional Facts Per Serving
- Calories: 181
- Fat: 6g
- Carb: 31g
- Protein: 4g

Monggo guisado or mug bean stew is a favorite dish. This dish can be cooked using shrimp or pork. If you are vegan, then omit both pork and shrimp.

FILIPINO MUNG BEAN STEW

Cook time: 15 minutes	Servings: 2

Ingredients
- Coconut oil – ½ tbsp.
- Garlic – 1 ½ cloves, minced
- Onion – 1/3, minced
- Pork – 1/3 lb. ground
- Mung beans – 2/3 cup, rinsed
- Water – 1 ½ cups
- Moringa leaves – 2/3 pack or spinach
- Sea salt to taste

Method
1. Press Sauté and melt the coconut oil in the Instant Pot.
2. Add onions and garlic and sauté until translucent.
3. Add pork and sauté until lightly browned.
4. Turn off the sauté.
5. Add the moringa leaves, water, and mung beans. If using spinach, then add at the end.
6. Cover and cook on Bean/Chili for 10 minutes.
7. Do a natural release.
8. Season with salt and serve.

Nutritional Facts Per Serving
- Calories: 375
- Fat: 9.3g
- Carb: 46.2g
- Protein: 27.9g

You can cook this tasty Filipino dish in the Instant Pot. Prepare for 5 minutes, cook for 25 minutes and your meal is ready!

FILIPINO ARROZ CALDO

Cook time: 30 minutes	Servings: 2

Ingredients
- Olive oil or butter – 1 tbsp.
- Onion – ½, chopped

- Ginger – ½ inch, sliced
- Chicken thigh – 3 pieces, cut in half
- Uncooked rice – ½ cup
- Water – 4 cups
- Lemon – ½ lemon
- Fish sauce – 1 ½ tbsps.
- Salt – 1 tsp.
- Pepper – 1 tsp.
- Chopped green onion as a topping

Method
1. Press Sauté and add oil in the Instant Pot.
2. Add ginger and onion and sauté for 2 minutes.
3. Place chicken (skin side down) and sauté for 1 minute.
4. Add fish sauce, salt, pepper, lemon juice, rice, and water. Mix.
5. Cover and press Soup. Cook for 25 minutes on normal.
6. Once cooked, do a natural release.
7. Open and skim about ½ cup of the liquid from the top.
8. Serve.

Nutritional Facts Per Serving
- Calories: 423
- Fat: 10.1g
- Carb: 44g
- Protein: 36.7g

This Sri Lankan creamy spiced Dal Curry is easy to cook and delicious to eat. It is spiced with fenugreek seeds and cinnamon.

Sri Lankan Red Lentil Curry

| Cook time: 30 minutes | Servings: 2 |

Ingredients
- Red lentils – ¾ cup
- Fenugreek seeds – ¼ tsp.
- Black peppercorns – 1/3 tsp.
- Cayenne to taste
- Turmeric – ¼ tsp.
- Oil – 1 tsp.
- Mustard seeds – ½ tsp.
- Curry leaves – 6 to 8

- Small red onion – ½ chopped
- Cinnamon stick – 2 inches
- Water – 1 ½ cups
- Salt to taste
- Coconut milk – ¼ cup
- Tomato -1, chopped
- Lemon juice – ½ tsp.
- Shredded coconut – 1 tbsp.

Method
1. Wash and soak the red lentils.
2. Grind the black pepper, fenugreek, cayenne, turmeric into a powder and set aside
3. Press sauté on your Instant Pot.
4. Heat oil over medium heat.
5. Add mustard seeds, curry leaves and mix. add the powdered fenugreek seeds and cook and stir for 10 seconds.
6. Add salt, cinnamon, and onions. Mix to coat with spices. Cook for about 3 minutes.
7. Deglaze with a bit of water.
8. Add the lemon juice, half of the tomato, salt, water, milk, and lentils.
9. Close the lid and cook on high pressure for 3 minutes, then do a quick release after 5 minutes.
10. Fold in the rest of the tomatoes and lemon.
11. Test and adjust seasoning.
12. Add some shredded coconut and serve.

Nutritional Facts Per Serving
- Calories: 316
- Fat: 9g
- Carb: 43g
- Protein: 16g

Cooked sticky rice is wrapped in a delicate wrapper to make it a delicious side meal.

SHANGHAI SIU MAI (CHINESE)

Cook time: 45 minutes	Servings: 10 dumplings

Ingredients
- Glutinous rice – 1/3 cup
- Chinese sausage – 2/3, diced
- Shitake mushrooms – 1, diced
- Liquid – ½ cup (from soaking mushrooms)
- Cooking oil – 2/3 tbsp.

- o Shu Mai wrappers – 8

Aromatics
- o Garlic – 2 cloves, chopped

Seasonings
- o Sugar – 1/3 tsp.
- o Soy sauce – ½ tsp.
- o Oyster sauce – 1/3 tbsp.
- o Dark soy sauce – 1/3 tsp.

Method
1. In a dish, add the sticky rice, aromatics, and seasonings, and the liquid + water into the sticky rice mixture. Make sure the rice is covered with water.
2. Set a trivet inside the Instant Pot.
3. Place the dish on top of the trivet and close the IP.
4. Cook on High for 30 minutes.
5. Then do a natural release.
6. Remove the bowl.
7. To wrap: place some sticky rice mixture on the middle of each wrapper and wrap nicely. Continue until you finish the filling.
8. Steam the wrapper on a high heat for 8 to 10 minutes.
9. Serve.

Nutritional Facts Per Dumpling
- o Calories: 108
- o Fat: 3.4g
- o Carb: 17.2g
- o Protein: 2.7g

Make this Chinese pork ribs bitter melon soup with Instant Pot.

PORK RIBS WITH BITTER MELON SOUP

Cook time: 30 minutes	Servings: 2

Ingredients
- o Pork ribs – ½ lb.
- o Bitter melon – ½, prepared
- o Salt – 1 tsp.
- o Carrots – 1, chopped
- o Water to cover

Seasonings
- o Ground bean paste – 1 ½ tbsps.
- o Soy sauce – 1 tbsp.
- o Sugar – ½ tsp.

Aromatics
- o Coriander – 1 bunch (stems for soup, leaves for garnish)
- o Fried shallots – 2 tbsps.

Garnish
- o Coriander leaves

Method
1. Put the carrot, bitter melon, and pork in the IP and add water to cover everything.
2. Add the seasonings and aromatics. Mix.
3. Close the lid.
4. Cook on High for 30 minutes, if the ribs are cut into bigger pieces.
5. Do a natural release.
6. Taste and adjust seasoning.
7. Garnish with chopped coriander and serve.

Nutritional Facts Per Serving
- o Calories: 336
- o Fat: 23.9g
- o Carb: 15.9g
- o Protein: 14.7g

This is an Indian healthy cauliflower and potato made in Instant Pot.

CAULIFLOWER AND POTATO STIR FRY

Cook time: 15 minutes	Servings: 2

Ingredients
- o Cauliflower – 2 cups, cut into florets
- o Cubed potato – 1 cup
- o Ghee – 1 tbsp.
- o Cumin seeds – ½ tsp.
- o Green chili pepper – 1, split into two
- o Onion – ½, chopped
- o Tomato – ½ chopped
- o Ginger – 1 tsp. minced
- o Garlic – 1 tsp. minced
- o Dry mango powder – ½ tsp. or lemon juice

- o   Cilantro for garnish

Spices
- o   Ground turmeric – ¼ tsp.
- o   Red chili powder – ¼ tsp.
- o   Coriander powder – ½ tsp.
- o   Garam masala – ¼ tsp.
- o   Salt – ½ tsp.

Method
1. Press Sauté on your IP and heat oil.
2. Add green chili and cumin seeds, sauté for 30 seconds.
3. Add garlic paste, ginger, and diced onions. Stir them.
4. Add all the spices and chopped tomatoes.
5. Add potato cubes and mix.
6. Stir fry for 2 minutes.
7. Add cauliflower florets and mix.
8. Remove any stuck bits from the bottom.
9. Add 1/8 cup water and deglaze the pot if necessary.
10. Cover and press Manual.
11. Cook on Low for 2 minutes.
12. Do a natural release.
13. Add dry mango powder and garnish with cilantro.
14. Serve.

Nutritional Facts Per Serving
- o   Calories: 153
- o   Fat: 7.83g
- o   Carb: 19.42g
- o   Protein: 4.59g

This Indian egg curry is made by adding boiled eggs to a curry sauce. Curry sauce and the coconut milk make it a flavorful protein-rich dish.

EGG CURRY

Cook time: 25 minutes	Servings: 2

Ingredients
- o   Eggs – 3
- o   Ghee – 1 tbsp.
- o   Cumin seeds – ½ tsp.
- o   Green chili – 1, sliced
- o   Onion – ¾ cup, chopped

- Ginger – 1 tsp, minced
- Garlic – 1 tsp, minced
- Tomato – ¾ cup, diced
- Water – ½ cup, divided
- Coconut milk – ¼ cup
- Lemon juice – ½ tbsp.
- Cilantro – 1 tbsp. for garnish

Spices
- Ground turmeric – ¼ tsp.
- Coriander powder – 1 tsp.
- Kashmiri red chili powder – ¼ tsp.
- Garam masala – ¼ tsp.
- Salt – ¼ tsp.

Whole spices
- Cinnamon – ½ stick
- Bay leaf – 1
- Black peppercorns – ½ tsp.
- Green cardamom – 1

Method
1. Press Sauté on your IP.
2. Add oil, cumin seeds, and whole spices.
3. Add garlic, ginger, onion, and green chili once the cumin changes color.
4. Stir fry for 3 minutes.
5. Add spices and tomato.
6. Stir fry for 2 minutes.
7. Add ¼ cup water and deglaze the pot.
8. Place the trivet, and a steel bowl with eggs in it.
9. Cover with the lid and cook on High for 6 minutes.
10. Do a quick release.
11. Gently remove the bowl with the eggs. Cool the eggs and peel them.
12. With a fork, make holes in the egg surface.
13. Add ¼-cup water and coconut milk.
14. Add back the peeled eggs in the pot.
15. Press Sauté and stir fry for 3 minutes.
16. Turn off the IP.
17. Add lemon juice and garnish with cilantro.
18. Serve.

Nutritional Facts Per Serving
- Calories: 268

- Fat: 20g
- Carb: 13g
- Protein: 10g

This is a hearty lamb curry with vegetables.

LAMB CURRY (INDIAN)

| Cook time: 20 minutes | Servings: 2 |

Ingredients
- Cubed lamb stew meat – ½ lb.
- Garlic - 2 cloves, minced
- Fresh ginger – ½ inch, grated
- Coconut milk – 2 tbsps.
- Juice of – ½ lime
- Salt to taste
- Black pepper to taste
- Ghee – ½ tbsp.
- Diced tomatoes – 5 oz.
- Garam masala – 1 ½ tsps.
- Turmeric – 1 pinch
- Onion – 1/3, chopped
- Carrot – 1, chopped
- Zucchini – ½, chopped
- Cilantro to taste, chopped

Method
1. In a bowl, meat, combine lime juice, sea salt, black pepper, milk, ginger, and garlic. Cover and marinate in the refrigerator for 30 minutes or overnight.
2. Add the meat, marinate, ghee, garam masala, tomatoes with their juice, onion, and carrots in the IP.
3. Cover and cook on High for 20 minutes.
4. Do a natural release.
5. Open and press sauté.
6. Stir in diced zucchini and simmer for 5 to 6 minutes.
7. Garnish with chopped cilantro and serve.

Nutritional Facts Per Serving
- Calories: 230
- Fat: 9g
- Carb: 11g

- Protein: 25g

CHAPTER 8 CURRIES

With an Instant Pot, making curry doesn't have to be difficult. This recipe uses simple ingredients and produces a great tasting curry for weeknight emergencies.

COCONUT CHICKEN CURRY (THAI)

Cook time: 15	Servings: 2

Ingredients
- Full-fat coconut milk – 1/3 can
- Bone broth – ¼ cup
- Red curry paste – 1 ½ tsps.
- Fish sauce – ½ tbsp.
- Cracked black pepper – 1/3 tsp.
- Onion – 1/3, chopped
- Red bell peppers – 2/3, sliced
- Carrot – 1, chopped
- Green beans – ½ cup, chopped
- Garlic – 1 clove, chopped
- Fresh ginger – 1/3 inch, minced
- Chicken thighs – ½ lb.
- Juice of ½ lime
- Chopped basil to taste

Method
1. Place fish sauce, curry paste, bone broth, milk, and black pepper in the Instant Pot and whisk to mix.
2. Add chicken, ginger, garlic, green beans, carrots, bell peppers, and onion. Stir to mix.
3. Cover and press Poultry. Cook for 10 minutes.
4. Release pressure naturally when cooked.
5. Remove the chicken and shred it.
6. Add it back in the pot and mix.
7. Top with basil and lime juice.
8. Serve with rice.

Nutritional Facts Per Serving
- Calories: 464
- Fat: 35g
- Carb: 14g
- Protein: 22g

This is a Vietnamese sweet and salty braised pork recipe. You can use pork shoulder for a leaner version and coconut water if you can't find coconut soda.

Vietnamese Caramelized Pork

Cook time: 45 to 50 minutes	Servings: 2

Ingredients
- Pork belly – 2/3 lb. cut into 2-inch pieces
- Hard-boiled eggs – 2
- Sugar – 1/8 cup
- Garlic – 1 clove, chopped
- Shallot – 1/3, chopped
- Star anise pods – 1
- Black pepper – 1/3 tsp.
- Salt – 2/3 tsp.
- Soy sauce – ¼ tbsp.
- Coconut (flavored soda) – 4 ounces
- Water – 1 cup
- Fish sauce – 1/3 tsp.

Method
1. In a bowl, combine the soy sauce, black pepper, salt, shallot, garlic, and pork. Set aside to marinate.
2. Press sauté on high.
3. Add the marinated pork and sauté for 5 to 7 minutes, or until pork gets some color.
4. Deglaze with water and turn off the pot.
5. To make the sauce: caramelize the sugar in a pan until dark brown. Add ¼ cup water and mix to make a sauce.
6. Add the star anise pod, coconut soda, hard-boiled eggs and enough water to cover the pork.
7. Cook for 30 minutes on high pressure. Then do a natural release.
8. Add the fish salt and adjust seasoning.
9. Serve over rice.

Nutritional Facts Per Serving
- Calories: 524
- Fat: 28g
- Carb: 31.4g
- Protein: 40.6g

This flavorful and delicious Vietnamese chicken curry dish is a favorite choice for most Vietnamese people. The use of coconut milk is the defining characteristic of this curry dish.

Vietnamese Chicken Curry (Ca Ri Ga)

| Cook time: 16 minutes | Servings: 2 |

Ingredients
- Chicken thighs – ¾ pound, boneless and skinless, cut into 3 to 4-inch pieces
- Lemongrass stalks – 1, cut into pieces and pounded
- Coconut milk – 7 ounces
- Carrots – 2, chopped
- Potatoes – 2, peeled and chopped
- Onion – ½ diced
- Garlic – 2 cloves, minced
- Yellow curry powder – 1 ½ tbsps.
- Fish sauce – 1 ½ tbsps.
- Freshly grated ginger – ½ tsp.
- Granulated sugar – 1 tsp.
- Salt – ½ tsp.
- Bay leaf – 1
- Coconut oil – ½ tbsp.
- All-purpose flour – 1 tbsp.
- Cilantro for garnish

Method
1. In a bowl, add the ginger, garlic, salt, ½ of the curry powder, and chicken and marinate for at least 1 hour.
2. Press sauté on the Instant Pot and add coconut oil.
3. Brown the chicken on all sides for 5 minutes.
4. Set aside the chicken to one side.
5. Add the onions and cook until soft, about 3 minutes.
6. Add the flour and coat the chicken well.
7. Add the coconut milk, remaining curry powder, fish sauce, sugar, bay leaf, and lemongrass.
8. Cover and cook on Manual for 2 minutes on High pressure.
9. Once cooked, do a natural release and open the pot.
10. Add the carrots and potatoes and mix.
11. Cover and cook on Manual for 4 minutes on High pressure.
12. Do a natural release.
13. Check the seasoning and serve over Jasmine rice or French bread.
14. Garnish with cilantro and enjoy.

Nutritional Facts Per Serving
- Calories: 608

- Fat: 31.7g
- Carb: 45.7g
- Protein: 39.2g

This butter chicken is easy to make and flavorful. The recipe tastes just like a restaurant meal and a family favorite. This dish has the perfect blend of masala, creaminess and tomato flavor.

INDIAN BUTTER CHICKEN

| Cook time: 25 minutes | Servings: 2 |

Ingredients
- Ghee – 1 tbsp.
- Onion – ½ diced
- Minced garlic – 2 tsps.
- Minced ginger – ½ tsp.
- Skinless and boneless chicken thighs – ¾ pound, cut into quarters

Spices
- Coriander powder – ½ tsp.
- Garam masala – ½ tsp.
- Paprika – ½ tsp.
- Salt – ½ tsp.
- Turmeric – ½ tsp.
- Black pepper – 1 pinch
- Cayenne – 1 pinch
- Ground cumin – 1 pinch
- Tomato sauce – 6 ounces

Add later
- Chopped green bell peppers
- Heavy cream
- Fenugreek leaves
- Cilantro

(All are to taste)

Method
1. Press the sauté and add the ghee and onion to the Instant Pot.
2. Stir-fry onions until beginning to brown, about 6 to 7 minutes.

3. Add ginger, garlic, and chicken. Stir-fry the chicken until the outside is no longer pink, about 6 to 7 minutes.
4. Add the spices and mix.
5. Stir in the tomato sauce and cover with the lid.
6. Cook on high pressure for 10 minutes.
7. Do a quick release and open the lid.
8. Press sauté and the bell peppers and cook until soft.
9. Stir in the fenugreek leaves and cream.
10. Garnish with cilantro and serve.

Nutritional Facts Per Serving
- Calories: 243
- Fat: 15.7g
- Carb: 14.4g
- Protein: 12.1g

Kari Ayam – This is an Indonesian chicken curry recipe. Usually, it takes an hour to cook on stove top, but with Instant Pot, it takes only minutes.

INDONESIAN CURRY CHICKEN (KARI AYAM)

| Cook time: 15 minutes | Servings: 2 |

Ingredients
- Bone-in, skin-on drumettes, and wings (separated) – 1 lb. discard the tip
- Cooking oil – ½ tbsp.
- Onion – 1/3, chopped
- Garlic – 1 clove, chopped
- Kaffir Lime leaves – 1, edges tore to release flavor
- Curry leaves – a few
- Turmeric powder – 1/3 tsp.
- Small star anise – 1
- All-purpose chili sauce – 1/3 tbsp.
- Water – ½ cup
- Roma tomatoes – 1 halved
- Coconut cream – 1/3 cup
- Salt to taste

Method
1. Press sauté and add oil. Add garlic and onion to the hot oil and stir-fry for 1 minute. Add turmeric, curry leaves, lime leaves, and star anise. Stir-fry for another minute. Add the chicken pieces and mix well.

2. Pour in the water and add tomatoes.
3. Close the lid and cook on High pressure for 15 minutes.
4. When cooked, do a quick release.
5. Remove the lid, stir in the coconut cream and mix well.
6. Season with salt.
7. Serve.

Nutritional Facts Per Serving
- Calories: 242
- Fat: 9.5g
- Carb: 4.7g
- Protein: 32.7g

This is a super easy classic beef curry. Cooking in IP makes a creamy hearty tender beef curry.

BEEF CURRY (HONG KONG)

| Cook time: 35 minutes | Servings: 2 |

Ingredients
- Beef finger meat – 1 pound
- Potato – ½, chopped
- Unsalted chicken stock – ½ cup
- Coconut milk – 2 tbsps.
- Chu Hou Sauce – 1 tbsp.
- Curry powder – 1 tbsp.
- Bay leaves – 1
- Garlic cloves – 2
- Shallot – ½
- Fish sauce – ½ tbsp.
- White sugar – ½ tsp.

Thickener
- Cornstarch – 1 tbsp.
- Cold water – 2 tbsp.

Method
1. Press sauté on your IP and add oil.
2. Brown the meat in the IP. About 2 minutes on each side. Set aside.
3. Add shallot, garlic, and bay leaves in the IP. Stir-fry for a few minutes.
4. Cut the beef in bit size pieces.

5. Add the chu hou sauce, fish sauce, sugar, curry powder, and meat pieces in the IP. Stir fry for 1 minute. Add a bit of chicken stock and deglaze the pot.
6. Add the potato and mix well.
7. Cover and cook on High for 25 minutes, then do a natural release for 15 minutes.
8. Remove the beef and half of the potato chunks.
9. Press sauté and add coconut milk.
10. Mix and add the cornstarch with water.
11. Mix and adjust seasoning.
12. Add back the beef and potato to the pot.
13. Mix and serve.

Nutritional Facts Per Serving
- Calories: 336
- Fat: 15g
- Carb: 18.4g
- Protein: 32.1g

This spicy, flavorful, authentic Sri Lankan curry recipe can be made with or without coconut milk.

CHICKEN CURRY

Cook time: 15 minutes	Servings: 2

Ingredients
- Coconut oil – 1 tbsp.
- Onion – 2 tbsps.
- Garlic – 1 clove, minced
- Ginger – 1/3 inch, minced
- Bay leave – 1
- Roasted Sri Lankan curry powder – ½ tbsp.
- Cinnamon – ½ stick
- Salt – a pinch
- Cayenne pepper – 1/3 tsp.
- Paprika – 1/3 tbsp.
- Chicken – 2/3 lb. thigh or leg pieces
- Serrano pepper – ½
- Roma tomatoes – 1 sliced
- Brown sugar – ½ tbsp.
- Apple cider vinegar – ½ tsp.
- Coconut milk – 2 tbsps.
- Water – 2 tbsps.

Method
1. In the Instant Pot add the coconut oil and heat.
2. Add ginger, garlic, and onion to the heated oil and cook until softened.
3. Add chili or cayenne pepper, curry powder, curry leaves, cinnamon, and paprika. Cook for a few minutes.
4. Add the sugar, tomato, salt, green chili/serrano peppers, and chicken. Mix to coat.
5. Cover and cook on High pressure for 10 minutes.
6. Do a natural release.

Nutritional Facts Per Serving
- Calories: 265
- Fat: 12.9g
- Carb: 3.3g
- Protein: 32.3g

This is a quick and easy Sri Lankan style chicken curry recipe.

CHICKEN CURRY

Cook time: 15 minutes	Servings: 2

Ingredients
- Onion – 1, chopped
- Tomato – 1 chopped
- Garlic – 1 chopped
- Ginger – ½ inch chopped
- Curry leaf – 1
- Pandan leaf – 1
- Lemongrass – 1
- Cardamom – 3
- Cinnamon – ½ piece
- Chicken – 1 lb. cut up
- Canola oil – 1 tsp.
- Curry powder – ½ tbsp.
- Red chili powder – ½ tbsp.
- Salt – 1 tsp.
- Green mango powder – ½ tbsp.

Method
1. Add the oil in the Instant Pot and rest of the ingredients. Mix and do not add water.
2. Cover and cook on High pressure for 15 minutes.
3. Do a quick pressure release.

4. Enjoy.

Nutritional Facts Per Serving
- Calories: 319
- Fat: 8.4g
- Carb: 15.8g
- Protein: 44.7g

This Instant Pot Burmese beef potato curry is simple. Using aromatic spices and herbs makes it delicious.

BEEF POTATO CURRY

| Cook time: 50 minutes | Servings: 2 |

Ingredients
- Beef stew meat – 350 grams
- Potatoes – 150 grams, chopped
- Cooking oil – 1 tbsp.
- Onion – 1/3, diced
- Grated ginger – ½ tbsp.
- Garlic – 1 clove, minced
- Large tomato – 1/3 diced
- Water – 1/3 cup

Spices
- Turmeric – ½ tbsp.
- Madras curry powder – 1/3 tbsp.
- Cumin powder – 1/3 tsp.
- Cinnamon – 1/3 stick
- Paprika – ½ tbsp.

Herbs
- Bay leaves – 1
- Fresh cilantro leaves

Seasoning
- Salt – ½ tsp.
- Sugar – 1/3 tsp.

Serve with

- o   Lemons – 1, cut into wedges

Method
1. Press sauté on the IP.
2. Add oil and garlic, ginger, and onion.
3. Stir-fry for 3 minutes.
4. Add spices and tomato pieces and stir-fry for 2 minutes more.
5. Add the bay leaf, beef, and seasoning. Mix.
6. Add ½-cup water.
7. Cover and cook on High for 30 minutes.
8. Do a quick release and open.
9. Pres sauté. Add potato pieces and mix.
10. Cook for 15 to 20 minutes or until the potatoes are soft.
11. Taste and adjust seasoning.
12. Serve.

Nutritional Facts Per Serving
- o   Calories: 263
- o   Fat: 12.6g
- o   Carb: 17g
- o   Protein: 20.2g

This Mongolian beef recipe gets better when cooked in a traditional Chinese away.

MONGOLIAN BEEF

Cook time: 20 minutes	Servings: 2

Ingredients
- o   Coconut oil – ½ tbsp.
- o   Long red chili – 2 slices
- o   Grated ginger - 1 tsp.
- o   Beef skirt steak or flank steak – 250 grams, cut into thin strips
- o   Garlic – 2 cloves, grated
- o   Tamari sauce – 2 tbspss.
- o   Coconut sugar – 2 tbsps.
- o   Honey – ½ tbsp.
- o   Sesame oil – ½ tsp.
- o   Fish sauce – ½ tsp.

To finish it off
- o   Tapioca flour – 1 tbsp.
- o   Carrot – 1, cut into matchsticks

- o   Green onions – 1, cut into long pieces (green and pale green part only)
- o   Cooked rice to serve

Method
1. Press Sauté on your IP.
2. Add oil, then add chili and ginger and stir to mix.
3. Add garlic and beef strips. Cook and stir for 1 minute.
4. Except for the green onion, carrots, and tapioca, add the rest of the ingredients.
5. Cancel Sauté.
6. Cover and cook on Manual for 12 minutes on High.
7. Do a natural pressure release and open the lid.
8. Add the carrots and press Sauté.
9. Cook for 2 minutes.
10. In the meantime, combine tapioca with ¼-cup hot water in a bowl. Mix.
11. Add 4 tbsps. of a tapioca-water mixture and green onions the IP.
12. Mix and press cancel.
13. Serve with cauliflower rice or cooked rice.

Nutritional Facts Per Serving
- o   Calories: 228
- o   Fat: 9.3g
- o   Carb: 20.9g
- o   Protein: 17.6g

Chapter 9 Salad Recipes

This delicious recipe is made unique with the use of Vietnamese coriander. This salad dish is perfect for a cold or a rainy day.

Vietnamese Chicken Porridge & Salad (Cháo & Gỏi Gà)

Cook time: 25 to 30 minutes	Servings: 2

Ingredients for chicken porridge
- Chicken leg quarters – 2 (prepared)
- Jasmine rice - ½ cup (washed well)
- Ginger – 1 inch, sliced
- Onion – ½, quartered
- Shallot – 1, quartered
- Chicken soup base – 2 tbsp.
- Boiling water – 2 to 4 cups (depends how thick you want)
- Sugar, salt, mushroom seasoning, fish sauce to taste

Chicken salad
- Onion – ½, sliced
- Cabbage – ¼, finely shredded
- Vietnamese coriander – a few, chopped
- Fried shallot

Salad dressing
- Ginger – ½ inch, sliced
- Minced garlic – ½ tbsp.
- Fish sauce – 1 tbsp.
- Sugar – 1 tbsp.
- Lime juice - 1 tbsp.

Garnishes
- Fried shallot, chili, black pepper, chopped onion, and cilantro

Method
1. Season the chicken with salt.
2. In the Instant Pot, add soup base, ginger, shallot, onion, and chicken.
3. Pour boiling water to cover the ingredients.
4. Cover and press Manual. Cook on high pressure for 8 minutes, then do a natural release for 5 minutes.

5. Meanwhile, mix lime juice, sugar, and sauce to make the salad dressing. Add garlic and ginger and mix. Adjust seasoning and set aside.
6. Remove chicken and put it in cold water to stop cooking. Drain and set aside.
7. Remove shallot and onion from the broth and add soup base and rice.
8. Mix and cover.
9. Press Porridge and cook for 18 minutes. Do a natural release when cooked.
10. Meanwhile, shred chicken and mix with coriander, sliced onion, and cabbage.
11. Drizzle with dressing and toss to combine.
12. Open the lid and stir the porridge. Adjust seasoning if necessary.
13. On serving plates, arrange the porridge, and chicken.
14. Garnish and serve.

Nutritional Facts Per Serving
- Calories: 408
- Fat: 3.2g
- Carb: 66.7g
- Protein: 28.5g

JAPANESE POTATO SALAD

Cook time: 4 minutes	Servings: 2

Ingredients
- Russet potato – 1 medium, diced
- Kewpie Mayonnaise – 2 tbsps.
- Diced onions – 1 tbsp.
- Carrot – 1 tbsp. chopped
- Japanese cucumber – 1/3 thinly sliced
- Salt – ½ tsp. Divided
- Granulated sugar – a pinch
- Rice vinegar – ½ tsp.

Method
1. Sprinkle the cucumber slices with salt. Coat well and set aside for 10 minutes. Then squeeze out as much as liquid possible with paper towels.
2. Place 1 cup water into the IP.
3. Place the steamer basket in the IP.
4. Place the diced potatoes into the steamer basket.
5. Close and cook on Manual for 4 minutes on High.
6. Do a quick release. Open the lid and remove the potatoes.

7. Cool and drain the potatoes for a few minutes.
8. In a bowl, add rice vinegar, sugar, salt, and mayonnaise. Mix well.
9. Add the cucumber, carrots, onions, and potatoes.
10. Mix with a spoon.
11. Taste and adjust seasoning.
12. Refrigerate uncovered for 2 hours before serving.

Nutritional Facts Per Serving
- Calories: 134
- Fat: 5.1g
- Carb: 21g
- Protein: 2.3g

This salad recipe is easy to make. You cook the pork loin in IP. Then toss with cooked quinoa, cashews, green onions, cilantro, and cabbage.

CHOPPED CHINESE PORK SALAD

Cook time: 50 minutes	Servings: 2

Ingredients
- Pork loin – ½ lb. quartered
- Water – ¼ cup
- Soy sauce - 1 tbsp.
- Sesame oil – 1 tsp.
- Garlic powder – ¼ tsp.
- Fresh ginger – ½ tsp. grated
- Chinese 5 spice powder - a pinch
- Brown sugar – ½ tsp.

For the salad
- Cooked quinoa – ½ cup
- Shredded or chopped cabbage – ¼ lb.
- Carrot – ½, chopped
- Green onions – ½, chopped
- Cashews – 1 tbsp.
- Tamari sunflower seeds – ½ tsp.
- Chopped cilantro – 1 tbsp.

For the dressing
- Fresh lime juice to taste

- o   Soy sauce to taste
- o   Rice vinegar to taste
- o   Sesame seeds to taste
- o   Sesame oil to taste
- o   Sugar to taste
- o   Salt – to taste
- o   Vegetable oil to taste

Method
1. Make the pork: Place the chopped pork in the IP.
2. In a bowl, combine brown sugar, water, 5 spice, ginger, garlic powder, sesame oil, and tamari. Mix to make it smooth and pour over the meat.
3. Cover and cook on High for 50 minutes.
4. Prepare salad ingredients: While the pork is cooking, chop up every salad ingredients and place in a bowl.
5. Whisk all the salad dressing ingredients in a bowl and set aside.
6. When cooking is done, do a natural release.
7. Prepare the salad and serve.

Nutritional Facts Per Serving
- o   Calories: 428
- o   Fat: 15.4g
- o   Carb: 34.2g
- o   Protein: 37.7g

This crunchy Paleo and Whole30 Chinese chicken salad is packed with vegetables and full of texture.

PALEO CHINESE CHICKEN SALAD

| Cook time: 20 minutes | Servings: 2 |

Ingredients for the chicken
- o   Chicken thighs – ½ lb.
- o   Salt and pepper to taste
- o   Bone broth – ¼ cup

For the dressing
- o   Juice of ½ orange
- o   Olive oil – ½ tbsp.
- o   Coconut aminos – ½ tbsp.
- o   Dijon mustard – ½ tbsp.
- o   Rice wine vinegar – ¼ tbsp.

- o   Sesame oil – ¼ tsp.

For the salad
- o   Cabbage – ¼ cup, chopped
- o   Kale – 1 cup
- o   Celery – ¼ cup
- o   Carrots – ½, chopped
- o   Green onions – 1 ½ tbsps. diced
- o   Slivered almonds – 1 tbsp.

Method
1. Season the chicken with salt and pepper.
2. Place the chicken in the IP.
3. Add bone broth and cook for 20 minutes on High.
4. Remove the chicken and shred with two forks.
5. Combine all the dressing ingredients in a bowl.
6. Prep the rest of the ingredients.
7. Place all of the vegetables and chicken in a large bowl.
8. Toss to mix.
9. Add the dressing, top with slivered almonds and serve.

Nutritional Facts Per Serving
- o   Calories: 315
- o   Fat: 15.4g
- o   Carb: 6.6g
- o   Protein: 36.1g

Enjoy this summer heat with this Asian noodle salad. You could make this with any type of pasta.

Asian Sesame Noodle Salad

Cook time: 10 minutes	Servings: 2

Ingredients for the noodle
- o   Linguine – 1/3 lb.
- o   Water – 1 ½ cups

Peanut dressing
- o   Smooth peanut butter – 1 tbsp.
- o   Tamari – 1 tbsp.
- o   Warm water – 2 tbsps.
- o   Peeled fresh ginger – ½ tbsp. chopped
- o   Fresh minced garlic – ½ tsp.

- Rice wine vinegar – ½ tsp.
- Sesame oil – ½ tsp.
- Honey – ½ tsp.
- Crushed chili pepper flakes - 1 pinch

Noodle salad
- Vegetable oil – ½ tbsp.
- Sliced red pepper – 1 tbsp.
- Chopped green onions – 1 tbsp.
- Sesame seeds – ½ tsp. toasted
- Toasted peanuts – 1 tbsp. chopped
- Lime for garnish

Method
1. Press Manual on your IP.
2. Add pasta and water in the IP.
3. Cover and press Manual. Cook on High for 4 minutes.
4. Do a quick release.
5. Open and transfer paste in a bowl.
6. Rinse under cold water.
7. Place in a large bowl.
8. Toss with vegetable oil, then add the green onions and red bell pepper.
9. Puree all the dressing ingredients in a blender.
10. Pour the dressing over the pasta and vegetables.
11. Top with toasted sesame seeds.
12. Top with toasted peanuts and quartered lime and serve.

Nutritional Facts Per Serving
- Calories: 422
- Fat: 21.7g
- Carb: 45.4g
- Protein: 12.8g

This Thai brown rice salad is hearty and nutritious. The vegetables and peanut butter dressing make it delicious.

Thai Brown Rice Salad

Cook time: 15 minutes	Servings: 2

Ingredients
- Uncooked brown rice – ½ cup

- Fresh ginger – 1 slice
- Garlic clove – 1 clove
- Vegetable stock – ½ cube
- Water – ¾ cup

For the salad
- Cabbage – ¼ cup, chopped
- Carrot – 1/2, chopped
- Red bell pepper – 1/2, chopped
- Red onion – ¼, chopped
- Cherry tomatoes – 2, halved
- Black or white sesame seeds – ½ tsp.
- Finish with cilantro/coriander and chopped fresh mint

For the dressing
- Crunchy peanut butter – ½ tbsp.
- Honey – ½ tbsp.
- Minced garlic – 1 clove
- Grated ginger – ½ tsp.
- Red chili – to taste
- Juice of half a lime
- Soy sauce – 1 tbsp.
- Fish sauce – ½ tbsp.
- Sesame oil – ½ tsp.
- Olive oil – ½ tbsp.
- Water – 1 tbsp.
- Lime to serve

Method
1. Add the rice ingredients in the IP and mix.
2. Cover with the lid and press Manual.
3. Cook on High for 15 minutes.
4. Do a natural release for 10 minutes.
5. Open the lid and fluff the rice.
6. Transfer the rice to a bowl and cool down.
7. To make the salad dressing, soften the peanut butter, add the remaining salad ingredients, and whisk until smooth.
8. Serve.

Nutritional Facts Per Serving
- Calories: 287
- Fat: 7.5g
- Carb: 49.7g

- Protein: 7.4g

You can make this Asian Chicken salad in the slow cooker also. This recipe is easy to make and full of flavor.

ASIAN CHICKEN SALAD

| Cook time: 5 minutes | Servings: 2 |

Ingredients
- Sliced mushrooms – ½ cup
- Chopped carrots – ½ cup
- Red bell pepper – ½, chopped
- Boneless, skinless chicken breasts – ½ pound
- Fresh ginger – ½ tbsp. chopped
- Soy sauce – 1 tbsp.
- Rice wine vinegar – 1 tbsp.
- Honey – 1 tbsp.
- Chicken broth – ¼ cup
- Garlic – 1 clove, minced

Method
1. Place chopped vegetables in the bottom of the IP.
2. Top with chicken breasts.
3. Combine remaining ingredients in a bowl and mix well.
4. Pour sauce over chicken.
5. Cover and press poultry and cook for 5 minutes.
6. Do a quick pressure release.
7. Shred chicken and serve.

Nutritional Facts Per Serving
- Calories: 201
- Fat: 1.8g
- Carb: 16.9g
- Protein: 28.4g

This is delicious Thai quinoa, mango salad. This refreshing summer salad is packed with flavor and makes a great lunch.

THAI QUINOA MANGO SALAD WITH DRESSING

Cook time: 15 minutes	Servings: 2

Ingredients
- Quinoa – ¼ cup, uncooked
- Red pepper – ¼, chopped
- Medium carrot – ½, chopped
- Green onion – ½ stalk, chopped
- Mango – ½, sliced
- Jalapeno – ¼, chopped
- Cilantro – to taste

Dressing
- Peanut butter – 1 ¼ tbsp.
- Soy sauce – 1/3 tbsp.
- Rice vinegar – ¼ tbsp.
- Lime juice from 1 lime
- Ginger – ¼ tbsp., minced
- Honey – ¾ tbsp.
- Sesame oil – ¼ tsp.
- Sriracha to taste

Method
1. Add quinoa and water in the Instant Pot.
2. Cook for 1 minute on High, then do a natural release.
3. Chop everything and arrange in a bowl.
4. In a bowl, add all the dressing ingredients and mix.
5. Whisk to mix.
6. Pour the dressing over the prepared mango, veggies, and quinoa.
7. Toss the salad with the dressing.
8. Garnish with peanuts and serve.

Nutritional Facts Per Serving
- Calories: 175
- Fat: 6g
- Carb: 23g
- Protein: 6g

This sweet and savory Asian salad recipe is easy to cook in your Instant Pot.

ASIAN SPAGHETTI SALAD WITH DRESSING

| Cook time: 1 minute | Servings: 2 |

Ingredients for the spaghetti
- Spaghetti noodles – 3 ounces, uncooked
- Water – 1 cup
- Salt to taste

Other ingredients
- Thinly sliced cabbage – 1/3 cup
- Green onion – ¾, chopped
- Avocado – ½ sliced
- Shredded carrots – 1 tbsp.
- Shredded edamame – 2 tbsps.
- Sliced almonds – ½ tbsp.
- Sesame seeds for topping
- Sesame ginger dressing
- Oil – 1 tbsp.
- Rice vinegar – 1 tbsp.
- Soy sauce – 1 tbsp.
- Brown sugar to taste
- Mince garlic – ½ tsp.
- Ground ginger to taste
- Sesame oil to taste

Method
1. To cook the pasta, put noodles, water, and salt in the IP.
1. Close and press Manual.
2. Cook 1 minute.
3. Do a natural release.
4. Open the noodles and drain if necessary. Set aside.
5. Combine almonds, edamame, carrots, avocado, onion, cabbage, and spaghetti.
6. Whisk the dressing ingredients in a bowl and drizzle over the salad.
7. Toss to coat.
8. Sprinkle with sesame seeds and serve.

Nutritional Facts Per Serving
- Calories: 178
- Fat: 12.9g
- Carb: 12.5g
- Protein: 4g

This Asian salad is made with cashews, cilantro, onion, carrots, quinoa, and cabbage and dressed in a vinaigrette dressing.

Asian Slaw Quinoa Salad

Cook time: 12 minutes	Servings: 2

Ingredients
For quinoa

- Quinoa – ½ cup, rinsed
- Water – ½ cup

Other ingredients

- Cabbage – 1 cup, shredded
- Carrots – 2 tbsps. shredded
- Fresh cilantro to taste, chopped
- Cashews – 1 tbsp. toasted and chopped
- Black sesame seeds to taste
- Green onion – ½, sliced, stalk and steam separated

For the vinaigrette

- Rice vinegar – 1 tbsp.
- Fresh ginger to taste, grated
- Garlic to taste, minced
- Maple syrup to taste
- Salt and pepper to taste
- Extra virgin olive oil – 1 tbsp.
- Sesame oil – 1 tsp.

Method
1. Combine the quinoa and water in the Instant Pot and cover.
2. Cook on High pressure for 1 minute.
3. Do a natural release.
4. Open the lid and remove the quinoa in a bowl.
5. In a bowl, combine green onions, seeds, cashews, cilantro, carrots, quinoa, and cabbage.
6. In another bowl, mix the dressing ingredients. Whisk until creamy.
7. Drizzle the salad with dressing and serve.

Nutritional Facts Per Serving
- Calories: 258
- Fat: 11.6g
- Carb: 31.4g
- Protein: 7.2g

CHAPTER 10 SAUCES

Once you taste this homemade hoisin sauce, you will never use a store-bought sauce again. Additionally, this sauce is made with commonly available ingredients.

HOMEMADE HOISIN SAUCE (CHINESE)

Total time: 5 minutes	Yield: ½ cup

Ingredients
- Light soy sauce – ¼ cup
- Natural peanut butter – 2 tbsps.
- Honey – 1 tbsp.
- Rice vinegar – 2 tsps.
- Sesame oil – 2 tsps.
- Garlic – 1 clove, grated
- Black pepper – 1/8 tsp.
- Miso paste – 1 tsp. or five spice powder – ¼ tsp. or Thai chili sauce – 1 tsp.

Method
1. Combine all ingredients in a bowl and mix well.
2. Store in an airtight bottle in the fridge.

Nutritional Facts Per Serving (1 tbsp.)
- Calories: 50
- Fat: 3.2g
- Carb: 3.8g
- Protein: 1.9g

This orange sauce is versatile. You can use it with stir fry, chicken or even roasted vegetables.

ORANGE CHICKEN SAUCE (CHINESE)

Cook time: 5 minutes	Yield: 2 ½ cup

Ingredients
- Vegetable oil – 1 tbsp.
- Garlic – 4 cloves, minced
- Minced garlic – 2 tbsps.

Sauce mix

- o   Dried tangerine peel or grated orange zest – ½ cup (soaked in hot water for 20 minutes, then drained and sliced)
- o   Orange juice – 1 cup
- o   Rice vinegar or distilled white vinegar– ¾ cup
- o   Light soy sauce – ¼ cup
- o   Shaoxing wine – ¼ cup
- o   Sugar – ½ cup
- o   Cornstarch – 2 tbsps. and ½ tbsp.
- o   Fine sea salt – 1 tsp.

Method
1. In a bowl, add ¼ cup sliced tangerine skin.
2. Add the soaked tangerine skin and the rest of the sauce ingredients to a bowl. Add cornstarch and mix well.
3. Heat oil in a saucepan and add ginger and garlic. Cook until you get a strong fragrance.
4. Stir the sauce again and pour into the pan.
5. Cook and stir until thick.
6. Transfer the sauce into a bowl.
7. Store in an airtight jar when cooled.

Nutritional Facts Per Serving (2 tbsp.)
- o   Calories: 83
- o   Fat: 1.1g
- o   Carb: 17.6g
- o   Protein: 0.8g

This homemade black bean sauce is extremely popular because it is versatile. You can use it for steaming, grilling, baking, and frying.

BLACK BEAN SAUCE (CHINESE)

Cook time: 15 minutes	Yields: 2 servings

Ingredients
- o   Fermented black beans – 1 cup (rinsed, drained, and chopped)
- o   Vegetable oil – 1/3 cup
- o   White onion – ¼ cup, minced
- o   Shaoxing wine – ¼ cup
- o   Light soy sauce – ¼ cup
- o   Sugar – ¼ cup
- o   Garlic – 1 head, minced
- o   Ginger – 1 thumb, minced

Method
1. In a saucepan, heat oil and dried chili peppers over medium heat until warm.
2. Lower heat and cook and stir until chili peppers are dark, but not black.
3. Discard the chili peppers.
4. Add the onion and black beans.
5. Cook and stir until the sauce appears dry.
6. Add sugar, soy sauce, and wine. Simmer and stir for about 10 minutes or until onion is tender. Careful not to burn the sauce.
7. Add ginger and garlic, cook and stir until the onion is very tender.
8. Transfer the sauce to a bowl and cool completely.
9. Store the sauce in an airtight jar in the fridge.

Nutritional Facts for Entire Recipe
- Calories: 1612
- Fat: 75.8g
- Carb: 185.5g
- Protein: 47.1g

This is a traditional white sauce and popular in the Philippines.

FILIPINO WHITE SAUCE RECIPE

Cook time: 10 minutes	Yields: 2 cups

Ingredients
- Flour – ¼ cup
- Butter – ¼ cup
- Milk – 2 cups
- Salt – ½ tsp.

Method
1. Add the butter in a saucepan and melt over low heat.
2. Add flour and mix.
3. Slowly add milk and stir.
4. Add salt and cook until thickens.

Nutritional Facts for The Entire Recipe
- Calories: 765
- Fat: 56.3g
- Carb: 47.9g
- Protein: 19.7g

This great tasting Japanese sweet and sour stir-fry sauce will be your go-to stir-fry sauce.

JAPANESE SWEET AND SOUR SAUCE

Ready in: 11 minutes	Yield: 1 cup

Ingredients
- Vinegar – 4 tbsps.
- Soy sauce – 4 tbsps.
- Brown sugar – 6 tbsps.
- Salt – 2 tsp.
- Water – 2/3 cup
- Garlic powder – 1 dash
- Ginger - dash
- Cornstarch to thicken

Method
1. In a saucepan, mix ginger, garlic, water, salt, sugar, soy sauce, and vinegar.
2. Heat on the stove.
3. Add cornstarch to thicken and use as a dipping sauce.
4. Or you can avoid including cornstarch and use it as a stir-fry sauce.

Nutritional Facts Per Serving (387 gram)
- Calories: 371.4
- Fat: 0.1g
- Carb: 85.9g
- Protein: 7.8g

This gochujang sauce is a popular sauce in Korea. It is used in Korean bulgogi, sandwiches, tacos, rice bowls and more.

SPICY KOREAN BIBIMBAP SAUCE

Cook time: 0 minutes	Yield: ¾ cup

Ingredients
- Korean red-hot pepper paste – 4 tbsps.
- Sesame oil – 2 tbsps.
- Brown sugar – 2 tbsps.
- Soy sauce – 1 tbsp.
- Water – 1 tbsp.
- Rice vinegar – 2 tsps.
- Minced garlic – 2 tsps.

- o Toasted sesame seeds – 1 tbsp.

Method
1. In a bowl, add the ingredients and whisk to combine.
2. Cover and keep in the refrigerator.

Nutritional Facts for the Entire Recipe
- o Calories: 536
- o Fat: 32.9g
- o Carb: 58.8g
- o Protein: 7.8g

Cincalok is a Malaysian dipping sauce. The sauce is made using fermented tiny shrimp. Beginners may not like the odor of the sauce, but once mixed it is actually great when added to lime juice and other ingredients.

CINCALOK DIPPING SAUCE

Total time: 5 minutes	Servings: ½ cup

Ingredients
- o Malaysian fermented tiny shrimp - 1/8 cup
- o Fresh lime juice – ½ of a lime
- o Fresh small red chilies – 1 or 2, prepared
- o Garlic – 1 clove, minced
- o Shallot – 1 small, finely sliced

Method
1. In a bowl, add the ingredients and mix well.
2. Use with your dishes.

Nutritional Facts for the Entire Recipe
- o Calories: 119
- o Fat: 1.8g
- o Carb: 7.8g
- o Protein: 19.9g

There are several versions of chili sauces in Thailand. They are also known as Nam prik pao chili sauce. This sauce is best with noodle dishes, soups and anything you want to spice up.

THAI CHILI SAUCE (NAM PRIK PAO)

| Cook time: 8 minutes | Yield: 1 small jar (6 portions) |

Ingredients
- Coconut or canola oil – ¼ cup, plus a little more
- Garlic – 4 cloves, chopped
- Shallots -2, chopped
- Dried whole or crushed red chilies – 3 tbsps. powdered
- Shrimp paste – 1 tsp.
- Fish sauce – 2 tbsps.
- Palm or brown sugar – 2 to 3 tbsps.
- Tamarind paste – 1 tsp.
- Lime juice 1 ½ tbsps.

Method
1. In a pan, heat oil over a medium heat.
2. Add the garlic and shallots. Fry for 2 to 3 minutes.
3. Remove shallots and garlic and place in a bowl (Keep the oil in the pan).
4. In a food processor, combine prepared chili with the water, lime, tamarind, sugar, fish sauce, and shrimp paste. Add the fried shallots and garlic.
5. Pulse to make a thick paste.
6. Return the paste to the frying pan and mix with the oil over low heat.
7. Gently simmer until you get an even consistency.
8. Add a little water or oil to adjust the consistency.
9. Taste and adjust the sauce.

Nutritional Facts for the Entire Recipe
- Calories: 700
- Fat:55.4g
- Carb: 47.4g
- Protein: 9.2g

This sweet chili sauce is available in Asian food markets. However, instead of buying store brands; make this easy recipe on your own. This sweet Thai chili sauce goes well with many Thai dishes and excellent with fish, seafood, and chicken.

THAI SWEET CHILI SAUCE (NAM HIM KAI)

Cook time: 15 minutes	Yield: ½ cup

Ingredients
- White or rice vinegar – ½ cup
- White sugar – ½ cup plus 2 tbsps.
- Water – ¼ cup
- Fish sauce – 3 tbsps.
- Sherry – 2 tbsps.
- Garlic – 3 cloves, minced
- Dried crushed chili – ½ to 1 tbsp.
- Cornstarch – 1 ½ tbsps. dissolved in 3 to 4 tbsps. cool water

Method
1. Except for the cornstarch-water mixture, place all ingredients in a saucepan.
2. Bring to a rolling boil.
3. Lower heat to medium and boil until reduced by half, about 10 minutes.
4. Lower heat to low and add the water-cornstarch mixture.
5. Cook and stir for 2 minutes.
6. Remove from heat and taste.
7. Cool and store in a jar.

Nutritional Facts for the Entire Recipe
- Calories: 566
- Fat: 1g
- Carb: 135g
- Protein: 3g

Most Western peanut sauces are made from peanut butter. But this Thai peanut sauce is made with real peanuts. You can use this with beef, chicken or as a dip for vegetables.

SALTY THAI PEANUT SAUCE

Cook time: 0 minute	Servings: 4 to 6 as a dip

Ingredients
- Dry roasted peanuts – 1 cup (unsalted)
- Water – 1/3 cup

- Garlic – 2 cloves, minced
- Dark soy sauce – ½ tsp.
- Sesame oil – 2 tsp.
- Brown sugar – 1 to 2 tbsp.
- Fish sauce – 2 to 12 ½ tbsp.
- Tamarind paste – ½ tsp.
- Cayenne pepper – ½ tsp.
- Coconut milk – 1/3 cup

Method

1. Place all the ingredients in a food processor.
2. Process until smooth.
3. Taste and adjust salt, lime juice, sugar or fish sauce.
4. Serve.

Nutritional Facts Per Serving

- Calories: 237
- Fat: 17g
- Carb: 17g
- Protein: 9g

CHAPTER 11 SOUPS AND STEWS

This is a warming and hearty Korean short rib soup. Traditionally it is slow cooked for hours, but you can also cook it in an Instant Pot.

SHORT RIB SOUP (GALBITANG IN KOREAN)

Cook time: 30 minutes	Servings: 2

Ingredients
- Beef short ribs – 0.6 lb. excess fat trimmed
- Water – 3.2 cups
- Yellow onion – 0.4, with skin
- Green onion – 0.8, for cooking broth
- Green onion – 0.8, for garnish, chopped
- Ginger – 0.8 inch, sliced
- Korean radish – 0.2, cut into chunks
- Garlic – 0.8 tbsp. chopped
- Guk ganjang – 0.8 tsp. (Korean soy sauce)
- Korean sea salt – 0.4 tsp.

Method
1. Soak ribs in cold water for an hour to remove excess blood.
2. Meanwhile prep the onions, ginger, and radish.
3. In the Instant Pot, add the yellow onion, ribs, ginger, green onion, radish, and water.
4. Close and press Soup. It will cook for 30 minutes.
5. Once done, release the pressure and open.
6. Skim off fat from soup.
7. Season with salt, garlic, and guk.
8. Serve.

Nutritional Facts Per Serving
- Calories: 990
- Fat: 51g
- Carb: 30g
- Protein: 99g

This is an Indonesian noodle soup recipe, cooked with chicken and vegetables.

INDONESIAN CHICKEN NOODLE SOUP (MIE SOP AYAM MEDAN)

| Cook time: 30 minutes | Servings: 2 |

Ingredients
- Egg noodles – ½ lb. cooked according to package directions
- Rice noodle stick – ½ lb.
- Cooking oil – ½ tbsp.
- Bone-in, skin-on chicken – 1 ½ lbs. thighs, leg or drumsticks
- Cinnamon – ½ stick
- Lemongrass – 1 stalk, prepared
- Chinese or regular celery – 1 ½ stalks
- Water – 4 cups
- Better than bouillon – ½ tbsp.
- Salt to taste
- Cooking oil for frying

To be ground in a food processor
- Shallots – 5, peeled
- Garlic – ½ blub

Spices and herbs
- Cardamoms – 1 ½
- Bay leaves – 3
- Cloves – 5
- Star anise – ½
- Whole white peppercorns – ½ tsp.

Garnishes
- Chinese celery – 1 bunch, chopped
- Fried shallots crisp
- Indonesian sweet soy sauce to drizzle

Green Chili
- Green chili – 25 grams
- Salt – 1/8 tsp.

Method
1. Destem the green chili and boil in water for 5 minutes or until soft. Add to a blender with salt and blend until a paste.

2. Press sauté on the Instant Pot.
3. Heat 1 tbsp. oil in a skillet and sauté ground spices for 1 minute or until fragrant.
4. Add the chicken, lemongrass, cinnamon, and water to the pot. Add all the herbs and spices.
5. Close and cook on high pressure for 20 minutes.
6. Release pressure naturally when cooked.
7. Remove the chicken and set aside before frying. Strain the soup and discard the solids.
8. Deep-fry the chicken until golden brown. You already cooked the chicken so deep-fry to get the color.
9. Arrange chicken with noodles. Garnish with chopped celery leaves, sweet soy sauce and fried shallot crisps.
10. Serve with chili on the side.

Nutritional Facts Per Serving
- Calories: 741
- Fat: 10.9g
- Carb: 128.5g
- Protein: 49.7g

This is a traditional Korean spicy beef soup. Usually difficult, Instant Pot makes it hassle-free. Made with beef, vegetables, and mild spices, this is a household favorite.

Korean Beef Cabbage Radish Soup (Yukgaejang)

Cook time: 10 minutes	Servings: 2

Ingredients
- Beef stew meat – 2 oz. cut thin
- Radish – ¾ cup, cut into squares
- Small green cabbage – ¼ lb. chopped
- Soybean sprouts (kongnamul) – 1 oz. rinsed and drain
- Green onions – ¼, chopped
- Water – ¾ cup

Seasoning
- Garlic – 2 tsps. Chopped
- Korean soy sauce – ½ tbsp.
- Sea salt – 1/3 tsp.
- Korean red chili pepper – ½ tsp.
- Sesame oil – ½ tsp.
- Garlic powder – ¼ tsp.

Method
1. Press sauté on the Instant Pot and add the sesame oil.
2. Sauté radish for 1 to 2 minutes.
3. Add beef to the IP and also add soy sauce and red chili pepper.
4. Sauté radish and beef until the beef pieces are cooked.
5. Add water, garlic, sprouts, green onions, and cabbage.
6. Add garlic powder, salt and close the lid.
7. Select Soup and cook for the reduced time of 10 minutes.
8. Release pressure naturally.
9. Mix with a ladle and serve with rice.

Nutritional Facts Per Serving
- Calories: 103
- Fat: 5g
- Carb: 7g
- Protein: 7g

Nihari is a one-pot meat stew cooked with a variety of spices. The dish is flavorful, delicious and rich with vitamins and minerals.

PAKISTANI BEEF OR MUTTON STEW (NIHARI)

| Cook time: 1 hour 20 minutes | Servings: 2 |

Ingredients
- Beef or mutton pieces with bone – 200 grams
- Oil – 1 tbsp.
- Garlic paste – ¼ tbsp.
- Ginger paste – ¼ tbsp.
- Salt – ¼ tsp.
- Cumin powder – ¼ tsp.
- Coriander powder – 1 pinch
- Red chili powder – 1 pinch
- Kashmiri chili powder – ¼ tsp.
- Turmeric powder – 1 pinch
- Nihari masala – ½ tbsp.
- Bay leaf – 1
- Grated nutmeg – 1 pinch
- Water – 1 ½ cups
- Black cardamom to taste
- Chilies – ½

- Fried onions – 1 tsp.
- Lemon juice – 1 tsp.
- Flour – 1 tsp. dissolved in 2 tbsps. water

Nihari Masala
- Whole star anise – 1
- Whole long peppers – 1
- Coriander seeds - a few
- Cumin seeds a few
- Fennel seeds a few
- Whole black peppers – 1
- Whole cloves - 1
- Cardamom seeds a few
- Nigella seeds a few
- Cinnamon stick – ½ inch
- Strands mace - ½
- Coriander for garnish
- Ginger slices for garnish

To make the Nihari masala
- Blend all the spices.

Method
1. Heat a pressure cooker and add meat.
2. Add salt, garlic, ginger, and oil.
3. Add the Nihari masala and ground spices.
4. Coat the meat and bones with the spices.
5. Add black cardamom, nutmeg and bay leaf. Mix.
6. Add water.
7. Cover and cook 1 hour on medium heat.
8. Carefully let out air and remove the lid.
9. Add flour-water mixture, lemon juice, fried onions, and chilies.
10. Cook uncovered for 15 minutes.
11. Serve garnish with ginger slices and coriander.

Nutritional Facts Per Serving
- Calories: 206
- Fat: 14g
- Carb: 4g
- Protein: 13g

This is deeply flavorful Chicken Rendang. This Indonesian-Malaysian chicken stew dish is cooked using coconut milk and spices.

CHICKEN RENDANG

| Cook time: 45 minutes | Servings: 2 |

Ingredients
- Boneless, skinless chicken thighs or breasts – 0.75 lbs. cut into cubes
- Cooking oil – 2 tbsp.
- Cinnamon stick – ½
- Cloves – 1 ½, chopped
- Star anise – 1 ½
- Cardamom pods – 1 ½
- Lemongrass – ½, white parts only, pounded and cut into strips
- Coconut milk – ½ cup
- Water – ½ cup
- Kaffir lime leaves – 2 ½ bruised
- Toasted grated coconut kerisik – 2 ½ tbsp.
- Sugar – ½ tbsp.
- Salt to taste

Spice Paste
- Shallots – 3
- Galangal – ½ inch
- Lemongrass – 1 ½ white parts only
- Garlic – 2 cloves
- Ginger – ½ inch
- Dried chilies – 5, seeded

Method
1. Add all the spice paste ingredients in a food processor and blend well.
2. Press sauté and add the oil.
3. Add blended paste to the hot oil and stir-fry for 2 to 3 minutes.
4. Stir in lemongrass, cinnamon, cloves, star anise, cardamom, water, and coconut milk.
5. Add the chicken and mix.
6. Cover and cook on high for 15 minutes.
7. When cooked, do a quick release.
8. Stir in salt, sugar, toasted coconut, and lime leaves.
9. Press sauté and reduce the sauce for 5 minutes. Stirring often.
10. Enjoy.

Nutritional Facts Per Serving
- Calories: 598

- Fat: 38.1g
- Carb: 8.2g
- Protein: 55.5g

This chicken soup is delicious and even better the next day. You can use more spinach with the recipe if you want.

CHICKEN GNOCCHI SOUP

| Cook time: 20 minutes | Servings: 2 |

Ingredients
- Chicken breasts – 1
- Chicken stock – 1 cup
- Chopped celery – 1/3 cup
- Chopped onion – ½ cup
- Butter – 1 ½ tbsps.
- Salt and pepper to taste
- Thyme – 1 tsp.
- Half and half – 1 ½ cups
- Shredded carrots – ½ cup
- Gnocchi – ½ package
- Spinach – 1 cup, chopped

Method
1. Press Sauté on your pressure cooker.
2. Sauté the onions and celery in the butter.
3. Add the chicken breasts when the vegetables are ¾ cooked.
4. Then add the thyme and stock.
5. Cover and cook on Manual for 15 minutes on low.
6. Do a quick release and shred the chicken.
7. Press sauté mode and add the carrots and half-and-half.
8. Mix and add the gnocchi.
9. Boil for about 5 minutes or until the gnocchi is cooked through.
10. Add spinach and stir.
11. Serve.

Nutritional Facts Per Serving
- Calories: 461
- Fat: 32.4g
- Carb: 15g
- Protein: 28.2g

This is a simple, but healthy instant pot soup. This beef soup offers a great balance with savory, sour and sweet flavors.

Borscht Soup (Hong Kong)

| Cook time: 20 minutes | Servings: 2 |

Ingredients
- Beef shank – ½ pound
- Cabbage – 200g, cut into pieces
- Onion – ¼, chopped
- Russet potato – ½, chopped
- Tomato – 1, quartered
- Carrot – 1, chopped
- Celery – 1, sliced
- Garlic – 2 cloves
- Bay leaves – 1
- Unsalted chicken stock – 2 cups
- Tomato paste – 1 tbsp.
- Olive oil – ½ tbsp.
- Paprika – 1 tsp.
- Salt and black pepper to taste

Method
1. Press Sauté on your Instant Pot and add oil.
2. Season the beef with salt and pepper and add to the hot oil.
3. Brown the meat on all sides.
4. Remove the meat and add onions to the IP.
5. Sauté for 3 minutes.
6. Then add carrot, garlic, celery, bay leaf, paprika, and tomato sauce.
7. Sauté for 2 minutes then add tomato.
8. Cut the beef into bite size pieces.
9. Add a bit of chicken stock to deglaze the pot.
10. Add back the beef pieces and add the stock.
11. Place potato chunks and cabbage pieces on top.
12. Pressure cook at High for 12 minutes then do a natural release.
13. Open the lid and press sauté.
14. Bring the soup to a boil and gently mix. Boil for 5 minutes more.
15. Taste and adjust seasoning.

Nutritional Facts Per Serving
- Calories: 237
- Fat: 5g
- Carb: 30g

- Protein: 19g

This is very easy delicious Instant Pot red bean soup from Hong Kong. This soup is comforting and satisfying.

RED BEAN SOUP (HONG KONG)

Cook time: 50 minutes	Servings: 2

Ingredients
- Adzuki beans – ¼ cup, soaked and drained
- Dried mandarin peel - ½ piece (rehydrated in cold water for 20 minutes) then scrub off the bitter white part
- Cold water – 2 cups
- Brown sugar – 40 grams
- Kosher salt to taste

Method
1. Add the brown sugar, salt, peel, and beans in the pot.
2. Add the water and cook on High pressure for 30 minutes.
3. Do a natural release for 20 minutes.
4. Press sauté and bring the mixture to a boil.
5. Boil until thickens, about 20 minutes. Stir a few times.
6. Taste and adjust seasoning.
7. Serve.

Nutritional Facts Per Serving
- Calories: 142
- Fat: 4g
- Carb: 31g
- Protein: 20g

This classic Korean stew is so flavorful and rich. Known as Kimchi Jjigae, it takes only a fraction of time when cooked in Instant Pot.

KIMCHI JJIGAE

Cook time: 20 minutes	Servings: 2

Ingredients
- Kimchi – 1 ½ cups, cut up

- Fatty pork or beef – 4 ounces, cut up
- Sesame oil – ½ tbsp.
- Korean red chili pepper flakes – 1 tsp. or to taste
- Juice from kimchi – 2 tbsp.
- Water – 1 cup
- Soy sauce – ½ tbsp.
- Minced garlic – ½ tbsp.
- Tofu- 4 ounces, sliced
- Scallions – 1, chopped
- Black pepper to taste
- Sugar – 1 tsp.

Method
1. Press the sauté on the Instant Pot.
2. Add the kimchi and pork along with the red pepper flakes and sesame oil and cook for 5 minutes.
3. Add the garlic, soy sauce, water, and kimchi juice.
4. Cover and press Soup.
5. Cook for 10 minutes.
6. Open the lid and add scallions and tofu.
7. Cover and cook 5 minutes more.

Nutritional Facts Per Serving
- Calories: 176
- Fat: 7.8g
- Carb: 19.8g
- Protein: 9g

This Indonesian vegetable tamarind soup is called Sayur Asem.

INDONESIAN VEGETABLE TAMARIND SOUP

| Cook time: 5 minutes | Servings: 2 |

Ingredients
- Cooking oil – 1 tsp.
- Raw peanuts – 1 ½ oz.
- Long beans – 1 ½ oz. cut into 2-inch pieces
- Sweet corn – 1, cut into 1-inch pieces
- Large chayotes – 1, cubed
- Cabbage leaves – 3, cut into pieces
- Tomato – 1, quartered

- Bay leaves – 1 or 2
- Water – 4 cups
- Seedless tamarind paste – 1 tbsp. plus 1 ½ tbsp. warm water
- Brown sugar – 1 tbsp.
- Salt to taste

Ground spices
- Galangal – ½ thumb size (mashed and removed after cooking)
- Shallot – 1
- Bird's eye chili – ½
- Red chilies – 2
- Garlic – 1 clove
- Kemiri/candlenuts – 2
- Shrimp paste – ½ tsp.

Method
1. Process all the ground spices in a food processor to make a fine paste. Add a bit of water if needed.
2. Mix warm water and tamarind paste. Get the tamarind juice and discard the solid.
3. Press sauté on your IP. Add oil.
4. Add the paste and stir fry for 1 minute.
5. Add the beef broth and bay leaves.
6. Bring to a boil then add in the rest of the vegetables and other ingredients.
7. Cover and cook on High for 5 minutes.
8. Taste and adjust seasoning.
9. Serve with rice.

Nutritional Facts Per Serving
- Calories: 337
- Fat: 18.8g
- Carb: 37g
- Protein: 10.9g

CHAPTER 12 NOODLES RECIPES

This is a traditional Vietnamese spicy beef noodle soup. The recipe uses a lot of spices, it is comforting and heartwarming.

SPICY BEEF NOODLE SOUP/BUN BO HUE (VIETNAMESE)

Cook time: 40 minutes	Servings: 2

Ingredients
Broth ingredients

- Beef shank – 1 lb.
- Oxtail – 2/3 lb.
- Daikon radish – 7 oz.
- Lemongrass – 1 ½ stalk, cut into pieces
- Beef broth powder – 1 tbsp.
- Salt – 1 ½ tsp.
- Fish sauce - 1 ½ tbsps.
- Rock sugar – 2 small

For the spicy soup pasta
- Minced lemongrass – 1 ½ tbsp.
- Vegetable oil – 3 tbsps.
- Minced shallot – ½ tbsp.
- Minced garlic – ½ tbsp.
- Annatto oil – ½ tbsp.
- Hue seasoning powder - ½ tbsp.
- Chili flakes – ¼ tsp.

Noodles and toppings
- Rice noodles – ½ package
- Vietnamese ham – ½ small roll

Method for parboiling
1. Add the oxtail in a pot and fill with water.
2. Bring to a boil. Discard the water and rinse under cold water.

Method
1. In an Instant Pot, place all broth ingredients. Fill the pot with water (up to maximum).
2. Cover and press Stew. Cook for 25 minutes and do a natural release for 15 minutes. Then do a quick release.
3. Remove the beef shank. Place in a bowl with cold water and slice thinly.

To make the spicy soup paste
1. Heat oil in a pan over medium heat.
2. Add lemongrass, shallot, and garlic. Sauté until golden brown.
3. Lower heat and add chili flakes and seasoning. Remove from the heat.
4. Add this paste to the broth.
5. Taste and adjust seasoning.
6. Prepare noodles according to package directions.
7. Arrange and serve

Nutritional Facts Per Serving
- Calories: 386
- Fat: 12.3g
- Carb: 49.5g
- Protein: 20.8g

INDONESIAN NOODLES (MIE GORENG)

Cook time: 15 minutes	Servings: 2

Ingredients
Sauce mixture

- Soy sauce – 1 tbsp.
- Oyster sauce – 1 tbsp.
- Sweet soy sauce – ½ tbsp.
- Sesame oil – ½ tsp.
- Sriracha chili sauce – ½ tsp.
- Low sodium chicken broth – ¼ cup

Mix the above ingredients and set aside

Ingredients
- Egg noodles – 6 oz. prepared according to package instructions. Set aside
- Vegetable oil – 1 tbsp.
- Sesame oil – ½ tsp.
- Shrimps – 6 pieces
- Medium chicken breasts – 1, boneless and skinless, cut into pieces
- Small onion – ½, chopped
- Garlic – 1 clove, chopped

- Grated carrots – ½ cup
- Sliced cabbage or bok choy – 1 cup
- Bean sprouts – ½ cup
- Scallions – 1 stalk, separated green and white parts, sliced
- Salt and pepper to taste

Method
1. Season the shrimp with salt and pepper.
2. Press sauté on the Instant Pot.
3. Add sesame oil and vegetables.
4. Add shrimp and cook 1 minute on each side. Remove the shrimp and set aside.
5. Add the garlic, white parts of scallions, onion, and sliced chicken. Sauté until the chicken is almost cooked. Scrape the bottom of the pot to remove any stuck bits.
6. Add bean sprouts, cabbage, and carrots. Stir –fry for 5 minutes.
7. Add noodles and pour sauce mixture on top.
8. Mix all the ingredients.
9. Cover and cook on High pressure for 5 minutes.
10. Add the shrimps.
11. Serve hot.

Nutritional Facts Per Serving
- Calories: 437
- Fat: 10.6g
- Carb: 54.7g
- Protein: 29.7g

This is Burmese chicken curry soup noodle dish also known as Ono Kyauk-Swé. This is a popular traditional Burmese soup.

CHICKEN CURRY SOUP NOODLES

Cook time: 20 minutes	Servings: 2

Ingredients
- Corn oil – 1 tbsp.
- Yellow onion – ½, diced
- Garlic – 2 cloves, minced
- Turmeric – 1 tsp.
- Paprika - ½ tsp.
- Chili powder – 1 tsp.
- Chicken stock – 2 cups
- Water – ½ cup

- Fish sauce – 2 tbsps.
- Salt to taste
- Coconut milk – ½ cup
- Egg – 1, beaten
- Hard-boiled egg – 1
- Chickpea flour – 2 tbsps.
- Chicken breast – ½ lb. chopped

Noodles
- Egg noodles for 2, cooked

Garnishes
- Cilantro leaves, hard boiled eggs, red onions, limes, toasted chili flakes, crunchy noodles

Method
1. Press Sauté and add oil.
2. Sauté onions for 4 minutes, then add then the garlic.
3. Stir-fry for 2 minutes, then add the chili flakes, paprika, and turmeric. Stir to combine and make a thick paste.
4. Add the fish sauce and chicken stock and mix.
5. Allow to come up to a slow boil on the Instant Pot.
6. In another bowl, mix water and chickpea flour. Whisk to mix.
7. Mix the beaten egg and coconut milk into this bowl and whisk until creamy.
8. Mix the egg mixture, coconut milk, and the flour mixture into the pot. Add salt.
9. Add the diced chicken meat to the pot and cover.
10. Cook on High pressure for 15 minutes.
11. Do natural release when done and mix in the sliced hard-boiled egg.
12. Cook the egg noodles in another pot according to package instructions.
13. Serve in bowls, garnish with garnish items.

Nutritional Facts Per Serving (without the noodles)
- Calories: 496
- Fat: 35.1g
- Carb: 8g
- Protein: 38.3g

This delicious Chinese garlic Instant Pot noodles recipe is easy to make. This is a quick weeknight meal for you to enjoy.

GARLIC NOODLES

Cook time: 6 minutes	Servings: 2

Ingredients
- Water – ½ cup
- Chicken broth – ½ cup
- Garlic – 3 cloves, minced
- Soy sauce – 1 tbsp.
- Brown sugar – 1 tbsp.
- Oyster sauce – 1 tbsp.
- Sesame oil – ½ tsp.
- Chili paste – ½ tsp.
- Thin spaghetti noodles – 4 oz. broken in half
- Sesame seeds and green onion for topping

Method
1. In the Instant Pot, combine chili paste, sesame oil, oyster sauce, sugar, soy sauce, garlic, broth, and water. Whisk to mix.
2. Place broken spaghetti noodles on top.
3. Make sure they are covered by the liquid.
4. Cover and cook on High for 6 minutes.
5. Do a quick release.
6. Open the pot and stir noodles.
7. Serve top with green onions and sesame seeds.

Nutritional Facts Per Serving
- Calories: 251
- Fat: 3.1g
- Carb: 49.4g
- Protein: 9.3g

These Instant Pot noodles are sticky and have an umami flavor. You can use a variety of items as toppings.

CHILI GARLIC NOODLES (CHINESE)

Cook time: 3 minutes	Servings: 2

Ingredients
- Soy sauce – ¼ cup
- Brown sugar – 1 tbsp.
- White vinegar – 1 tbsp.
- Chili garlic paste – ½ tbsp.
- Olive oil – ½ tbsp.
- Water – 1 cup
- Uncooked brown rice noodles – 4 oz.
- Raw chicken breasts – ½ lb. cut into small pieces
- Red bell peppers – 1, sliced thinly
- Sesame seeds, green onions, and peanuts for garnish

Method
1. Except for the red pepper, place all the ingredients in the Instant Pot.
2. Cook for 3 minutes on manual and release steam.
3. Open and mix in the red bell pepper and mix gently.
4. Adjust oil or water if necessary.
5. Serve with garnishes.

Nutritional Facts Per Serving
- Calories: 286
- Fat: 5.2g
- Carb: 38.1g
- Protein: 19g

If you love Thai food and want to cook authentic Thai food in your home, then cook this Thai Peanut Noodles recipe.

THAI PEANUT NOODLES

Cook time: 10 minutes	Servings: 2

Ingredients
- Spaghetti – 4 ounces, broken in half
- Sesame oil – 1 tbsp.
- Garlic – 2 cloves, minced
- Fresh ginger – 1 tbsp. minced
- Red pepper – ¼, thinly sliced
- Honey – 2 tbsps.
- Peanut butter – 2 tbsps.
- Soy sauce – 2 tbsps.
- Vegetable broth – ½ cup

- Rice vinegar – 2 tbsps.
- Sriracha sauce – 2 tsps.
- Chopped cilantro – 1 tbsp.
- Lime juice – ½ tbsp.
- Peanuts for garnish

Method
1. Press Sauté on the IP and add sesame oil.
2. Add sliced peppers, garlic, and ginger. Stir-fry for 2 minutes.
3. Mix together rice vinegar, sriracha sauce, vegetable broth, soy sauce, peanut butter, and honey and add to the IP.
4. Break noodles in half and add to the pot.
5. Make sure they are covered with liquid. Add more liquid if needed.
6. Cover and cook for 5 minutes on High.
7. Serve topped with fresh cilantro, peanuts, and lime juice.

Nutritional Facts Per Serving
- Calories: 514
- Fat: 18g
- Carb: 74g
- Protein: 15g

This noodle dish is called Lo Mein. With an Instant Pot you cook everything in one pot and don't have to drain the noodles.

Lo Mein (Chinese)

Cook time: 10 minutes	Servings: 2

Ingredients
- Garlic – 1 clove, minced
- Sesame oil – ½ tbsp.
- Linguine pasta – 4 oz. broken in half
- Snow peas – ½ cup, trimmed
- Broccoli florets – ½ cup
- Carrots – 1, sliced thin
- Chicken broth - ¾ cup
- Grated ginger – ½ tsp.
- Low sodium soy sauce – 1 tbsp.
- Oyster sauce – ½ tbsp.
- Shaoxing rice wine – ½ tbsp.
- Light brown sugar – ½ tbsp.

Method
1. In the Instant Pot, add the sesame oil and garlic. Press sauté and stir-fry for 2 to 3 minutes.
2. Spread noodles and add vegetables.
3. In a bowl, add the brown sugar, rice wine, oyster sauce, soy sauce, ginger, and broth. Mix well. Taste and adjust seasoning.
4. Pour sauce into the pot.
5. Cover and cook on Manual for 5 minutes on High.
6. Do a quick release and stir the noodles a few times.
7. Stir until the water is gone.
8. Serve.

Nutritional Facts Per Serving
- Calories: 299
- Fat: 4.7g
- Carb: 53.7g
- Protein: 10.1g

This is the easiest and heartiest one pot dinner. Simply add everything in the pot and your dinner is ready after a few minutes.

CHICKEN NOODLE SOUP (CHINESE)

| Cook time: 20 minutes | Servings: 2 |

Ingredients
- Wheat or rice noodles – 3 oz.
- Chopped greens of your choice – 2 cups
- Eggs for topping
- Toasted sesame oil – ½ tsp.
- Chili oil for serving

Instant Pot ingredients
- Fresh and room temperature boneless skinless chicken breast or thigh – ¾ lb.
- Green onion – 1, chopped and separated
- Garlic – 1 clove, minced
- Ginger – 1 large slice, chopped
- Bay leaf – 1
- Chicken broth – 4 cups
- Shaoxing wine – 1 tbsp.
- Light soy sauce – ½ tbsp.
- Black pepper – 1 pinch
- Salt – 1 pinch

Method
1. Add all the Instant Pot ingredients and white parts of the green onion in the IP.
2. Cover and cook on High for 10 minutes.
3. Do a natural release, remove the meat and shred.
4. Press sauté on the IP.
5. When it starts to boil, add the wheat noodles and cook according to package instructions.
6. Add the eggs and green vegetables 2 minutes before the noodles are ready.
7. Cook until the vegetables are just cooked.
8. Taste and adjust seasoning.
9. Add green part of the green onion and drizzle with sesame oil.
10. Mix and serve topped with Sriracha sauce and chili oil.

Nutritional Facts Per Serving
- Calories: 456
- Fat: 13.9g
- Carb: 29.3g
- Protein: 51.1g

This Chinese noodle recipe uses ramen noodles. They are cooked with soy, sesame, and garlic and turn into a wonderful lunch of noodles.

CHINESE GARLIC SESAME NOODLES

| Cook time: 4 minutes | Servings: 2 |

Ingredients
- Ramen noodles – 2 packages, break in half (discard seasoning packets)
- Water – 2 cups
- Soy sauce – ¼ cup
- Sesame oil – 1 tsp.
- Garlic – 1 tsp.
- Sesame seeds and chives for garnish

Method
1. Add the noodles, water, soy sauce, garlic and oil in the IP.
2. Close the lid and set to manual or 0 minutes.
3. Do a quick release.
4. Stir noodles.
5. Serve garnish with sesame seeds and chives.

Nutritional Facts Per Serving
- Calories: 335
- Fat: 16g

- Carb: 39g
- Protein: 10g

These noodles are delicious and a gluten-free dinner option. This dish is even easier than a stir-fry dish.

SPICY HONEY GARLIC NOODLES (CHINESE)

Cook time: 15 minutes	Servings: 2

Ingredients
- Sesame oil – 1/3 tbsp.
- Low sodium soy sauce – 1 1/3 tbsps.
- Garlic – 2 cloves, minced
- Honey – ½ tbsp.
- Chili garlic sauce – 1/3 tbsp.
- Medium-sized chicken breasts – ½, diced
- Water – ½ cup
- Rice noodles – 80 grams
- Sesame seeds for garnish
- Broccoli – 1/3 head, chopped
- Red and yellow bell pepper – 1/3, sliced

Method
1. In the Instant Pot, add the oil, garlic, honey, soy sauce, garlic sauce, water, chicken, and rice noodles.
2. Make sure the noodles are covered with water.
3. Cover and cook on High pressure for 2 minutes.
4. Do a quick release and open the lid.
5. Add the broccoli and bell peppers. Stir to mix.
6. Push the vegetables under the noodles.
7. Cover and let sit for 5 to 10 minutes.
8. Serve.

Nutritional Facts Per Serving
- Calories: 404
- Fat: 15g
- Carb: 40g
- Protein: 26g

CHAPTER 13 VEGETARIAN RECIPES

Make this delicious, crunchy broccoli in just 20 minutes in your Instant Pot or pressure cooker.

BROCCOLI WITH GARLIC

Cook time: 5 minutes	Servings: 2

Ingredients
- Broccoli – 1 head, cut into 2 cups of florets
- Water – ½ cup
- Garlic – 6 cloves, minced
- Peanut oil – 1 tbsp.
- Rice wine – 1 tbsp.
- Fine sea salt

Method
1. Add ½ cup water in the IP.
2. Place steamer rack into the pressure cooker.
3. Place the broccoli florets onto the steamer rack.
4. Cover and cook on low pressure for 0 minutes.
5. Do a quick release.
6. Place the broccoli in the cold water to stop cooking. Drain and set aside.
7. Remove the water from the IP and towel dry the inner pot.
8. Heat up your pressure cooker on sauté.
9. Add 1 tbsp. oil, and garlic.
10. Stir-fry for 30 seconds. Don't burn.
11. Add the broccoli and 1 tbsp. rice wine.
12. Stir for 30 seconds.
13. Season with salt and serve.

Nutritional Facts Per Serving
- Calories: 147
- Fat: 7.4g
- Carb: 18.4g
- Protein: 5.6g

This is a Sri Lankan budget-friendly, and nutritious vegetable dish. The dish is called mallung or mallum in Sri Lanka. This cabbage dish is made delicious by using spices like turmeric and mustard seeds.

Coconut Cabbage

Cook time: 15 minutes	Servings: 2

Ingredients
- Coconut oil – ½ tbsp.
- Brown onion – ½, sliced
- Salt – ½ tsp.
- Garlic – 1 clove, diced
- Red chili – ¼, sliced
- Yellow mustard seeds – ½ tbsp.
- Mild curry powder – ½ tbsp.
- Turmeric powder – ½ tbsp.
- Cabbage – ½, sliced
- Carrot – ½, sliced
- Lemon juice – 1 tbsp.
- Desiccated unsweetened coconut – ¼ cup
- Olive oil – ½ tbsp.
- Water – ½ cup

Method
1. Press sauté on your Instant Pot.
2. Add oil and onion and half the salt.
3. Sauté for 3 to 4 minutes.
4. Add the spices, chili, and garlic and stir fry for 30 seconds.
5. Add the olive oil, coconut, lime juice, carrots, and cabbage and stir through.
6. Add the water and stir through. Press Cancel.
7. Cover and cook on High pressure for 5 minutes.
8. Do a natural release for 5 minutes
9. Serve.

Nutritional Facts Per Serving
- Calories: 410
- Fat: 31.7g
- Carb: 32.3g
- Protein: 6.9g

This Japanese vegan curry dish is comforting, flavorful, and perfect for weekday dinner.

Vegan Japanese Curry

Cook time: 12 minutes	Servings: 2

Ingredients
- Oil – 1 tsp. divided
- Onion – ¼, sliced
- Garlic – 2 cloves, minced
- Finely chopped ginger – ½ tbsp.
- Flour – ½ tbsp.
- Garam masala – 1 tsp.
- Turmeric 1 pinch
- Chopped carrots – ½ cup
- Potato – ½ cup, cubed
- Chickpeas – 7 oz. drained
- Tomato paste – 1 tsp.
- Vegan Worcestershire sauce - 1 tsp.
- Water – 1 cup
- Salt to taste
- Apple sauce – 1 ½ tbsps.
- Peas – 1 tbsp.
- Rice, pickled ginger, and radish for serving

Method
1. Press sauté on IP.
2. Add oil and add onion to the hot oil.
3. Stir fry until translucent.
4. Add ginger and garlic and mix. Cook for 30 seconds.
5. Move onions to the side and add more oil.
6. Add the flour and mix into the oil.
7. Then mix with the garlic, ginger, and onion. Stir fry for 30 seconds.
8. Add the spices and mix.
9. Add the water, salt, sauces, chickpeas, and vegetables. Mix and remove the stuck flour from the bottom.
10. Cancel sauté.
11. Close and cook on High for 6 to 7 minutes.
12. Once cooked do a natural release.
13. Open the lid and press sauté.
14. Add the peas, and apple sauce and bring to a boil.
15. Taste and adjust spice and salt.
16. Add some pepper and sweetener if needed.

17. Garnish with scallions, radishes and sesame seeds.
18. Serve with rice.

Nutritional Facts Per Serving
- Calories: 209
- Fat: 5g
- Carb: 33g
- Protein: 9g

This is butter chicken, but vegan version. The recipe gives all the butter chicken flavor minus the chicken.

BUTTER CHICKPEAS (INDIAN)

Cook time: 50 minutes	Servings: 2

Ingredients
- Dried chickpeas – 1 cup, soaked overnight, then drained and rinsed
- Oil – 1 tbsp.
- Onion – ½, diced
- Minced garlic – 1 ½ tsp.
- Minced ginger – ½ tsp.

Spices
- Garam masala – ½ tsp.
- Coriander powder – ½ tsp.
- Paprika – ½ tsp.
- Salt – ½ tsp.
- Turmeric – ½ tsp.
- Black pepper – to taste
- Cayenne – to taste
- Ground cumin – to taste
- Tomato sauce – 1
- Water – ¾ cup

Add later
- Green bell pepper – ½, chopped
- Coconut cream – ¼ cup, unsweetened
- Pinch of dried fenugreek leaves
- Cilantro for garnish

Method
1. Press the sauté button.
2. Add the oil and heat.
3. Add the onion and stir fry for 6 to 7 minutes.
4. Add the spices, ginger, and garlic and add the tomato sauce, chickpeas, and water.
5. Cover with the lid and cook on High for 35 minutes.
6. Do a natural pressure release.
7. Add fenugreek leaves, cream, and bell pepper. Mix well.
8. Garnish with cilantro and serve.

Nutritional Facts Per Serving
- Calories: 470
- Fat: 13.3g
- Carb: 70.8g
- Protein: 21.4g

This Indian vegetable biryani is flavorful, aromatic, and tasty.

VEGETABLE BIRYANI

| Cook time: 15 minutes | Servings: 2 |

Ingredients
- Basmati rice – ½ cup (soaked for 15 minutes, then drained)
- Oil – 1 tbsp.

Whole Spice
- Cardamom pods – 2
- Whole cloves – 2
- Bay leaf – 1
- Cinnamon stick – ¼
- Cumin seeds – ¼ tsp.
- Fennel seeds – ¼ tsp.
- Onion – ½, thinly sliced
- Minced garlic – 1 tsp.
- Minced ginger – ½ tsp.

Ground spices
- Salt – ½ tsp.
- Coriander powder – ½ tsp.
- Paprika – ½ tsp.

- Garam masala – to taste
- Black pepper – to taste
- Cayenne – to taste
- Ground cumin - to taste
- Turmeric – to taste

Vegetables
- Bell pepper – ½, cut into strips
- Baby carrots – ½ cup
- Frozen veggies – ½ cup
- Gold potatoes – ¼ pound, cut in half
- Water – ½ cup
- Cilantro leaves, mint leaves
- Ghee coated cashews and raisins

Method
1. Press Sauté and add the oil to the pot.
2. Add the whole spice to the hot oil and stir.
3. Once the cumin is brown, add the onions, and stir-fry for 5 to 7 minutes.
4. Add the ground spices, ginger, garlic, and stir.
5. Add the vegetables, rice, and water and stir.
6. Cover and cook 6 minutes at High.
7. Do a natural release.
8. Open and add mint, cilantro, cashews, and raisins.
9. Mix and serve.

Nutritional Facts Per Serving
- Calories: 305
- Fat: 8.3g
- Carb: 52.8g
- Protein: 5.9g

This Indian Kidney bean curry dish has a thick masala gravy and is full of flavors.

KIDNEY BEAN CURRY

Cook time: 45 minutes	Servings: 2

Ingredients
- Dried kidney beans – 1 cup, soaked overnight
- Onion – ½, roughly chopped
- Serrano pepper or green chili – ¼

- Oil – 1 ½ tbsp.
- Cumin seeds – ½ tsp.
- Bay leaf – 1
- Minced garlic – 1 tsp.
- Minced ginger – 1 tsp.

Spices
- Salt – 1 tsp.
- Coriander powder – ½ tsp.
- Garam masala – ½ tsp.
- Paprika – ½ tsp.
- Black pepper – ¼ tsp.
- Turmeric – ½ tsp.
- Cayenne – 1 pinch
- Fresh tomato puree – 1 cup
- Water – 1 cup
- Cilantro for garnish

Method
1. Blend the serrano pepper and onion in a food processor until smooth. Set aside.
2. Press the Sauté on the IP.
3. Add the oil and heat.
4. Add the cumin seeds and heat until browned.
5. Add the blended serrano pepper and onion and stir fry for 8 to 10 minutes.
6. Add the spices, ginger, garlic, and bay leaf.
7. Add the tomato puree and stir fry for 5 minutes.
8. Add the water and kidney beans.
9. Cover with the lid and cook on High for 30 minutes.
10. Do a natural release.
11. Garnish with cilantro and serve.

Nutritional Facts Per Serving
- Calories: 455
- Fat: 15g
- Carb: 60.5g
- Protein: 21.3g

This Indian popular vegetable korma is a part of Mughal cuisine. This dish is made with cream, nuts, and dried fruits.

VEGETABLE KORMA

| Cook time: 20 minutes | Servings: 2 |

Ingredients

Onion tomato sauce

- Onion – ½, roughly chopped
- Garlic – 2 cloves, chopped
- Ginger – 1 inch, chopped
- Tomato -1/2 chopped
- Serrano pepper or green chili – ¼ tsp.

Cashew Sauce

- Water – ½ cup
- Cashews – ¼ cup
- Heavy cream – 2 tbsps.
- Ghee – 1 ½ tbsps.
- Cashews – 2 tbsps.
- Golden raisins - 2 tbsps.
- Cumin seeds – ¼ tsp.

Spices

- Paprika – 1 tsp.
- Salt – 1/2 tsp.
- Coriander powder – ½ tsp.
- Turmeric powder – ¼ tsp.
- Garam masala – ¼ tsp.
- Cayenne – a pinch
- Ground cardamom - a pinch
- Chopped potato – 1 cup
- Water – ½ cup
- Chopped vegetables – 2 cups (broccoli, green beans, peas, carrots)
- Dried fenugreek leaves – ¼ tsp.
- Cilantro for garnish

Method

1. To make the tomato sauce: in a blender, add the serrano, tomato, ginger, garlic, and onion and blend until smooth. Set aside.
2. Prepare the cashew sauce: blend heavy cream, cashews, and water until smooth. Set aside.
3. Press the sauté on the Instant Pot.

4. Add the ghee, golden raisins and cashews.
5. Stir fry until the cashews turn golden.
6. Remove the raisins and cashews from the pot and set aside.
7. Add the cumin seeds to the pot.
8. Once they start to brown, add the tomato and onion mixture.
9. Stir fry for 7 to 8 minutes.
10. Add all the remaining spices and the potatoes. Mix well.
11. Add the water and cover.
12. Cook on High for 5 minutes.
13. Do a quick release.
14. Add the remaining chopped vegetables.
15. Cover and cook on High for 2 minutes.
16. Do a quick release.
17. Stir in fenugreek leaves, and cashew sauce.
18. Garnish with ghee-coated raisins, and cashews and cilantro.
19. Serve.

Nutritional Facts Per Serving
- Calories: 380
- Fat: 24.6g
- Carb: 31.1g
- Protein: 8.6g

This Indian recipe is called Aloo baingan masala. It is made with spiced eggplant and potatoes.

SPICED POTATO AND EGGPLANT

Cook time: 5 minutes	Servings: 2

Ingredients
- Oil – ½ tbsp.
- Cumin seeds – ¼ tsp.
- Serrano pepper – ½, minced
- Golden potatoes – ½ pound, chopped
- Eggplant – ¾ pound, chopped
- Water – ¼ cup
- Onion masala – ¼ cup (recipe below)
- Salt – ½ tsp.
- Garam masala – ¼ tsp.
- Cilantro for garnish

Method
1. Press the Sauté and add oil.
2. Add serrano pepper and cumin seeds to the hot oil.
3. Add the remaining ingredients once the cumin seeds are brown.
4. Cover with the lid and cook on High for 4 minutes.
5. Do a quick release.
6. Mix well.
7. Garnish and serve.

Nutritional Facts Per Serving
- Calories: 155
- Fat: 3.8g
- Carb: 29.5g
- Protein: 3.4g

This Indian Punjabi Dal recipe is made with only a few ingredients, but full of flavor.

LANGAR DAL

| Cook time: 30 minutes | Servings: 2 |

Ingredients
- Ghee – 2 tbsps. divided
- Cumin seeds – ½ tsp.
- Urad dal – ½ cup, soaked in cold water overnight
- Chana dal – 2 tbsp.
- Water – 2 cups
- Onion masala – ½ cup
- Salt – ¾ tsp.
- Garam masala – ¾ tsp.
- Cayenne – ¼ tsp.
- Cilantro and heavy cream for garnish

Method
1. Press the sauté button on the IP.
2. Add 1 tbsp. ghee to the pot and add cumin seeds to the melted ghee.
3. Add the remaining ingredients to the pot when the cumin seeds are brown.
4. Cover and cook on High for 30 minutes.
5. Do a natural release.
6. Stir in the remaining ingredients.
7. Garnish with the cilantro and heavy cream and serve.

Nutritional Facts Per Serving
- Calories: 338
- Fat: 13.6g
- Carb: 39.1g
- Protein: 16g

This Indian egg biryani is flavorful, delicious and easy to make.

EGG BIRYANI

| Cook time: 20 minutes | Servings: 2 |

Ingredients
- Basmati rice – 1 cup, soaked for 15 minutes
- Ghee – 2 tbsps.

Whole spices
- Cardamom pods – 5
- Whole cloves – 4
- Bay leaf – 2
- Cinnamon stick – ½ inch
- Cumin seeds – ½ tsp.
- Fennel seeds – ½ tsp.
- Oil – 2 tbsps.
- Onion – 1, thinly sliced
- Minced garlic – 2 tsps.
- Minced ginger – 1 tsp.
- Tomato – 1, diced

Ground spices
- Salt – 1 ½ tsp.
- Coriander powder – 1 tsp.
- Paprika – 1 tsp.
- Garam masala – ½ tsp.
- Black pepper – ¼ tsp.
- Cayenne – ¼ tsp.
- Ground cumin – ¼ tsp.
- Turmeric – ¼ tsp.
- Water – 1 cup
- Eggs - 6
- Cilantro leaves, chopped

- Mint leaves, chopped
- Ghee coated raisins and cashews

Method
1. Press the sauté button and add the oil to the Instant Pot.
2. Add the whole spices and stir.
3. Add the onions once the cumin seeds are brown.
4. Stir-fry for 5 to 7 minutes.
5. Add the ground spices, ginger, garlic, and tomato.
6. Cook for 2 to 3 minutes.
7. Add the rice and water.
8. Then place a steamer basket on top of the rice.
9. Place the eggs in the steamer basket.
10. Cover and cook on High for 10 minutes.
11. Do a quick release.
12. Remove the eggs, cool and peel them. You can stir fry the eggs if necessary.
13. Place the peeled eggs back into the rice and mix well.
14. Garnish with ghee coated cashews and raisins, mint, and cilantro.
15. Serve.

Nutritional Facts Per Serving
- Calories: 835
- Fat: 41.9g
- Carb: 91.4g
- Protein: 25.7g

Chapter 14 Desserts and Snacks

This is Filipino rice pudding. This dish is sweet, delicious and you will enjoy making this recipe. The fresh mango slices and caramel topping makes this recipe delicious.

Filipino Sweet Rice Cake

| Cook time: 75 + minutes | Servings: 4 |

Ingredients
- Asian sweet rice – 1 ½ cups
- Coconut milk – 2 cans
- White sugar – ½ cup
- Light brown sugar – ½ cup
- Vanilla – 1 tsp.
- Water – 3 cups

Caramel topping sauce

Ingredients
- Brown sugar – 1 cup
- Half-and-half – ½ cup
- Butter – 4 tbsp.
- Pinch salt
- Vanilla extract – 1 tbsp.

Method
1. Fill your pot with 3 cups of water.
2. In a bowl, add rice and sugar. Mix well.
3. Add the vanilla and coconut milk, mix well and cover with aluminum foil.
4. Add a wire stand to your pot. Make sure the stand is high enough so the bowl will not touch the water at the bottom.
5. Cover and press Manual for 75 minutes.
6. Do a natural release and cool for 15 minutes.
7. Open the pot and check the middle.
8. If it needs more time, then cover and let sit for 10 minutes more.
9. Remove when the rice is cooked completely.
10. Add a caramel topping and serve.
11. Caramel topping: mix all the ingredients in a pan over medium heat.
12. Cook and whisk until dark, about 5 to 7 minutes.

Nutritional Facts Per Serving
- Calories: 573

- o Fat: 28.6g
- o Carb: 82.4g
- o Protein: 3.9g

This is a Filipino Leche Flan dish. This dish is made only on special occasions such as Thanksgiving, or Christmas. Use an oven safe bowl when making this recipe.

FILIPINO LECHE FLAN

Cook time: 16 to 35 minutes	Servings: 5

Ingredients
- o Egg yolks – 10
- o Condensed milk – 1 can
- o Evaporated milk – 1 can
- o Sugar – ½ cup
- o Vanilla – 1 tsp.
- o Water – 2 cups
- o Caramel

Method
1. Whisk the egg yolks, but do not over mix.
2. Gently add both the milks. Mix well.
3. Mix in sugar and vanilla. Do not over mix.
4. Add the water in the pressure cooker and add the trivet.
5. Pour in caramel in 2 bowls so the bottom is covered.
6. Add the mixture in two bowls evenly.
7. Cover each bowl with foil. Tap to release any extra bubbles.
8. Gently place the bowl on the trivet.
9. Cover and cook on Manual for 16 minutes.
10. Then do a natural release for 10 minutes.
11. Remove and check with a toothpick.
12. If they are still not cooked, then repeat the cooking time.
13. When cooked, cool and place in the refrigerator overnight.
14. Serve.

Nutritional Facts Per Serving
- o Calories: 290
- o Fat: 23g
- o Carb: 4g
- o Protein: 16g

This is a very easy Instant Pot pudding recipe. This soybean pudding is drizzled with sweet ginger syrup.

Tofu Pudding (Singaporean)

| Cook time: 15 minutes | Servings: 4 |

Ingredients

Soy milk

- Dry soybeans – 1 cup
- Cold water for soaking – 3 cups
- Cold water – 6 cups
- Salt - 1 pinch

Tofu pudding
- Agar-agar powder – 1 tsp.
- Granulated sugar – 2 to 3 tbsp.

Ginger syrup
- Rock sugar – 200 grams
- Water – 1 cup
- Brown sugar – 3 tbsps.
- Ginger – 3 tbsps. crushed

Method
1. Soak the soybeans: in the pressure cooker, add 3 cups cold water and 1 cup dried soybeans.
2. Close the lid and cook at High pressure for 0 minute.
3. Do a 30-minute natural release. Discard the soaking water and rinse the beans under cold water.
4. To make the pudding: in a blender, blend the soybeans with 2 cups of water until smooth.
5. To cook: place the steamer basket in the Instant Pot.
6. Add 4 cups of cold water and 1 pinch of salt.
7. Add the soybean mixture.
8. Close and pressure cook on High for 5 minutes.
9. Then do a 25-minute natural release.
10. Syrup: add the ingredients in a saucepan and bring to a simmer over medium heat.
11. Stir until sugar melts. Lower heat and simmer for 2 minutes more.
12. Discard ginger and simmer until thickens, about 5 to 10 minutes more.
13. Remove from the heat and cool the syrup.
14. Strain the soy milk.
15. Add agar-agar power to a saucepan and add the soy milk.
16. Stir and bring the mixture to a simmer and mix well.
17. Add granulated sugar to sweeten the pudding.

18. Cool and serve.

Nutritional Facts Per Serving
- Calories: 402
- Fat: 6.3g
- Carb: 78.9g
- Protein: 11.6g

This Sri Lankan dish is called Watalappan in Sri Lanka. This dish is made with spices such as nutmeg and cardamom and sweetened with traditional Kitul jiggery.

WATALAPPAN (SRI LANKAN)

| Cook time: 15 minutes | Servings: 2 |

Ingredients
- Eggs – 2
- Brown molasses sugar or kitul jiggery – 125 gramss (shaved with a knife)
- Canned coconut milk – ½ cup
- Cardamom powder –1 pinch
- Salt – 1 pinch
- Roasted cashews for garnish

Method
1. Heat a pan on medium heat.
2. Add 2 tbsps. water and shaved jiggery.
3. Melt until dissolved. Remove from heat and cool.
4. Whisk in the coconut milk.
5. In another bowl, whisk the eggs, with cardamom and salt.
6. Add the coconut milk mixture to the eggs and whisk to combine. Don't make it frothy.
7. Strain the mixture and pour into two ramekins or one large dish.
8. Add 2 cups of water in the Instant Pot and place the steaming insert.
9. Place the ramekins on the insert.
10. Close and seam for 15 minutes.
11. Release pressure and remove the ramekins.
12. Cool and serve.

Nutritional Facts Per Serving

- Calories: 439
- Fat: 19.6g
- Carb: 64g
- Protein: 7.8g

Called Ji Dan Gao, this Instant Pot Chinese Matcha Sponge Cake is lightly flavored and spongy.

CHINESE SPONGE CAKE

Cook time: 20 minutes	Servings: 5

Ingredients
- Eggs – 2
- Sugar – 120 grams
- Matcha powder – 1 tbsp.
- Sprite – 100 ml
- Cake flour – 120 gram

Method
1. In a bowl, place the matcha, sugar, and eggs.
2. Beat with a hand mixer for 1 minute on medium speed.
3. Then increase the speed and beat on high for 20 minutes to make it as light as the sponge.
4. The batter will be double in volume.
5. Lower the speed to low and gradually add in soda drink and flour.
6. Just mix so there is no lump remains.
7. Prepare a 5 to 6-inch container and line with parchment paper.
8. Pour batter into the prepared container and break up any bubbles.
9. Place the trivet in the Pot.
10. Add 3 cups of water.
11. Gently place the cake container on top of the trivet.
12. Close and press Steam.
13. Cook on High for 20 minutes.
14. Do a natural release.
15. Remove and cool.
16. Serve.

Nutritional Facts Per Serving
- Calories: 216
- Fat: 2.2g
- Carb: 44.7g
- Protein: 5g

This traditional Chinese rice pudding dessert recipe is made with nuts, fruits, and seeds.

RICE PUDDING (BA BAO FAN)

Cook time: 1 hour 6 minutes	Servings: 4

Ingredients
- Glutinous rice – 1 cup, rinsed and drained
- Water – 2 cups, and more as needed
- Brown sugar – 1 ½ tbsps.
- Butter – 1 tbsp.
- Red bean paste – 1 cup

Dried fruits
- Dried candied mango – 2 slices
- Golden raisins – 1 tbsp.
- Goji berries – 1 tbsp.
- Dried cranberries – 1 tbsp.
- Dried longan – 2 tbsp.
- Chinese red dates – 4
- Chinese black dates – 4

Soak all the dried fruits in warm water for 30 minutes.

Syrup
- Sugar – ¼ cup
- Water – ½ cup

Dried fruit for the syrup
- Golden raisin – 1 tbsp.
- Dried cranberries – 1 tbsp.

Serve with
- Condensed milk

Method
1. Add the water in the IP.
2. Put the trivet in.
3. Add the rice in a stainless-steel bowl and add enough water to cover the rice. Mix to make sure all the rice is submerged in water.
4. Place the bowl on top of the trivet.
5. Close the lid and cook on High pressure for 15 minutes.
6. Do a natural release.

7. Open the lid and stir in the butter and brown sugar.
8. To assemble: add more 2 cups more water in the IP.
9. Add the soaked dried fruit and red bean paste with the rice pudding.
10. If you want to decorate then arrange rice, dried fruit, and red bean paste in layers.
11. Smooth with a rubber spatula.
12. Cover and press Steamer.
13. Cook for 30 minutes.
14. Prepare the syrup: in a saucepan, place dried fruits, sugar and water.
15. Cook on medium heat until the mixture gets a syrup consistency.
16. Serve the rice pudding with syrup and condensed milk.

Nutritional Facts Per Serving
- Calories: 276
- Fat: 3.4g
- Carb: 58g
- Protein: 4.5g

Making this traditional Chinese Lunar New Year cake is easy.

CHINESE NEW YEAR CAKE (KUE BAKUL)

| Cook time: 1 hour 10 minutes | Servings: 7x 3 inch round cake |

Ingredients
- Glutinous rice flour – 300 grams
- Water – 300 mls
- White sugar – 300 grams
- Dark brown sugar – 100 grams
- Long sheet of banana leaves – 4 to 5 (blanch in hot boiling water for 5 minutes, then pat dry)

Method
1. Cut the banana leaves into 7-inch width and about 7 to 8-inch length. Arrange them on the bottom of a 7 X 3 inch round cake pan so they cover the bottom and all the sides.
2. In a saucepan, place the water and sugar and bring to a boil to melt the sugar.
3. Remove from the heat and cool completely.
4. Gradually add the flour into the sugar mixture.
5. Stir to mix until smooth.
6. Pour the batter into the prepared aluminum pan and cover with aluminum foil.
7. Pour 1 cup of water into the IP.
8. Set the trivet.
9. Place the cake pan on top of the trivet.
10. Cover and cook on High for 45 minutes.

11. Do a natural release.
12. Remove and cool for 24 hours to harden.
13. Serve.

Nutritional Facts for the Entire Recipe
- Calories: 2595
- Fat: 2g
- Carb: 639.9g
- Protein: 21.4g

This silky-smooth egg custard recipe takes only 4 ingredients and 4 steps to make.

CHINESE EGG CUSTARD

| Cook time: 16 minutes | Servings: 4 to 5 |

Ingredients
- Eggs – 3, beaten
- Whole milk – 1 ½ cup, divided
- A pinch of salt
- Sugar – 4 tbsps. or 5 tbsps. for more sweetness

Method
1. In a pan, add sugar, 1 cup milk, and a pinch of salt.
2. Whisk and heat until sugar melts.
3. Add the remaining milk and mix.
4. The mixture should cool to touch.
5. Slowly pour the milk mixture into the beaten eggs and whisk.
6. Then strain the milk-egg mixture.
7. Pour the mixture into 4 to 5 ramekins.
8. Cover the ramekins tightly with foil.
9. Add 1 cup of water in the Instant Pot.
10. Place a trivet in the IP.
11. And gently place the ramekins on the trivet.
12. Cover and cook on Low for 0 minutes.
13. Do a natural release.
14. Open and serve.

Nutritional Facts Per Serving
- Calories: 119
- Fat: 4g
- Carb: 13g
- Protein: 5g

This Asian popsicle recipe is made with just 5 ingredients. They are full of sweet and nutty beans and are delicious.

ADZUKI BEANS COCONUT POPSICLES

Cook time: 55 minutes	Servings: 10 Ice Pops

Ingredients
- Adzuki beans – 240 grams
- Cold running water – 5 cups
- Brown rock sugar in pieces – 2 ½ to 3 ½ pieces (70 grams each)
- Coconut milk – ¾ cup, plus 1 tbsp.
- Cornstarch – 1 ½ tbsps. plus 2 tbsps. water

Method
1. Rinse the beans under cold water and drain.
2. Place 5 cups of water and beans in the pressure cooker.
3. Close and cook on High for 20 minutes.
4. Do a natural release for 15 minutes.
5. Open the lid and press sauté.
6. Add the brown rock sugar.
7. Stir and boil for 10 minutes or until sugar melts.
8. Mix in the coconut milk and adjust the sweetness.
9. Mix the cornstarch with water.
10. Gradually add to the Instant Pot mixture.
11. Turn off the heat.
12. Cool the mixture completely.
13. And fill the popsicle molds.
14. Freeze for 6 hours and serve.

Nutritional Facts Per Serving
- Calories: 144
- Fat: 5.8g
- Carb: 24.8g
- Protein: 1g

This is a popular Taiwanese street food made with 6 ingredients. Serve with yummy sauce.

TAIWANESE CORN ON THE COB

Cook time: 20 minutes	Servings: 2 to 4

Ingredients
- Corn on the cob – 4 ears

Sauce

- Light soy sauce – 3 tbsps.
- Shacha sauce – 2 tbsps.
- Sugar – 1 tbsp.
- Garlic powder – 1 tsp.
- Sesame oil – ¼ tsp.

Method
1. Add 1 cup water into the pressure cooker.
2. Place a trivet in the pressure cooker.
3. Place 4 ears of corn on the cob onto the trivet.
4. Close and cook on High for 1 to 2 minutes.
5. Do a quick release.
6. Open the lid and remove.
7. Preheat the oven to 450F.
8. In a bowl, mix all the sauce ingredients.
9. Brush the sauce all over the corn on the cob.
10. Place them in a baking rack.
11. Bake for 5 to 10 minutes.
12. Serve.

Nutritional Facts Per Serving
- Calories: 85
- Fat: 0.8g
- Carb: 19.1g
- Protein: 3.3g

Chapter 15 Keto Asian Recipes

This is a low-carb, Ketogenic, delicious chicken dish cooked in less than 30 minutes. The secret of this dish is the use of a lot of tomato and ginger.

Keto Pakistani Karachi Chicken

| Cook time: 15 minutes | Servings: 2 |

Ingredients
- Oil – 1 tbsp.
- Grated ginger – 2 tbsp.
- Boneless, skinless chicken thighs – ½ lb. cut into pieces
- Canned diced tomatoes – ¾ cup
- Ground cumin – 1/3 tsp.
- Garam masala – 1/3 tsp.
- Cayenne – 1/3 tsp.
- Salt – 1/3 tsp.

For finishing
- Chopped cilantro or parsley – 1 tsp.
- Lemon juice – 1 tbsp.
- Garam masala – 1/3 tsp.
- Fresh ginger to taste, thinly cut

Method
1. Add oil to a hot Instant Pot.
2. Add the thinly sliced ginger and cook for 2 to 3 minutes.
3. Add the spices, tomatoes, and chicken and stir well.
4. Close the lid and cook on High for 5 minutes.
5. When done, do a natural release for 10 minutes.
6. Garnish with finishing ingredients and serve.

Nutritional Facts Per Serving
- Calories: 202
- Fat: 9g
- Carb: 5g
- Protein: 22g

Traditionally cooked in a tandoor (oven), this is now can be cooked using an Instant Pot. This dish is succulent, moist and a favorite for the whole family.

PAKISTANI TANDOORI CHICKEN

Cook time: 30 minutes	Servings: 2

Ingredients
- Chicken drumsticks – 8 (1 lb.), skinned and dried with a paper towel
- Plain yogurt – ¼ cup
- Ginger – ¼ tbsp. grated
- Garlic – ¼ tbsp. minced
- Kashmiri red chili powder – ½ tbsp.
- Turmeric – ¼ tsp.
- Garam masala – ½ tsp.
- Salt – 1 tsp.
- Lemon juice – ½ tbsp.
- Oil – ½ tbsp.
- Water – 1 cup

Method
1. In a bowl, add the oil, lemon juice, salt, garam masala, turmeric, chili powder, garlic, ginger, and yogurt. Mix well.
2. Make 2 to 3 slits on each chicken piece and coat with marinade. Marinate up to 24 hours in the refrigerator and remove chicken 30 minutes before cooking.
3. Add 1 cup water to the Instant Pot and grease the trivet with cooking oil. place the trivet in the IP.
4. Arrange the marinated chicken pieces on the trivet.
5. Close and cook on High for 15 minutes, then do a natural release.
6. Enjoy tandoori chicken with low-carb chutney and lime wedges.

Nutritional Facts Per Serving
- Calories: 331
- Fat: 11g
- Carb: 3g
- Protein: 50g

This Instant Pot chicken curry is made using whole spices and a simple tomato-onion gravy. The secret of this recipe is you need to sauté both onions and tomatoes for a bit longer, about 4 minutes each.

Chicken Curry (Indian)

Cook time: 20 minutes	Servings: 2

Ingredients
- Chicken – ½ pound, cut into bite-size pieces
- Ghee or oil – 1 ½ tbsp.
- Green chili pepper – 1, small chopped
- Ginger – ½ inch, chopped
- Garlic – 2 cloves, chopped
- Onion – ½, chopped
- Medium tomato – 1, chopped
- Water – ½ cup
- Lemon juice – ½ tbsp.
- Cilantro – 1 tbsp. for garnish

Whole spices
- Black cardamom – 1
- Bay leaf – 1
- Cloves – 3
- Black peppercorns – 3
- Cumin seeds – ¼ tsp.

Spices
- Coriander powder – 1 tsp.
- Cayenne or red chili powder – ¼ tsp.
- Garam masala – ¼ tsp.
- Ground turmeric – a pinch
- Salt – ½ tsp.

Method
1. Press Sauté and add the oil to the Instant Pot.
2. Add whole spices and sauté for 30 seconds.
3. Add the garlic, ginger, onion, and green chili and sauté for 4 minutes. Stirring continuously.
4. Add the spices and chopped tomato. Cook and stir for 4 more minutes.
5. Add the chicken and sauté for 2 minutes. Add water and stir to mix.
6. Cover and cook on manual for 5 minutes on High pressure.
7. Do a quick release. Open and stir in the lemon juice.
8. Garnish with cilantro and serve.

Nutritional Facts Per Serving
- Calories: 386
- Fat: 30g
- Carb: 8g
- Protein: 19g

Chicken Kadai or chicken Karachi is a spicy curry recipe made with fresh ginger and fragrant spices. It is a popular Pakistani and North Indian curry dish.

Chicken Karachi

Cook time: 20 minutes	Servings: 2

Ingredients
- Olive oil – 1 ½ tbsps.
- Yellow onion – ½, diced
- Ginger – 1 tbsp. diced
- Garlic – 1 tbsp. minced
- Boneless, skinless chicken thighs – ¾ pound, cut into pieces
- Canned diced tomatoes – ¾ cup
- Ground cumin – ½ tsp.
- Ground coriander – ½ tsp.
- Garam masala – ½ tsp.
- Kashmiri red chili powder – ½ tbsp.
- Ground turmeric – a pinch
- Kosher salt – ¾ tsp.

Garnish
- Chopped cilantro to taste
- Ginger to taste, sliced

Method
1. Press sauté on your Instant Pot and add oil to heat.
2. Add garlic, ginger, and onion and cook for 2 to 3 minutes or until onions are translucent.
3. Add the ground turmeric, red chili powder, garam masala, ground coriander, ground cumin, tomato, chicken and salt. Mix well.
4. Close the pot and cook on Manual for 5 minutes on High pressure.
5. Do a quick pressure release when cooked. Then release all remaining pressure and open the lid.
6. Press Sauté mode and cook for 5 minutes to thicken the curry.
7. Garnish with ginger and cilantro.

8. Serve hot with cauliflower rice or almond bread.

Nutritional Facts Per Serving
- Calories: 347
- Fat: 18g
- Carb: 11g
- Protein: 34g

This Indonesian Oxtail soup or Sup Buntut is delicious and low-carb. Just like any other Asian dish, this soup has sweet and salty flavors.

INDONESIAN OXTAIL SOUP (SUP BUNTUT)

Cook time: 1 hour 10 minutes	Servings: 2

Ingredients

Spice Paste

- Shallots – 4
- Garlic – 2 cloves
- Young ginger – ¼ inch
- Nutmeg – ¼ tsp.

Soup

- Oxtail pieces – 300 grams
- Carrots – 1, sliced
- Cinnamon – ½ stick
- Whole cloves – 2
- Tomatoes – 1, sliced
- Oil – ½ tbsp.
- Salt – ½ tsp.
- Sugar substitute – 1 tsp.
- Ground white pepper – ½ tsp.
- Fish sauce – ½ tbsp.
- Fried shallots for garnishing
- Coriander leaves for garnishing
- Water – 2 cups

Method
1. Place the oxtail in the IP and add water.
2. Close and cook on Manual for 50 minutes on High pressure.
3. Release pressure naturally.
4. Skim off the layer of oil

5. Drain the oxtail and stock.
6. Clean the inner pot and press sauté.
7. Add oil and sauté the cloves, cinnamon and spice paste ingredients for 5 minutes.
8. Add the stock and oxtail back into the pot.
9. Add the pepper, sugar substitute, salt, carrot, and fish sauce.
10. Close and on Manual, cook for 10 minutes on High pressure.
11. Do a quick release.
12. Skim off any remaining scum or oil.
13. Add the tomato and mix.
14. Ladle soup into bowls and garnish with fresh red chilies, coriander, and shallots.

Nutritional Facts Per Serving
- Calories: 351
- Fat: 24.9g
- Carb: 10.8g
- Protein: 23g

This pork butt recipe is delicious and fatty. You will get a lot of oil when you have done the cooking. Use a spoon to drain the fat if you don't like too much fat.

FILIPINO PORK ADOBO

Cook time: 30 minutes	Servings: 2

Ingredients
- Pork butt – 1 lb. cut into large cubes
- Soy sauce – 1 tbsp.
- Apple cider vinegar – 1 tbsp.
- Minced garlic – 1 tbsp.
- Bay leaves – 1
- Black pepper to taste
- Oregano – ¼ tsp.
- Coconut oil to taste

Method
1. Sauté pork with oil for 5 minutes in the Instant Pot.
2. Add all the other ingredients and mix.
3. Cancel sauté and press Meat.
4. Cook for 25 minutes
5. Do a natural release for 10 minutes, then do a quick release.
6. Serve.

Nutritional Facts Per Serving
- Calories: 348
- Fat: 22g
- Carb: 2.6g
- Protein: 32.8g

This is a juicy and tender Instant Pot pork chop recipe from Hong Kong. This recipe is made with a sweet-savory umami sauce.

PORK CHOPS

| Cook time: 15 minutes | Servings: 2 |

Ingredients
- Boneless pork chops – 2 (1.25 inch thick) tenderize the pork chops with a knife
- Small onion – ½ sliced
- Olive oil – ½ tbsp.
- Balsamic vinegar – ½ tbsp.
- Worcestershire sauce – ½ tbsp.
- Liquid aminos – ½ tbsp.
- Erythritol – ½ tsp.
- Unsalted chicken stock – ½ cup
- Cornstarch – 1 tsp. plus 1 tbsp. water mixed
- Kosher salt

Marinade
- Liquid aminos – ½ tbsp.
- Shaoxing wine – ½ tbsp.
- Salt to taste
- Erythritol to taste
- Ground white pepper to taste
- Sesame oil – ¼ tsp.

Method
1. Mix the chops with marinade ingredients and marinate for 20 minutes.
2. Press Sauté and add oil to the pot.
3. Brown the pork chops on both sides. Remove and set aside.
4. Add sliced onions and sauté. Add salt and pepper to taste.
5. Cook for 1 minute.
6. Add the vinegar and deglaze the pot.

7. Add the chicken stock, liquid aminos, Worcestershire sauce, and erythritol. Mix well. Taste and adjust seasoning.
8. Add the pork chops and cook on High pressure for 1 minute. Do a natural release for 10 minutes. Remove pork chops and set aside.
9. Press Sauté. Taste and adjust seasoning.
10. Mix the cornstarch and water.
11. Then mix it into the onion sauce one-third at a time.
12. Serve the pork chops.

Nutritional Facts Per Serving
- Calories: 294
- Fat: 13g
- Carb: 9g
- Protein: 31g

This fish curry is an Instant Pot version of traditional fish curry from the southern part of India. You can add more heat by adding more serrano chilies or jalapeno.

INDIAN FISH CURRY

| Cook time: 10 minutes | Servings: 2 |

Ingredients
- Coconut oil – 1 tbsp.
- Curry leaves – 5
- Onion – ½ cup, chopped
- Garlic – ½ tbsp. chopped
- Ginger – ½ tbsp. chopped
- Jalapeno or serrano chili pepper – 1, chopped
- Tomato – ½ cup, chopped
- Ground coriander – ½ tsp.
- Ground cumin – 1 pinch
- Turmeric – ¼ tsp.
- Black pepper – ¼ tsp.
- Salt – ½ tsp.
- Water – for deglazing
- Canned coconut milk – ½ cup
- Fish fillets – ¾ lb. cut into 2-inch pieces
- Lime juice – ½ tsp.
- Fresh cilantro leaves and tomato slices for garnish

Method
1. Press Sauté on your IP.
2. Add coconut oil and heat up.
3. Add curry leaves and stir fry for 20 seconds.
4. Add green chilies, ginger, garlic, and onions to the IP.
5. Stir fry until onions are translucent.
6. Add tomatoes and sauté until the tomatoes start to break down and release juice.
7. Add the salt, black pepper, turmeric, cumin, and coriander.
8. Sauté for 30 seconds, or until fragrant.
9. Deglaze with a little water.
10. Stir in coconut milk.
11. Add the fish pieces.
12. Make sure the milk goes under the fish pieces.
13. Close and cook pressure cook for 2 minutes.
14. Do a quick release and open the lid.
15. Add the lime juice and gently mix.
16. Serve the fish and gravy in bowls.
17. Garnish with fresh tomato slices, and chopped cilantro.

Nutritional Facts Per Serving
- Calories: 190
- Fat: 11g
- Carb: 6g
- Protein: 16g

This Korean savory pork dish is flavorful. Cooked in a pressure cooker, it is deliciously tender.

KOREAN SPICY PORK (DAE JI BULGOGI)

| Cook time: 30 minutes | Servings: 2 |

Ingredients for the marinating and cooking
- Pork shoulder – ½ lb. cut into ½ inch slices
- Onion – ½, sliced thin
- Minced ginger – ½ tbsp.
- Minced garlic – ½ tbsp.
- Liquid aminos – ½ tbsp.
- Rice wine – ½ tbsp.
- Sesame oil – ½ tbsp.
- Splenda – 1 packet
- Gochujang – 1 tbsp.

- o Cayenne or gochugaru – ½ tsp.
- o Water – 1/6 cup

For the finishing
- o Onion – ½, thinly sliced
- o Sesame seeds – ½ tbsp.
- o Sliced green onions – 4

Method
1. Mix up all the cooking and marinade ingredients in the IP.
2. Allow to sit for 1 hour to a day.
3. Cook on high pressure for 20 minutes.
4. Do a natural pressure release and open the lid.
5. Heat up a pan and add the pork cubes and sliced onion in it.
6. Allow to get very hot and add ½ cup of the sauce from the IP.
7. The sauce will caramelize and mix well with the pork.
8. Once the sauce has evaporated, sprinkle with green onions and sesame seeds.
9. Serve.

Nutritional Facts Per Serving
- o Calories: 189
- o Fat: 9g
- o Carb: 9g
- o Protein: 15g

This Taiwanese Beef stew dish is flavorful, tender and delicious.

TAIWANESE BEEF STEW

Cook time: 45 minutes	Servings: 2

Ingredients for aromatics
- o Medium yellow onion – ½, chopped
- o Large garlic cloves – 5, chopped
- o Finely chopped ginger – 1 tbsp.
- o Red chili pepper or jalapeno – ½, chopped
- o Cinnamon stick – ½ inch
- o Bay leaf – 1
- o Scallions – 2, chopped, white and green parts separated

Other
- o Carrots – 2, chopped
- o Tomatoes – 2, chopped

- o Fresh shitake – 2 oz. chopped
- o Avocado oil for sautéing
- o Cilantro garnish

Beef
- o Beef shank – 1.2 lb. bone in
- o Salt and ground pepper to taste

Stew seasonings
- o Beef stock – 1/3 cup
- o Coconut aminos – 2 tbsp.
- o Five spice powder – ½ tsp.
- o Coarse salt – ½ tsp.

Method
1. Season the beef shank with salt and pepper on all sides.
2. Mix well coconut aminos, beef stock, salt, and five-spice powder. set aside in a bowl.
3. Press sauté on your IP.
4. Add 1 tbsp. avocado oil and sear the beef for 3 minutes per side. Set aside.
5. Add more oil if necessary and sauté white scallion parts, bay leaf, cinnamon, chili pepper, ginger, garlic, and onion. Season with salt and pepper and sauté until fragrant. Press Cancel.
6. Scrape the bottom of the pot to remove any stuck bit.
7. Place beef on top of the aromatics.
8. Add shiitake, tomatoes, and carrots.
9. Seal and press Manual.
10. Cook on High for 45 minutes.
11. Wait 15 minutes then do a quick release.
12. Remove the beef and debone.
13. Add them back to the pot.
14. Garnish with cilantro and green scallion parts.
15. Serve over cauliflower rice.

Nutritional Facts Per Serving
- o Calories: 289
- o Fat: 7g
- o Carb: 8g
- o Protein: 40g

CONCLUSION

In this delightful Asian Instant Pot cookbook, you will learn to enjoy a variety of dishes that offer a wide range of flavors, textures, aromas, and colors. Designed for easy weeknight eating, this unique cookbook's wide range of dishes from a variety of Asian cuisines will appeal to all the home cooks. Each of these 130 recipes has been streamlined for home cooks of all experience levels. You don't have to order take outs anymore, just gather your ingredients, add them into your Instant Pot and an authentic Asian meal is ready within minutes! These recipes are sure to please picky eaters and gyoza connoisseurs alike! Impress friends and family with these satisfying and easy-to-make recipes.

Book №3

INTRODUCTION

People say money is life, but in reality, life is about scrumptious good food. Good food means a good life, and by good food, we mean healthy, luxurious and delicious Indian cuisine. Eternally delicious food involving tasty Indian spices equals incredible and appetizing dishes.

No other cuisine comes up with a wide variety of flavors like sour, sweet, spicy and hot all the same time. One of the main spices which are used in almost every dish of Indian cuisine is 'Garam Masala.' The best Dal (lentil) and vegetarian recipes use garam masala as the main spice to make it flavorful. Indian recipes have the best enviable flavors, and this is often due to the spices used to make the dishes.

India is one of those countries which have a wide variety of dishes to try and experience different flavors in all of them. This book has all the best Indian dishes which are luscious and delectable. Even non-vegetarians will find this book useful because it contains chicken, meat and Indian fish recipes.

Why should vegetarians have all the mouth-watering and succulent food? Foodies must grab this book, because it has everything you need for a palatable Indian dish. The book contains the best Indian recipes which will make you want to try them right now. Enjoy the widest variety of savory food with the best flavors of Indian spices and ingredients.

INDIAN CUISINE

India, the land of spices has a unique place in the world of culinary culture. Whenever we think about Indian cuisine, the thoughts of aromatic dishes lavishly treated with spices and herbs stay dominant in the forefront. It has a variety of mouth-watering dishes, peppered in herbs and spices, that are considered as gourmet meals all over the world.

The Dravidian and Aryan civilization has influenced Indian recipes. A lot of factors influence the Indian culinary culture and the hot weather in India is the greatest among them, enabling some of the spices and ingredients to grow.

Being a large country with different culture, faiths, and lifestyles, you can find different styles of cuisines in India. Each of these cuisines maintains its uniqueness which stands as its cultural identity.

Let us now discuss the two major divisions namely North Indian and South Indian food.

NORTH INDIAN FOOD

Northern India is known for its extreme type of climate and rainfall. Cooking style differs from each state, and the choice of herbs and spices are also very distinct. India has a significant subdivision in food like vegetarian and non-vegetarian types.

Kashmiri Food: Kashmiri dishes have a long-lasting impact of Persian, Afghanistan and Central Asian culinary styles. The culinary knowledge of Kashmiri pundits profoundly influences it. A lot of dried fruits and poppy seeds find their way into every dish you'll find there.

Mughlai Food: Since the Mughals invaded and ruled India, the country has adapted its style of having non-vegetarian dishes. Use of 'garam masala,' kewra water, and other spices are prominent in their culinary form.

Punjabi Food: There are a large variety of dishes in the culinary culture of Punjab which satiates the vegetarian as well as non-vegetarian taste buds. The use of freshly harvested sag leaves, herbs, and various lentils are quite evident. Punjabi food is relished all over the country and is readily available in the restaurants.

Gujarati Food: Gujarati food has a collection of typical lip-smacking dishes and is mainly vegetarian. In Gujarati cooking, it adopts a different style of flavors, and you will love the various blends.

Rajasthani Food: Rajasthani food is primarily vegetarian. A Rajasthani thali is well known for its delicious food and blend of spices in its curries and desserts. The usage of ghee is very much prominent here.

Maharashtrian Food: Maharashtra has its own specialty, and you will love the easy to afford and popular street food specialties like Vada-paw and Paw-bhaji. Here, any person will enjoy a filling meal at the most affordable price.

Goan Food: Anybody who loves seafood will find Goa heavenly. Goa specializes in wine and gigantic prawns with a plethora of other seafood. Cooked in authentic spices with a blend of coconut oil, the Goan food stands at a class of its own.

Bengali Food: Bengal is famous for its fish dishes. Various sea and river water fishes are available and are a regular component in every household. The usage of Panchforon (five spices) and mouthwatering sweet dishes are amongst the specialties of Bengal.

SOUTH INDIAN FOOD

The majority of South Indian food consists of – dosa, idli, vada, medu vada, rasam, uttapam, sambhar, chutney and boiled rice. Well, there are variations in the states - Andhra Pradesh, Tamilnadu, Telangana, Kerala, and Karnataka.

Karnataka Food: The food of Karnataka is mostly the same as other South Indian states. Some specialty prevails in Coorg and Mysore which are famous for their pork dishes and special dosas. The main accompaniments are the spicy pickles, curries, and buttermilk.

Kerala Food: The specialty of Kerala is the use of coconut in almost every dish. Non-vegetarian dishes have got characteristically rich spices and of course a blend of typical coconut flavor. The Malabar style of cooking will tantalize your taste buds.

Tamil Food: If you're fond of vegetarian food, then Tamilnadu must be a heaven for you. The specialties there are idli, dosa, and rasam. Try the Pongal, vada sambhar for a mouth-watering experience. If you like hot and sour, then Tamilnadu food will never fail to impress you.

Telangana Food: Telangana has its own food styles apart from the regular south Indian staple foods. Their specialty is a soup with the ingredient tamarind. You will be amazed by the unique meat dishes which have a blend of all spices, coconut milk, and Kari leaves giving them a rich flavor.

Andhra Pradesh Food: Andhra food stands very close to Telangana food as both states reflect a common culture and their meals are a staple diet for entire Southern India. Enjoy the specialty like tamarind rice, Koora and the various styles of gravy and fries with lentils.

If you travel to Andaman and Nicobar islands, you will find similar sort of dishes which are considered the main food of Southern India. Seafood is popular over there, and they use dried fruits for topping to make the dishes attractive. There are some tribal influence in the local food, and you will enjoy the authentic seafood served with traditional herbs.

India specializes in a diverse range of different styles of food. If you think of biriyani, this differs depending on whether it is done in the Malabar (north Kerala), Lucknow or Hyderabad styles. With vegetarian food, Gujrat and Rajasthan offer a fiercely competitive style. If you want a variety of fish dishes, compare and contrast those from Bengal, Kerala and other eastern states of India.

If you want an easy and affordable breakfast, South Indian dishes have no match. If you're looking for a job or business in the financial capital of the country, satisfy your belly with affordable lip-smacking street food. Indian food has rightly influenced the world for its spicy flavor and incredible rich varieties. You will have a lip-smacking time with some of the best Indian recipes throughout this book.

WHAT FOOD AND SPICES ARE MAINLY USED IN INDIAN CUISINE?

The Indian cuisine is characterized by its subtle and sophisticated use of spices and herbs to transform an otherwise standard recipe instantly. If you ask, I would say that the heart of Indian cuisine lies in the spices used. Any Indian food is incomplete without the unique blend of spice mixture. Indians not only use it to spice up their food, but they also spice up drinks and even sweets with their exquisite spices well known for its wonderful aromatics.

'Masala' is a quite common word used in Indian cuisine which is a Hindi word meaning 'spice.' So, whenever a combination of spices or condiments are mixed it falls under the general category 'masala.' Indian cuisine consists of an extensive range of spices using in both whole and ground form and often combined into a complex spice mixture.

USING INDIAN SPICES

Most of the Indian spices are dry roasted to release their aroma and essential oils contained, before they are ground (some exceptions exist like nutmeg). While some spices can be easily blended using a mortar, it is usually recommended to use a powerful spice blender to make sure that you have a thoroughly ground spice mixture as some spices can be very hard to blend to a powder form.

So here goes the popular Indian spices used in Indian cuisine.

Turmeric:

Turmeric looks similar to ginger root, but it can be identified by its bright orange-yellow color. It is used in Indian dishes for its antibacterial properties and intensive color it gives to dishes. It is mainly used in powder form for the Indian dishes.

Chili powder:

Indian chili powder is the next most common spice after turmeric, which is an essential spice made from spicy ground chilies. You can find different varieties of chilies.

Cardamom:

Cardamom is an incredible aromatic spice with a spicy sweet flavor that enhances sweet and savory dishes. Black and green cardamom are the 2 varieties commonly used in Indian cuisine. Green is the most commonly used variety that is used in lassi, chicken curry, meat dishes, and Indian desserts, etc.

hole green cardamom is used while preparing 'garam masala' (hot spices), or you can also open the pod and use the black seeds. While green cardamom is mild, black cardamom is very powerful. It's mostly just the seeds that are used when using black cardamom, and if it is used as a whole, it is recommended to remove it from the food before serving as it is very spicy and strong.

Cassia Bark:

Cassia bark is an enticing spice, commonly known as Chinese cinnamon and it is similar to cinnamon but a bit different from it. Cassia is easily distinguishable by this rough and tree bark-like texture and known for its milder flavor. Cassia bark can be used in all Indian dishes like vegetable curries and meat varieties.

Cumin Seeds:

Cumin seeds are a commonly used Indian spice in North Indian cuisine and are distinguishable by their distinctive and robust flavor. Cumin seeds should have more aroma while roasting and give a sweet flavor to dishes. It can be use either whole or in powdered form, and it is one of the main ingredients in Indian Garam masala.

Black mustard seeds:

In India, black mustard seeds are more widely used than the large yellow mustard seeds which are very common in western countries. Black mustard seeds have a strong but pleasing flavor and are well known for their digestive qualities. They can be spluttered (fried until they make a hissing nose) in oil and are using for tempering in south Indian dishes. It is an inevitable spluttering ingredient for tempering curries, vegetables and to flavor pickles.

Cloves:

Cloves are a common spice used in Indian dishes that have a medicinal and robust flavor that comes from the essential oils contained in them. Cloves are used either as whole or blended into spice mixtures. Cloves also need to be used in the right quantities as they might overpower other mild spices in a dish.

Asafetida:

Commonly known as Hing, which has a unique place in Indian cuisines. It is prominent for its digestive properties and it enhances flavor in some of Indian dishes. Not all recipes call for Hing, but it is commonly used when cooking beans and lentils, Sambhar and pickles.

Other complementary spices using in Indian dishes are;

- Coriander seeds
- Fenugreek seeds
- Carom seeds
- Fennel seeds
- Nigella seeds
- Nutmeg
- Peppercorns
- Saffron
- Bay leaves

While cooking Indian recipes, spices have to use in the right quantities to get the precise balance of taste. Some spices are extremely hot; hence their use in food should be always be kept to a moderate level. The aroma of the spices increases the flavor and taste of the food. They are healthy because the spices have therapeutic health benefits. Spices are one of the necessary ingredients of Indian recipes, which makes it unique in taste.

Chicken – Indian Style

1. Butter Chicken

Preparation: 40 minutes | Cooking: 20 minutes | Servings: 8

Ingredients:

Marinade section:

- Fresh chicken – 1½ pounds
- Fresh ginger paste - ½ teaspoon
- Garlic paste – ½ teaspoon
- Red chili powder – 1 teaspoon
- Curd – 2 cups
- Salt – to taste

Sauce section:

- Fresh butter – 6 ounces
- Pureed tomato – 1 pound
- Black cumin seeds – ½ teaspoon
- Sugar – ½ teaspoon
- Sliced green chilies – 4
- Crushed fenugreek leaves – ½ teaspoon
- Fresh cream – 3½ ounces

Cooking directions:

The first step is to marinate the chicken:

- In a mixing bowl, put red chili powder, ginger and garlic paste, curd and salt.
- Mix thoroughly.
- Now put the chicken pieces into the mix and coat with the marinade.
- Refrigerate the marinated chicken for 6 hours in a closed container.

The next step is to prepare the sauce:

- For the gravy preparation, turn on your Instant Pot in SAUTE mode.
- Add butter, when the display panel shows 'hot.'
- When the butter starts to melt, add tomato puree and sauté till the raw smell goes.
- Add cumin seeds and red chili powder.
- Now add salt as per your taste and mix it well with the butter. The whole process will take about 3-5 minutes.

- After mixing the ingredients with the butter add the chicken pieces, sliced green chilies, and crushed fenugreek leaves. Make sure it has enough liquid for cooking.
- Stop sautéing by pressing the START/STOP button.
- Close the lid and set the Instant Pot to Poultry manual mode and set timer to 5 minutes.
- When the set time elapses, wait for 10 minutes for natural release of the pressure.
- Again change the cooking mode to SAUTÉ and continue cooking for about 5 minutes without closing the lid. Make sure the sauce consistency is okay.
- Add fresh cream to the sauce before serving.
- Serve and enjoy the yummy curry with hot rice or a butter naan.

Nutritional Values:

Calories: 346.20 |Carbs: 5.2g |Fats: 26.2g |Protein: 21.8g | Cholesterol: 116.7 mg | Fiber: 0 g | Sodium: 582.6mg

2. INSTANT POT CHICKEN MASALA

Preparation: 20 minutes | Cooking: 30 minutes | Servings: 4

Ingredients:

- Chicken pieces with bone – 1½ pounds
- Medium sized onions – 3
- Tomatoes (chopped) – 3
- Green chilies – 2
- Coriander seeds – 2 tsp
- Cumin seeds – 2 tsp
- Black peppercorns – 12
- Dried red chilies – 5
- Ginger garlic paste – 2 tablespoons
- Cashew nut paste – 2 tablespoons
- Oil – 3 tablespoons
- Salt – to taste

Cooking directions:

- Select the Instant Pot SAUTÉ mode on low heat for a minute.
- Pour oil, when the display shows 'hot,' and fry coriander seeds, cumin seeds, and peppercorns for 2-3 minutes.
- Now add dried chilies and roast it for about 1 minute until it releases the fragrance.
- Stop sauté by pressing START/STOP when the fragrance emanates and allow it cool for some time.
- When the heat has settled down, grind the powder coarsely and keep it aside.

- Now put the chopped tomatoes in a blender and puree them.
- Again, keep the setting on SAUTÉ mode on high heat for a minute.
- Pour oil and when the oil becomes hot add finely chopped onions and sauté for about 2 minutes until the onion becomes soft and translucent.
- Now add garlic, green chilies and ginger paste. Stir continuously for a minute.
- Add a little water and continue sautéing for a minute.
- Now add all the ground spices and sauté for half a minute.
- Put the chicken into the mix, stir occasionally and cook for 2-3 minutes.
- Pour the puree over the chicken.
- Stop SAUTÉ mode by pressing START/STOP.
- Close the lid and pressure valve.
- Cook on high pressure for about 5 minutes.
- Let the pressure release naturally.
- Add salt, cashew nut paste, and adequate water and cover the lid.
- Select sauté mode on high heat and cook for about 15 minutes.
- Serve hot with fried rice or plain rice.

Nutritional values:

Calories: 1605 |Carbohydrates: 55.7 grams | Protein: 206.9 grams | Fat: 61.5 grams| Fibers: 18.9 grams

3. CHICKEN CHETTINAD

Preparation: 15 minutes | Cooking: 30 minutes | Servings: 4

Ingredients:

- Chicken pieces with bone – 1 pound
- Finely chopped large onion – 1
- Finely chopped tomatoes – 2
- Curry leaves – a handful
- Bay leaf – 1
- Oil – 2 tablespoons

To prepare the marinade:

- Turmeric – 1 teaspoon
- Chili powder – ¼ teaspoon
- Curd – 1 tablespoon
- Fresh ginger paste – 1 teaspoon
- Garlic paste – 1 teaspoon
- Salt – to taste

Chettinad masala (Roast and grind)

- Poppy seeds – 1 tablespoon
- Grated coconut – ¼ cup
- Coriander seeds – 1 tablespoon
- Fennel seeds – 1 teaspoon
- Cumin – ¾ teaspoon
- Peppercorns – ½ teaspoon
- Red chilies – 4 to 5
- Cardamoms, green – 3
- Cloves – 4
- Cinnamon stick – 1 inch

Cooking directions:

- Marinate the chicken with turmeric, chili powder, curd, salt, ginger, and garlic paste in a mixing bowl and set aside for 15 minutes.
- In the Instant Pot, select SAUTÉ mode low heat and press start.
- Dry roast coriander seeds and red chilies for a minute. When it starts to release the fragrance, add cardamoms, cumin, pepper, cinnamon, cloves and continue stirring for 2-3 minutes. Finally, add the poppy seeds and roast for 2 minutes. Transfer the contents into a plate.
- In the sauté mode fry the coconut for 2-3 minutes until it releases the aroma.
- Add the contents in a blending jar and make a fine powder, or you can add little water and make a paste.
- Now the masala is ready.
- To prepare the Chettinad dish, in your Instant Pot, select SAUTÉ mode low heat and heat oil for a minute.
- Add bay leaf and chopped onions and continue sautéing for about 3-4 minutes, until it becomes brown and transparent.
- Add the marinated chicken and fry for 5 minutes.
- Now add tomatoes, turmeric, salt, and chili powder.
- Add the masala and curry leaves.
- Pour 1 cup of water.
- Cancel sauté mode by pressing START/STOP.
- Close the lid and pressure valve.
- Select cooking to poultry mode high pressure for 5 minutes.
- When the whistle starts blowing, quick release the pressure.
- Now change the cooking mode to sauté low heat for 10-15 minutes.
- As the sauce thickens, we can add water for the desired consistency. Add curry leaves for a pleasant aroma.
- Serve hot with ghee rice or naan.

Nutritional information:

Calories: 570 | Cholesterol: 125 mg | Sodium: 136 mg | Proteins: 34 grams | Carbs: 13 grams | Potassium: 657mg | Fat: 42g | Dietary fiber: 5g | Sugars: 4g

4. Mughlai Zaafrani Chicken

Preparation: 10 minutes |Cooking: 40 minutes |Servings: 4

Ingredients:

- Chicken fresh, cut into pieces with bone – 2 pounds
- Soaked Saffron in milk – 12 strands
- Black pepper – 5
- Cinnamon – 1 inch
- Ginger paste – 1 teaspoon
- Garlic paste – 1 teaspoon
- Onion, sliced – 1 cup
- Soaked Cashew nuts – 15
- Kashmiri red chili powder – 2 teaspoons
- Coriander ground – 2 teaspoons
- Garam masala powder – ½ teaspoon
- Ghee – 3 tablespoons
- Oil – 2 tablespoons
- Cloves – 4
- Black /green cardamom – 2
- Salt – to taste
- Kewra essence – 5 drops
- Water – 1 cup

Cooking directions:

- Place an insert pan in the Instant Pot and select SAUTÉ mode.
- In the pan pour some oil and heat up on low temperature.
- When the pan becomes hot add onion and sauté about 4-5 minutes or until it becomes golden brown.
- Keep it aside.
- Again select SAUTÉ mode and pour oil and ghee heat at high temperature.
- When the pan becomes hot add cardamoms, black pepper, cinnamon, and cloves.
- Sauté it for 1-2 minute.
- Increase the temperature and add chicken and fry for 5 minutes.
- In a blender, add fried onions and soaked cashew nuts to make a fine floury paste.
- Add the paste into the cooking chicken and continue cooking for about 5 minutes. Stir occasionally.
- Add ginger, garlic paste with a little salt.
- Fry about 2-3 minutes till the raw smell goes.
- Now, add curd, Kashmiri red chili powder, coriander powder, garam masala powder, and salt.
- Add a cup of water.

- Cancel sauté mode.
- Cover the lid, close the pressure vent and select poultry mode and set the timer for 5 minutes.
- When the timer blows, quick release the pressure from the Instant Pot.
- Open the lid, and add cardamom powder, saffron, and essence and simmer for another 10 minutes.
- Garnish the dish with your choice and serve hot with chapatti or paratha.

Nutritional Values:

Calories: 468 | Carbs: 5g | Cholesterol: 118mg | Potassium: 364mg |Fat: 38g | Protein: 24g | Sodium: 118mg |Dietary fiber: 1g

5. CHICKEN CURRY WITH COCONUT MILK

Preparation: 40 minutes | Cooking: 30 minutes | Servings: 4

Ingredients:

Marinade section:

- Boneless chicken – 1½ pounds
- Turmeric powder – 2 teaspoons
- White vinegar - 1 teaspoon
- Black pepper powder – ½ teaspoon
- Salt – taste

For paste mix:

- Pearl onions – 10
- Garlic – 5 cloves
- Ginger – one piece
- Fennel seeds – ½ teaspoon

Other items:

- Curry leaves – 10 to 15
- Green chilies, julienned – 4
- Cubed potatoes – 2
- Chopped red onions – 2
- Tomatoes, chopped – 2 medium
- Garam masala powder – 1 teaspoon
- Cumin powder – ½ teaspoon
- Turmeric powder - ½ teaspoon
- Coriander powder – 1 tablespoon
- Red chili powder – ½ teaspoon

- Coconut oil – 2 tablespoons
- Plain coconut milk – 2 cups
- Salt - to taste

For tempering:

- Pearl onion, sliced – 2
- Coconut oil – 2 tablespoons
- Curry leaves – 6-8

Cooking directions:

- Take a medium bowl and marinate the chicken pieces by adding turmeric powder, pepper powder, vinegar and salt, and mix and keep it aside for half an hour.
- Next, crush the pearl onions, garlic, ginger, and fennel seeds and make a paste.
- Now, in the Instant Pot select SAUTÉ mode, add coconut oil and heat on medium-high temperature.
- Add chopped onions, curry leaves, and green chilies and sauté about 3-5 minutes till the onions become transparent and turn golden brown.
- In this stage, add turmeric, coriander, cumin, red chili, and garam masala powders.
- Sauté the mixture well for about 2-3 minutes, until it emanates the fragrance.
- Add the crushed coarse paste and garlic and sauté for about 3-4 minutes till the raw smell disappears.
- Now, add finely chopped tomatoes and add a little salt to make the tomatoes soft.
- Stir and continue sautéing for about 4-5 minutes to make it a paste/pulp form.
- Now, add the marinated chicken pieces and the potatoes with adequate water and salt.
- Stop sautéing.
- Close the lid and pressure valve and select poultry mode.
- Select the time to 5 minutes.
- When the timer whistle beeps, you can quick release the pressure of the Instant Pot.
- Change the cooking mode to sauté and set low heat.
- Now add coconut milk and stir well. Cook for five minutes and stop cooking.
- In another pan, you can prepare the tempering ingredients.
- Sauté coconut oil in a non-stick pan.
- When the pan becomes hot, add chopped pearl onions and curry leaves to it.
- Once the onion turns its color, pour the mixture to the chicken curry. After that, cover the curry with a lid to get the flavor. The tempering will take about 2-3 minutes.
- Serve hot with naan, chapatti, rice or bread.

Nutritional values:

Calories: 735| Fat: 54g | Cholesterol: 166mg | Carbs: 32g| Sugars: 10g| Fiber: 7g | Protein: 32g |Potassium: 1057mg | Sodium: 848mg

MEAT – INDIAN STYLE

1. INSTANT POT BEEF FRY KERALA STYLE

Preparation: 15 mins | Cooking: 1 hour & 20 mins |
Servings: 6

Ingredients

- Beef (cut into small cubes) -2.2 pounds
- Onion, nicely sliced -2 large
- Tomatoes, chopped -2 large
- Ginger paste-2 tablespoons
- Garlic paste-2 tablespoons
- Green chilies-2-3
- Coriander seeds-3 tablespoons
- Fennel seeds-4 tablespoons
- Cloves-8
- Green cardamom seeds-6
- Cinnamon-1" stick
- Black peppercorns-25

For tempering:

- Large onion- 1 (chopped finely)
- Curry leaves-50
- Coconut, (1" julienned) -1 cup
- Mustard seeds-1 tablespoon
- Sunflower/vegetable cooking oil-4 tablespoons

Cooking directions:

- Place the insert pan in your Instant Pot and set the cooking to manual SAUTÉ mode on low heat.
- When the pan becomes hot, put the fennel, cloves, coriander seeds, cardamom seeds, peppercorns, and cinnamon and start roasting for about 5 minutes.
- Stir all the spices occasionally until it gets a slightly darker color and starts to emanate the fragrance.
- Now stop sautéing and let it cool.
- After cooling the ingredients, grind it to a fine powder.
- Into a large bowl, transfer the powdered spices, and add tomatoes, ginger, green chilies, garlic paste, and sliced onions. Combine the spices.
- Now, put the meat and combine with the ingredients and keep it aside.

- Let it marinate for one hour or more.
- Now again in your Instant Pot, select the manual sauté mode.
- When the Insert Pot become hot pour in some cooking oil.
- Now add mustard seeds, curry leaves and wait until it finishes spluttering.
- After that, add the finely chopped onions to it and fry till it becomes translucent.
- Add the sliced coconut into the pan and cook so that it starts to turn a pale yellow color. All these processes will take about 10 minutes.
- Put the marinated meat and the remaining marinade into the insert port and combine with tempering mix.
- Do not add water while cooking as the meat will release enough juice/water.
- Now change the sauté mode to high heat and cook for about 1 hour. Stir occasionally, until the meat becomes brown.
- Remember, the entire dish should turn to a dark brown color.
- It is a dry dish; hence there won't be any gravy in it. So if water is there, make sure to dry it off.
- Serve hot for dinner or lunch.

Nutritional value:

Calories: 496 | Carbohydrate: 20g | Protein: 53g | Fat: 23g |Cholesterol: 149mg | Sodium: 243mg |Dietary fiber: 6g | Calcium: 106mg

2. GOAN PORK INSTANT POT VINDALOO

Preparation: 30 m minutes | Cooking: 30 minutes|
Servings: 4

Ingredients:

- Boneless pork loin roast,(cut into 1-inch cubes) -2 pounds
- Onions, chopped-4
- Vegetable oil-1/4 cup
- Dried Kashmiri chili peppers, stemmed and seeded-16
- Cinnamon stick-1 (1 inch) piece
- Cumin seeds-1 teaspoon
- Whole cloves-6
- Ground turmeric- ½ teaspoon
- White vinegar-1 tablespoon
- Whole black peppercorns- ½ teaspoon
- Fresh ginger minced- 1 (2 inches)
- Garlic minced-10 cloves
- Boiling water-2 cups
- Green chili peppers, seeded and cut into strips-2

- White vinegar- ¼ cup
- salt to taste

Cooking directions:

- Grind all the ingredients like Kashmiri chilies, cumin, cinnamon stick, clove, turmeric, and peppercorns, with an electric grinder to make it a fine powder.
- Transfer the fine spice powder into a medium bowl.
- Add salt to taste.
- Add white vinegar and combine thoroughly to make a marinade paste.
- Put the chopped pork into the marinade mix and coat the pork evenly.
- Keep the marinated pork in a closed container and refrigerate about 10-12 hours.
- For a better result always marinate for a more extended period.
- In your Instant Pot pan pour vegetable oil.
- Set the cooking to manual high SAUTÉ mode.
- When the oil becomes hot, stir onions for about 3-5 minutes until it turns translucent.
- Now add garlic, ginger and sauté about 10 minutes or until the ingredients become golden brown and the flavour starts to release.
- Now transfer the marinated pork along with the remaining marinade into the Instant Pot.
- Stir continuously and cook for about 5 minutes.
- When the pork starts to become firm, pour in some water.
- Cover the pot, stop sautéing and close vents.
- Select normal meat/stew mode and set the cooking to 15 minutes.
- After 15 minutes, allow the pressure release naturally. It will take about 20-30 minutes.
- By now the pork becomes soft.
- Open the lid and pour in ¼ cup of vinegar and add julienned chili pepper.
- Stir the dish.
- Again set the cooking to sauté mode low heat for 5 minutes.
- When the chili becomes soft, you can add salt to taste.
- Press START/STOP to stop the cooking.
- Your vindaloo is ready. If the sauce is not thick, sauté it some more time until the sauce gets the required consistency.

Nutritional value:

Calories: 264 | Carbohydrate: 9.2g | Protein: 19.7g | Sugars: 6.9g | Fat: 16.4g | Cholesterol: 54mg |Sodium: 51mg | Potassium: 454mg |Dietary fiber: 1.9g

3. Instant Pot Gosht

Preparation: 3¼ hours | Cooking: 40 minutes | Servings: 6-8

Ingredients

- Mutton (large cut pieces) - 2¼ pounds
- Garlic paste – 2 tablespoons
- Yogurt-1 cup
- Lemon juice-2 tablespoons
- Sunflower oil (or any cooking oil) – 3 tablespoons
- Garam masala- 2 teaspoons
- Cumin powder-1 teaspoon
- Coriander powder-2 teaspoons
- Turmeric powder - ¼ teaspoon
- Green chilies lengthwise cut-4
- Chopped tomatoes-2 medium
- Salt to taste
- Ginger juliennes for garnishing
- Clean chopped fresh coriander to decorate

Cooking directions:

- In a large bowl, combine garlic paste, lemon juice, yogurt, garam masala to a paste.
- Add salt to taste.
- Now marinate the mutton pieces.
- Cover the bowl and marinate for 3 hours. For a better result, you can marinate it for more hours.
- Now pour sunflower oil into the insert pan of your Instant Pot.
- Set cooking mode to manual SAUTÉ medium heat for 3-4 minutes.
- Put green chilies to the pan when the oil becomes hot.
- Continue cooking until the chilies stop spluttering.
- Now put the whole mutton and marinade into the insert pan and cook about 7 minutes by stirring continuously.
- After that, you can add the remaining ingredients such as cumin powder, coriander powder, turmeric powder, and the tomatoes.
- Stir well and continue cooking for 5 minutes.
- Pour some water over the meat.
- Press stop to cancel sauté mode.
- Cover the lid and seal the vent.
- Select MEAT/STEW high-pressure cook option for 20 minutes.
- Once the cooking time has elapsed, allow it to settle for about 20 minutes.
- Maintain the consistency that you like by sautéing or adding water.

- Once the cooking is over, garnish with coriander and ginger julienne.
- Serve hot.

Nutritional value:

Calories: 408 | Carbohydrate: 10g | Protein: 34g | Fat: 25g | Sodium: 244mg | Calcium: 87mg

4. Instant Pot/Pressure Cooker Mutton Korma

Preparation: 10 minutes | Cooking: 40 minutes | Servings: 4

Ingredients:

- Mutton or lamb - 2¼ pounds
- Yogurt-1 cup
- Turmeric - ¼ teaspoon
- Coriander powder-1 tablespoon
- Red chili powder-1 teaspoon
- Cloves- 6
- Cardamoms - 6
- Cinnamon - 2 inch
- Black cardamoms-2
- Green chili slit-1
- Pepper corn-(lightly crushed) - ½ teaspoon
- Fresh ginger garlic paste-1 tablespoon
- Salt – to taste

Other Ingredients

- Onions, sliced – 3 medium
- Oil as needed
- Strand mace or Javithri-1
- Nutmeg - ⅛ teaspoon
- Cardamom ground - ¼ teaspoon
- Ghee – 3 tablespoons
- Water – 2 cups

Cooking directions:

For marinade:

- Clean, wash and drain mutton to marinate.
- In a large bowl, put the mutton and spices such as cinnamon, cardamoms, pepper, and cloves.
- Mix the ingredients with the mutton.
- Now put the remaining spices like red chili powder, coriander powder, turmeric, red chili powder, and salt into the bowl.

- Add the green chili and yogurt.
- Mix all the spices very well with the mutton and keep it aside for at least for two hours. For better results, you can marinate it for extended hours.

Cooking procedure:

- Put some ghee over the marinade and combine it thoroughly.
- Set your Instant Pot to SAUTÉ mode low heat.
- After a minute pour in oil.
- When the oil becomes hot, put the nicely chopped onion and add a little salt.
- Stir continuously and sauté for 2-3 minutes. Adding salt will let the onion cook quickly.
- Continue cooking until the onion becomes golden brown.
- Transfer it to an electric mix, coarsely pulse the onion.
- Put the mutton and marinade into the insert pot and sauté it for about 10 minutes.
- Stop sautéing by pressing START/STOP.
- Now close the lid and seal the vent.
- Change the mode to MEAT/STEW manual pressure cook for 20 minutes.
- Don't bother to add water, as mutton and yogurt will generate the required amount of liquid for cooking.
- After 20 minutes allow it to release the pressure naturally.
- Add water if required and sauté for 4-5 minutes to boil the sauce. (You need to do this only if the consistency is too thick)
- Check its tenderness; if it is not cooked well, you can continue cooking for another 10-20 minutes until it becomes soft.
- Now put nutmeg and mace over it.
- Continue cooking in sauté mode for 2-3 minutes.
- Add ¼ cardamom power at this stage and turn off the stove.
- Allow the mutton korma to settle so that the meat can absorb the spices.
- Serve hot along with rice, chapatti or bread.

Nutritional value:

Calories: 596 | Carbohydrate: 15g | Protein: 24g | Sugars: 7g | Fat: 48g |Cholesterol: 128mg |Sodium: 464mg | Potassium: 559mg | Dietary fiber: 3g

5. Spicy Beef Curry Slow Cooking

Preparation: 15 minutes | Cooking: 4¾ hours | Servings: 4

Ingredients:

Beef and marinade:

- Beef (small cut pieces) - 2¼ pounds
- Coriander ground – 1 teaspoon
- Turmeric ground - ½ teaspoon
- Cumin ground - ½ teaspoon
- Yogurt - ¾ cup
- Salt – to taste

Curry section:

- Coconut/Sunflower oil – 4 tablespoons
- Coriander ground – 2 tablespoons
- Turmeric ground - ¾ teaspoons
- Cumin ground - 1½ teaspoons
- Onion, sliced -1 large
- Tomatoes, chopped - ¾ pound
- Cardamom ground - 3
- Garam masala-2 teaspoon
- Black pepper, fresh ground - ½ teaspoon
- Dried chilies (whole) -4
- Green chili, fresh (finely chopped) -1
- Garlic, finely chopped - 3 cloves
- Ginger, minced -1 tablespoon
- Tomato paste-2 tablespoons
- Beef stock- 2¼ cup
- Lemon juice -1 lemon
- Cilantro leaves – for garnishing.

Cooking directions:

- In a large bowl, put all the marinade ingredients, except meat and yogurt, and combine well.
- Now add yogurt and mix well forming to a paste.
- Add beef and combine well.
- Cover the bowl and refrigerate it for about two hours. You can marinade it for an extended amount of time, for a better effect.
- Now place an insert pan in the Instant Pot and set the cooking to sauté mode high heat.
- When the pan becomes hot, pour some cooking oil.

- You may add a little cooking oil over the marinated beef and start cooking for about 6 minutes.
- Now add a sliced onion into the cooking pot. Slow down the temperature to low-medium and continue cooking for about 5 minutes.
- Add in the spices like cumin, coriander, cardamom, Garam masala, turmeric, whole and chopped chilies, black pepper, garlic, and ginger. Combine the spices with a spatula.
- Again cook it for 3-4 minutes, until it starts to release the aroma.
- Add some tomato paste, lemon juice, and the stock and bring to a simmer.
- Now close the lid and the vent.
- Now set the cooking to slow mode.
- Set the timer for 5-6 hours. (You can also cook the same on high temperature by setting the pot to 3-4 hours)
- Add little salt and pepper to taste.
- Garnish with cilantro leaves while serving.
- Serve hot along with rice.

Nutritional value:

Calories: 224 | Carbohydrate: 18.5g | Protein: 29.7g | Sugars: 6.9g | Fat: 3.7g |Cholesterol: 1mg |Dietary Fiber: 2.2g | Sugars: 6.9g |Potassium: 234mg |Sodium: 427mg

Indian Fish Curry Recipes

1. Indian Fish Curry

Preparation: 10 minutes | Cooking: 20 minutes | Servings: 3

Ingredients:

- Pieces of firm white fish – 1 pound
- Powdered turmeric – 1 teaspoon
- Yogurt – 2 cups
- Olive oil – 6 teaspoons
- Cumin Seeds – 1 teaspoon
- Asafetida – ½ teaspoon
- Cloves – 2
- Grated ginger – 2 teaspoons
- Coriander powder – 2 teaspoons
- Water – 8 ounces
- Spice mixture – 1 teaspoon
- Pieces of green chilies -4
- Chopped cilantro leaves – 4 teaspoons
- Water – 8 ounces
- Salt – as required

Cooking directions:

- In a medium bowl, put fish fillets, salt, and turmeric.
- Rub salt and turmeric on the fish and keep it aside.
- Add little salt and yogurt in the bowl.
- Set the Instant Pot to sauté mode.
- Pour 2 teaspoons of olive oil and fry the fish fillets for about 4-5 minutes until its color gets changed, then keep it aside.
- Pour rest of the olive oil into the insert pot and when the oil becomes hot, add cumin seeds, asafetida, cloves, and grated ginger. Stir it well for 30 seconds.
- Add yogurt, cook the sauce and add coriander powder for 5 minutes.
- Add 8 ounces of water and sprinkle the salt, spices, mixtures, and chilies.
- Now, add in the fish and close the Instant Pot.
- Seal the vent and select manual low pressure for 5 minutes.
- After hearing the beep sound, stop cooking and allow natural pressure release.
- Open the lid and garnish with cilantro leaves.
- Serve hot.

Nutritional value:

Calories: 278 | Carbohydrate: 9g | Protein: 25g | Fat: 16g |Cholesterol: 91mg | Dietary Fiber: 2g |Sodium: 667mg

2. INSTANT POT FISH TIKKA

Preparation: 5 minutes | Cooking: 10 minutes | Servings: 4

Ingredients:

- Boneless fish – 8 pieces
- Cumin powder - ½ teaspoon
- Cooking oil – 3 tablespoons
- Lemon juice – 2 tablespoons

Marinade preparation:

- Yogurt thick – 1 cup
- Onion, grind to paste – 1 medium
- Olive oil – 4 tablespoons
- Ginger paste, fresh – 1 tablespoon
- Lemon juice, fresh – 4 tablespoons
- Garlic paste, fresh – 1 tablespoon
- Red food coloring – as required

Required spices:

- Turmeric powder - ½ teaspoon
- Cumin powder – 1 teaspoon
- Coriander powder – 1 teaspoon
- Red chili powder – 1 tablespoon
- Cinnamon ground - ¼ teaspoon
- Nutmeg powder - ¼ teaspoon
- Salt – to taste

Cooking directions:

- Clean and wash the fish. Pat dry.
- In a medium bowl put all the marinade items and combine to make a smooth paste.
- Now add the spices to the paste.
- Put the boneless fish into the marinade mix one by one and coat the paste on all sides of the fish.
- Cover the bowl and refrigerate for one hour. For a better marinade result, keep the fish in the refrigerator for more hours.

Direction for making the Fish:

- In your Instant Pot, place a steam rack.

- Pour some water below the rack level.
- Now put the marinated fish in a baking bowl over the rack.
- Close the Instant Pot and pressure valve.
- Set high-pressure cooking for 4 minutes.
- When hearing the timer beep, quick release the pressure.
- Press cancel to stop cooking and open the pot.
- Remove the fish from the steam rack.
- Add the remaining marinade and sauté for 3-4 minutes.
- Once the fish has reached the desired consistency, remove it a serving plate.
- Sprinkle with cumin powder and drizzle some lemon juice.
- Serve hot.

Nutritional values:

Calories: 134 | Carbohydrate: 4g | Protein: 1g | Fat: 13g |Sodium: 707mg | Sugars: 2g | Cholesterol: 1mg

3. Coconut Milk Fish Curry

Preparation: 10 minutes | Cooking: 15-20 minutes | Servings: 4

Ingredients:

- Fresh fish fillet – ¾ pound
- Sliced Onion – 1
- White mushrooms – 2 cups
- Butter – 1 tablespoon
- Minced ginger – 1½ teaspoon
- Curry powder, mild – 2 tablespoons
- Coconut milk, low fat – 9 ounces
- Chopped green beans – 2 cups
- Sliced carrot – ½ cup
- Oyster sauce – 2 tablespoons
- Soy Sauce – 2 teaspoons
- Water - ½ cup
- Salt – to taste
- Fresh curry leaves – for seasoning
- Mustard seeds – for seasoning

Cooking directions:

- Wash and drain the fish properly.
- Cut it into medium-large size pieces.
- Set your Instant Pot to sauté mode high.

- Add butter when you see the 'hot' display.
- When the butter becomes hot, add ginger, onion and stir it well for 4-5 minutes.
- Change the sauté setting to low and add curry powder and stir well for 2-3 minutes. Let the curry powder mix with ingredients in the pan.
- Add ½ cup of water, soy sauce, coconut milk and mix it.
- Now add mushrooms, green beans, carrot and boil the mixture. Sauté it for 10 minutes for a soft texture.
- Add oyster sauce, and fish.
- Close the Instant Pot and seal the vent.
- Set low-pressure cooking for 4 minutes.
- When the timer beeps, quick release the pressure.
- Now in a small cracking pan, put some oil and bring to medium temperature.
- When the oil becomes hot, put ¼ teaspoon mustard seeds and let it crack.
- After the mustard seed has spluttered, put the fresh curry leaves in. Let it sizzle.
- When the sizzling is over, transfer the entire things into the prepared fish curry.
- Serve hot.

Nutritional values:

Calories: 415 | Carbohydrate: 19.8g | Protein: 29.5g | Fat: 26g | Cholesterol: 118mg | Potassium: 999mg | Dietary fiber: 6.5g | Sugars: 8g | Sodium: 314mg

4. INSTANT POT FISH COCONUT CURRY

Preparation: 10 minutes | Cooking: 10 minutes | Servings: 4

Ingredients:

- Pieces of Tilapia filets – 1 pound
- Olive oil – 1 tablespoon
- Coconut milk – 12 ounces
- Onion medium size – ½
- Red chili powder - ½ teaspoon
- Coriander powder – 1 tablespoon
- Turmeric ground – ½ teaspoon
- Sliced pepper, green – ½
- Ginger garlic paste – 1 tablespoon
- Sliced yellow pepper – ½
- Cumin powder – 1 teaspoon
- Spice mixture – 1 teaspoon
- Cilantro – 3 sprigs
- Mint leaves – 8
- Lime juice – ½ teaspoon
- Mustard seeds – ½ teaspoon

- Curry leaves – 10
- Salt – to taste

Cooking directions:

- Slice onion and the bell pepper nicely.
- Select sauté mode high in the Instant Pot.
- When the display appears 'hot,' pour oil.
- When the oil becomes hot, put the mustard seeds and let it crack.
- Put the curry leaves to sizzle. All this process will take 2-3 minutes.
- Add ginger and garlic paste and cook for 30 seconds by stirring vigorously.
- Now pour coconut milk and mix carefully. Put the pieces of tilapia, cilantro and mix gently. If you stir vigorously, it can spoil the fish.
- And add mint leaves.
- Press Start/Stop to cease the sauté mode.
- Now close the lid of the instant pot and lock the pressure vent too.
- Set the pressure high on manual mode and cook for 3 minutes.
- Once 3 minutes elapsed, quick release the pressure.
- Open the lid and drizzle lemon juice.
- Serve hot along with rice or bread.

Nutritional values:

Calories: 333 | Cholesterol: 56mg | Carbohydrate: 6g | Protein: 25g | Fat: 24g | Sodium: 660mg | Fat: 17g | Potassium: 627mg | Fiber: 1g | Sugars: 1g

5. FISH MOLEE

Preparation: 10 minutes | Cooking: 30 minutes | Servings: 4

Ingredients:

- Fish (seer fish/king fish) – 1 pound
- Vegetable oil – 2 tablespoons
- Coconut milk – ½ cup
- Green chilies, sliced to half – 3-4
- Sliced onion – 2 cups
- Kashmiri red chili powder – 2 teaspoons
- Chopped ginger – 1
- Chopped garlic – 5-6 cloves
- Chopped tomato – 1 cup
- Turmeric powder – ½ teaspoon
- Black pepper ground – ½ teaspoon
- Lemon juice – 2 teaspoons
- Curry leaves – 10

- Coriander leaves, fresh
- Water - ½ cup
- Salt – to taste

Cooking directions:

- Select sauté mode in the Instant Pot.
- Wait for a minute and put curry leaves, green chilies, and onion and sauté it for 2 minutes.
- Fry the ingredients until their color changes.
- Add tomato and cook it for less than a minute.
- Now add Kashmiri chili powder, turmeric powder, ground black pepper and continue stirring. Make sure not to burn the spices. Sauté on a low temperature. The total process will take 6-8 minutes.
- When the frying fragrance emanates, pour ½ cup of water and coconut milk into the mix.
- To stop sautéing, press START/STOP icon.
- Add the fish.
- Close the lid and pressure vent.
- Select slow pressure cook for 5 minutes.
- When the timer starts to beep, quick release the pressure.
- Open the lid and add lemon juice.
- Change to sauté mode without closing the lid and cook for two minutes.
- After the beep 'cancel' sautéing and garnish with coriander leaves.
- Serve hot for dinner or lunch.

Nutritional value:

Calories: 388 | Carbohydrate: 16g | Protein: 28g | Fat: 25g | Dietary fiber: 3g |Cholesterol: 62mg | Potassium: 788mg | Sodium: 215mg | Sugars: 5g

Rice Indian Recipes

1. Chicken Biriyani

Preparation: 30 minutes | Cooking: 25 minutes | Servings: 4

Ingredients:

- Basmati rice, long grain – 3 cups
- Chicken – 2 ½ pounds
- Yogurt – 2 cups
- Water – 3 cups
- Cooking oil – 1 cup
- Ghee – 2 tablespoons
- Garlic and ginger paste- 1 teaspoon
- Red pepper – 2 teaspoons
- Biryani spices– 4 teaspoons
- Bay leaves – 2
- Chopped red onions -2
- Salt –to taste

Cooking directions:

- Prepare the marinade in a bowl by mixing garlic and ginger paste, red pepper, biriyani spices, yogurt and salt.
- Add chicken and marinate evenly.
- Refrigerate the marinade for 30 minutes.
- In your Instant Pot, select sauté mode high temperature.
- When the display appears 'hot,' add cooking oil and chopped onion.
- Sauté for 10 minutes until it becomes golden brown.
- Keep a ¼ portion of the golden brown onion in a separate bowl for garnishing biriyani.
- Pour 2 tablespoons of ghee to the remaining onion in the pot.
- Add bay leaves and half portion of the marinated chicken along with the marinade sauce.
- Combine the chicken with the onion thoroughly and also deglaze the pan with the spatula. Remove all the possible brown onions stuck to the side of the Instant Pot.
- When all the brown portions have been cleaned from the pot, add the remaining chicken along with marinade sauce.
- Press START/STOP to cease sautéing.
- Close the Instant Pot and pressure valve.
- Select manual pressure cook for 5 minutes.
- Use quick release when you hear the beep sound.

- Open the lid and gently put in the washed rice.
- Pour 3 cups of water in.
- Add salt and stir.
- Close the lid and select manual pressure cook for 6 minutes.
- When hearing the timer beep, opt for the quick pressure release.
- If the top layer of the rice is not cooked well, you may gently mix the rice to the bottom of the chicken.
- Close the lid for some time so that rice will get cooked thoroughly.
- Before serving, garnish with caramelized onion.
- Serve biryani hot.

Nutritional value:

Calories: 2080 | Carbohydrate: 232g | Protein: 137g | Sugars: 34g | Fat: 68g | Cholesterol: 399mg | Sodium: 760mg |Dietary fiber: 22g

2. Jeera Rice

Preparation: 5 minutes | Cooking: 10 minutes | Servings: 2

Ingredients:

- Vegetable oil- 2 tablespoons
- Cooking oil – 1 cup
- Cumin(whole) – ½ teaspoon
- White basmati rice -2 cups
- Water – 2½ cups
- Salt –to taste

Cooking directions:

- Wash the rice, drain and keep aside.
- Select sauté mode high in the Instant Pot.
- When the display appears 'hot,' pour oil and put cumin seeds in.
- Sauté it until it starts to splutter for 2-3 minutes. Do not let it burn or turn dark brown.
- Add rice in the sauté pan and fry it about 1 minute
- After that add salt and water.
- Pres START/STOP to stop sauté mode.
- Close the Instant Pot and seal the vent.
- Select manual low pressure for 5 minutes.
- When the timer beeps, quick release the pressure.
- Open the lid and fluff the rice and allow it to settle.
- Serve hot for good taste.

Nutritional value:

Calories: 927 | Carbohydrate: 148g | Protein: 13g | Sugars: 0.3g | Fat: 29g | Cholesterol: 0 mg |Fiber: 3g |Sodium: 166mg

3. GHEE RICE

Preparation: 5 minutes | Cooking: 15 minutes | Servings: 3

Ingredients:

- Basmati rice – 1½ cup
- Ghee– 3 tablespoons
- Onion, sliced – ½ cup for garnishing
- Sliced onion- ½ cup for rice
- Water – 2 cups
- Ginger paste - ¼ teaspoon
- Cashew – ½ cup
- Raisins - ¼ cup
- Biryani flower -1
- Sauf (fennel seeds) - ½ teaspoon
- Bay leaf -1
- Cloves - 4
- Cinnamon sticks -2 inches long
- Salt to taste

Cooking directions:

- Wash rice and drain water and soak it for 30 minutes.
- In your Instant Pot, select sauté mode high.
- Pour in ghee and when ghee becomes hot add cashews and stir continuously for 3-4 minutes to fry until they becomes golden color. Keep it aside.
- After that add raisins, and stir, until it swells up. Transfer it into a plate and keep it aside.
- Do the same process with onions and after frying them to a golden brown keep them aside on a plate. Onions, cashew and raisins are for garnishing purpose.
- In the same pan mix all spices and stir them continuously and take care not to let them burn.
- Further, add garlic paste in it stir for a while.
- Add rice to this mixture and fry for 2 to 3 minutes. Stir the mixture gently else rice will break.
- Stop sauté mode by pressing START/STOP.
- Pour in water and salt.
- Close the Instant Pot lid and seal the pressure vent.
- Select manual pressure and cook for 5 minutes.
- When the timer beeps, quick release the pressure.
- Open the lid and fluff the rice gently.
- Allow it to settle.

- Before serving, garnish it with cashew, raisins, and onion.
- For delicious and soft ghee rice, serve hot.

Nutritional value:

Calories: 585 | Carbohydrate: 91 g | Protein: 9 g | Sugars: 2 g | Fat: 20 g | Cholesterol: 38mg |Sodium: 23mg |Potassium: 335mg

4. Lemon Rice

Preparation: 15 minutes | Cooking: 10 minutes | Servings: 5

Ingredients:

- Cooked brown basmati rice -3 cups
- Kosher salt – ¾ teaspoon
- Canola oil – 2 tablespoons
- Lemon juice – ¼ cup
- Black mustard seeds - ½ teaspoon
- Cashew/peanuts - ⅓ cup
- Sliced garlic -2 cloves
- Green chili, small - 1
- Cumin seeds - ½ teaspoon
- Fresh curry leaves -10 leaves
- Chana dal, roasted (split chickpeas) - 2 tablespoons
- Urad dal (split black gram) – 1 tablespoon
- Ground turmeric – ¼ teaspoon

Cooking directions:

- In a bowl, mix salt and lemon juice. Mix until salt dissolves in the lemon juice.
- In the Instant Pot, select sauté mode high.
- When the display appears 'hot,' pour oil.
- Put mustard seed to splutter.
- After spluttering, select the sauté mode to low and add the remaining mustard seeds, chili, pepper, cumin seeds, garlic, curry leaves, chana dal, and urad dal. Sauté for about 3-4 minutes.
- Add cashew/peanuts into the pot and stir for about 2-3 minutes.
- Now press START/STOP to cease heating and add turmeric, lemon juice, and rice and mix it properly to get delicious lemon rice.
- Serve hot.

Nutritional value:

Calories: 220 | Carbohydrate: 29g | Protein: 4g | Sugars: 2g | Fat: 11g | Cholesterol: 0 mg |Protein: 4g | Fiber: 2g | Calcium: 11mg | Sodium: 170mg | Potassium: 79mg

5. South Indian Curd Rice

Preparation: 5 minutes | Cooking: 15 minutes | Servings: 2

Ingredients:

- Curd/yogurt- 1½ cup
- White rice - ¼ cup
- Brown rice - ¼ cup
- Salt to taste
- Water - 1½ cup

Vegetables for curd rice:

- Grated carrot -2 tablespoons
- Cucumber, grated – ¼ cup
- Coriander leaves, fresh – finely chopped - ¼ cup

Curd rice tempering:

- Hing (asafetida) – pinch
- Green or red chili, julienned - 1
- Urad dal (split black gram) - 1 teaspoon
- Mustard - ½ teaspoon
- Ginger crushed - ½ teaspoon
- Cumin - ½ teaspoon
- Chana dal (split chickpeas) - ¾ teaspoon
- Curry leaves -1 sprig

Cooking directions:

- Wash rice and soak it for 20 -30 minutes.
- After soaking, drain the rice and keep ready.
- Pour 1½ cup of water in the Instant Pot Cooker.
- Put the rice and add salt as required.
- Cover the Instant Pot lid and also seal the pressure vent.
- Select the high-pressure manual for 5 minutes.
- When the timer beeps, quick release pressure.
- Cool it completely and if you wish you can mash it lightly.
- Add curd to the prepared rice and mix it thoroughly.
- Press START/STOP to stop sautéing.
- Put another insert pan in the Instant Pot.

- Select sauté low and when the display shows 'hot,' pour oil.
- When the oil becomes hot, put cumin and mustard seed. When they start to splutter, add urad dal and Chana dal.
- Fry until it becomes golden brown for about 3-4 minutes.
- Soon after that add ginger, chili and curry leaves and sauté for 1 minute.
- After the curry leaves have sizzled, add one pinch of asafetida and sauté for 1 minute.
- Press START/STOP to cease sautéing.
- Add all the ingredients of vegetable for curd to the seasoning mix and stir and transfer to the yogurt rice.
- The South Indian style curd rice is ready to serve.

Nutritional value:

Calories: 310 | Carbohydrate: 49 g | Protein: 11 g | Sugars: 11 g | Fat: 7 g | Cholesterol: 26 mg | Sodium: 126mg | Potassium: 445mg | Dietary fiber: 1g

BEANS RECIPES

1. BEANS THORAN

Preparation: 15 minutes | Cooking: 13 minutes | Serves: 8

Ingredients:

- Green beans, cut into small pieces – ½ pound
- Red chili, cut into half - 1
- Green chili, cut into small rounds – 1
- Grated coconut – ½ cup
- Mustard seeds – 1 teaspoon
- Chili powder – 1 teaspoon
- Cumin seeds - ½ teaspoon
- Olive oil – 1 tablespoon
- Salt - taste

Cooking directions:

- Select SAUTÉ mode high temperature in the Instant Pot.
- When the display shows 'hot,' pour a tablespoon of olive oil.
- Once the oil becomes hot add mustard seed to pop.
- Then add red chili and stir continuously for 2-3 minutes.
- When the aroma of chili emanates, stir in green beans.
- Now add salt, chili powder, grated coconut along with cumin seeds.
- Cover and cook for 8-10 minutes in low heat.
- Once the green beans are tender, turn off the heat and serve the dish hot with rice or roti as preferred.

Nutritional value:

Calories: 85 | Total Fats: 4.2g | Net Carbs: 11.3g | Protein: 3.1g | Fiber: 0.7g | Cholesterol: 0g | Sodium: 10.9mg | Potassium: 3.1mg | Sugars: 0g

2. Spicy Green Beans

Preparation: 15 minutes | Cooking: 7 minutes | Serves: 4

Ingredients:

- Green beans, fresh, chopped into 1 inch pieces – 1 pound
- Red chili, dried and crushed – 1
- Vegetable oil - ¼ cup
- Mustard seed – 1 tablespoon
- Sugar - ½ teaspoon
- Garlic, finely chopped – 4 cloves
- Black pepper ground - ½ teaspoon
- Salt – to taste
- Water – 1 cup

Cooking directions:

- In your Instant Pot, select SAUTÉ mode high.
- When the display appears 'hot,' pour oil.
- When the oil becomes hot, add mustard seed to splutter.
- Now add chopped dry chili and stir for 2-3 minutes.
- When the chili changes its color to dark, add the chopped garlic, black pepper and stir for about 1-2 minutes until the garlic becomes brown.
- Stop sautéing by pressing START/STOP
- Pour water.
- Add the chopped green beans, salt, and sugar.
- Close the Instant Pot lid and pressure vent.
- Select PRESSURE COOK low mode for 2 minutes.
- Quick release the pressure when the timer beeps.
- Open the cover and allow to settle the heat.
- Serve hot.

Nutritional values:

Calories: 171 | Cholesterol: 0mg | Sodium: 589mg | Carbohydrates: 10.7g | Dietary Fiber: 4.7g | Protein: 2.9g | Potassium: 255mg | Sugars: 2g

3. Beans Patoli Curry

Preparation: 120 minutes | Cooking: 25 minutes | Serves: 8

Ingredients:

- Green beans – ½ pound
- Red chili – 1 teaspoon
- Chickpeas – ¼ pound
- Turmeric ground – ½ teaspoon
- Green chilis – 4
- Cooking oil – 2 tablespoons
- Cumin seeds – 1 teaspoon
- Asafetida – ¼ teaspoon
- Mustard – 1 teaspoon
- Curry leaves – 5-6 leaves
- Salt – 1 teaspoon
- Coriander leaves – 4-5 leaves
- Urad dal (black gram) – 3 teaspoon

Cooking directions:

- Start the cooking process by soaking the black gram in a medium bowl for about 2 hours.
- In the Instant Pot select SAUTE.
- Pour oil with the display shows 'hot.'
- Now, add the mustard, and let it splutter.
- After spluttering add urad dal (black gram), 2 chilies (red), cumin seeds and the curry leaves and fry it for 2 minutes until the aroma starts to rise.
- Press START/STOP and cease sautéing.
- Cut the green beans into small sizes (2cms) as needed. Remove both ends.
- Wash and drain the Bengal gram and discard the water.
- Using a grinder, mix the spices like the red chili (8), curry leaves, around 4 green chilies, cumin seeds, asafetida, salt, and turmeric powder without adding water.
- Now, marinate the chopped beans with the spice mix.
- In your Instant Pot, select SAUTÉ high mode.
- When the display appears 'hot,' put the beans with spice mix into the pan and sauté for 4-5 minutes.
- Let the beans cook for around 15 minutes to make it soft and tender.
- Once done, let it cool and mash the mixture vigorously to turn it into a dry paste.
- Cover the pan with a lid and let it cook for another 3 minutes.
- Once cooked, open the lid and garnish with chopped coriander leaves.
- Serve it hot.

Nutritional value:

Calories: 87.81 | Total Fats: 7g | Net Carbs: 5.41 | Protein: 1.81g | Fiber: 1.89g | Cholesterol: 6.79g | Sodium: 4.6mg | Potassium: 1mg | Sugars: 0.65g

4. CLUSTER BEANS FRY

Preparation: 10 minutes | Cooking: 20 minutes | Serves: 4

Ingredients:

- Green beans – ¾ pounds
- Cooking oil – 1 tablespoon
- Carom seeds, crushed – ¼ teaspoon
- Turmeric powder - ¼ teaspoon
- Asafetida – ¼ teaspoon
- Coriander ground - 1½ teaspoon
- Cumin powder – ½ teaspoon
- Chili powder (red) – 1 teaspoon
- Sugar – 1 teaspoon
- Ginger garlic paste – 2 teaspoons
- Water – ¼ cup
- Fresh coriander leaves – 2 teaspoons
- Salt – 1 teaspoon

Cooking directions:

- Wash and cut the green beans into half inch size.
- On an Instant Pot, select SAUTÉ mode high.
- Pour oil, when the 'hot' display appears.
- Once the oil becomes hot, add the crushed carom seeds, turmeric powder, asafetida, and the ginger garlic paste.
- Sauté the mixture for 2-3 minutes until it starts to release the aroma.
- After sautéing, add sugar, red chili powder and the cumin-coriander powder in the pot. Let it cook for another minute.
- Add the finely chopped beans in the pan and stir it vigorously to let the mixture cover the beans entirely.
- Add ¼ cup water in the pan as you see the dish drying up and continue to stir the mix.
- Stop sautéing by pressing the START/STOP button.
- Close the lid and seal pressure valve.
- Select pressure cooker manual high for 5 minutes.
- When the timer beeps, release the pressure naturally.
- Open the lid and stir the dish.
- The cluster beans are ready to serve.

Nutritional value:

Calories: 57 | Total Fats: 13g | Net Carbs: 2g | Protein: 0.5g | Fiber: 1.89g | Cholesterol: 8g | Sodium: 5mg | Potassium: 0mg | Sugars: 3.6g

5. Green Beans with Potatoes

Preparation: 10 minutes | Cooking: 15 minutes | Serves: 5

Ingredients:

- Green beans chopped – 3½ cups
- Potatoes – 2 small
- Cooking oil – 2 teaspoons
- Asafetida – ¼ teaspoon
- Mustard seeds – ½ teaspoon
- Garlic – 3 cloves
- Red chili powder – ¼ teaspoon
- Turmeric ground – ½ teaspoon
- Cumin ground – ½ teaspoon
- Coriander ground – ½ tablespoon
- Salt – to taste
- Water – ¼ cup
- Fresh cilantro, chopped – as required for garnishing.
- Lemon juice (fresh) – 2 teaspoons

Cooking directions:

- Wash and cut the beans in generous size by removing both ends.
- Try to keep the pieces limited to ¼ inch long or smaller as needed. The smaller the size, the quicker it will cook. However, the size entirely depends upon you.
- Peel potatoes and dice into ¾ inch pieces.
- Let us cook it in an instant pot.
- Select 'SAUTÉ' (normal) mode on the Instant Pot.
- When the Instant Pot displays 'hot,' pour cooking oil in first and when the oil becomes hot add the following ingredient like mustard seeds, minced garlic, and asafetida. Let the mixture fry for 2 minutes before adding another batch.
- Once done, add the green beans, red chili powder, ground turmeric and diced potato in the mix alongside ¼ teaspoon of salt and stir it well to let the spices absorb into the beans and potatoes. Cook it for 2 minutes.
- After a while, you may add water to the mix and close the lid. Set the timer of 2 minutes using the 'sauté' button on the pot.

- Once the time has elapsed, let the pressure release naturally for about 5 minutes and later on manually release the pressure.
- Again select sauté mode and cook the vegetables for 2 minutes.
- Once you feel the potatoes and the beans are tender enough, add the ground coriander and ground cumin and continue to stir.
- Mix it well and let it stay on low heat for extra 2-3 minutes.
- Add salt to taste and freshly squeezed lemon juice at the top.
- Press START/STOP to cease sautéing.
- Garnish it with freshly cut cilantro.
- Serve hot.

Nutritional value:

Calories: 99 | Total Fats: 2g | Net Carbs: 14g | Protein: 6g | Fiber: 0.5g | Cholesterol: 0g | Sodium: 1g | Potassium: 7mg | Sugars: 0g

DAL RECIPES

1. GUAJARATI DAL

Preparation: 10 minutes | Cooking: 20 minutes | Servings: 4

Ingredients:

- Turmeric powder - ½ teaspoon
- Tuvar dal (split red gram) - 1 cup
- Chili powder - ½ teaspoon
- Green chili paste - ½ teaspoon
- Chopped tomato - ½ cup
- Grated jaggery - 1 teaspoon
- Ginger paste - ½ teaspoon
- Boiled peanuts - 2 tablespoons
- Lemon juice - 2 tablespoons
- Chopped coriander - 2 tablespoons
- Salt- as per taste
- Water – 4 cups

For tempering:

- Hing (asafetida) - ¼ teaspoon
- Ghee - 2 tablespoons
- Mustard seeds - ½ teaspoon
- Fenugreek seeds - ¼ teaspoon
- Dry red chilies - 2 to 3
- Cumin seeds - ½ teaspoon
- Cinnamon - 1 inch
- Cloves - 2 to 3

Cooking Directions:

- Select sauté mode in the Instant Pot.
- Add the mentioned amount ghee when the pot signals 'hot.'
- Once the ghee starts to melt, add mustard seed. When it begins spluttering add fenugreek seeds, Hing (asafetida), and cumin seeds and keep stirring them continuously for a minute.
- After a minute, add cloves, dry red chili, and cinnamon stick to the pan and fry it for a minute as well.
- Stop sautéing by pressing the START/STOP button.
- Put washed tuvar dal (split red gram) in the Instant Pot.

- Add red chili powder, turmeric powder, tomato, ginger paste and green chili paste to the pressure cooker.
- Add about four cups of water and add salt to taste.
- Close the lid and also seal the pressure valve.
- Select PRESSURE COOK manual high for 15 minutes.
- When the timer beeps, go for a natural pressure release.
- Once the pressure has released naturally, open the cooker and whisk the dal.
- Add lemon juice, jaggery, and boiled peanuts to the dal.
- Before serving, mix them well.
- Garnish using fresh coriander leaves.
- Serve hot along with steamed rice or phulka (chapatti).

Nutritional Value:

Calories: 262 | Carbohydrate: 34g | Protein: 13g | Sugars: 4g | Fat: 8g | Dietary Fiber: 15g | Cholesterol: 19mg | Sodium: 55mg | Potassium: 587mg

2. Instant Pot Daal Tadka

Preparation: 15 minutes | Cooking: 5 minutes | Servings: 6

Ingredients:

- Moong dal (split green gram) - ½ cup
- Chana dal (split chickpeas) - ½ cup
- Garlic - 2 cloves
- Masoor dal (split red lentil) - ½ cup
- Cumin seeds - 1 tablespoon
- Green chili - 1 large
- Turmeric powder - ¼ teaspoon
- Extra virgin olive oil - 1½ tablespoon
- Tomato - 1 large
- Water - 4 cups
- Salt – to taste

Cooking Directions:

- On the Instant Pot, select SAUTÉ mode high.
- Pour about one and a half tablespoons of olive oil when the display signals 'hot.'
- When the oil becomes hot, add chopped garlic, cumin seeds, and chopped chili to the pan and wait until the cumin seeds pop up. It will take about 1-2 minutes.
- Now stop sautéing by pressing START/STOP button.

- In the Instant Pot mix, add washed moong dal, chana dal and masoor dal as per the mentioned quantity.
- Put the finely diced tomato to the pot and add water.
- Add salt to taste.
- Close the lid and seal the pressure valve.
- Select PRESSURE COOK high manual for 8 minutes.
- When the timer beeps, go for a natural pressure release, which is about 10 minutes.
- Open the top and mash the cooked lentils.
- Before serving, add some finely chopped cilantro above for garnishing.

Nutritional Value:

Calories: 118.9 | Carbohydrate: 15.3g | Protein: 5.5g | Fat: 4.8g | Dietary Fiber: 3.6g | Cholesterol: 0.1mg | Sodium: 479.3mg

3. Daal Makhani

Preparation: 5 minutes | Cooking: 25 minutes | Servings: 4

Ingredients:

- Tomatoes, crushed tomatoes - 14 ounces
- Dry lentils (red lentils) - 1 cup
- Fresh ginger, grated - 1 tablespoon
- Garlic, minced - 1 tablespoon
- Cayenne pepper - 1 teaspoon
- Unsalted butter - 4 tablespoons
- Water - 3 cups
- Heavy cream - ⅓ cup
- Fresh cilantro, minced - 2 tablespoons
- Fresh black pepper ground - as required
- Salt - as per taste

Cooking Directions:

- In the Instant Pot, select sauté mode high.
- When it becomes 'hot,' add unsalted butter, minced garlic, black pepper ground, cayenne pepper, and fresh ginger. Sauté for about 2 minutes, until you can feel the aroma.
- Add tomatoes and cook about 3 minutes, until it becomes soft pulp.
- Stop sautéing mode by pressing START/STOP.
- Put the mentioned amount of lentils in and pour in 3 cups of water.
- Close the lid and seal the pressure valve.
- Select PRESSURE COOK high manual for 8 minutes.
- When the timer gives a warning beep, go for a natural pressure release.

- Open the lid and mash the cooked lentils.
- Check the consistency of the mixture, and if required, cook on sauté mode low for about 5-10 minutes, depending on the consistency requirements.
- Press START/STOP to cancel sautéing.
- Stir in the cream and then garnish it with cilantro before serving.

Nutritional Value:

Calories: 263 | Carbohydrate: 18.5g | Protein: 6.7g | Fat: 19.1g | Dietary Fiber: 5.7g | Cholesterol: 58mg | Sodium: 262mg

4. Panjabi Dal Tadka

Preparation: 10 minutes | Cooking: 15 minutes | Servings: 4

Ingredients:

- Moong dal (split green gram) - ½ cup
- Arhar dal (split red gram) - ½ cup
- Oil - 2 tablespoons
- Ginger, grated - 1 teaspoon
- Onion, chopped - ½ cup
- Green chili, chopped - 1 teaspoon
- Turmeric powder - ½ teaspoon
- Chopped tomato - ½ cup
- Red chili powder - 1 teaspoon
- Lemon juice - 1 tablespoon
- Water – 3 cups
- Salt - as required
- Cumin seeds - 1 teaspoon
- Ghee - 2 tablespoons
- Hing (asafetida) - ¼ teaspoon
- Chopped garlic - 2 teaspoons
- Red chilies, dry - 2 to 3
- Fresh coriander - 2 tablespoons

Cooking Directions:

- Set your Instant Pot to sauté mode high.
- Add ghee when the display shows 'hot.'
- Put cumin seeds, chopped garlic, ginger, and asafetida and sauté for 2 minutes until the chopped garlic becomes light brown.
- Add dry red chilies sauté for 1 minute until it releases the aroma.
- Now add onion and sauté it for 2-3 minute until it becomes light golden brown.

- Now, add tomato and green chili and cook it for another two to three minutes
- Add red chili powder and turmeric powder to the pan.
- Press START/STOP to cancel sautéing.
- Put washed and drained dal into the Instant Pot.
- Pour three cups of water into the cooker and salt as per your taste requirement.
- Close the lid and seal the pressure vent.
- Select PRESSURE cook manual high for 5 minutes.
- When the timer beeps, go for a natural pressure release.
- The pressure will release naturally within 5 minutes.
- Open the top and mash the dal using the backside of a ladle.
- Sprinkle lemon juice into the pan and mix well.
- Garnish the dal with freshly chopped coriander leaves and serve hot.

Nutritional Value:

Calories: 129 | Carbohydrate: 6g | Protein: 1g | Sugars: 2g | Fat: 11g | Cholesterol: 28mg | Potassium: 168mg | Dietary Fiber: 1g | Sodium: 25mg

5. Instant Pot Dal Fry

Preparation: 2 minutes | Cooking: 15 minutes | Servings: 1

Ingredients:

- Green pepper (also known as bell peppers) - ¼ cup
- Chopped onions - ¼ cup
- Ghee - 1 tablespoon
- Diced tomatoes - 1
- Cumin seeds - 1 teaspoon
- Washed toor dal (split red gram) - ½ cup
- Onion, thinly chopped - ½
- Cinnamon - 1 teaspoon
- Garlic – 3 cloves
- Curry leaves – 6
- Green chili pepper, split sliced - 1
- Hing (Asafetida) - ¼ teaspoon
- Water – 3 cups
- Coriander leaves fresh – to garnish

Cooking Directions:

- On the Instant Pot, select sauté mode high.
- Add oil when the display shows 'hot.'

- When the oil becomes hot add cumin seeds, garlic cloves, cinnamon, green chili, asafetida, and curry leaves.
- Sauté for about 2 minutes until the garlic becomes light brown.
- Now add chopped onion and sauté for 2 minutes, until it becomes golden brown.
- Add the chopped tomato and continue sautéing for another 2 minutes.
- Put the washed toor dal in and combine all.
- Pour in water and add salt.
- Press START/STOP to cancel sauté mode.
- Close the lid and seal the pressure vent.
- Select Pressure cook manual high for 5 minutes.
- When the timer beeps, release the pressure naturally. It will take about 5 minutes.
- Open the top, add salt to taste and garnish with fresh coriander leaves.

Nutritional Value:

Calories: 196.1 | Carbohydrate: 31.4g | Protein: 7.4g | Fat: 6.1g | Cholesterol: 0.0mg | Sodium: 15.2mg | Dietary Fiber: 9.5g

VEGETABLE RECIPES

1. SOUTH INDIAN SAMBAR

Preparation: 10 minutes | Cooking: 15 minutes | Servings: 4 to 5

Ingredients:

For Sambar Recipe:

- Toor dal (split red gram) - 1 cup
- Sambar powder – 2 tablespoons
- Turmeric powder - ½ teaspoon
- Coconut, fresh, grated - ¼ cup
- Red chili powder – 1 teaspoon
- Tamarind paste - 1 to 2 tablespoons
- Salt - as per taste
- Coriander leaves - ¼ cup
- Cooking oil – 2 tablespoons
- Water – 4 cups

Vegetables: (Chop all the vegetables to moderate size)

- Drumsticks - 1 to 2
- Shallots - 12 to 15
- Red pumpkin - 3 to 4
- Ladies' fingers (Okra) - 2 to 3
- Chopped tomato - 1 medium
- Green chili - 1
- Carrots – 2
- Beans – 12-15
- Potatoes - 3

For Tempering:

- Curry leaves - 1 sprig
- Oil or ghee - 2 tablespoon
- Mustard seeds - ½ teaspoon
- Jeera (cumin) - ½ teaspoon
- Hing (asafetida) - 2 pinches
- Methi seeds (Fenugreek seeds) - 1 pinch
- Dry red chili – 1

Cooking Directions:

- Make a fine coconut paste by adding little water in an electric mixer. Keep it ready to use.
- In your Instant Pot, select sauté mode high.
- Pour cooking oil when the display illuminates 'hot.'
- Add tempering ingredients starting with mustard seed, cumin, fenugreek and sauté for 1-2 minutes.
- Now add asafetida, dry red chili and sauté for 1 minute. Let the dry red chili become dark brown to release the aroma.
- Finally, put in curry leaves and sizzle.
- Add the chopped vegetables and cook for about 2-3 minutes until the vegetables become soft. The taste and flavor of the sambar will be delicious if all of the vegetables are soft cooked.
- Now add the washed lentils, turmeric powder, sambar powder, tamarind pulp/extract, coconut paste, water, and salt.
- Combine it. Make sure the salt and tamarind are in the right quantities.
- Press START/STOP button to cancel the sauté mode.
- Close the lid and pressure valve.
- Select PRESSURE cook manual high for 8 minutes.
- When the timer blows, go for a natural pressure release.
- Open the top and garnish with fresh chopped coriander leaves.

Nutritional Value:

Calories: 187 | Carbohydrate: 32g | Protein: 10g | Sugars: 6g | Fat: 2g | Dietary Fiber: 11g | Cholesterol: 4mg | Sodium: 385mg | Potassium: 934mg

2. AVIAL (MIXED VEGETABLE) CURRY

Preparation: 15 minutes | Cooking: 20 minutes | Servings: 3

Ingredients:

- Turmeric powder - ½ teaspoon
- Water - 2 to 3 cups
- Mixed vegetables (elephant foot yam, carrot, yellow cucumber, drumstick, potato, chayote) - 2 cups
- Salt - as per taste
- Water – for cooking purpose 2-3 cups

For the Paste:

- Yogurt - ¼ cup
- Grated coconut - ½ cup
- Cumin seeds - ½ teaspoon
- Green chilies - 2 to 3

For Garnishing:

- Coconut oil - 2 teaspoons
- Curry leaves – 10

Cooking Directions:

- Wash the vegetables three – four times.
- Cut the vegetables into 3 inch long pieces.
- Put the vegetables in the Instant Pot.
- Close the lid and also the pressure valve.
- Select pressure cook manual for 4 minutes.
- When the timer beeps, quick release the pressure.
- Add the required amount of salt to the vegetables, once cooked.
- Grind cumin, green chilies, yogurt, and coconut together until it turns into a fine paste.
- Add the paste into the cooked vegetables.
- Set the Instant Pot to SAUTÉ mode high for two minutes and keep stirring.
- In another small pan, heat 1 teaspoon coconut oil on the stovetop.
- When the oil becomes hot add mustard seed to splutter.
- Next add curry leaves in the oil to sizzle.
- Transfer the entire tempering mix on to the avial.
- Pour the remaining 1 teaspoon of raw coconut oil over the avial and stir.
- The avial is ready to serve.

Nutritional Value:

Calories: 665 | Carbohydrate: 70g | Protein: 17g | Sugars: 9g | Fat: 40g | Dietary Fiber: 24g | Cholesterol: 7mg | Sodium: 541mg | Potassium: 1097mg

3. KADAI MUSHROOM CURRY

Preparation: 10 minutes | Cooking: 20 minutes | Servings: 4

Ingredients:

- Julienned capsicum - 1 large
- Button mushrooms - ½ pound
- Coriander seeds, dry roasted - 1 tablespoon
- Red chilies, roasted - 2 to 3
- Onion, finely chopped - 1 medium
- Garam masala powder - ½ teaspoon
- Ginger garlic paste - 1 teaspoon
- Tomatoes - 3 medium
- Oil - ½ tablespoon
- Kasuri methi (fenugreek leaves) - 1 teaspoon

- Salt – to taste

For Garnishing:

- Coriander leaves - 2 tablespoons
- Ginger juliennes - few

Cooking directions:

- Wash the mushrooms two to three times and cut into small pieces.
- Take the mentioned amounts of tomatoes and puree them using a blender.
- Now grind the roasted coriander and chilies into a fine powder.
- Select cooking mode to SAUTÉ high on the Instant Pot.
- Pour oil when the display appears 'hot.'
- Add the finely chopped onions and sauté for about 4 minutes until the onions turn brown.
- Add ginger garlic paste to the pan and fry it for nearly a minute or until the raw aroma of the paste disappears.
- Now add the grounded coriander-chili mix into the pan.
- Continue stirring and add the tomato puree.
- At this point put in the julienned capsicum and chopped mushrooms.
- Add about ½ to ¾ cups of water.
- Put in the required amount of salt.
- Press START/STOP to cancel sautéing.
- Close the lid and select PRESSURE cook manual high for 2 minutes.
- When the timer beeps release the pressure quickly, use the quick release option.
- Open the lid and add fenugreek powder along with garam masala powder.
- Again select sauté low.
- Stir it for about a minute and then garnish using coriander leaves.
- The Instant Pot mushroom curry is ready to serve.
- Serve hot along with naan or chapatti.

Nutritional Value:

Calories: 59.5 | Carbohydrate: 9.2g | Protein: 3g | Fat: 2.1g | Dietary Fiber: 2.1g | Cholesterol: 0.0mg | Sodium: 103.9mg

4. NAVARATAN KORMA

Preparation: 40 minutes | Cooking: 30 minutes | Servings: 5 to 6

Ingredients:

Vegetables:

- Frozen peas or shelled peas - ½ cup
- Peeled and chopped carrots - 2 medium
- Green beans - ¼ cup
- Diced potato - 1 large
- Baby corn - 8 to 9
- Chopped cauliflower - 1 cup

Other Ingredients:

- Green chilies, chopped - 2 to 3
- Onion, thinly sliced - 2 medium
- Fresh curd - ½ cup
- Ginger garlic paste - ½ tablespoon
- Garam masala powder - ¼ teaspoon
- Fresh low-fat cream - ⅓ cup
- Red chili powder - 1 teaspoon
- Turmeric powder - ½ teaspoon
- Water - 1 cup
- Ghee - 2 tablespoons
- Salt – to taste

For Paste:

- Almonds - 10 to 12
- Poppy seeds - 1 tablespoon
- Melon seeds - 1 tablespoon
- Cashews - 10 to 12
- Water - ¼ cup

For Whole Garam Masala:

- Black cardamom - 1
- Green cardamoms - 2 to 3
- Cinnamon - 1 inch
- Cloves - 3
- Mace - 2 single strands

- Bay Leaf - 1

For Garnishing:

- Peeled and blanched almonds - 6 to 7
- Ghee - 1 tablespoon
- Ginger julienne - 2 teaspoons
- Cashew nuts - 10
- Pistachios - 10
- Chopped pineapple - ½ cup
- Raisins - 1 tablespoon
- Walnut halves - 10
- Mint leaves - 1 tablespoon
- Melon seeds - ½ tablespoon
- Saffron strands - a pinch

Cooking Directions:

Preparing the paste:

1. Soak all the dry fruits in hot water for about thirty to forty minutes.
2. Later on, the outer layer of almonds must be peeled off completely before adding them into a grinder jar.
3. Thoroughly drain the other nuts and seeds mixture and then add them into the grinder jar as well.
4. Add about ¼ cups of water and grind them until they turn into a smooth fine paste.
5. Add more water if required to attain an excellent paste consistency.
6. Keep this paste aside.

Cooking the main recipe:

- Place the insert pot in the Instant Pot and set the cooking mode to SAUTÉ high.
- When the display shows 'hot,' add the mentioned amount of ghee and heat for half a minute.
- Once the ghee starts to melt, add whole garam masala and fry it for 1-2 minutes until you hear the crackling sound.
- Add the onions to the pan and sauté for about 3-4 minutes until they turns golden brown.
- Now, add finely chopped green chilies and ginger garlic paste to the pan and sauté for about 2-3 minutes, until the raw aroma disappears.
- At this point add the ground nuts-seeds paste.
- Add mentioned amounts of curd along with the nuts-seeds paste and keep stirring it on low heat for a minute.
- Then, add red chili powder and turmeric to the pan and stir for a minute.
- Add all the vegetables to the pan and stir continuously for three minutes.
- You need to keep stirring to avoid the mixture from sticking at the bottom of the pan.
- Next, add about one cup of water to the pan and season it using salt.
- Now stop sautéing mode by pressing START/STOP.

- Close the lid and also seal the pressure valve.
- Select PRESSURE cook high for 3 minutes.
- When the timer beeps, allow for a natural pressure release.
- After that, again select sauté mode high.
- Stir in cream to the mix of sauce and sauté for a minute.
- Put off the Instant Pot by pressing START/STOP.
- Sprinkle some garam masala powder over the recipe and keep it aside by covering with a lid.

Garnishing the recipe:

1. On a stovetop, put a small frying pan and heat about one tablespoon of ghee.
2. Add six to seven blanched almonds to the pan and sauté until they turn to a pale golden color.
3. Slide these almonds to one side of the pan and add ten cashews, ten pistachios, ten walnut halves and sauté until the cashews turn golden brown.
4. Add about one tablespoon of raisins and half a tablespoon of melon seeds to the pan and sauté them for a few seconds.
5. Add half a cup of chopped pineapples and sauté it for about a minute.
6. Next, add one tablespoon of mint leaves, two teaspoons of julienned ginger and a pinch of kesar (saffron) strands.
7. Sauté for a minute under low heat.
8. Pour this into the pan of Navaratan korma.
9. Serve the Navaratan korma hot with naan, tandoori roti or parathas.

Nutritional Value:

Calories: 275.2 | Carbohydrate: 21.8g | Protein: 5.3g | Sugars: 1.8g | Fat: 20.1g | Dietary Fiber: 4.2g | Cholesterol: 7.4mg

5. Vegetable Korma

Preparation: 20 minutes | Cooking: 40 minutes | Servings: 4

Ingredients:

For Paste:

- Cashews - 15
- Desiccated coconut - 5 tablespoons
- Roasted chana dal (chickpeas) - ½ tablespoon
- Poppy seeds - 2 teaspoons
- Fennel seeds (saunf) - 1 teaspoon
- Coriander seeds - ½ tablespoon
- Cloves - 3
- Cumin seeds - ½ teaspoon

- Black peppercorns - 4 to 5
- Green cardamoms - 2
- Stone flower - 1
- Capers (Marathi moggu) - 1
- Garlic - 3 to 4 cloves
- Green chilies - 2
- Chopped ginger - ¾ inch
- Water - ½ cup

Vegetables:

- Diced potato - ¾ cup
- Cauliflower florets - ½ cup
- French beans - ¼ cup
- Green peas - ⅓ cup
- Chopped carrots - ½ cup

Other Ingredients:

- Finely chopped onion - ⅓ cup
- Oil - 2 tablespoons
- Curry leaves - 7 to 8
- Diced tomatoes - ⅓ cup
- Red chili powder - ½ teaspoon
- Turmeric powder - ¼ teaspoon
- Water - 1½ cup
- Fresh curd - 2 tablespoons
- Chopped coriander leaves - 2 to 3 tablespoons
- Salt – to taste

Cooking Directions:

Preparing the Veg Korma:

1. Soak the cashews in hot water for about twenty to thirty minutes. Later on, drain and keep them aside.
2. Rinse the afore mentioned amounts of cauliflower florets and then soak in hot water for about fifteen to twenty minutes. Drain the florets and keep them aside as well.
3. Rinse the other vegetables, peel them and chop into small pieces.
4. Add all the ingredients mentioned under the paste section into a wet grinder jar.
5. Pour in about ½ cup of water and grind them into a fine paste.

Cooking the Korma:

1. Select sauté mode high on your Instant Pot.
2. Wait for the display to show 'hot,' and pour in two tablespoons of oil.
3. Put in the chopped onions and sauté for 3-4 minutes until the onions turn a light brown color.

4. Add about seven to eight curry leaves and stir them for a minute.
5. Next, add finely chopped tomatoes, ½ a teaspoon of red chili powder and ¼ teaspoon of turmeric powder into the cooker.
6. Sauté for two to three minutes.
7. Afterwards, add the finely grounded paste into the Instant Pot and stir continuously.
8. Reduce the heat setting to low and keep stirring for four to five minutes until the raw aroma of the paste disappears.
9. Later on, add two tablespoons of fresh curd and make sure it mixes well with the masala.
10. Add all the chopped vegetables and stir for one to two minutes.
11. Add one and a half cups of water to make a thin sauce.
12. Season the sauce with salt as per your taste.
13. Now, it's time to pressure cook the vegetable korma.
14. Stop sautéing by pressing START/STOP.
15. Close the lid and select pressure cook manual high for 4 minutes.
16. When the timer beeps, allow for a natural pressure release.
17. Once the pressure gets settled down, open up the lid and check the consistency of the sauce.
18. If the sauce is light, then you can simmer the vegetable korma in SAUTÉ mode for a few more minutes, without closing the lid.
19. If the sauce looks thick, then you can add a cup of water and simmer it on SAUTÉ mode for a few minutes. (Depending on the thickness of the sauce, you can add water or cook further to maintain the consistency of korma.)
20. The texture must be medium and not thin or too thick.
21. Once you have attained the desired consistency level, add two to three tablespoons of chopped coriander leaves and stir.
22. Serve hot along with chapattis or pooris.

Nutritional Value:

Calories: 279.42 | Carbohydrate: 44.8g | Protein: 15.3g | Sugars: 3.9g | Fat: 9.4g | Dietary Fiber: 8.1g | Cholesterol: 2.5mg

INDIAN DESSERTS

1. GULAB JAMUN

Preparation: 30 - 35 minutes | Cooking: 15 minutes | Servings: 8

Ingredients:

- Milk (full-fat milk) - 6 tablespoon
- Bread - 8 pieces
- Water - $1/5$ cup
- Sugar - 1 cup
- Almonds, sliced - 4
- Cardamom powder - 1 teaspoon
- Raisins - 8
- Oil - 5 cups
- Chopped almonds - ¼ cup

Cooking Directions:

- Take a pan and add sugar and water to it.
- On a stovetop, set to medium heat and keep stirring to form a sugar syrup.
- Once the sugar gets dissolved, and forms into a syrup consistency spread green cardamom powder over it.
- Take the bread on a separate plate and cut and remove the crusts. Then cut the remaining bread into small pieces.
- Pour the mentioned quantity of milk all over the pieces and make it into a dough.
- You need to add milk slowly to create a dough-like texture with the bread.
- Now with the bread dough, make small rounded balls.
- Flatten the dough and put almonds and raisins in and again make it a ball.
- Set the Instant Pot to SAUTÉ low.
- When the display shows 'hot,' pour in oil and wait for it to sizzle.
- Add the rounded ball dough to the oil and fry it.
- When the dough ball becomes slightly brown increase the temperature to high and continue with the frying process, until it becomes golden brown.
- Press START/STOP for stopping the sautéing.
- Now remove it from the pan.
- Put it directly into the Gulab Jamun syrup already prepared.
- Keep the Gulab Jamun on low heat for about 5 minutes.
- The more the Gulab Jamun rest on the sugar syrup, it will have a better taste.
- Garnish the Gulab Jamun with dry fruits.

Nutritional Value:

Calories: 230 | Carbohydrate: 40g | Protein: 3g | Sugars: 28g | Fat: 7g | Dietary Fiber: 1g | Cholesterol: 1mg | Sodium: 175mg | Potassium: 72mg

2. Instant Pot Gajar Halwa

Preparation: 15 minutes | Cooking: 30 minutes | Servings: 3

Ingredients:

- Milk - 2½ cups
- Grated carrots - 2¼ pounds
- Sugar - 8 tablespoons
- Chopped cashews - 8 to 10
- Chopped almonds – 8-10
- Pistachios, chopped - 7 to 8
- Cardamom powder – ½ teaspoon
- Saffron – a pinch
- Ghee/oil - 3 to 4 tablespoons

Cooking Directions:

1. Prepare the carrots after washing thoroughly.
2. Peel the skin and grate the carrots.
3. Set your Instant Pot to SAUTÉ mode high.
4. Wait for the 'hot' display to appear, pour in ghee and the carrot.
5. Cook for about 3 minutes by covering the lid.
6. Press START/STOP to cease sautéing.
7. Now add milk, close the lid and vent.
8. Select PRESSURE COOK manual high for 5 minutes.
9. After hearing the beeping, do a quick pressure release.
10. Open the lid and add cardamom, sugar, cashews, almonds, pistachios, saffron and raisins.
11. Mix in all the ingredients.
12. Select SAUTÉ mode high and cook for 6-7 minutes until the gajar halwa thickens.
13. Keep stirring the mixture until it turns dry.
14. Now add the dry fruits and cook for about 5 minutes.
15. Serve cold.

Nutritional Value:

Calories: 188 | Carbohydrate: 32g | Protein: 5g | Sugars: 27g | Fat: 8g | Dietary Fiber: 2g | Cholesterol: 5mg | Sodium: 158mg | Potassium: 450mg

3. Sweet Pongal

Preparation: 5 minutes | Cooking: 25 minutes | Servings: 5

Ingredients:

- Yellow moong dal (split yellow gram) - ¼ cup
- Rice - ½ cup
- Ghee - 2 tablespoons
- Chopped jaggery - 1 cup
- Nutmeg - a pinch
- Cardamom powder - ½ teaspoon
- Raisins - 2 tablespoons
- Broken cashew nuts - 2 tablespoons
- Water - 3¼ cups

Cooking directions:

1. Set Instant Pot to SAUTE mode high.
2. Put the yellow moong dal and rice into it when the display shows 'hot.'
3. Sauté it for about four minutes.
4. Press START/STOP and cancel the sautéing.
5. After cooling the roasted ingredients, wash the dried items and strain it.
6. Put the strained yellow moong dal-rice mixture along with three cups of water in the Instant Pot.
7. Close the lid and pressure valve.
8. Now select RICE mode on the Instant Pot.
9. When the timer beeps, allow it to release the pressure naturally.
10. Once the pressure has settled down, open up the lid and mash the dal and rice using a spoon. Keep it aside.
11. Now on the stovetop place a non-stick pan and heat about ¼ cups of water in it.
12. Add one tablespoon of ghee and jaggery to the pan and cook it on medium heat for about two minutes.
13. Keep stirring the mixture continuously.
14. Add the yellow moong dal and rice mixture to the pan, along with nutmeg powder and cardamom powder.
15. Mix them and cook it on medium temperature for two to three minutes.
16. Keep them aside.
17. Put another nonstick pan on stovetop and heat on medium temperature.
18. When the pan becomes hot add one tablespoon of ghee.
19. Sauté raisins and cashews in it for two minutes.
20. Add these fried cashews and raisins to the prepared mix, and the Sweet Pongal is ready to serve.

Nutritional Value:

Calories: 272 | Carbohydrate: 48.7g | Protein: 3.8g | Fat: 6.9g | Dietary Fiber: 1.4g | Cholesterol: 0mg | Sodium: 2.1mg

4. Kaju Barfi

Preparation: 15 minutes | Cooking: 10 minutes | Servings: 20

Ingredients:

- Sugar - ½ cup
- Water - ½ cup
- Cashew nuts, broken - 1 cup
- Ghee - 2 tablespoons
- Cardamom powder - ½ teaspoon

Cooking Directions:

1. Prepare the cashew nuts by blending in a mixer.
2. On your Instant Pot, select sauté mode high.
3. Add sugar and water to the pan. Sauté for about three minutes.
4. Keep stirring it.
5. Once the sugar forms to syrup consistency, add the blended cashew powder into it.
6. Mix it well together and cook it on medium temperature for two minutes, by continuously stirring it.
7. Afterward, add cardamom powder and mix well for about 2 minutes.
8. Press START/STOP to cancel sautéing.
9. Take a plate and spread melted ghee.
10. Transfer the mixture to the plate and spread evenly.
11. Let the mixture cool for about two to three minutes.
12. Once the heat settled down, cut it into eight equal diamond size pieces.
13. Serve hot or cold.

Nutritional Value:

Calories: 48 | Carbohydrate: 5.7g | Protein: 1.1g | Fat: 2.3g | Dietary Fiber: 0.1g | Cholesterol: 0mg | Sodium: 0.6mg

5. Paal Payasam (South Indian Dessert in Milk)

Preparation: 5 minutes | Cooking: 13 minutes | Servings: 4

Ingredients:

- Long grained rice (basmati) - ¼ cup
- Full fat milk - 4½ cups
- Saffron - ¼ teaspoon
- Warm full-fat milk - ¼ cup
- Cardamom powder - ½ teaspoon
- Sugar - ½ cup

Cooking Directions:

1. The long-grained rice must be soaked in water for about thirty minutes and then drained. Keep this aside.
2. On your Instant Pot, select SAUTÉ mode low.
3. When the display shows 'hot,' add milk and warm for about 3-4 minutes.
4. Combine saffron to the milk.
5. Press STOP/START to stop sautéing.
6. Put the drained rice to the Instant Pot with saffron mixed milk.
7. Add sugar and cardamom powder.
8. Stir all the ingredients.
9. Close the lid and seal the pressure vent.
10. Select PORRIDGE mode high pressure for 20 minutes.
11. When the timer beeps, go for a quick pressure release.
12. Open the lid and mix the dessert.
13. Serve hot or cold.

Nutritional Value:

Calories: 408 | Carbohydrate: 43.4g | Protein: 10.9g | Fat: 15.5g | Dietary Fiber: 0.4g | Cholesterol: 38mg | Sodium: 45.7mg

SOUP RECIPES

1. TOMATO SOUP

Preparation: 25 minutes | Cooking: 20 minutes | Servings: 4

Ingredients:

- Finely chopped onion - 1 small
- Tomato - 4 large
- Bay Leaf - 1
- Garlic cloves - 2 to 3
- Butter - 1 tablespoon
- Corn starch (corn flour + water) - 1 teaspoon
- Water - 1 cup
- Sugar - ½ tablespoon
- Cream - 1 tablespoon
- Powdered black pepper - as per taste required
- Bread - 1 or 2 slices
- Salt – to taste
- Water – 6 cups

Cooking Directions:

Preparing tomato puree:

- Wash tomatoes and remove the stems.
- Select SAUTÉ high on your Instant Pot.
- After seeing 'hot' display add about 6 cups of water.
- Add a teaspoon of salt and bring to boil.
- Once the water starts to boil add the tomatoes.
- Press START/STOP to cancel sautéing.
- Close the pot using a lid.
- Let the tomatoes stay in hot water for about twenty to thirty minutes
- Later on, drain the water and let the tomatoes cool down.
- During this waiting period, you can finely chop the garlic and onions and keep it aside.
- Once the tomatoes cool down, peel the outer part and slice down the eye part as well.
- Add the tomatoes to a blender jar and blend them until the tomatoes turn into a thick texture.
- Keep this thick and smooth puree aside.

Bread toasting:

- Bread can toast using a frying pan.

- For that select SAUTÉ mode low on your Instant Pot.
- Place bread when you see the 'hot' display.
- Toast the bread for about 1 minute by flipping until it turns brown or becomes crisp on both sides.
- Press START/STOP to cancel sautéing.
- Once the bread is toasted, slice the toast into strips for easy dipping.

Making tomato soup:

- Take about one teaspoon of cornflour and mix it well with two tablespoons of water to bring a smooth paste of cornstarch.
- Now on your Instant Pot, select SAUTÉ mode low.
- Put in 1 tablespoon of butter when 'hot' appears on the display.
- When the butter starts to melt, add a bay leaf and sauté for 1 minute.
- Later on, add finely chopped garlic to the pan and sauté 1 or 2 minutes.
- Add finely chopped onions to the pan and sauté for 3-4 minutes until it turns translucent.
- After a few seconds, add the blended tomato puree to the pot.
- Keep stirring the puree for a minute and then add water, pepper, and salt.
- Keep the temperature on a low heat for about 5-8 minutes and wait until the soup reaches a boiling stage.
- Add the prepared cornflour paste to the soup.
- Stir it well together and simmer the soup for about three to four minutes or until the soup attains a thick texture.
- Add sugar to the soup and stir.
- Now, add 1 tablespoon of cream into the soup and simmer it for a minute.
- Turn off the heat and pour the hot tomato soup into a soup bowl.
- Put the toasted bread pieces into the soup.
- Garnish the tomato soup with coriander leaves.
- The soup is ready to serve.

Nutritional Value:

Calories: 72.6 | Carbohydrate: 61.3g | Protein: 1.9g | Sugars: 9.8g | Fat: 0.7g | Dietary Fiber: 1.5g | Cholesterol: 0.0mg | Sodium: 667mg | Potassium: 277mg

2. BEETROOT CARROT GINGER SOUP

Preparation: 10 minutes | Cooking: 60 minutes | Servings: 4

Ingredients:

- Olive oil - 1 tablespoon
- Beetroot - 1 pound

- Carrots, coarsely chopped - 1 pound
- Finely chopped onion - 1 cup
- Ginger, fresh, minced - 1 tablespoon
- Water - 6 cups
- Minced garlic - 1 large clove
- Sour cream - 4 teaspoons
- Orange rind - 1 teaspoon
- Ground black pepper - as per taste required
- Salt - if required

Preparing Directions:

- Wash and peel the outer layers of beetroots and chop into large chunks.
- Discard the greens.
- On your Instant Pot, select SAUTÉ mode high.
- When the display illuminates 'hot,' add olive oil.
- Now stir in chopped onions until it turns light brown for 2 minutes.
- Add ginger, carrots, and garlic to the skillet and sauté for 2 minutes.
- Press STOP/START to cease sautéing.
- Add water and diced beetroots to the Instant Pot.
- Add orange rind to the soup and continue stirring.
- Cover the Instant Pot and also seal the pressure vent.
- Select PRESSURE COOK high for 5 minutes.
- After the beep, quick release the pressure.
- Transfer the mix to a blender and puree the soup.
- Taste the soup and add seasoning as per your taste required.
- If you prefer salt, add some salt.
- Garnish with sour cream.
- The soup is ready to serve hot.

Nutritional Value:

Calories: 141 | Carbohydrate: 25g | Protein: 2.4g |Fat: 3.8g | Dietary Fiber: 6.2g | Cholesterol: 0.0mg | Sodium: 1608.9mg

3. MUTTON SHORBA

Preparation: 10 minutes | Cooking: 40 minutes | Servings: 5

Ingredients:

- Mutton ribs - ½ pound
- Finely chopped onion - 1 large
- Cloves - 5

- Cinnamon stick - 1 inch
- Pepper powder - 1 tablespoon
- Ginger – 1 tablespoon
- Garlic paste – 1 tablespoon
- Red chili powder - 1 teaspoon
- Cumin powder - 1 teaspoon
- Oil - 2 tablespoons
- Finely chopped mint leaves - ¼ cup
- Finely chopped coriander leaves - ½ cup
- Lemon - 2 slices
- Salt - as per taste
- Water – 4 cups

Preparing Directions:

1. Set cooking to SAUTÉ mode high on your Instant Pot.
2. When the display 'hot' illuminates, add oil and chopped onions.
3. Sauté it for a minute or until the onions turn light brown.
4. Now, add cumin, pepper, and red chili powders to the pan and sauté them for a minute.
5. Add ginger, and garlic paste along with a pinch of turmeric powder. Sauté for 3 minutes.
6. Afterward, add crushed cinnamon, and cloves and continue sautéing.
7. Pour 4 cups of water and mutton.
8. Add salt as required and stir the soup.
9. Press START/STOP for canceling the sauté mode.
10. Close the lid and pressure valve.
11. Select SOUP mode high pressure.
12. When the alarm beeps allow natural pressure release.
13. Open the lid and carefully transfer the mutton to a plate.
14. After cooling remove the meat from the bone and put it back to the cooker.
15. Add coriander leaves, mint and select SAUTÉ low for 5 minutes.
16. Press START/STOP to cancel sautéing.
17. Your soup is ready to serve.

Nutritional Value:

Calories: 274 | Carbohydrate: 10g | Protein: 27g | Sugars: 0g | Fat: 14g | Dietary Fiber: 0g | Cholesterol: 0.0mg | Sodium: 1705mg | Potassium: 0mg

4. Instant Pot Lentil Soup

Preparation: 10 minutes | Cooking: 25 minutes | Servings: 4

Ingredients:

For Moong Dal Puree:

- Chopped onions - ½ cup
- Carrot - ¼ cup
- Yellow moong dal - 3 tablespoons

Other Ingredients:

- Oil - 2 teaspoon
- Corn flour - ½ tablespoon
- Chopped garlic - ½ teaspoon
- Chopped onions - ½ cup
- Cooked barley - 2 tablespoons
- Chopped celery - 2 tablespoons
- Salt – as required
- Water – 2¼ cups

Preparing Directions:

For Moong Dal Puree:

- Wash the moong dal and then soak it in water for about two to three hours.
- Afterwards, drain the water from the moong dal and combine it with carrots and onions in an Instant Pot Cooker.
- Add two cups of water to the cooker.
- Close the lid and seal the pressure valve.
- Set pressure cooking manual high mode for 15 minutes.
- After beeping allow it cool naturally for 10-15 minutes.
- Wait until the steam escapes and then open the pressure cooker.
- Allow the cooked dal mix to cool and then blend it using a mixer to form a fine puree.

Preparing the soup:

1. Take cornflour and mix it with ¼ cup of water in a separate bowl.
2. Now, set your Instant Pot to sauté high.
3. When 'hot' appears on the display add garlic, onions, and celery to the pan and sauté it on medium temperature for a minute.
4. Later on, add the dal puree to the pan and mix it well.
5. Change the sauté mode to low and let the soup cook on low heat for about 2-3 minutes until it boils.

6. Keep stirring the soup occasionally to avoid lumps forming.
7. Add salt, barley, previously mixed cornflour mixture, and pepper to the soup.
8. Mix them well and cook it under low heat for 5 minutes till it simmers.
9. Press start/stop to cease sautéing.
10. The soup is ready to serve hot.

Nutritional Value:

Calories: 106 | Carbohydrate: 16.2g | Protein: 3.9g | Fat: 2.8g | Dietary Fiber: 1.7g | Cholesterol: 0.0mg | Sodium: 5.5mg

5. Curried Chicken Soup

Preparation: 10 minutes | Cooking: 30 minutes | Servings: 4

Ingredients:

- Chicken breast - ½ pound
- Garlic - 1 clove
- Finely diced onion - 1 large
- Finely diced ginger - 2 inches
- Canola oil - 2 tablespoons
- Curry powder - 1 teaspoon
- Cayenne pepper – 1 teaspoon
- Cloves - 2
- Chicken stock - 2½ cup
- Whipping cream - ½ cup
- Cornstarch - 2 teaspoons
- Red lentils - ½ cup
- Cilantro - as required for garnishing
- Black sesame seeds – ¾ teaspoon

Preparing Directions:

- In your Instant Pot, select sauté mode low.
- Wait for 'hot' to appear on the display and add some oil to heat it.
- Sauté the diced vegetables for 3-4 minutes.
- Add chicken to the pan and sauté it for about two to three minutes.
- Sauté with cayenne pepper, salt, cloves, and curry powder for 2-3 minutes.
- Stir in the cream for 3 minutes.
- After that, pour the stock into the pan.
- Bring to boiling and then slow the temperature and simmer for about fifteen minutes.
- For improving the consistency of the soup, add cornstarch.
- Press start/stop for canceling the sauté mode.

- Splutter sesame seeds in a little oil in a pan and spread over the soup for tempering.
- Garnish with cilantro.
- Serve hot.

Nutritional Value:

Calories: 390 | Carbohydrate: 29g | Protein: 25g | Fat: 20g | Dietary Fiber: 10g | Sodium: 300mg

Keto Indian Recipes

1. Keto Mutton Masala

Preparation: 2 hours | Cooking: 50 minutes | Servings: 4

Ingredients:

For Marinating:

- Mutton with bones – 1 pound
- Chili powder – 1 teaspoon
- Turmeric powder – 1 teaspoon
- Yogurt – 3 tablespoons
- Salt: to taste

For Ghee Roast:

- Onion, finely sliced – 1 small
- Coriander powder – 1 teaspoon
- Ghee – 3 tablespoon
- Cumin powder – 1 teaspoon
- Cloves – 3 or 4 pods
- Cinnamon – 1 stick
- Black cardamom – 2 pods
- Bay leaves – 1
- Ginger garlic paste – 1 tablespoon
- Tomatoes (pulped to paste) – 2
- Garam masala powder – 1 teaspoon
- Peppercorns – 4 or 5
- Water – 1¼ cups

Cooking directions:

For Marinating:

1. Put the mutton in a bowl and add the marinade mix.
2. Rub the mix thoroughly with the mutton and refrigerate for two hours for better 341argination.

For Ghee Roast:

1. In the Instant Pot, select sauté mode high and wait for half second for 'hot' to appear on the display.

2. Add ghee to melt and add spices.
3. Sauté it for 2-3 minutes until it starts to produce the aroma.
4. Turn the heat to low and add onion and keep stirring them slowly for about 3-4 minutes, until they turn soft.
5. Add the mentioned amount of ginger garlic paste and cook it together for about two to three minutes. Stir continuously; otherwise, it will stick in the cooker.
6. Later on, add the mutton that has been marinated previously to the Instant Pot and roast it for about five minutes until the meat changes its color
7. When the mutton changes its color, add cumin, garam masala, and coriander powder. Mix them well and cook for about five minutes. Stir continuously.
8. Add tomatoes as a pulp (cut two small tomatoes and grind them to make a paste). Mix them well for five minutes. (Alternatively, you can mash the tomatoes in the cooker. When the tomatoes become soft after cooking, you can mash them with a spoon/spatula)
9. Press start/stop to cancel sautéing.
10. Add water until the mutton gets thoroughly covered.
11. Close the Instant Pot lid and seal the pressure vent.
12. Set pressure cook high manual mode for 25 minutes.
13. After hearing the timer beep, allow it to do a natural pressure release. It will take about 10-20 minutes.
14. Open the cooker and garnish the mutton with finely chopped coriander leaves.
15. Serve hot. Ideal to serve with nan/bread or rice.

Nutritional Value:

Calories: 330 | Carbohydrate: 8g | Protein: 28.7g | Sugars: 3.9g | Fat: 330g | Cholesterol: 80mg | Sodium: 1285mg | Dietary fiber: 1.8g

2. KETO INSTANT POT PANEER BHURJI

Preparation: 5 minutes | Cooking: 25 minutes | Servings: 3

Ingredients:

- Cottage cheese or Paneer - ½ pound
- Butter or Ghee - 2 tablespoons
- Coriander powder - 1 teaspoon
- Turmeric, grounded - ½ teaspoon
- Tomato - ½ cup
- Onion (finely sliced) - ½ cup
- Capsicum or Green Pepper (julienned) – 2
- Ginger, fresh, finely chopped - ½ tablespoon
- Cheddar cheese - 1¾ ounce
- Finely chopped garlic - ½ tablespoon
- Chili (julienned) - 1

- Cumin seeds - 1 teaspoon
- Kashmiri red chili powder - ½ teaspoon
- Salt - as per taste required
- Fresh coriander leaves (chopped) - for seasoning

Cooking Directions:

1. In a medium bowl, grate the paneer.
2. Select sauté mode in your Instant Pot.
3. Wait for the display to appear as 'hot.'
4. Add butter/ghee when the pan becomes hot.
5. Now, add the sliced onion and sauté it for 4-5 minutes until it becomes translucent.
6. Add cumin seeds to the pan and keep stirring for two minutes.
7. Add garlic, ginger and green chili and fry them all together for 1 minute until the fragrance emanates.
8. Now add chili powder, turmeric and coriander powder and stir continuously for 2-3 minutes.
9. When the spices become dry and roasted, add the chopped tomatoes.
10. Cover up the pan and let it cook on a low heat for about five to six minutes. Don't forget to stir occasionally.
11. Add the paneer, green pepper and salt to the pan
12. Add cheese and let it cook for about three to four minutes
13. Finally, add fresh coriander and one tablespoon of butter to the pan. Sauté for 2 minutes.
14. Stop/Cancel sauté to cease cooking.
15. Stir them well and serve it hot.

Nutritional Value:

Calories: 463 | Carbohydrate: 4g | Protein: 22g | Fat: 39g | Fiber: 1g

3. Spiced Mustard Greens

Preparation: 5 minutes | Cooking: 15 minutes | Servings: 6

Ingredients:

Greens:

- Finely chopped Mustard green leaves - 6 cups
- Finely chopped spinach - 4 cups
- Green chilies, chopped – 2

For Masala Seasoning:

- Coarsely chopped onion - 1 medium
- Butter or ghee - 2 teaspoons
- Ginger garlic paste - 2 tablespoons

- Turmeric powder - ½ teaspoon
- Coriander powder - 3 teaspoons
- Garam masala - 1 teaspoon
- Red chili powder - ½ teaspoon
- Cumin seeds - 1 teaspoon
- Water - ¾ cups
- Corn flour - 2 tablespoons
- Salt - 1 teaspoon or as per taste required

Cooking Directions:

For preparing the greens:

1. Rinse and wash spinach leaves and mustard greens to remove any dirt.
2. Afterward, remove the stems from the mustard greens and spinach.
3. Finely chop it and keep ready to cook.
4. Add chopped green chilies.
5. Now microwave them together for about two minutes.
6. Take a hand blender and puree the greens to an excellent consistency as required.

For preparing the masala:

1. Set Instant Pot to sauté mode.
2. When the display shows 'hot,' add ginger garlic paste to the pot and sauté it for about thirty seconds.
3. Later on, add coarsely chopped onions and sauté them for thirty seconds.
4. Finally, add spices, salt, and water.
5. Stir them well together and then press the SAUTE button again to cancel the operation.
6. Close the lid and set the valve to a sealing position
7. Set pressure cook manual high for about two minutes.
8. After two minutes, quick release the pressure.
9. Open up the lid after the pressure has released completely.
10. Turn on the SAUTE button.
11. Add finely ground cornmeal and sauté it for about one minute.
12. Add a little amount of water as per the required consistency.
13. Add pureed greens and sauté them for about two minutes
14. Once the flavors set together, the recipe is ready to serve.
15. Serve hot with nan or bread.

Nutritional Values:

Calories: 61 | Carbohydrate: 8g | Protein: 2g | Sugars: 2g | Fat: 2g | Cholesterol: 4mg | Sodium: 472mg | Fiber: 3g |Potassium: 365mg |Fiber: 3g

4. Keto Indian Lamb Curry

Preparation: 15 minutes | Cooking: 1 hour 20 minutes | Servings: 14

Ingredients:

For Marination:

- Olive oil - 2 tablespoons
- Coriander powder - 2 teaspoons
- Turmeric ground - 1 teaspoon
- Finely chopped ginger - 2 teaspoons
- Cumin powder - 2 teaspoons
- Crush garlic - 3 cloves
- Onion powder - 1 teaspoon
- Cardamom fine powder - 1 teaspoon
- Paprika ground - 1 teaspoon
- Kashmiri chili powder - 1 teaspoon

For Curry:

- Lamb shoulder (chopped) - 4 pounds
- Ghee - 3 tablespoons
- Diced onion - 1 medium
- Heavy cream - 1 cup
- Cinnamon ground - 1 teaspoon
- Kashmiri chili powder - 1 teaspoon
- Pepper - 1 teaspoon
- Flaked almonds - 1/2 cup
- Roughly chopped cilantro - 3 tablespoons
- Salt – to taste

Cooking Directions:

For Marination:

1. Put all marinade ingredients in a medium size bowl and mix them well.
2. Add chopped lamb to the ingredients and mix them.
3. Keep the marinated lamb in a fridge for about one hour. The marination can also be refrigerated overnight. If you can marinate for a longer time, it will give a better marinade effect.

For Curry:

1. Select sauté mode high on your Instant Pot.
2. When the display turns 'hot,' add ghee.

3. Once the ghee completely melts down, add cinnamon, onion and chili powder. Sauté it for about 2-3 minutes.
4. Add marinated lamb, pepper, and salt and stir them all together.
5. Stop sautéing.
6. Close the lid and pressure vent of the Instant Pot.
7. Select manual pressure cook for 20 minutes.
8. When the timer beeps, allow it to release the pressure naturally.
9. Open the lid and add heavy cream.
10. Sauté it without the lid for about 6 minutes.
11. Add flaked almonds and stir them well with the sauce.
12. Garnish the curry with coriander leaves.
13. Serve hot.

Nutritional Values:

Calories: 480 | Carbohydrate: 2g | Protein: 30g | Sugars: 0.2g | Fat: 38g | Cholesterol: 150mg | Sodium: 586mg | Fiber: 1g | Potassium: 380mg

5. Keto Indian Butter Chicken

Preparation: 25 minutes | Cooking: 35 minutes | Servings: 4

Ingredients:

For Spice Mixing:

- Black pepper ground - ¼ teaspoon
- Mix garam masala powder - 1½ tablespoons
- Cumin ground - 1 teaspoon
- Coriander powder - ½ teaspoon
- Turmeric - 1/2 teaspoon
- Fenugreek - ¼ teaspoon
- Cinnamon - ¼ teaspoon

For Chicken Marination:

- Chicken breast, boneless and skinless – 1 pound
- Spice mix powder - ¾ (Use from the 2 tablespoons)
- Fresh lemon juice - 2 tablespoons
- Crushed garlic - 2 large cloves
- Sour cream - 3 tablespoons
- Salt: ½ teaspoon

For Sauce:

- Butter - 4 tablespoons

- Diced onion - 1 medium
- Grated fresh ginger - 1 inch
- Crushed garlic - 3 large
- Crushed red pepper flakes - ¼ teaspoon
- Chicken bone broth - 1½ cup
- Tomato paste - 4 tablespoons
- Remaining spice mix - ¾ tablespoon
- Whipping cream - ½ cup
- Salt - ½ teaspoon

For Serving:

- Sliced red onions – For garnishing
- Cilantro leaves – Few as required

Cooking Directions:

1. In a medium bowl mix all the spice powders and keep ready.
2. In another large bowl, mix all the ingredients mentioned under the chicken section with the chicken.
3. Cover them up and refrigerate for about two hours. For a better marinade effect, refrigerate for a more extended period.

Preparing the sauce:

1. In your Instant Pot select sauté mode high.
2. When the display shows 'hot,' add ghee and onion.
3. Keep stirring for about 3 minutes until the onion turns brown
4. Stir in ginger, garlic and the ¾ tablespoon spice mix to the insert pan and continue sautéing for about one minute.
5. Later on, add crushed red pepper flakes, salt, and tomato paste. Continue stirring for 2 minutes.
6. Now add chicken broth.
7. Bring them all to a boiling state and then reduce the heat to simmer.
8. Let it cook for about ten minutes.
9. After that turn off the Instant Pot.
10. Now put the marinated chicken into the insert pot. Close the lid and pressure vent.
11. Select poultry mode default setting and press start. The default setting is 15 minutes.
12. After cooking release the pressure using the quick release option.
13. Remove the chicken into a bowl.
14. Once the sauce has cooled down, blend the sauce with butter and whipping cream with an immersion blender.
15. After combining add back the chicken to the sauce.
16. The chicken is ready to serve.
17. Garnish with fresh cilantro leaves and sliced red onions.
18. Serve hot.

Nutritional Values:

Calories: 469 | Carbohydrate: 9.8g | Protein: 37.7g | Fat: 31g | Sodium: 676mg | Fiber: 1.7g | Potassium: 583mg

CONCLUSION

This book contains the best Indian recipes which are enhanced with unique Indian spices. These flavorsome dishes will make your inner soul satisfied and happy. Not only does the book have best Indian vegetarian and non-vegetarian recipes but it also contains recipes of Indian desserts.

The book will make you feel like saying the expression, 'Small Package Big Explosion (Dhamaka)'. Indian desserts are undoubtedly very delectable and scrumptious. Indian cuisine has the blend of flavorful spices, and the mixture turns out to be the best amongst all.

The best part about Indian Cuisine is that there is always something extra with the average meal. Pickles and chutney are something which is one of the most famous side dishes or extra accompaniments with meals. The contemporary dishes are all about flavors and essence of the spices used in the recipes.

Making food simply and concisely is what Indian Cuisine is about. You simply cannot miss this book which has the best Indian recipes.

With utmost thankfulness and acknowledgment, I thank you and appreciate you from my inner soul for giving your precious time and attendance to this book. Your expression of liking the recipes of this book will always motivate me to explore more on Indian cuisine.

Book №4

Introduction

An Insight into Vietnamese Cuisine:

Vietnamese cuisine is very rich in aromas and taste and every dish has its own sternly desirable appeal. Despite the fact that the landscape of the country is very versatile, the Vietnamese cuisine is rich in lemongrass, cilantro, simmered beef bones, mint and the most important, the fish sauces. The food always has a balanced proportion of sweetness, fish-sauciness, aromatics, sourness, and heat. The basic theme of the cuisine is based on the 'yin and yang' principles, i.e. warm and cool, salty and sweet, and fermented and fresh. In the coming portions, we are going to describe this in detail.

The Vietnamese cuisine is very healthy and is solely based on fresh ingredients and a lesser amount of added butter, fats and oils. All the spices and herbs are carefully picked for adding a particular flavor to the dishes. All the herbs and spices are keenly combined with precision to have a particular balanced taste in the dishes. There are various fast food restaurants in the country but they aren't that crowded. You are going to find people having their meals together with their families and prefer a balanced meal instead of going out for fast food.

Just like the Chinese cuisine, the Vietnamese cuisine is based on the five flavor elements; i.e. bitter, sweet, salty, sour, and spicy. The cooking methods and techniques have been passed from generations to generations and the present day Vietnamese chefs are highly expert in making the best of the Vietnamese traditional dishes.

Geographical Importance:

The Vietnamese cuisine can be better understood by looking at the geographical position of the country. Vietnam is a very small, skinny country just like Italy, and having an S-shaped map. The country has China to its north, Cambodia, and Laos to the western side, and the South China Sea as its eastern border. The coastline of the country is approximately 3,000 km long and is stretched towards the downside, with Hanoi in the northern part. Saigon (also known as Hoi Chi Minh City) with rugged central highlands is located in the southern part. "The rice bowl of the country" also known as the fertile delta of Mekong is located in the bottom-most part.

The cuisines of the northern part are highly influenced by the Chinese cuisines with noodle-oriented soups and stir-fries. If you start your journey down, the cuisine gets more influence from neighboring Thailand and Cambodia, adding more flavors and taste. The southern part of the country has a tropical climate and is rich in jackfruit trees, abundant rice paddies, herb gardens, and coconut groves. The cuisines of southern Vietnam are generally sweeter, i.e., having an extra amount of palm sugar in savory dishes, the pho has generally sweeter broths, and the highly demanded coconut candies which are taffy-like, are prepared with coconut cream.

French Impact:

You cannot take out the French factor if you are considering the Vietnamese cuisine. The French colonization of Vietnam started in the Eighteenth century by the arrival of missionaries and lasted till around the initial years of the 1950s, i.e., 1954. The colonization had a strong influence on the lifestyle, cuisines, architecture, flavors, and land of the locals. The most prominent one is the banh mi, which has a highly crusty French baguette as its foundation. The Vietnamese have taken a step above this sandwich and added their own taste to it by adding fish patties, cilantro, grilled pork, sardines, chili-spiked carrots, and various other fillings.

Another remarkable impact of the French colonization on the Vietnamese cuisine is the pho (it is pronounced as 'fuh', the 'ph' giving an 'f' sound). The pho is basically comprised of French-minded meat broths and blended with Vietnamese rice noodles. A theory proposes that the word 'pho' is the phonetic imitation of the word 'feu' which is used for 'fire' in the French language like 'pot-au-feu'. Various people ponder that the French colonizers had slaughtered a huge chunk of animals to satisfy their tastes for steaks. The Vietnamese cooks were highly resourceful and would utilize the bones, ascraps, and the rest of the rejected parts to prepare pho.

Broths play a pivotal role in the Vietnamese cuisine and have critical importance in courtship. The mothers chose the wives of their sons on the basis of the wife's expertise in the preparation of broth' Preparing a lackluster broth is going to discard your chances of getting married to a guy! The experts in broth could state the exact stage of the broth by merely sniffing it. In conclusion, the Vietnamese are very strict and serious about their broths.

Basic Ingredients:

The basic or the building ingredients of almost every dish in Vietnam is fish and rice sauce. Wherever you travel in Vietnam, almost every food is themed on fish and rice sauces.

After Thailand, Vietnam is the second largest rice exporting nation in the world. Rice has grown abundantly in almost every part of the country. But, the fertile Mekong Delta located in the southern part of the country is the best rice producing area i.e. capable of producing enough rice for the entire population of Vietnam which is about 87 million people. That is not the end, despite feeding the entire country, the Delta produces a large quantity of rice which allows it to be further exported to various countries.

You can easily see that rice is a part of every meal, irrespective of its time, be it breakfast, lunch, dinner or even desserts. Of course, there is the presence of rice noodles, sticky rice, puffed rice snacks, rice paper wrappers, rice wine, fried rice, rice porridge, and regular ol' rice. It is almost hard to stay away from rice for a few hours while you are in Vietnam.

Rice is so culturally involved with them that they even say 'cơm muối' i.e. 'rice and salt', instead of gesundheit in response to sneezing. For instance, it means that if you want to bless someone or wish them better health, simply say rice and salt and that is going to fade away all the disease they are having.

The salt consumption in the entire Vietnamese cuisine usually comes from the fish sauce. A fermented, funky, and salty fish sauce which is also called nước mắm in the Vietnamese language is abundantly used in salad dressings, marinades, spring roll dips, broths, and almost every other dish you can possibly point out in the Vietnamese cuisine. Fish sauce is so important that the national condiment which is called the 'nước chấm' in the Vietnamese language is prepared from fish sauce which is slightly diluted with a mere splash of garlic, sugar, lime juice, and chilies.

The best, and high-quality fish sauce is made in Phu Quoc, which is basically an island closely located near the Cambodian border. The water surrounding Phu Quoc has an abundant amount of plankton and seaweed, which keeps the abundant population of anchovy very happy. You can make fish sauce from any fish, but the best fish sauce is made from anchovies that are harvested near the Phu Quoc Island. The Vietnamese love their fish sauce as much as the Americans love cheese.

The fish sauce is produced in various factories where salt and tiny fishes are aged for around 6 months in wooden barrels. These fish sauces are the best in the country and are high in demand due to their presence in almost every food in Vietnamese cuisine.

Aromatics and Herbs:

There is a geographical history associated with the herbs and spices used in Vietnamese cuisine. Vietnam had been usually isolated and wasn't a great partner in the spice trading. As a general rule, anything that is produced in Vietnam is going to be a good point to ponder about what would be the best spot for it in the cuisine. Ingredients like chili powders and chilies were added later on in the Vietnamese cuisine when spice traders expanded their business to include Vietnam. The Vietnamese foods are comprised of an abundant amount of aromatics, spices, and herbs. They can either be in the steamy pots of pho or enclosed with a pancake called Banh xeo or even wrapped into spring rolls.

All the ingredients in the Vietnamese cuisine are very fresh. Almost every food of the Vietnamese contain herbs, spices, and various other aromatics and the best dish is served only when all the ingredients are highly fresh.

Some of the important herbs, aromatics, and chilies used in the Vietnamese cuisine are as follows:

1. **Mint:**
   There are various verities of mint that are produced in Vietnam. They include fuzzy, lemony tasted, spicy tasted, etc.
2. **Cilantro:**
   It is used in various spring rolls, soups, salads, and various other dishes. They are also used abundantly in garnishing. It depends on your genetics if the cilantro tastes soapy or not.
3. **Lime Leaf:**

   It is shiny and bright green in appearance and is used in some oils that are bitter.

4. **Basil:**
   Although it is generally more popular in Thailand, in the Vietnamese cuisine, it is used on herb plates and in pho.
5. **Fish leaf or fish mint:**
   Clear from the name, this herb is having a certain pungent smell and taste like fishes. It tastes exactly like a fish.
6. **Garlic Chives:**

They have onion and garlic flavor and are flat leaves.
7. **Scallions and green onions.**
8. **Lemongrass:**

As from the name, they smell and tastes like lemon. They are used in both savory and sweet dishes.

9. **Turmeric:**

They are also knowns as poor man's saffron. They add a peppery flavor and certain vivid godliness to various fried foods.

10. **Dill:**

They are not that popular in other South Asian cuisines but they are certainly used in the Vietnamese cuisine in a fish dish known as Cha Ca. this herb is treated as a vegetable instead of an herb in this dish.

11. **Saigon Cinnamon:**

They are various varieties of cinnamon in the world but this one is particularly associated with Vietnamese cuisine. They are having a certain earthy, woody aroma and flavor and is mostly used in pho.

12. **Galangal and ginger:**

They are both knobby rhizomes and are pervasive in the Vietnamese cuisine.

13. **Tamarind Pulp:**

Although, this isn't used that much in the Vietnamese cuisine, yet this sweet-sour pulp is an ingredient in making curries and soups.

14. **Annatto Seeds:**

They are used in foods to provide a specific lemony flavor and for coloring foods.

15. **Chili Powder:**

It is used not only for color but also for having a spicy flavor. Chili powder is more famous and used in the southern parts of the country as the northern parts still rely on black pepper as the major spice.

16. **Star anise:**

They are usually used in stews and soups to add a certain licorice flavor. They also are an important ingredient in various meat dishes too.

17. **Coconut Sugar:**

It is very popular in southern parts of the country for making soups but is not used abundantly as rock sugar. Rock sugar is very famous in the country and is used as a sweetener in desserts and drinks. It is also used in various savory dishes.

18. **Salt:**

Although it is used sparingly yet, it is a key ingredient in Vietnamese cuisine. There are very limited dishes which have no salt in them. Irrespective of this, the Vietnamese cuisine is considered to be healthier than the American cuisine due to the limited amount of salt used.

19. **Black pepper:**

The usage of black pepper is almost the same as its usage in American cuisine. It is widely used in stews and soups as well as in various meat dishes. Black pepper was the only spice used in Vietnamese cuisine before the introduction of chili powder. It hasn't lost its importance despite the introduction of fruits to the cuisine and the Vietnamese love their peppercorns even now.

Seasoning Blends:

Seasoning blends are not that much used in the Vietnamese cuisine as single spices. Generally, food is flavored with a small amount of one or two spices and a lot of herbs. As in Indian cuisine where spice blends are pretty common, the Vietnamese cuisine doesn't involve spice blends generally. There is a 'Vietnamese Pork Rub' available in the market which is a spice blend based on the Vietnamese cuisine. It is created by Vietnamese chefs who have mastered the art of cooking various pork dishes. Pork is a very important part of the cuisine and this spice blend contains the exotic flavors of the Vietnamese cuisine. This blend can be used for seasoning grilled pork chops and pork tenderloin. It can also be used as an ingredient in pork gravies too.

Sauces:

Sauces are the most crucial part of the Vietnamese cuisine and it is incomplete without them. The Vietnamese cuisine is actually based on these sauces having a salty taste for providing a base touch but many dishes also include these sauces as a finishing touch.

1. The most abundantly used sauce is the **fish sauce** which is like a thick condiment. It is used in pho or even or grilled pork dishes apart from being the base for various stews and soups.
2. **Soy sauce** is also used in Vietnamese cuisine. It is generally used in veggies and has an umami flavor with a salty taste.
3. **Shrimp sauce** is used for marinating and sautéing meats and is actually a paste of salt and shrimp.
4. **Chili sauce** is also used abundantly in the Vietnamese cuisine. It gives out a reddish color to various light veggie broths or soups, apart from giving out a nice kick.

Vietnamese cuisine has evolved a bit and contains a small amount of MSGs, contrary to the common prejudice. "Gia vi" or "Bot canh" which is a mixture of pepper, salt and a little number of MSGs are used in the Vietnamese cooking widely I and in particular, the northern part of the country. The most popular spice choice for the Vietnamese cooks is poultry powder, sugar, pepper, gia yi, pepper and salt and a smaller dose of MSGs.

All the spies mentioned above are used in the Vietnamese cuisine but their usage may vary from place to place depending upon the landscape. As said earlier, black pepper is still used as the main spice in the northern parts of the country while the southern part uses chili powder. Importantly, the northern Vietnamese like their food saltier and less sweet than the rest of the country.

Central Vietnamese like their food savor, spicy and colorful. They prefer cooking with dried chilies instead of fresh ones for adding an extra spicy taste to their foods. Cooking methods in the southern part of the country are strongly influenced by Chinese, Thai and Cambodian cuisines. So, southern Vietnamese like their food spicy by adding more red chilies, and sweet by adding coconut milk or sugar in their foods.

Dairy:

There is no concept of fresh dairy but the cuisine includes an abundant quantity of sweetened condensed milk. There is a specific egg coffee available in Hanoi which is made by whipping a raw egg on the topmost layer of condensed and sweetened milk

It's important to note that there isn't any impact of Camembert or Brie by the French colonists. Clearly, there isn't any high usage of cheese, cream, or butter in the Vietnamese cuisine but the calcium intake is compensated by consuming fish shells and bones. Normally, you don't have to remove the tail of the shrimp, eat it completely so it will give you a crunchy taste.

In the case of fresh milk, you can easily spot lots of cans of sweetened condensed milk which is mostly used in the 'white coffee'. The sweet and thick layer of the milk is blended with locally grown dark roast coffee. This coffee is separately brewed via a metal drip filter for servings into various cups. In general, the amount of milk is higher than the amount of coffee in the cups. Although the coffee is amazing and sweeter in taste, it is very strong.

Fruits:

Fruits are used both as veggies and in desserts in the Vietnamese cuisine. In general, unripe fruits are used as a veggie. For example, a green banana flower or papaya is used as the base of various salads instead of leafy greens. These fruits are usually ripe in taste and are blended with chili, dried shrimp, fish sauce, chopped peanuts, and garlic.

For ripe fruits, according to their wondrous and sweet taste, they are used for desserts. Generally, meals are followed by a large platter of fruits and a teapot instead of cookies or cakes. These include slices of mango, banana, watermelon, pineapple, papaya, lychees, and rambutans.

The unjust thing done to the Vietnamese cuisine available in the United States is that it is reduced merely to stir fry and rice because the cuisine has such rich-flavored and aromatic foods to offer other than rice and stir fry. In comparison with other various cuisines which are a part of the culture of the US, Vietnamese cuisine also has a a small standing in it.

Chicken Recipes

Caramelized Chicken

Servings: 8

Prep Time: 40 minutes

Ingredients:

For Marinade:

- 4 tablespoons fish sauce
- 3 red chilies, minced
- 4 tablespoons fresh ginger, minced finely
- 4 teaspoons garlic, minced finely
- 2 tablespoons sugar
- 8 (5-ounce) chicken thighs

For Sauce:

- 2 tablespoons canola oil
- 1/3 cup sugar
- 1 cup chicken broth
- 1 small yellow onion, sliced into petals

For Garnishing:

- ¼ cup fresh cilantro, chopped

Directions:

1. For the marinade: place all the ingredients except the chicken breasts in a large bowl and mix until well combined.
2. Add the chicken breasts and mix well.
3. Refrigerate to marinate for about 6-8 hours.
4. Remove the chicken breasts from bowl, reserving marinade.
5. Add the oil in the Instant Pot and select "Sauté". Now, add 4 chicken breasts, skin side down and cook for about 4-5 minutes or until golden brown.
6. With a slotted spoon, transfer the chicken breasts onto a plate.
7. Repeat with the remaining chicken breasts.
8. For sauce: in the pot, add the sugar and cook until the sugar begins to melt, stirring continuously.
9. Add the chicken broth with the reserved marinade and with a spatula, scrape the brown bits from the bottom.
10. Select the "Cancel" and stir in the chicken breasts.
11. Secure the lid and turn to "Seal" position.
12. Select "Poultry" and just use the default time of 20 minutes.

13. Press the "Cancel" and allow a "Natural" release.
14. Carefully remove the lid and serve hot with the garnishing of cilantro.

Nutrition Information

- Calories: 371
- Fat: 14.4g
- Saturated Fat: 3.3g
- Cholesterol: 126mg
- Sodium: 1032mg
- Carbohydrates: 16g
- Fiber: 0.8g
- Sugar: 13.1g
- Protein: 42.2g

MARINATED CHICKEN CURRY

Servings: 8

Prep Time: 36 minutes

Ingredients:

For Chicken Marinade:

- 1 tablespoon fresh ginger, grated
- 6 garlic cloves, minced finely
- 1 tablespoon yellow curry powder
- Salt, as required
- 3 pounds skinless, boneless chicken thighs, cut into pieces

For Curry:

- 2 tablespoons coconut oil
- 1 large onion, chopped
- 3 tablespoons all-purpose flour
- 2 fresh lemongrass stalks, sliced into 3-inch pieces and pounded
- 4 tablespoons yellow curry powder
- 1 bay leaf
- 4 tablespoons fish sauce
- 4 teaspoons granulated sugar
- Salt, as required
- 2 (13½-ounce) cans coconut milk
- 6 red potatoes, peeled and cut into bite sized pieces
- 6 medium carrots, peeled and cut into bite sized pieces
- 2 scallions (green part), chopped

Directions:

1. For the marinade: place all the ingredients except the chicken breasts in a large bowl and mix until well combined.
2. Add the chicken pieces and coat with marinade generously.
3. Refrigerate to marinate for about 1-2 hours.
4. Add the oil in the Instant Pot and select "Sauté". Now, add the chicken pieces and cook or about 5 minutes.
5. With the spoon, push the chicken to one side of the pot.
6. In the pot, add the onions and cook for about 3 minutes.
7. Stir in the four and cook for about 2 minutes, stirring continuously.
8. Select "Cancel" and stir in the lemongrass pieces, curry powder, bay leaf, fish sauce, sugar and coconut milk.
9. Secure the lid and turn to "Seal" position.
10. Cook on "Manual" with "High Pressure" for about 2 minutes.
11. Press the "Cancel" and allow a "Natural" release for about 5 minutes and then, allow a "Quick" release.
12. Carefully remove the lid and add the potatoes and carrots.
13. Secure the lid and turn to "Seal" position.
14. Cook on "Manual" with "High Pressure" for about 4 minutes.
15. Press the "Cancel" and allow a "Natural" release for about 5 minutes and then, allow a "Quick" release.
16. Carefully, remove the lid and serve hot with the garnishing of scallions.

Nutrition Information

- Calories: 750
- Fat: 39.6g
- Saturated Fat: 26.8g
- Cholesterol: 151mg
- Sodium: 920mg
- Carbohydrates: 45g
- Fiber: 9.1g
- Sugar: 10.7g
- Protein: 56.2g

CHICKEN & BELL PEPPER CURRY

Servings: 4

Prep Time: 30 minutes

Ingredients:

- 2 (8-ounce) boneless, skinless chicken breasts
- 3 tablespoons fish sauce
- 2 tablespoons red curry paste
- 2 tablespoons brown sugar
- 1 (13½-ounce) can full-fat coconut milk
- 3 cups mixed bell peppers, seeded and julienned

- 1 cup red onion, sliced and
- 1 tablespoon fresh lime juice

Directions:

1. In the pot of Instant Pot, place chicken, curry paste, brown sugar, fish sauce and coconut milk and stir to combine.
2. Secure the lid and turn to "Seal" position.
3. Cook on "Manual" with "High Pressure" for about 8 minutes.
4. Press the "Cancel" and allow a "Quick" release.
5. Carefully remove the lid of Instant Pot and with a spoon, place the chicken breasts into a bowl.
6. Select "Sauté" and stir in bell peppers, onion and lime juice.
7. Cook for about 3-5 minutes.
8. Meanwhile, cut the chicken breasts into bite sized pieces.
9. Add the chicken meat into pot and stir to combine.
10. Select the "Cancel" and serve hot.

Nutrition Information

- Calories: 548
- Fat: 35.9g
- Saturated Fat: 22.5g
- Cholesterol: 101mg
- Sodium: 1159mg
- Carbohydrates: 21.8g
- Fiber: 3.9g
- Sugar: 13.8g
- Protein: 37.3g

LEMONGRASS CHICKEN

Servings: 5

Prep Time: 35 minutes

Ingredients:

- 1 thick lemongrass stalk, papery outer skins and rough bottom removed, trimmed to the bottom 5-inch
- 1 tablespoon fresh ginger, chopped
- 4 garlic cloves, crushed
- 3 tablespoons soy sauce
- 2 tablespoons fish sauce
- 1 cup full-fat coconut milk
- 10 (4-ounce) skinless chicken drumsticks
- Salt and ground black pepper, as required
- 1 teaspoon coconut oil

- 1 large onion, sliced thinly
- 2 tablespoons fresh lime juice

Directions:

1. In a food processor, add the lemongrass, ginger, garlic, soy sauce and fish sauce and pulse until a smooth sauce forms.
2. Sprinkle the chicken drumsticks with salt and pepper evenly.
3. Add the oil in the Instant Pot and select "Sauté". Now, add the onion and cook for about 4-5 minutes.
4. Select the "Cancel" and place the drumsticks, followed by the sauce.
5. Secure the lid and turn to "Seal" position.
6. Cook on "Manual" with "High Pressure" for about 15 minutes.
7. Press the "Cancel" and allow a "Quick" release.
8. Carefully remove the lid and mix in the lime juice.
9. Serve hot.

Nutrition Information

- Calories: 530
- Fat: 25.4g
- Saturated Fat: 14.4g
- Cholesterol: 200mg
- Sodium: 1300mg
- Carbohydrates: 8.3g
- Fiber: 2g
- Sugar: 3.4g
- Protein: 65g

GLAZED CHICKEN BREASTS

Servings: 3

Prep Time: 25 minutes

Ingredients:

- 2 (7-ounce) boneless, skinless chicken breasts
- 2 tablespoons fresh ginger, grated
- 1 garlic clove, minced
- 1/3 cup chicken broth
- ¼ cup honey
- ¼ cup soy sauce
- 2 tablespoons fish sauce
- 1 tablespoon canola oil
- 2 teaspoons cornstarch
- 2 tablespoons water

Directions:

1. In the pot of Instant Pot, place all the ingredients except the cornstarch and water and stir to combine.
2. Secure the lid and turn to "Seal" position.
3. Cook on "Manual" with "High Pressure" for about 8 minutes.
4. Press the "Cancel" and allow a "Quick" release.
5. Meanwhile, in a bowl, add the cornstarch and water and mix well.
6. Carefully remove the lid and with the tongs, transfer the chicken breasts onto a plate.
7. Cut the chicken breasts into desired sized slices.
8. Add the cornstarch mixture into pot, stirring continuously.
9. Select "Sauté" and cook for about 1-2 minutes.
10. Select the "Cancel" and stir in the chicken slices.
11. Serve hot.

Nutrition Information

- Calories: 419
- Fat: 14.9g
- Saturated Fat: 3.2g
- Cholesterol: 118mg
- Sodium: 2300mg
- Carbohydrates: 29.9g
- Fiber: 0.7g
- Sugar: 24.2g
- Protein: 41.2g

Meat Recipes

Braised Beef Brisket

Servings: 8

Prep Time: 1½ hours

Ingredients:

- 1 tablespoon sesame oil
- 1 small onion, sliced
- 1 tablespoon fresh ginger, minced
- 4 garlic cloves, smashed
- 1 (2½-pound) beef brisket
- ½ cup hoisin sauce
- 3 tablespoons fish sauce
- 2 tablespoons hot sauce
- ¼ cup water
- Salt and ground black pepper, as required

Directions:

1. Add the oil in the Instant Pot and select "Sauté". Now, add the onion and cook for about 1-2 minutes.
2. Add the ginger and garlic and cook for about 2 minutes.
3. Select the "Cancel" and stir in the remaining ingredients.
4. Secure the lid and turn to "Seal" position.
5. Cook on "Manual" with "High Pressure" for about 60 minutes.
6. Press the "Cancel" and allow a "Natural" release for about 10 minutes and then, allow a "Quick" release.
7. Carefully remove the lid and place the brisket onto a cutting board for about 5-10 minutes.
8. Select "Sauté" and cook for about 10 minutes or until desired thickness of cooking sauce.
9. Cut the brisket into thin pieces against the grain.
10. Serve the brisket slices with alongside the sauce.

Nutrition Information

- Calories: 324
- Fat: 11.1g
- Saturated Fat: 3.7g
- Cholesterol: 127mg
- Sodium: 988mg
- Carbohydrates: 9.2g
- Fiber: 0.8g
- Sugar: 5.1g
- Protein: 44.2g

SHREDDED CHUCK ROAST

Servings: 6

Prep Time: 50 minutes

Ingredients:

- ¼ cup soy sauce
- 2 tablespoons fresh lime juice
- 2 tablespoons fresh apple juice
- 2 tablespoons rice vinegar
- 1 tablespoon curry paste
- 1 tablespoon fresh ginger, minced
- 1 tablespoon garlic, minced
- Salt, as required
- 1 tablespoon canola oil
- 1 jalapeño pepper, chopped
- 2 pounds beef chuck roast, cubed

Directions:

1. For sauce: in a bowl, add all the ingredients except the oil, jalapeño pepper and roast and beat until well combined.
2. Add the oil in the Instant Pot and select "Sauté". Now, add the jalapeño pepper and cook for about 1-2 minutes.
3. Add the chuck roast and cook for about 1-2 minutes.
4. Select the "Cancel" and place the sauce on top.
5. Secure the lid and turn to "Seal" position.
6. Cook on "Manual" with "High Pressure" for about 30 minutes.
7. Meanwhile, preheat the oven to broiler and line a baking sheet with a foil piece.
8. Press the "Cancel" and allow a "Natural" release for about 10 minutes and then, allow a "Quick" release.
9. Carefully remove the lid and with 2 forks, shred the meat.
10. Mix the meat with sauce and serve

Nutrition Information

- Calories: 639
- Fat: 46g
- Saturated Fat: 17g
- Cholesterol: 156mg
- Sodium: 727mg
- Carbohydrates: 12.1g
- Fiber: 0.5g
- Sugar: 8.3g
- Protein: 40.6g

Caramelized Pork

Servings: 6

Prep Time: 55 minutes

Ingredients:

- 2 tablespoons canola oil
- 2 pounds pork butt, cut in 1-inch pieces
- Salt and ground black pepper, as required
- 4 tablespoons brown sugar
- 3 garlic cloves, minced
- 2 tablespoons fish sauce
- ½ cup chicken broth
- ½ cup water
- 1 small onion, sliced
- 1 scallion (green part), chopped

Directions:

1. Add the oil in the Instant Pot and select "Sauté". Now, add the pork, salt and black pepper and cook for about 3-4 minutes or until browned completely.
2. Add the brown sugar and cook for about 2 minutes or until pork turn a golden brown color, stirring continuously.
3. Stir in the garlic and cook for about 1 minutes.
4. Select the "Cancel" and stir in the fish sauce, broth and water.
5. Secure the lid and turn to "Seal" position.
6. Cook on "Manual" with "High Pressure" for about 20 minutes.
7. Press the "Cancel" and allow a "Natural" release for about 10 minutes and then, allow a "Quick" release.
8. Carefully remove the lid and select "Sauté".
9. Stir in the onions and cook for about 5-10 minutes or until desired thickness of sauce.
10. Select the "Cancel" and serve with the garnishing of scallion.

Nutrition Information

- Calories: 369
- Fat: 14.9g
- Saturated Fat: 3.7g
- Cholesterol: 139mg
- Sodium: 624mg
- Carbohydrates: 8g
- Fiber: 0.4g
- Sugar: 6.7g
- Protein: 48.1g

Braised Pork Belly

Servings: 8

Prep Time: 55 minutes

Ingredients:

- 2 shallots, chopped finely
- 3 garlic cloves, minced
- 2 tablespoons fish sauce
- 1 teaspoon thick soy sauce
- Salt and ground black pepper, as required
- 2½ pounds lean pork belly, cut into 1-inch squares
- 7 tablespoons granulated sugar
- 2 cups coconut water
- 1 scallion (green part), chopped

Directions:

1. In a large bowl, add the shallots, garlic, fish sauce, soy sauce, salt and black pepper and mix until well combined.
2. Stir in the pork pieces and coat with the mixture generously.
3. Place the sugar in the Instant Pot and select "Sauté". Cook for about 10-15 minutes or until sugar starts to become dark in color, stirring frequently.
4. Add the pork belly pieces and cook for about 5 minutes, stirring continuously.
5. Select the "Cancel" and stir in the coconut water.
6. Secure the lid and turn to "Seal" position.
7. Cook on "Manual" with "High Pressure" for about 35 minutes.
8. Press the "Cancel" and allow a "Natural" release for about 15 minutes and then, allow a "Quick" release.
9. Carefully remove the lid and serve with the garnishing of scallion.

Nutrition Information

- Calories: 713
- Fat: 38.3g
- Saturated Fat: 16.5g
- Cholesterol: 164mg
- Sodium: 2700mg
- Carbohydrates: 14.3g
- Fiber: 0.7g
- Sugar: 12.3g
- Protein: 66.3g

Shredded Pork

Servings: 8

Prep Time: 1¼ hours

Ingredients:

- 1 tablespoon garlic, minced
- ¼ cup fish sauce
- 1 tablespoon fresh lime juice
- 2 tablespoons sugar
- 1 teaspoon five-spice powder
- Freshly ground black pepper, as required
- 2½ pounds pork butt
- 1 tablespoon canola oil

Directions:

1. For sauce: in a bowl, add all the ingredients except the oil and pork and beat until well combined.
2. In the pot of the Instant Pot, place the pork butt and top with the sauce evenly.
3. Secure the lid and turn to "Seal" position.
4. Cook on "Manual" with "High Pressure" for about 60 minutes.
5. Press the "Cancel" and allow a "Natural" release.
6. Carefully remove the lid and with a spoon, place the pork butt into a bowl.
7. With 2 forks, shred the meat.
8. In a large skillet, heat oil over medium heat and stir in the shredded meat.
9. Add desired amount of cooking liquid and cook for about 1-2 minutes.
10. Serve hot.

Nutrition Information

- Calories: 305
- Fat: 11.2g
- Saturated Fat: 3.3g
- Cholesterol: 130mg
- Sodium: 774mg
- Carbohydrates: 3.7g
- Fiber: 0g
- Sugar: 3.3g
- Protein: 44.7g

FISH RECIPES

STEAMED SEA BASS

Servings: 4

Prep Time: 20 minutes

Ingredients:

For Sea Bass:

- 1 teaspoon fresh ginger, minced
- 1 teaspoon garlic, minced
- 1 tablespoon rice wine
- 1 tablespoon soy sauce
- 1 tablespoon fish sauce
- Freshly ground black pepper, as required
- 1 pound whole sea bass
- 2 cups water

For Sauce:

- 1 teaspoon fresh ginger, julienned finely
- ¼ cup light soy sauce
- 1 tablespoon rice wine
- 1 tablespoon water
- 1 scallion, julienned
- ¼ cup canola oil

Directions:

1. For marinade: in a baking dish, add all the ingredients except the fish and water and mix well.
2. Add the fish and mix well.
3. Set aside for about 20-30 minutes.
4. In the bottom of Instant Pot, arrange a steamer basket and pour water.
5. Place the fish in steamer basket.
6. Secure the lid and turn to "Seal" position.
7. Cook on "Manual" with "Low Pressure" for about 2 minutes.
8. Press the "Cancel" and allow a "Quick" release.
9. Meanwhile, in a small bowl, add the ginger, soy sauce, wine, and 1 tablespoon of water and mix well.
10. Carefully remove the lid and transfer the fish onto a serving platter.
11. Place the ginger mixture over the fish.
12. Now, arrange the scallion over the fish.
13. In a frying pan, add the oil over medium heat and cook until just heated.
14. Pour oil over the fish and serve.

Nutrition Information

- Calories: 372
- Fat: 18.7g
- Saturated Fat: 2g
- Cholesterol: 46mg
- Sodium: 1683mg
- Carbohydrates: 27.3g
- Fiber: 0.3g
- Sugar: 15.8g
- Protein: 23.9g

CARAMELIZED SALMON

Servings: 4

Prep Time: 20 minutes

Ingredients:

- 1/3 cup light brown sugar
- 3 tablespoons fish sauce
- 1 tablespoon coconut oil, melted
- 1 tablespoon fresh lime juice
- 1½ tablespoons soy sauce
- 1 teaspoon fresh ginger, grated
- 1 teaspoon fresh lime zest, grated
- Freshly ground black pepper, as required
- 4 (6-ounce) skinless salmon fillets
- 1 scallion (green part), chopped

Directions:

1. Place all the ingredients except the salmon and scallion in a bowl and mix until well combined.
2. Place the sugar mixture in the Instant Pot and select "Sauté". Cook for about 2-3 minutes, stirring frequently.
3. Select the "Cancel" and stir in the salmon fillets.
4. Secure the lid and turn to "Seal" position.
5. Cook on "Manual" with "Low Pressure" for about 1 minute.
6. Press the "Cancel" and allow a "Natural" release for about 5 minutes and then, allow a "Quick" release.
7. Carefully remove the lid and select "Sauté".
8. Cook for about 1 minute.
9. With a slotted spoon, transfer the salmon fillets onto a platter.
10. Cook the sauce for about 3 minutes.
11. Select the "Cancel" and pour the caramel sauce over the salmon fillets.
12. Serve with the garnishing of the scallion.

Nutrition Information

- Calories: 388
- Fat: 21.5g
- Saturated Fat: 6.7g
- Cholesterol: 98mg
- Sodium: 1482mg
- Carbohydrates: 13.5g
- Fiber: 0.3g
- Sugar: 12.4g
- Protein: 34.4g

CATFISH IN CARAMEL SAUCE

Servings: 4

Prep Time: 20 minutes

Ingredients:

- 3 garlic cloves, minced and divided
- 2 scallions (white part), minced
- 3 tablespoons fish sauce
- 1 tablespoon sugar
- ½ teaspoon coconut caramel sauce
- Freshly ground black pepper, as required
- 1 pound catfish fillets
- 1 tablespoon coconut oil
- 1 shallot, minced
- ½ cup coconut water

Directions:

1. Place half of the garlic, scallions, fish sauce, sugar, caramel sauce and black pepper in a large bowl and mix well.
2. Add the fish and coat with mixture generously.
3. Set aside to marinate for about 15-30 minutes.
4. Add the oil in the Instant Pot and select "Sauté". Now, add the shallot and remaining garlic and cook for about 1 minute.
5. Add the fish with marinade sauce and cook for about 2 minutes.
6. Flip the fish and cook for about 2 minutes.
7. Select the "Cancel" and stir in the coconut water.
8. Secure the lid and turn to "Seal" position.
9. Cook on "Manual" with "Low Pressure" for about 3 minutes.
10. Press the "Cancel" and allow a "Quick" release.
11. Carefully, remove the lid and select "Sauté".
12. Cook for about 3-5 minutes, occasionally pouring the sauce over the fish.
13. Select the "Cancel" and serve.

Nutrition Information

- Calories: 178
- Fat: 17.5g
- Saturated Fat: 4.2g
- Cholesterol: 58mg
- Sodium: 1100mg
- Carbohydrates: 8.4g
- Fiber: 0.6g
- Sugar: 4.5g
- Protein: 22.1g

Fish Curry

Servings: 4

Prep Time: 20 minutes

Ingredients:

- 1 (14½-ounce) can coconut milk
- 2 tablespoons fresh lime juice
- 2 teaspoons Sriracha
- 1 teaspoon soy sauce
- 1 teaspoon fish sauce
- 1 teaspoon honey
- 2 garlic cloves, minced
- 1 tablespoon curry paste
- 1 teaspoon ground ginger
- 1 teaspoon ground turmeric
- Salt and ground white pepper, as required
- 1 pound sea bass, cut into 1-inch cubes
- ¼ cup fresh cilantro, chopped

Directions:

1. In a large bowl, add the coconut milk, lime juice, Sriracha, soy sauce, fish sauce, honey, garlic, curry paste, ginger, turmeric, salt and white pepper and beat until well combined.
2. In the pot of Instant Pot, place the fish pieces and top with the sauce.
3. Secure the lid and turn to "Seal" position.
4. Cook on "Manual" with "High Pressure" for about 3 minutes.
5. Press the "Cancel" and allow a "Quick" release.
6. Carefully remove the lid and serve with the garnishing of cilantro.

Nutrition Information

- Calories: 473
- Fat: 37.2g

- Saturated Fat: 23.9g
- Cholesterol: 0mg
- Sodium: 264mg
- Carbohydrates: 10.2g
- Fiber: 3.1g
- Sugar: 5.1g
- Protein: 28.1g

FISH & VEGGIE CURRY

Servings: 6

Prep Time: 1½ hours

Ingredients:

- 1½ pounds catfish fillets
- 2 cups carrots, peeled and sliced
- 1 red bell pepper, seeded and sliced
- 1 medium zucchini, chopped
- 2 tablespoons green curry paste
- 1 tablespoon fish sauce
- 2 (14-ounce) cans coconut milk
- 2 cups water

Directions:

1. In the pot of Instant Pot, add all the ingredients and stir to combine.
2. Secure the lid and turn to "Seal" position.
3. Select "Soup" and just use the default time of 60 minutes.
4. Press the "Cancel" and allow a "Quick" release.
5. Carefully remove the lid and serve hot.

Nutrition Information

- Calories: 500
- Fat: 41.3g
- Saturated Fat: 29.6g
- Cholesterol: 53mg
- Sodium: 543mg
- Carbohydrates: 15.1g
- Fiber: 4.4g
- Sugar: 7.9g
- Protein: 21.7g

Rice Recipes

Coconut Rice with Peas

Servings: 6

Prep Time: 15 minutes

Ingredients:

- 2 cups jasmine rice
- 1 (15-ounce) can lite coconut milk
- ½ cup water
- 1 cup frozen peas, thawed
- 1 tablespoon fresh lime juice
- 2 tablespoons fresh cilantro, chopped

Directions:

1. In the pot of Instant Pot, add the rice coconut milk and water and stir to combine.
2. Secure the lid and turn to "Seal" position.
3. Cook on "Manual" with "High Pressure" for about 4 minutes.
4. Press the "Cancel" and allow a "Natural" release.
5. Carefully remove the lid and immediately, stir in the peas and lime juice.
6. Serve with the garnishing of cilantro.

Nutrition Information

- Calories: 397
- Fat: 17g
- Saturated Fat: 15g
- Cholesterol: 0mg
- Sodium: 31mg
- Carbohydrates: 55.8g
- Fiber: 5.7g
- Sugar: 3.6g
- Protein: 7g

Veggie Rice

Servings: 4

Prep Time: 25 minutes

Ingredients:

- 4 teaspoons vegetable oil, divided
- ½ cup onion, chopped finely
- 1 tablespoon fresh ginger, minced finely
- 2 teaspoons garlic, minced finely
- 1½ cups jasmine rice, rinsed
- ¾ cup frozen peas
- ¾ cup frozen carrots
- 3 tablespoons soy sauce
- 1 tablespoon oyster sauce
- ½ teaspoon sesame oil
- Freshly ground black pepper, as required
- 1¾ cups water
- 2 eggs, beaten

Directions:

1. Place 1 tablespoon of the vegetable oil in the Instant Pot and select "Sauté". Now, add the onion and cook for about 2 minutes.
2. Stir in the ginger and garlic and cook for about 1 minute.
3. Select the "Cancel" and stir in the remaining ingredients except the eggs.
4. Secure the lid and turn to "Seal" position.
5. Cook on "Manual" with "High Pressure" for about 5 minutes.
6. Press the "Cancel" and allow a "Natural" release for about 10 minutes and then, allow a "Quick" release.
7. Carefully remove the lid and let the rice rest for a few minutes.
8. Meanwhile, in a nonstick frying pan, heat the remaining oil over medium heat and cook the beaten eggs for about 2 minutes or until scrambled, staring continuously.
9. Add the scrambles eggs into the pot with the rice and stir to combine.
10. Serve immediately.

Nutrition Information

- Calories: 368
- Fat: 7.5g
- Saturated Fat: 1.7g
- Cholesterol: 82mg
- Sodium: 772mg
- Carbohydrates: 64.3g
- Fiber: 5.8g
- Sugar: 3.5g
- Protein: 10.1g

Chicken Rice

Servings: 8

Prep Time: 45 minutes

Ingredients:

For Chicken:

- 1 (5-pound) whole chicken, trimmed and cut in half
- 1 onion, halved
- 1 (2¼-inch) piece fresh ginger, cut in half
- 1 teaspoon ground turmeric
- Salt, as required
- 9 cups boiling water

For Dressing:

- 4 tablespoons water
- 2 tablespoons rice vinegar
- 2 tablespoons sugar
- ½ white onion, sliced thinly

For Rice:

- 3 tablespoons canola oil
- 5 garlic cloves, minced
- 2½ cups jasmine rice, rinsed
- ½ cup sweet rice, rinsed
- ½ teaspoon ground turmeric
- Salt, as required
- ½ cup fresh cilantro, chopped

For Sauce:

- 4 tablespoons sugar
- 3 tablespoons fresh lime juice
- 3 tablespoons fish sauce
- 5 garlic cloves, mashed
- ¼ teaspoon fresh ginger, julienned

Directions:

1. In the pot of Instant Pot, place the chicken alongside the onion, ginger, turmeric, salt and billing water.
2. Secure the lid and turn to "Seal" position.
3. Cook on "Manual" with "High Pressure" for about 10 minutes.
4. Press the "Cancel" and allow a "Natural" release for about 5 minutes and then, allow a "Quick" release.
5. Meanwhile, for dressing: in a bowl, add the water, vinegar and sugar and mix well.

6. Stir in the onion slices and set aside for about 15 minutes.
7. Carefully remove the lid and place the chicken onto a platter to cool.
8. Through a sieve, strain the broth into a bowl and remove the solids.
9. With paper towels, wipe the inner pot of Instant Pot.
10. Add the oil in the Instant Pot and select "Sauté". Now, add the garlic and cook for about 1 minute.
11. Add the jasmine rice and sweet rice and sauté for about 4 minutes.
12. Select the "Cancel" and stir in 3 cups of the broth, turmeric and 1 teaspoon of the salt.
13. Secure the lid and turn to "Seal" position.
14. Cook on "Manual" with "Low Pressure" for about 12 minutes.
15. Press the "Cancel" and allow a "Quick" release.
16. Meanwhile, for the sauce: place all the ingredients in a bowl and mix well.
17. Carefully remove the lid and transfer the rice onto a platter.
18. Meanwhile, remove the bone from the chicken and shred the meat.
19. In a large bowl, add the shredded meat, onion mixture and cilantro and mix well.
20. Divide the rice and chicken mixture onto serving plates.
21. Top with the sauce and serve.

Nutrition Information

- Calories: 887
- Fat: 26.4g
- Saturated Fat: 6.2g
- Cholesterol: 252mg
- Sodium: 787mg
- Carbohydrates: 68.2g
- Fiber: 3.5g
- Sugar: 10.5g
- Protein: 87.4g

CHICKEN & RICE PORRIDGE

Servings: 4

Prep Time: 40 minutes

Ingredients:

- 4 chicken leg quarters
- 1 white onion
- 2 shallots
- 1 (1-inch) piece fresh ginger, halved
- 8-10 cups boiling water
- 4 tablespoons chicken soup base, divided
- ¾ cup jasmine rice, rinsed
- ¼ cup sweet rice, rinsed
- 1 teaspoon fish sauce

- ½ teaspoon sugar
- Salt, as required
- 2 scallions (green part), chopped

Directions:
1. In the pot of Instant Pot, place the chicken, onion, shallot, ginger, 2 tablespoons of the chicken soup base and billing water.
2. Secure the lid and turn to "Seal" position.
3. Cook on "Manual" with "High Pressure" for about 8 minutes.
4. Press the "Cancel" and allow a "Natural" release for about 5 minutes and then, allow a "Quick" release.
5. Carefully remove the lid and place the chicken into the bowl of the cold water.
6. Drain the chicken and set aside to cool.
7. With a slotted spoon, remove the onion and shallots from the broth.
8. In the pot, add the rice and remaining chicken soup base and stir to combine.
9. Secure the lid and turn to "Seal" position.
10. Select "Porridge" and just use the default time of 18 minutes.
11. Meanwhile, remove the bone from the chicken and shred the meat.
12. Press the "Cancel" and allow a "Natural" release.
13. Carefully remove the lid and mix in the shredded meat, fish sauce, sugar and salt.
14. Serve with the garnishing of scallion.

Nutrition Information
- Calories: 379
- Fat: 13.1g
- Saturated Fat: 3.5g
- Cholesterol: 85mg
- Sodium: 1000mg
- Carbohydrates: 42.5g
- Fiber: 2.6g
- Sugar: 2.2g
- Protein: 22.8g

FISH CONGEE

Servings: 4

Prep Time: 40 minutes

Ingredients:

- ¾ cup rice, rinsed and drained
- 1½ pounds fish bones, scrubbed, rinsed and drained
- 1 shallot, halved
- 1 (½-inch) piece fresh ginger, sliced thinly
- 1 tablespoon fish sauce
- Salt, as required
- 6 cups boiling water
- Freshly ground black pepper, as required
- 1 pound grouper fillet, cut into ½-inch thick pieces
- 2 tablespoons fresh cilantro, chopped

Directions:

1. In the pot of Instant Pot, place all the ingredients except the fish fillets and cilantro.
2. Secure the lid and turn to "Seal" position.
3. Select "Porridge" and just use the default time of 20 minutes.
4. Press the "Cancel" and allow a "Natural" release.
5. Meanwhile, Sprinkle the fish pieces with a pinch of salt and black pepper.
6. Carefully remove the lid and select "Sauté".
7. With a slotted spoon, remove the fish bones.
8. Add the fish pieces and cook for about 2-3 minutes.
9. Select the "Cancel" and serve hot with the garnishing of cilantro.

Nutrition Information

- Calories: 266
- Fat: 1.7g
- Saturated Fat: 0.4g
- Cholesterol: 53mg
- Sodium: 460mg
- Carbohydrates: 28.9g
- Fiber: 0.5g
- Sugar: 0.2g
- Protein: 31g

Side Dishes Recipes

Glazed Chicken Wings

Servings: 6

Prep Time: 40 minutes

Ingredients:

- 1 cup water
- 2 pounds chicken wings
- ¼ cup sugar
- ¼ cup fish sauce
- 3 garlic cloves, crushed
- 2 tablespoons canola oil
- 5 garlic cloves, minced

Directions:

1. In the bottom of Instant Pot, arrange a steamer trivet and pour 1 cup of water.
2. Arrange the chicken wings on top of the trivet in a single layer.
3. Secure the lid and turn to "Seal" position.
4. Cook on "Manual" with "High Pressure" for about 5 minutes.
5. Meanwhile, preheat the oven to broiler. Line a baking sheet with a piece of foil.
6. Press the "Cancel" and allow a "Quick" release.
7. Carefully remove the lid and transfer the wings onto a plate.
8. With paper towels, pat the chicken wings dry.
9. For sauce: in a large bowl, add the sugar, fish sauce and crushed garlic cloves and mix well.
10. Add the wings and coat with the sauce generously.
11. Remove the wings from the bowl, reserving any remaining sauce.
12. Arrange the wings onto the prepared baking sheet and broil for about 5 minutes per side.
13. Remove the wings from the oven and set aside.
14. In a skillet, heat the oil over medium heat and sauté the minced garlic for about 1-2 minutes.
15. Add the wings and reserved sauce and cook for about 1 minute, stirring continuously.
16. Serve hot.

Nutrition Information

- Calories: 370
- Fat: 15.9g
- Saturated Fat: 3,4g
- Cholesterol: 135mg
- Sodium: 1050mg
- Carbohydrates: 10.1g
- Fiber: 0.1g

- Sugar: 8.8g
- Protein: 44.6g

ZESTY MEATBALLS

Servings: 8

Prep Time: 420 minutes

Ingredients:

For Meatballs:

- 1½ pounds ground pork
- 2 tablespoons fresh ginger, grated
- 1 tablespoon garlic, minced
- 1 tablespoon lemongrass paste
- 1 teaspoon fresh lime zest, grated
- 2 tablespoons fresh lime juice
- 1 tablespoon soy sauce
- ½ tablespoon chili paste
- Salt, as required

For Cooking:

- 1½ cups beef broth
- 1 tablespoon soy sauce
- ½ tablespoon fish sauce

Direction:

1. For meatballs: in a large bowl, add all the ingredients and with your hands, mix until well combined.
2. Make golf ball sized meatballs from the mixture and arrange onto a large parchment paper lined baking sheet.
3. Freeze or about 20 minutes.
4. In the pot of Instant Pot, place the meatballs and top with broth, soy sauce and fish sauce.
5. Secure the lid and turn to "Seal" position.
6. Cook on "Manual" with "High Pressure" for about 5 minutes.
7. Press the "Cancel" and allow a "Natural" release for about 10 minutes and then, allow a "Quick" release.
8. Carefully remove the lid and serve.

Nutrition Information

- Calories: 467
- Fat: 11.5g
- Saturated Fat: 3.8g
- Cholesterol: 228mg
- Sodium: 674mg

- Carbohydrates: 2.4g
- Fiber: 0.3g
- Sugar: 0.7g
- Protein: 83.1g

GARLICKY SPINACH

Servings: 4

Prep Time: 15 minutes

Ingredients:

- 2 tablespoons vegetable oil
- 1 tablespoon garlic, chopped finely
- 1¼ pounds fresh spinach
- 2 tablespoons fish sauce
- 2 tablespoons water
- Salt and ground black pepper, as required

Directions:

1. Add the oil in the Instant Pot and select "Sauté". Now, add the garlic and cook for about 1 minute.
2. Select the "Cancel" and stir in the spinach, fish sauce, water, salt and black pepper.
3. Secure the lid and turn to "Seal" position.
4. Select "Steam" and just use the default time of 1 minute.
5. Press the "Cancel" and allow a "Quick" release.
6. Carefully remove the lid and select the "Sauté".
7. Cook for about 1-2 minutes.
8. Select the "Cancel" and serve hot.

Nutrition Information

- Calories: 99
- Fat: 7.4g
- Saturated Fat: 1.4g
- Cholesterol: 0mg
- Sodium: 846mg
- Carbohydrates: 6.2g
- Fiber: 3.2g
- Sugar: 1g
- Protein: 4.6g

Soy Sauce Braised Broccoli

Servings: 4

Prep Time: 20 minutes

Ingredients:

- 1 cup water
- 4 cups broccoli florets
- 1 tablespoon peanut oil
- 4 garlic cloves, minced
- 1 teaspoon fresh ginger, grated
- 1 tablespoon soy sauce
- ½ tablespoon fish sauce
- ½ tablespoon rice wine

Directions:

1. In the bottom of Instant Pot, arrange a steamer basket and pour water.
2. Place the broccoli florets in steamer basket.
3. Secure the lid and turn to "Seal" position.
4. Cook on "Manual" with "High Pressure" for about 3-4 minutes.
5. Press the "Cancel" and allow a "Quick" release.
6. Carefully remove the lid and transfer the broccoli onto a plate.
7. Remove the steamer basket and water and with paper towels, pat the pot dry.
8. Add the oil in the Instant Pot and select "Sauté". Now, add the garlic and ginger and sauté for about 30 seconds.
9. Add broccoli and remaining ingredients and cook for about 1-2 minutes.
10. Select the "Cancel" and serve hot.

Nutrition Information

- Calories: 73
- Fat: 3.7g
- Saturated Fat: 0.6g
- Cholesterol: 0mg
- Sodium: 446mg
- Carbohydrates: 8g
- Fiber: 2.5g
- Sugar: 2.3g
- Protein: 3.1g

SAUTÉED MUSHROOMS

Servings: 6

Prep Time: 25 minutes

Ingredients:

- 1 tablespoon vegetable oil
- 2 garlic cloves, chopped finely
- 1 red chili, chopped
- 24 ounces fresh mushrooms, sliced
- 2 tablespoons water
- 2 tablespoons soy sauce
- 1 tablespoon fish sauce
- Freshly ground black pepper, as required

Directions:

1. Add the oil in the Instant Pot and select "Sauté". Now, add garlic and red chili and cook for about 1 minute.
2. Add the mushrooms and cook for about 1-2 minutes.
3. Select the "Cancel" and stir in remaining ingredients.
4. Secure the lid and turn to "Seal" position.
5. Select "Steam" and just use the default time of 2 minutes.
6. Press the "Cancel" and allow a "Quick" release.
7. Carefully remove the lid and select "Sauté".
8. Cook for about 3-4 minutes.
9. Select the "Cancel" and serve hot.

Nutrition Information

- Calories: 50
- Fat: 2.6g
- Saturated Fat: 0.5g
- Cholesterol: 0mg
- Sodium: 539mg
- Carbohydrates: 4.7g
- Fiber: 1.2g
- Sugar: 2.2g
- Protein: 4.1g

Salads & Eggs Recipes

Chicken & Veggie Salad

Servings: 4

Prep Time: 35 minutes

Ingredients:

For Chicken:

- 2 (8-ounce) boneless, skinless chicken breasts
- Salt, as required
- 1 cup water

For Dressing:

- 1/3 cup fish sauce
- 1/3 cup fresh lime juice
- 2 red chilies, seeded and chopped finely
- 2 tablespoons brown sugar

For Salad:

- 2 carrots, peeled and cut into matchsticks
- ½ large head cabbage, shredded finely
- 1 cup fresh cilantro leaves
- 1 cup fresh mint leaves

Directions:

1. For chicken: Lightly sprinkle the chicken breasts with salt..
2. In the bottom of Instant Pot, arrange a steamer trivet and pour the water.
3. Place the chicken breasts on top of the trivet.
4. Secure the lid and turn to "Seal" position.
5. Cook on "Manual" with "High Pressure" for about 12 minutes.
6. Press the "Cancel" and allow a "Quick" release.
7. Carefully remove the lid and transfer the chicken breasts onto a cutting board.
8. Chop the chicken breasts into desired sized pieces.
9. For dressing: in a bowl, add all the ingredients and beat until sugar is dissolved.
10. In a large serving bowl, place the chopped chicken and all salad ingredients and mix.
11. Pour the dressing and toss to coat.
12. Serve immediately.

Nutrition Information

- Calories: 293
- Fat: 8.7g
- Saturated Fat: 2.4g

- Cholesterol: 101mg
- Sodium: 2000mg
- Carbohydrates: 16.3g
- Fiber: 4.8g
- Sugar: 9.8g
- Protein: 36.3g

CHICKEN & NOODLES SALAD

Servings: 4

Prep Time: 40 minutes

Ingredients:

For Chicken:

- 1 pound chicken thighs
- Salt and ground black pepper, as required
- 1 tablespoon vegetable oil
- ½ cup water

For Dressing:

- 4 garlic cloves, chopped
- 1/3 cup vegetable oil
- 1/3 cup fresh lime juice
- ¼ cup fish sauce
- 2 tablespoons rice vinegar
- 2 tablespoons brown sugar
- 3 serrano peppers, sliced thinly

For Salad:

- 6 ounces rice noodles, soaked for 15 minutes and drained
- 2 cups carrots, peeled and julienned
- 2 cups cabbage, shredded
- 2 cups lettuce, shredded
- ½ cup fresh mint leaves, chopped

Directions:

1. For chicken: Sprinkle the chicken thighs with salt and black pepper.
2. Add the oil in the Instant Pot and select "Sauté". Now, add the chicken thighs and cook for about 1 minute per side.
3. Transfer the chicken thighs onto a plate.
4. In the bottom of Instant Pot, arrange a steamer trivet and pour the water.
5. Place the chicken thighs on top of the trivet.
6. Secure the lid and turn to "Seal" position.
7. Cook on "Manual" with "High Pressure" for about 9 minutes.

8. Press the "Cancel" and allow a "Natural" release for about 10 minutes and then, allow a "Quick" release.
9. Carefully remove the lid and transfer the chicken thighs onto a cutting board.
10. Chop the chicken thighs into desired sized pieces.
11. For the dressing: in a food processor, add all the ingredients except the Serrano peppers and pulse until smooth.
12. Transfer the dressing into a large serving bowl and stir in the Serrano pepper slices.
13. With a kitchen scissors, cut the drained noodles into shorter pieces.
14. In a large skillet, heat a small amount of the dressing over medium-high heat and stir-fry the noodles for about 5 minutes.
15. Remove from the heat and set aside.
16. In the bowl of the remaining dressing, add the chicken, salad ingredients and noodles and gently toss to coat.
17. Serve immediately.

Nutrition Information

- Calories: 548
- Fat: 32.5g
- Saturated Fat: 7g
- Cholesterol: 101mg
- Sodium: 1540mg
- Carbohydrates: 26.4g
- Fiber: 3.8g
- Sugar: 9.3g
- Protein: 35.8g

BEEF SALAD

Servings: 4

Prep Time: 20 minutes

Ingredients:

For Beef:

- 1 pound flank steaks, trimmed and cut into ¼-inch thick strips
- Freshly ground black pepper, as required
- ½ tablespoon canola oil
- 2 garlic cloves, minced
- ¼ cup water
- ¼ cup soy sauce
- 2 tablespoons fresh lime juice
- 1 tablespoon honey

For Dressing:

- 2 garlic cloves, crushed

- 2 red chilies, seeded and sliced finely
- 3 tablespoons fish sauce
- 3 tablespoons soy sauce
- 3 tablespoons fresh lime juice
- 3 tablespoons rice vinegar
- 2 tablespoons soft brown sugar

For Salad:

- 6 cups lettuce, shredded
- 2 cups carrots, peeled and shredded
- 1 large tomato, cubed
- 1 cucumber, peeled and sliced thinly
- ½ cup fresh cilantro, chopped
- ½ cup fresh mint, chopped

Directions:

1. Season steak evenly with black pepper..
2. Add the oil in the Instant Pot and select "Sauté". Now, add the steak, salt and black pepper and cook for about 5 minutes.
3. Transfer the steak into a bowl.
4. In the pot, add the garlic and cook for about 1 minute.
5. Select the "Cancel" and stir in beef, water, soy sauce, lemon juice and honey.
6. Secure the lid and turn to "Seal" position.
7. Cook on "Manual" with "High Pressure" for about 12 minutes.
8. Press the "Cancel" and allow a "Quick" release.
9. Carefully remove the lid and transfer the steak onto a plate.
10. For dressing: in a bowl, add all the ingredients and beat until sugar is dissolved.
11. In a large serving bowl, place the steak slices and all salad ingredients and mix.
12. Pour the dressing and toss to coat.
13. Serve immediately.

Nutrition Information

- Calories: 360
- Fat: 11.6g
- Saturated Fat: 4.1g
- Cholesterol: 15mg
- Sodium: 2700mg
- Carbohydrates: 26g
- Fiber: 4g
- Sugar: 15.8g
- Protein: 36.4g

Shrimp Salad

Servings: 4

Prep Time: 25 minutes

Ingredients:

For Shrimp:

- 1 cup water
- ¾ pound medium frozen shrimp, peeled and deveined
- 1 tablespoon butter, melted
- 2 tablespoons fresh lime juice
- Salt and ground black pepper, as required

For Dressing:

- 1/3 cup fresh mint
- 3 tablespoons red onion, chopped
- 1 garlic clove, peeled
- ¼ cup olive oil
- 2 tablespoons fresh lime juice
- 1 tablespoon rice vinegar
- 1 teaspoon fish sauce
- ¼ teaspoon honey
- 1/8 teaspoon chili paste

For Salad:

- 6 cups romaine lettuce, chopped
- 2 cups zucchini, julienned
- 2 cucumbers, sliced thinly
- 1 large carrot, peeled and julienned
- 1 red chili, sliced thinly
- ½ cup raw unsalted peanuts, toasted

Directions:

1. In the bottom of Instant Pot, arrange a steamer trivet and pour water
2. Arrange the shrimp on top of trivet in a single layer.
3. Drizzle with melted butter and lemon juice. Sprinkle with salt and black pepper.
4. Secure the lid and turn to "Seal" position.
5. Select "Steam" and just use the default time of 2 minutes.
6. Press the "Cancel" and allow a "Natural" release.
7. Carefully remove the lid and transfer the shrimp onto a plate.
8. For the dressing: in a food processor, add all the ingredients except the Serrano peppers and pulse until smooth.
9. In a large bowl, add all the salad ingredients and shrimp and mix well.
10. Drizzle with the dressing and toss to coat.

11. Serve immediately.

Nutrition Information

- Calories: 401
- Fat: 26.4g
- Saturated Fat: 5.4g
- Cholesterol: 187mg
- Sodium: 377mg
- Carbohydrates: 17.9g
- Fiber: 4.6g
- Sugar: 6.7g
- Protein: 26.8g

Chicken & Veggie Omelet

Servings: 3

Prep Time: 20 minutes

Ingredients:

- 5 eggs
- 2 tablespoons coconut milk
- 1 teaspoon fish sauce
- 1 garlic clove, chopped finely
- Salt and ground black pepper, as required
- 1 tablespoon vegetable oil
- 1/3 cup cooked chicken, shredded
- 1/3 cup mung bean sprouts
- ¼ cup mixed fresh herbs (mint, basil and cilantro leaves), chopped finely
- 1 scallion, chopped finely

Directions:

1. In a bowl, add eggs, coconut milk, fish sauce, garlic, salt and black pepper and beat until well combined.
2. Place the oil in the Instant Pot and select "Sauté" to heat the oil.
3. Select the "Cancel" and place the egg mixture.
4. Secure the lid and turn to "Seal" position.
5. Select "Steam" and just use the default time of 5 minutes.
6. Meanwhile, in a bowl, add the remaining ingredients and mix well.
7. Press the "Cancel" and allow a "Quick" release.
8. Carefully remove the lid and transfer the omelet onto a plate.
9. Place the chicken mixture over one half of omelet and fold it.
10. Serve immediately.

Nutrition Information

- Calories: 204
- Fat: 14.9g
- Saturated Fat: 5.4g
- Cholesterol: 285mg
- Sodium: 323mg
- Carbohydrates: 3.4g
- Fiber: 0.9g
- Sugar: 1.1g
- Protein: 15.3g

Soup & Stew Recipes

Chicken & Noodles Soup

Servings: 4

Prep Time: 40 minutes

Ingredients:

For Broth:

- 2 tablespoons canola oil
- 2 medium yellow onions, halved
- 1 (2-inch) piece fresh ginger, cut into ¼-inch slices
- 1 tablespoon coriander seeds
- 5 whole cloves
- 3 cardamom pods, lightly smashed
- 3 star anise pods
- 1 cinnamon stick
- 6 (5-ounce) bone-in, skin-on chicken thighs
- 3 tablespoons fish sauce
- 1 tablespoon sugar
- 8 cups water
- Salt and ground black pepper, as required

For Serving:

- 8 ounces rice noodles, prepared according to package's directions
- 3 scallions, sliced
- ½ cup bean sprouts
- ½ cup mixed fresh herbs (mint, cilantro and basil), chopped
- 1 lime, cut into wedges

Directions:

1. Add the oil in the Instant Pot and select "Sauté". Now, add the onions, cut side down, with the ginger and cook for about 4 minutes, without moving.
2. Stir in the whole spices and cook for about 1 minute.
3. Select the "Cancel" and stir in the chicken, fish sauce, sugar and water.
4. Secure the lid and turn to "Seal" position.
5. Cook on "Manual" with "High Pressure" for about 15 minutes.
6. Press the "Cancel" and allow a "Natural" release for about 10 minutes and then, allow a "Quick" release.
7. Carefully remove the lid and place the chicken thighs onto a plate.
8. Through a fine mesh strainer, strain the broth and season with the salt and black pepper.
9. Remove the bones from the chicken and then chop the meat.

10. Divide the cooked noodles and chopped into 4 serving bowls and top with the hot broth.
11. Serve with the topping of the scallions, bean sprouts and herbs.

Nutrition Information

- Calories: 593
- Fat: 23.3g
- Saturated Fat: 4.9g
- Cholesterol: 189mg
- Sodium: 1257mg
- Carbohydrates: 28.5g
- Fiber: 4.1g
- Sugar: 6.3g
- Protein: 65.3g

BEEF & NOODLES SOUP

Servings: 8

Prep Time: 1 hour 35 minutes

Ingredients:

For Broth:

- 1 tablespoon vegetable oil
- 4 pounds beef shanks
- 1 large onion, sliced thinly
- 1 tablespoon fresh ginger, sliced thinly
- 10½ cups water, divided
- ¼ cup fish sauce
- 2 tablespoons soy sauce
- 1 tablespoon sugar
- 2 star anise pods
- 1 cinnamon stick
- 4 whole cloves
- 1 teaspoon whole black peppercorns
- Salt, as required
- 1½ pounds beef brisket
- 10 cups of water

For Bowls:

- 1 pound thin rice noodles, prepared according to package's directions
- 2 cups bean sprouts
- 1 cup fresh cilantro leaves
- ½ cup fresh basil leaves
- 2-3 Serrano chilies, sliced thinly

- 2 tablespoons soy sauce

Directions:

1. Add the oil in the Instant Pot and select "Sauté". Now, add the beef shanks and sear for about 3 minutes per side.
2. With a slotted spoon, transfer the shanks into a bowl
3. In the pot, add the onions and ginger and cook for about 5-6 minutes.
4. Add ½ cup of water and scrape the browned bits from the bottom.
5. Select the "Cancel" and stir in the cooked beef shanks, fish sauce, soy sauce, sugar, whole spices and salt.
6. Arrange the beef brisket on top and place the remaining water.
7. Secure the lid and turn to "Seal" position.
8. Cook on "Manual" with "High Pressure" for about 60 minutes.
9. Press the "Cancel" and allow a "Natural" release.
10. Carefully remove the lid and transfer the shanks and brisket onto a plate.
11. Through a fine mesh strainer, strain the broth.
12. Remove the bones from the shanks and shred it.
13. Cut the brisket into thin slices against the grain crosswise.
14. Divide the cooked noodles and meat into 8 serving bowls and top with the hot broth.
15. Top each bowl with bean sprouts, herbs and Serrano chilies.
16. Drizzle with the soy sauce and serve.

Nutrition Information

- Calories: 728
- Fat: 21.8g
- Saturated Fat: 7.6g
- Cholesterol: 253mg
- Sodium: 1391mg
- Carbohydrates: 20.8g
- Fiber: 1.2g
- Sugar: 2.8g
- Protein: 106g

SHRIMP & CRAB SOUP

Servings: 6

Prep Time: 1 hour

Ingredients:

- 2 pounds pork ribs
- 4 tablespoons vegetable oil, divided
- 3 large shallots, halved
- 1 carrot, peeled and chopped roughly
- 5 teaspoons granulated sugar, divided

- Salt, as required
- 2 tablespoons fish sauce, divided
- 11 cups water, divided
- 1 cup cornstarch
- 2 pounds raw shrimp, peeled and deveined
- 1 shallot, chopped
- 5 garlic cloves, minced
- 1 pound lump crabmeat
- 10 ounces Udon noodles, prepared according to package's directions

For Topping:

- 3 scallions, chopped
- ½ cup fresh mint leaves, chopped
- 1 lime, cut into wedges

Directions:

1. In a pan of the boiling water, add the pork ribs and cook for about 4 minutes.
2. Drain the pork ribs and rinse well.
3. Place 1 tablespoon of the oil in the Instant Pot and select "Sauté". Now, add the halved 3 shallots and cook for about 2-3 minutes.
4. Select the "Cancel" and stir in the pork ribs, carrot, 4 teaspoons of sugar, salt, 1 tablespoon of fish sauce and 10 cups of water.
5. Secure the lid and turn to "Seal" position.
6. Cook on "Manual" with "High Pressure" for about 25 minutes.
7. Meanwhile, in a bowl, add the shrimp, 1 teaspoon of sugar, salt and remaining fish sauce and mix well.
8. Set aside for about 10 minutes.
9. Heat 3 tablespoons of oil in a large pan over medium heat and sauté the chopped shallot for about 3 minutes.
10. Stir in the garlic and sauté for about 1 minute.
11. Add the marinated shrimp and cook for about 2-3 minutes.
12. With tongs, transfer the shrimp into a bowl.
13. In the same skillet, add the crabmeat and toss with shallot mixture.
14. Remove from the heat and set aside.
15. Press the "Cancel" and allow a "Natural" release for about 15 minutes and then, allow a "Quick" release.
16. Meanwhile, in a bowl, add the cornstarch and remaining water and mix well.
17. Carefully remove the lid and through a fine mesh strainer, strain the broth.
18. Return the broth into the Instant Pot and select "Sauté".
19. Add the cornstarch mixture, stirring continuously and cook for about 2-3 minutes.
20. Divide the cooked noodles, shrimp and crabmeat into 6 serving bowls and top with the hot broth.
21. Top each bowl with scallion, mint and lime wedges and serve.

Nutrition Information

- Calories: 732
- Fat: 27.9g

- Saturated Fat: 5.9g
- Cholesterol: 391mg
- Sodium: 2000mg
- Carbohydrates: 63.8g
- Fiber: 3.9g
- Sugar: 8.6g
- Protein: 67.1g

Beef Stew

Servings: 4

Prep Time: 35 minutes

Ingredients:

- 1 turnip, peeled and cut into chunks
- 2 carrots, peeled and cut into chunks
- ¼ cup beef broth
- 1 pound beef chuck stew meat
- 1 onion
- 1 tablespoon fresh ginger, minced
- 1 tablespoon garlic, minced
- 2 tablespoons tomato paste
- 1 tablespoon lemongrass paste
- 2 whole star anise
- 1 teaspoon curry powder
- Salt and ground black pepper, as required
- 2 tablespoons fish sauce
- 1½ cups water
- ½ cup coconut water
- ½ cup fresh cilantro, chopped

Directions:

1. In a small, heatproof container, place the carrots, turnip and broth. Set aside.
2. In the pot of Instant Pot, place the remaining ingredients except the cilantro and stir to combine.
3. Arrange a steamer trivet on top of beef mixture.
4. Place the container of vegetables on top of the trivet.
5. Secure the lid and turn to "Seal" position.
6. Cook on "Manual" with "High Pressure" for about 15 minutes.
7. Press the "Cancel" and allow a "Natural" release for about 10 minutes and then, allow a "Quick" release.
8. Carefully remove the lid and place the vegetable mixture into the stew.
9. Serve hot with the garnishing of cilantro.

Nutrition Information

- Calories: 305
- Fat: 15.6g
- Saturated Fat: 6.2g
- Cholesterol: 81mg
- Sodium: 940mg
- Carbohydrates: 12.8g
- Fiber: 3g
- Sugar: 6.3g
- Protein: 27.8g

PORK STEW

Servings: 8

Prep Time: 1 hour 10 minutes

Ingredients:

- 1 tablespoon coconut oil
- ¼ pound shiitake mushrooms, stems removed and halved
- ¼ cup shallots, sliced thinly
- 4 garlic cloves, smashed
- 1 tablespoon fresh ginger, sliced
- 3 pounds pork shoulder, cubed into 2-inch size
- 3 tablespoons fish sauce
- 1 cup coconut water
- 3 carrots, peeled and cut into ½-inch slices diagonally
- ½ cup fresh cilantro, chopped

Directions:

1. Add the oil in the Instant Pot and select "Sauté". Now, add the mushrooms and shallots and cook for about 3-5 minutes.
2. Stir in the garlic and ginger and cook for about 1 minute.
3. Add the pork cubes and cook for about 1-2 minutes.
4. Select the "Cancel" and stir in the fish sauce and coconut water.
5. Secure the lid and turn to "Seal" position.
6. Cook on "Manual" with "High Pressure" for about 40 minutes.
7. Press the "Cancel" and allow a "Natural" release for about 15 minutes and then, allow a "Quick" release.
8. Carefully remove the lid and with a spoon, transfer the pork cubes into a bowl.
9. In the pot, add the carrots and stir to combine.
10. Secure the lid and turn to "Seal" position.
11. Cook on "Manual" with "High Pressure" for about 2 minutes.
12. Press the "Cancel" and allow a "Natural" release for about 10 minutes and then, allow a "Quick" release.
13. Carefully remove the lid and mix in the pork cubes.

14. Serve hot with the garnishing of cilantro.

Nutrition Information

- Calories: 547
- Fat: 38.2g
- Saturated Fat: 14.9g
- Cholesterol: 153mg
- Sodium: 722mg
- Carbohydrates: 7.8g
- Fiber: 1.4g
- Sugar: 2.9g
- Protein: 40.9g

Noodles Recipes

Garlicky Noodles

Servings: 4

Prep Time: 20 minutes

Ingredients:

- 1 cup chicken broth
- 1 cup water
- 6 garlic cloves, minced
- 2 tablespoons brown sugar
- 2 tablespoons soy sauce
- 1 tablespoon fish sauce
- 1 teaspoon sesame oil
- 1 teaspoon chili paste
- 8 ounces noodles, broken in half
- 2 scallions, chopped

Directions:

1. In the pot of Instant Pot, place all the ingredients except the noodles and scallion and beat until well combined.
2. Place the noodles evenly on top of mixture.
3. Secure the lid and turn to "Seal" position.
4. Cook on "Manual" with "High Pressure" for about 6 minutes.
5. Press the "Cancel" and allow a "Quick" release.
6. Carefully remove the lid and mix the noodles with mixture.
7. Serve with the garnishing of scallions.

Nutrition Information

- Calories: 134
- Fat: 2.9g
- Saturated Fat: 0.5g
- Cholesterol: 17mg
- Sodium: 1012mg
- Carbohydrates: 22.2g
- Fiber: 1g
- Sugar: 5.6g
- Protein: 5g

Noodles with Vegetables

Servings: 4

Prep Time: 20 minutes

Ingredients:

- 3 tablespoons peanut butter
- 2½ tablespoons soy sauce
- 1½ tablespoons rice vinegar
- 1 tablespoon fish sauce
- 1½ tablespoons honey
- ½ tablespoon chili paste
- Salt, as required
- 2 tablespoons vegetable oil
- 1 teaspoon fresh ginger, minced
- 4 garlic cloves, minced
- 2 medium carrots, peeled and sliced thinly
- 1 medium red bell pepper, seeded and sliced thinly
- 2 scallions, chopped
- 8 ounces noodles, broken into half
- 1½ cups water
- 2 tablespoons fresh lime juice
- 2 tablespoons fresh cilantro, chopped

Directions:

1. For sauce: in a bowl, add the peanut butter, soy sauce, vinegar, fish sauce, honey, chili paste and sat and beat until well combined.
2. Add the oil in the Instant Pot and select "Sauté". Now, add the garlic and ginger and cook for about 1 minute.
3. Add in the carrots, bell pepper and scallion and cook for about 1-2 minutes.
4. Select the "Cancel" and stir in the sauce.
5. Place the spaghetti over vegetable mixture and pour water on top.
6. Gently, press the noodles under water.
7. Secure the lid and turn to "Seal" position.
8. Cook on "Manual" with "High Pressure" for about 4 minutes.
9. Press the "Cancel" and allow a "Quick" release.
10. Carefully remove the lid and mix in the lime juice.
11. Serve with the garnishing of cilantro.

Nutrition Information

- Calories: 281
- Fat: 14.5g
- Saturated Fat: 2.9g
- Cholesterol: 17mg

- Sodium: 1050mg
- Carbohydrates: 32g
- Fiber: 3g
- Sugar: 11.9g
- Protein: 7.5g

VERMICELLI NOODLES WITH VEGGIES

Servings: 4

Prep Time: 20 minutes

Ingredients:

- 1 tablespoon vegetable oil
- 1 onion, chopped finely
- ¾ cup carrot, peeled and julienned
- ¾ cup red bell peppers, seeded and julienned
- 2 red chilies, chopped
- 2 cups vermicelli noodles
- ¼ teaspoon ground turmeric
- Salt, as required
- 1 tablespoon fish sauce
- 1 tablespoon soy sauce
- 2¼ cups water
- 2 scallions, sliced

Directions:

1. Add the oil in the Instant Pot and select "Sauté". Now, add the onions and cook for about 2 minutes.
2. Add in the carrot, bell pepper and red chili and cook for about 2 minutes.
3. Select the "Cancel" and stir in the remaining ingredients except the scallions.
4. Secure the lid and turn to "Seal" position.
5. Cook on "Manual" with "High Pressure" for about 1 minute.
6. Press the "Cancel" and allow a "Quick" release.
7. Carefully remove the lid and mix in the scallions.
8. Serve hot.

Nutrition Information

- Calories: 198
- Fat: 3.5g
- Saturated Fat: 0.7g
- Cholesterol: 0mg
- Sodium: 629mg
- Carbohydrates: 34.9g
- Fiber: 3.1g

- Sugar: 3.8g
- Protein: 6.1g

Honey Noodles with Chicken

Servings: 4

Prep Time: 20 minutes

Ingredients:

- 2 (6-ounce) skinless, boneless chicken breasts, chopped
- 3 tablespoons soy sauce
- 1 tablespoon fish sauce
- 1 tablespoon sesame oil
- 2 tablespoons honey
- ½ teaspoon chili paste
- 6 garlic cloves, minced
- 2 cups water
- 1 (8-ounce) package rice noodles
- 1 head broccoli, cut into small florets
- <u>1 yellow bell pepper, seeded and thinly sliced</u>
- <u>1 orange bell pepper, seeded and thinly sliced</u>
- <u>1 tablespoon sesame seeds</u>

Directions:

1. In the pot of Instant Pot, place the chicken breasts, soy sauce, fish sauce, oil, honey, chili paste, garlic cloves and water and mix well.
2. Place the rice noodles on top and gently, press into the water.
3. Secure the lid and turn to "Seal" position.
4. Cook on "Manual" with "High Pressure" for about 2 minutes.
5. Press the "Cancel" and allow a "Quick" release.
6. Carefully remove the lid and immediately, stir in the broccoli and bell peppers.
7. Immediately, secure the lid for about 5-10 minutes.
8. Remove lid and serve with the garnishing of sesame seeds.

Nutrition Information

- Calories: 427
- Fat: 6.4g
- Saturated Fat: 0.7g
- Cholesterol: 49mg
- Sodium: 1216mg
- Carbohydrates: 67.5g
- Fiber: 3.7g
- Sugar: 13.2g
- Protein: 25.5g

Noodles with Shrimp

Servings: 4

Prep Time: 25 minutes

Ingredients:

- 8 ounces rice noodles
- 4 tablespoons vegetable oil, divided
- 1/3 cup brown sugar
- 3 tablespoons rice vinegar
- 3 tablespoons fish sauce
- 2 tablespoons soy sauce
- 4 scallions, chopped and divided
- 2 garlic cloves, chopped
- 2 carrots, peeled and cut into thin strips
- 1 cup red bell pepper, seeded and sliced into thin strips
- 1 cup yellow bell pepper, seeded and sliced into thin strips
- 3 large eggs, beaten
- 1 pound shrimp, peeled and deveined
- 1 tablespoon fresh lime juice

Directions:

1. In a large bowl of boiling water, soak the rice noodles for about 5 minutes.
2. Drain the noodles and mix 1 tablespoon of oil. Set aside.
3. For sauce: in another bowl, add the brown sugar, vinegar, soy sauce and fish sauce and beat until well combined.
4. Place the remaining oil in the Instant Pot and select "Sauté". Then add 2 scallions and garlic and cook for about 1 minute.
5. Stir in the bell peppers and carrots and cook for about 2 minutes.
6. Push the mixture to the edge of the pan.
7. In the center of pan, place the beaten eggs and cook for about 1-2 minutes, stirring continuously.
8. Add the bell peppers and cook for about 1 minute.
9. Select the "Cancel" and stir in the shrimp.
10. Secure the lid and turn to "Seal" position.
11. Cook on "Manual" with "High Pressure" for about 1 minute.
12. Press the "Cancel" and allow a "Natural" release for about 5 minutes and then, allow a "Quick" release.
13. Carefully remove the lid and mix in the noodles and sauce.
14. Immediately secure the lid for about 10 minutes.
15. Remove lid and stir in the lime juice.
16. Serve with the garnishing of remaining scallions.

Nutrition Information

- Calories: 472

- Fat: 19.6g
- Saturated Fat: 4.4g
- Cholesterol: 378mg
- Sodium: 1800mg
- Carbohydrates: 38.2g
- Fiber: 2.6g
- Sugar: 17.5g
- Protein: 33.5g

Vegetables & Vegetarian Recipes

Stewed Squash

Servings: 6

Prep Time: 20 minutes

Ingredients:

- 2 tablespoons vegetable oil
- 1 tablespoon garlic, chopped
- 1 (2½-pound) butternut squash, peeled and cut into 1-inch cubes
- 2 tablespoons fish sauce
- 1 tablespoon sugar
- Salt and ground black pepper, as required
- ¾ cup vegetable broth

Directions:

1. Add the oil in the Instant Pot and select "Sauté". Now, add the garlic and cook for about 1 minute.
2. Add the squash cues and cook for about 1 minute.
3. Select the "Cancel" and stir in the remaining ingredients.
4. Secure the lid and turn to "Seal" position.
5. Cook on "Manual" with "High Pressure" for about 4 minutes.
6. Press the "Cancel" and allow a "Natural" release.
7. Carefully remove the lid and serve hot.

Nutrition Information

- Calories: 142
- Fat: 4.9g
- Saturated Fat: 1g
- Cholesterol: 0mg
- Sodium: 954mg
- Carbohydrates: 24.9g
- Fiber: 3.8g
- Sugar: 6.5g
- Protein: 2.9g

Vegetarian Curry

Servings: 4

Prep Time: 25 minutes

Ingredients:

- 2 tablespoons canola oil
- 3 tablespoons curry paste
- 1 (19-ounce) can coconut milk
- 14 ounces firm tofu, pressed and cubed
- 1 carrot, peeled and sliced
- 1 red bell pepper, seeded and chopped into 1-inch pieces
- 1 green bell pepper, seeded and chopped into 1-inch pieces
- 2 scallions, cut into 2-inch pieces
- 1 teaspoon fresh ginger, grated
- 1 tablespoon fresh lime juice
- 1 tablespoon fish sauce
- 1 teaspoon sugar

Directions:

1. Add the oil in the Instant Pot and select "Sauté". Now, add the curry paste and sauté for about 30 seconds.
2. Add the coconut milk and stir well.
3. Select the "Cancel" and stir in tofu, carrot, bell peppers, scallion and ginger.
4. Secure the lid and turn to "Seal" position.
5. Cook on "Manual" with "Low Pressure" for about 2 minutes.
6. Press the "Cancel" and allow a "Quick" release.
7. Carefully remove the lid and mix in the remaining ingredients.
8. Serve hot.

Nutrition Information

- Calories: 551
- Fat: 50g
- Saturated Fat: 29.9g
- Cholesterol: 0mg
- Sodium: 393mg
- Carbohydrates: 20.4g
- Fiber: 5.3g
- Sugar: 10.2g
- Protein: 12.9g

Tofu & Green Beans Curry

Servings: 5

Prep Time: 35 minutes

Ingredients:

For Green Beans:

- 1 pound fresh green beans, trimmed and chopped into 1½-inch pieces
- 1 cup water

For Curry:

- 1 (14-ounce) can coconut milk
- ½ cup water
- 3 tablespoons peanut butter
- 2 tablespoons plus 1 teaspoon curry paste
- 1 tablespoon coconut oil
- 2 dried red chilies, broken into pieces
- 1 small onion, chopped
- ¼ cup raw cashews
- 2 teaspoons fresh ginger, grated
- 2 teaspoons garlic, grated
- 3 teaspoons rice vinegar
- 1 teaspoon fish sauce
- 1 teaspoon soy sauce
- 1 teaspoon coconut sugar
- ¼ teaspoon ground turmeric
- 8 ounces extra-firm tofu, drained and cubed
- 1 tablespoon fresh lime juice

Directions:

1. For green beans: In the bottom of Instant Pot, arrange a steamer trivet and pour water.
2. Place green beans on top of the trivet.
3. Secure the lid and turn to "Seal" position.
4. Cook on "Manual" with "High Pressure" for about 5 minutes.
5. Press the "Cancel" and allow a "Quick" release.
6. Carefully, remove the lid and transfer the green beans into a bowl. Set aside.
7. Remove the water from the pot and with paper towels, pat dry it.
8. For curry: in a bowl, add the coconut milk, water, peanut butter, water and curry paste and beat until well combined. Keep aside.
9. Add the oil in the Instant Pot and select "Sauté". Now, add the dried red chili and cook for about 30 seconds.
10. Add the onion and cook for about 1 minute.
11. Add cashews and cook for about 1 minute.
12. Stir in the ginger and garlic and cook for about 1 minute.

13. Add the coconut milk mixture and cook for about 1 minute.
14. Select the "Cancel" and stir in remaining ingredients except the lime juice.
15. Secure the lid and turn to "Seal" position.
16. Cook on "Manual" with "High Pressure" for about 2 minutes.
17. Press the "Cancel" and allow a "Quick" release.
18. Carefully remove the lid and select "Sauté".
19. Stir in green beans and cook for about 1-2 minutes.
20. Select the "Cancel" and stir in lime juice before serving.

Nutrition Information

- Calories: 428
- Fat: 36g
- Saturated Fat: 21.1g
- Cholesterol: 0mg
- Sodium: 220mg
- Carbohydrates: 20.8g
- Fiber: 6.2g
- Sugar: 6.9g
- Protein: 12.1g

CARAMELIZED TOFU

Servings: 4

Prep Time: 25 minutes

Ingredients:

- ¾ cup water
- 2 tablespoons cornstarch
- 2 tablespoons granulated sugar
- 1 teaspoon fresh ginger, minced
- 2 garlic cloves, minced
- ¼ cup soy sauce
- 3 tablespoons rice wine vinegar
- ½ teaspoon red pepper flakes, crushed
- 2 tablespoons vegetable oil
- 16 ounces extra-firm tofu, pressed and cut into ½-inch thick pieces.

Directions:

1. In a bowl, add all the ingredients except the tofu and oil and beat until well combined.
2. Add the oil in the Instant Pot and select "Sauté". Now, add the tofu and cook for about 2-3 minutes or until browned from all sides.
3. Select the "Cancel" and stir in the sauce.
4. Secure the lid and turn to "Seal" position.
5. Cook on "Manual" with "High Pressure" for about 5 minutes.

6. Press the "Cancel" and allow a "Quick" release.
7. Carefully remove the lid and serve.

Nutrition Information

- Calories: 222
- Fat: 13.5g
- Saturated Fat: 2g
- Cholesterol: 0mg
- Sodium: 910mg
- Carbohydrates: 14.1g
- Fiber: 0.8g
- Sugar: 6.9g
- Protein: 12.4g

STEAMED SPRING ROLLS

Servings: 10

Prep Time: 25 minutes

Ingredients:

- 5 ounces dried rice vermicelli, soaked for 10 minutes and drained
- 1 cup carrot, peeled and grated
- ½ cup fresh bean sprouts
- 3 tablespoons fresh cilantro leaves, chopped
- 2 tablespoons soy sauce
- 1 tablespoons fresh lime juice
- 1 tablespoon chili jam
- 1½ tablespoons granulated sugar
- 1 tablespoon fried garlic
- 10 (10-inch) dried rice paper wrappers
- 2 cups water

Directions:

1. For the filling: place all the ingredients except the wrappers and water in a large bowl and mix well.
2. Fill a shallow bowl with warm water.
3. Dip 1 rice wrapper into the water until it is pliable.
4. Now, arrange the wrapper on a smooth surface.
5. Place about 1-2 tablespoons of filling in the center of the rice paper.
6. Carefully fold the wrapper around the filling.
7. Repeat with the remaining wrappers and filling.
8. In the bottom of Instant Pot, arrange the steamer basket and pour the water.
9. Place the rolls in steamer basket.
10. Secure the lid and turn to "Seal" position.

11. Select "Steam" and just use the default time of 3 minutes.
12. Press the "Cancel" and allow a "Natural" release.
13. Carefully remove the lid and serve warm.

Nutrition Information

- Calories: 119
- Fat: 0.2g
- Saturated Fat: 0.1g
- Cholesterol: 0mg
- Sodium: 238mg
- Carbohydrates: 27.5g
- Fiber: 0.8g
- Sugar: 3.9g
- Protein: 1.5g

Dessert Recipes

Sweet Soup

Servings: 5

Prep Time: 25 minutes

Ingredients:

- 1/3 cup tapioca strips, shredded
- 2 cups water
- 1 pound sweet potato, peeled cubed and soaked in salted water for 5 minutes
- ½-1 cup kelp strips, washed thoroughly, soaked in warm water for 5 minutes and rinsed
- ½ cup peeled split mung beans, rinsed
- 1 (13½-ounce) can coconut milk
- ½-¾ cup sugar
- ½ teaspoon vanilla extract
- 2 cups milk

Directions:

1. In the pot of Instant Pot, place the tapioca strips and water and stir to combine.
2. Secure the lid and turn to "Seal" position.
3. Cook on "Manual" with "High Pressure" for about 3 minutes.
4. Press the "Cancel" and allow a "Quick" release.
5. Carefully, remove the lid and mix in the sweet potato, seaweed strips, mung beans, coconut milk, sugar and vanilla extract.
6. Secure the lid and turn to "Seal" position.
7. Cook on "Manual" with "High Pressure" for about 5 minutes.
8. Press the "Cancel" and allow a "Natural" release for about 10 minutes and then, allow a "Quick" release.
9. Carefully remove the lid and select "Sauté".
10. Mix in the milk and bring to a gentle boil.
11. Select the "Cancel" and serve immediately.

Nutrition Information

- Calories: 487
- Fat: 20.6g
- Saturated Fat: 17.4g
- Cholesterol: 8mg
- Sodium: 132mg
- Carbohydrates: 70.4g
- Fiber: 9.5g
- Sugar: 43g

- Protein: 12.3g

RICE PUDDING

Servings: 6

Prep Time: 25 minutes

Ingredients:

- 3 cups whole milk
- ¾ cup jasmine rice, rinsed
- ½ cup granulated sugar
- 1 strip lime peel
- Pinch of salt
- 1 cup canned coconut milk
- 1 teaspoon vanilla extract
- 1/8 teaspoon ground cinnamon

Directions:

1. In the pot of Instant Pot, place the milk, rice, sugar, lime peel and salt and stir to combine.
2. Secure the lid and turn to "Seal" position.
3. Select "Porridge" and just use the default time of 15 minutes.
4. Press the "Cancel" and allow a "Natural" release for about 10 minutes and then, allow a "Quick" release.
5. Carefully remove the lid and discard the lime peel.
6. Stir in the coconut milk and vanilla extract.
7. Serve warm with the sprinkling of cinnamon.

Nutrition Information

- Calories: 310
- Fat: 13.5g
- Saturated Fat: 10.7g
- Cholesterol: 12mg
- Sodium: 82mg
- Carbohydrates: 42.5g
- Fiber: 1.9g
- Sugar: 24.5g
- Protein: 6.4g

Rice & Black-Eyed Peas Pudding

Servings: 6

Prep Time: 30 minutes

Ingredients:

For Pudding:

- 1 (15½-ounce) can black-eye peas, drained and rinsed thoroughly
- 1 cup sweet rice, rinsed and drained
- 1 cup sugar
- 1 teaspoon vanilla extract
- 4 cups water

For Coconut Sauce:

- 1 tablespoon cornstarch
- 2 tablespoons water
- 1 (14-ounce) can coconut milk
- ½ cup water
- 1 Pandan leaf
- 1 tablespoon sugar
- ½ teaspoon salt

Directions:

1. For the pudding: in the pot of Instant Pot, place all the ingredients and stir to combine.
2. Secure the lid and turn to "Seal" position.
3. Cook on "Manual" with "Low Pressure" for about 14 minutes.
4. Meanwhile, for coconut sauce: in a bowl, add the cornstarch and water and mix well.
5. In a pan, add the coconut milk, water, Pandan leaf, sugar and salt over medium heat and bring to a gentle boil.
6. Slowly, add the cornstarch mixture, stirring continuously.
7. Remove from the heat and set aside.
8. Press the "Cancel" and allow a "Quick" release.
9. Carefully remove the lid and quickly, put the pudding into a large serving bowl.
10. Add the coconut sauce and stir to combine.
11. Serve warm.

Nutrition Information

- Calories: 585
- Fat: 15.8g
- Saturated Fat: 14g
- Cholesterol: 0mg
- Sodium: 234mg
- Carbohydrates: 111.2g
- Fiber: 21.9g

- Sugar: 39g
- Protein: 21.3g

COFFEE FLAN

Servings: 7

Prep Time: 30 minutes

Ingredients:

- ¾ cup granulated sugar
- 1 cup plus 2 tablespoon water, divided
- 1 cup sweetened condensed milk
- 2 whole eggs
- 2 egg yolks
- 2 cups whole milk
- 2 tablespoons instant coffee powder
- 1 cup water

Directions:

1. In a pan, add the sugar and 2 tablespoon of the water over medium-low heat and cook until the sugar turns into a golden amber color.
2. Remove from the heat and immediately, place about 1½ tablespoons of the caramel into each of the 7 (4-ounce) ramekins.
3. Set aside to cool and harden.
4. In a large bowl, add the condensed milk, whole eggs and egg yolks and beat until smooth.
5. In a pan, add 1 cup of milk over medium heat and cook until it starts to bubble.
6. Remove from the heat and add the coffee powder, stirring continuously until dissolved.
7. Add the remaining milk and mix well.
8. Add the milk mixture into the bowl of egg mixture and mix until well combined.
9. Through a fine mesh sieve, strain the flan mixture.
10. Carefully place the mixture into the ramekins over caramel.
11. With 1 piece of the foil, cover each ramekin well.
12. In the bottom of Instant Pot, arrange the steamer trivet and pour the water.
13. Place the ramekins on top of the trivet.
14. Secure the lid and turn to "Seal" position.
15. Cook on "Manual" with "High Pressure" for about 6 minutes.
16. Press the "Cancel" and allow a "Natural" release for about 10 minutes and then, allow a "Quick" release.
17. Carefully remove the lid and place the ramekins onto a counter.
18. Carefully remove the foil and let them cool for about 60-90 minutes.
19. With 1 plastic wrap, cover each ramekin and refrigerate overnight.
20. Carefully place each flan onto a serving plate and serve.

Nutrition Information

- Calories: 296

- Fat: 8.6g
- Saturated Fat: 4.6g
- Cholesterol: 129mg
- Sodium: 103mg
- Carbohydrates: 48.6g
- Fiber: 0g
- Sugar: 49g
- Protein: 8.1g

COCONUT FLAN

Servings: 6

Prep Time: 25 minutes

Ingredients:

- 1 (13½-ounce) can coconut milk
- 14 ounces sweetened condensed milk
- 12 ounces evaporated milk
- 1 cup full-fat milk
- 3 eggs
- 1 cup sugar
- Pinch of salt
- ¼ teaspoon vanilla extract
- 2 cups water
- ½ cup desiccated coconut

Directions:

1. For caramel syrup: in a pan, add the sugar over medium heat and cook for 5 minutes or until it changes into a golden amber color, stirring frequently.
2. Remove from the heat and immediately, place the caramel syrup into a 6-inch aluminum cake tin evenly.
3. In a blender, add the remaining ingredients except the water and coconut and pulse until well combined.
4. Through a mesh strainer, strain the mixture into the cake tin over caramel syrup evenly.
5. With a piece of the foil, cover the cake tin.
6. In the bottom of Instant Pot, arrange the steamer trivet and pour the water.
7. Arrange the cake tin on top of the trivet.
8. Secure the lid and turn to "Seal" position.
9. Cook on "Manual" with "High Pressure" for about 15 minutes.
10. Press the "Cancel" and allow a "Natural" release.
11. Carefully remove the lid and transfer the cake tin onto a counter.
12. Carefully remove the foil and let it cool completely.
13. With 1 plastic wrap, cover the tin and refrigerate overnight.
14. Carefully place the flan onto a serving plate and sprinkle with coconut.

15. Cut into desired sized pieces and serve.

Nutrition Information
- Calories: 636
- Fat: 30.5g
- Saturated Fat: 22.9g
- Cholesterol: 124mg
- Sodium: 235mg
- Carbohydrates: 81.7g
- Fiber: 2g
- Sugar: 79.6g
- Protein: 14.9g

CONCLUSION

Vietnamese cuisine is very rich in aromas, taste and is very healthy despite the fact that the landscape of the country is very versatile, the Vietnamese cuisine is rich in lemongrass, cilantro, simmered beef bones, mint and least to forget, the fish sauces. The food always has a balanced proportion of sweetness, fish-sauciness, aromatics, sourness, and heat. The basic theme of the cuisine is based on the 'yin and yang' principles, i.e. warm and cool, salty and sweet, and fermented and fresh. Just like the Chinese cuisine, the Vietnamese cuisine is based on the five flavor elements i.e. bitter, sweet, salty, sour, and spicy.

Made in the USA
Middletown, DE
02 September 2019